MW00774007

DOUBTING SEX

Manchester University Press

DOUBTING SEX

INSCRIPTIONS, BODIES AND SELVES IN NINETEENTH-CENTURY HERMAPHRODITE CASE HISTORIES

Geertje Mak

MANCHESTER UNIVERSITY PRESS

Manchester and New York

distributed in the United States exclusively by Palgrave Macmillan

Published by Manchester University Press
Oxford Road, Manchester M13 9NR, UK
and Room 400, 175 Fifth Avenue, New York, NY 10010, USA
www.manchesteruniversitypress.co.uk

Distributed in the United States exclusively by
Palgrave Macmillan, 175 Fifth Avenue, New York,
NY 10010, USA

Distributed in Canada exclusively by
UBC Press, University of British Columbia, 2029 West Mall,
Vancouver, BC, Canada V6T 1Z2

British Library Cataloguing-in-Publication Data
A catalogue record for this book is available from the British Library

Library of Congress Cataloging-in-Publication Data applied for

ISBN 978 0 7190 8690 8 hardback

First published 2012

Typeset
by Graphicraft Limited, Hong Kong
Printed in Great Britain
by TJ International, Padstow

CONTENTS

Figures and tables	*Page* vi	
Acknowledgements	vii	
Introduction	1	
I INSCRIPTION	17	
1 Secrecy and disclosure: The politics of containment	19	
2 Early sex reassignments and the absence of a sex of self	43	
3 Herculine Barbin	66	
II BODY	91	
4 How to get the semen to the neck of the womb	95	
5 Justine Jumas: conflicting body politics	116	
6 The dislodgement of the person	136	
III SELF	157	
7 Sex assignment around 1900. From a legal to a clinical issue	165	
8 The turn inwards	185	
9 Scripting the self. N. O. Body's autobiography	205	
Conclusion	225	
Notes	233	
Bibliography	266	
Index	279	

FIGURES AND TABLES

FIGURES

1 Reason for disclosures in absolute and relative numbers   *Page* 139
2 Different medical disclosures in absolute numbers   140

TABLES

1 Different medical disclosures in absolute and relative numbers   140
2 Numbers of operations on hermaphrodites and discoveries of
   erroneous sex   152

ACKNOWLEDGEMENTS

This book has been part of my life for over ten years. Institutions, colleagues and friends have been indispensable all those years. Therefore I want to thank:

- Willem Frijhoff, for his open and supportive attitude with regard to my research proposal from the very beginning and the generous way of letting me go to the Radboud University;
- the Netherlands Organization for Scientific Research for financing the project;
- the colleagues attending Willem Frijhoff's cultural history seminar at the Free University for inspiring discussions, in particular Joris van Eijnatten and Magda Machielse;
- all the mostly invisible people working at libraries and archives that have provided me with books and documents, in particular from the university libraries of Utrecht, Amsterdam and Leiden, the Royal Library in The Hague, the Staatsbibliothek zu Berlin, the library of the New York Academy of Medicine, the Bibliothèque Interuniversitaire de Médecine in Paris, and the Bibliothèque Nationale de France – thank you, Muriel Piécoup and Bénédicte Bringtown-Agasson, working at the last, for your hospitality, hilarious stories about a megalomaniac building, help with retrieving documents and a long-lasting friendship;
- the Centre for the Study of Gender and Sexuality at New York University for their hospitality, support and working space, in particular Carolyn Dinshaw for interesting discussions and Svati Shah for sharing trans experiences and issues;
- Carole Vance for her generous invitation to join the weekly Program for the Study of Sexuality, Gender, Health and Human Rights at Columbia University, where I was so happy to be able to discuss my work with Robert Tobin, Alice Miller and David Churchill;
- my colleagues at the Institute for Gender Studies at the Radboud University in Nijmegen, where I have felt at home from the very start – Willy Jansen, Stefan Dudink, Liedeke Plate, Veronica Vasterling, Grietje Dresen, Mieke Verloo, Els Rommes, Tatjana van Strien, Yvonne Benschop, renée c. hoogland, Claudia Krops and all the others: thank you for inspiration, critical thinking, pragmatic advice and moral support in difficult times;
- Paula Yoni, Jennifer Gay, Steph Morris, Wendy Schaffer for painstakingly translating the French, German and Dutch quotations; Han van der Vegt for editing the first two chapters so thoroughly; Titus Verheijen for the correction of the entire manuscript so well and in such an incredible short time;

- my colleagues at the Department of History of the Radboud University, who show so much devotion and skill in teaching – thank you, Inger Leemans, Marit Monteiro, Remco Ensel and Martijn Eickhoff for co-teaching such interesting classes;
- organizers and participants of the Sexuality Network of the biannual European History Social Sciences Conference, in particular Dan Healey and Elise Chenier;
- Willem Frijhoff, Alison Redick, Randolph Trumbach, Willy Jansen, Liedeke Plate, Stefan Dudink and Veronica Vasterling, for discussing draft chapters, and Inger Leemans, Theo van der Meer, Annemarie Mol Chris Straayer, Rebecca Jordan-Young for reading earlier versions of this book;
- Manchester University Press, in particular Emma Brennan for always answering all my questions so promptly, and Julian Lock for going over the manuscript with a fine-tooth comb;
- Annemarie Mol, for long walks with good questions and intellectual challenge, and for being 'severe for the text and soft on the author' at a crucial moment;
- Chris Straayer, for reading drafts when I needed that so badly, for our dear trips, and for being my soulmate;
- Beck Jordan-Young, for fun, food, music, laughter, art and so many inspiring discussions, but most of all for being so bright and so light;
- Inger Leemans, for hilarious relativism, intellectual pleasure, surviving 'de flat', good food, wine, and more.

Many other people helped me living a good life. I owe a lot to my colleagues at Fatusch Productions, in particular Gülay Orhan, Jac Persson, Eray Ergeç, Mitchke Leemans and Caroline Visser. Thank you all for allowing me to be part of your incredible team in creatively fighting Dutch xenophobia and islamophobia, for the humour, the food, the hope and the courage. Family and friends surrounded me with their love and friendship, music, gardening, dog-care, painting, and more – I can only mention a few by name here: Berteke Waaldijk, Peter Romijn, Marieke van der Meer, Marika Dekkers, Marian van der Klein, Agnes Andeweg, Rolien Botma, Geert van Dijk, Sandra Ringeling, Tineke Mak and Nel Mak. Ansje Roepman, my mother Bettie Mak-Wits and Joke Oosterhuis, all so engaged with my earlier books, no longer live to see this one in print – their memory is very dear to me. Omar Al-Azhar and Nora Al-Azhar have made me part of the wonderful experience of their growing up as such characteristic personalities. Most of all I want to thank Ineke van Gelder for sharing all of this already for more than half my lifetime.

INTRODUCTION

This book started with a single question. Ten years ago, when I was writing
my book on masculine women on the European Continent in the nineteenth
century, I found to my utter surprise that in narratives about passing women
who sometimes lived as men for years the issue of an inner sexual identity
was *never* raised. Not one text wondered about or discussed the possible
inner motives of the woman involved, pointed to early childhood boyish
inclinations, discussed the difficulties of transvestism in terms of identity, or
tried to explain the passing in a more or less psychological way. Only at the
very end of the nineteenth century did the first narratives appear in which
the sex of a passing woman's self was questioned.[1] I kept wondering how,
then, the sexed body was related to the self before that time. If people did
not think of the category of sex as something that was also deeply fixed in
the interior of the self during early childhood, something which could not be
changed at will later in life without severe psychological trauma, how then
did they conceive of sex? How was physical sex related to individuals and
more in particular to their sense of self?

I decided to turn to narratives of hermaphrodites: nineteenth-century
medical case histories reporting on people whose physical sex had raised doubts
during their lifetime.[2] There, I supposed, I would find out how the relationship
between physical sex and self was conceived of, for in these cases of doubtful
bodily sex the seemingly self-evident category of sex was under pressure.
What happened if the physical sex of a person was questioned? What was the
role of the hermaphrodite her- or himself? What do such stories reveal about
notions of the self in relation to physical sex?

The stories I found about hermaphrodites were mainly medical case
histories. These led to a closer consideration of the other core element in this
project: physical sex. Initially overwhelmed by all the medical details, I slowly
started to sort out how medical techniques and practices changed over the
course of the nineteenth century and established sex in fundamentally different
ways. Hermaphroditism in 1900, I started to realize, was not the same thing
as it had been in 1800. How did that change affect my first question: that is,
the relationship between a physically doubtful sex and the notion of a self?

Thirdly, the relationship between physical sex and the person cannot be understood outside the social, moral and legal order in which an individual is embedded. In nineteenth-century Western Europe, two fundamental rules concerning the categories of sex seem to be obvious: first of all, legally, everyone is either a man or a woman and not something in between, and secondly, sexuality is only allowed in heterosexual relationships. Hermaphrodites challenged both rules, but had to be assigned a sex anyway. How was this distortion of the relationship between physical sex, the person's sex and the social, moral and legal order dealt with? And how was the sex a hermaphrodite belonged to decided?

Instead of criticizing a social, legal and cultural system that does not allow for gender categories outside the male and female dichotomy and which is implicitly heterosexual, I decided to doubt the category of sex itself. The topic of hermaphroditism or intersex itself makes one doubt sex: it helps to crack the smooth surface of something that seems so utterly self-evident and 'natural' as the fact that people are categorized as male or female at birth on the basis of their physical sex. Although this doubting always started off with someone noticing some sort of physical ambiguity, the central question in each of my case histories was, in the end: to which sex should this person belong? 'Sex' is then not the physical thing, but the *category* to which a person belongs. This has therefore become the core concept I wanted to question: on what grounds exactly, was the category of sex based? I therefore decided to analyze the source material in terms of rationales: not explicit standards, values, concepts or ideologies with regard to sex, but the implicit, tacit logics involved in the practices with regard to a person's sex (re)assignment.[3]

How did self, body and society play a role in the way people were assigned a sex in cases where their physical sex had raised doubt? How did these three interrelate, and how was that affected by the drastic changes in medical practices over the course of time? In my analysis, I discerned three main rationales, three implicit logics behind the way people were assigned a sex. It is through one or more of these that sex is understood as the category to which a person duly belongs.[4] These three are the rationales of the category of sex:

1 as an inscription in the social community;
2 as a representation of the body;
3 as a representation of the self.

The rationale of the body seems to be the easiest and most logical one: you have duly to represent the sex your body displays. Apart from the fact that this is of course already problematic in cases in which physical sex raises doubts, it is precisely this rationale which changes so fundamentally in practice over the course of time. It has therefore literally and figuratively become the heart of this book, constituting the middle section. The rationale of sex as true representation of the body mainly changed because of medicine's increasing capacity to detach the person from the medical establishment of sex. This did not, however, ameliorate sex diagnosis but conversely complicated it. The rationale of sex as a representation of the self turns out to be closely related to this dislodgement of the person from medical enactments of sex. The 'sex of self' was not increasingly suppressed, as might have been expected, but started to become an object of clinical concern in its own right for the first time in history. It is therefore described in the final section of this book. The rationale of sex as inscription will be the most unfamiliar to modern Western readers. It becomes apparent initially only as the remarkable *absence* of the other two rationales. How it functioned, when, and in what sort of social structure is analyzed in the first part of the book, which is mainly dedicated to the 'early' case histories from my source material from the period before roughly the 1870s.

These rationales and their mutual relationships will be extensively examined in the three subsequent parts of *Doubting Sex*. Many case histories display overlap, friction or conflict between these rationales. This is one of the reasons why the category of sex is fundamentally unstable: more than one basic logic is at work at the same time. Moreover, the balance between these logics of sex shows a major shift over the course of time, which demonstrates the historicity of the category of sex.

In the remainder of this introduction, I will address some methodological and theoretical issues constituting the context for this book. First I will introduce the reader to the sources that are the basis of the book: the medical case histories of over three hundred adult hermaphrodites published between the late eighteenth century and the start of the twentieth century. Then I will briefly review how *Doubting Sex* is aligned with the field of the history of the body and the history of the self, as well as with the history of same-sex sexuality, cross-dressing and hermaphroditism.

Franz Ludwig von Neugebauer's collection of hermaphrodite case histories

Franz Ludwig von Neugebauer's *Hermaphroditismus beim Menschen* ('Hermaphroditism in Humankind'), published in 1908, is an amazing book: almost 750 pages in length, it contains references to 1,885 publications from antiquity to 1908 on hermaphroditism and the 1,257 cases of hermaphrodites described in these publications.[5] It is written in German, but contains entries for literature in most European languages, such as English, French, German, Polish, Russian, Spanish, Italian and Dutch as well as Latin, and includes many illustrations. Some references are just titles, others contain extensive descriptions of the arguments of the original author as well as Neugebauer's

summaries of the case histories presented. Its introduction is an overview of
the scientific state of the art with regard to hermaphroditism, followed by the
bibliographical entries alphabetized by the author. Within these entries, the
case histories are individually numbered. The book ends with conclusions
drawn from the material collected and an extensive record ordering the
case histories by all kinds of entries, such as 'Clitorishypertrophy in female
pseudohermaphrodites', or 'Suicide or suicide attempts', or 'Hermaphroditism
and tuberculosis'. These entries refer to the numbers of the case histories.

    This book was the basis for my search for sources regarding hermaphrodit-
ism. I have selected all the references in languages I can read (Dutch, German,
French and English) and restricted myself to references to case histories in
which the person involved was alive at the time her sex was doubted and old
enough possibly to have a say in what happened (twelve and up). There are
rare exceptions to this rule, for example if the case history about a person
who had died contained her life history or if the story concerning a child
under twelve was very interesting for some reason. I selected 600 references.
I subsequently tried to find the original sources and managed to trace 289
of these. Some of these are entire books, others consist of no more than
three sentences. Some describe dozens of cases, others only refer to a single
case. Finally I decided to confine myself to clinical case histories, and to leave
out the cases describing hermaphrodites who exhibited themselves to
several doctors in exchange for money.[6] As it turned out, the majority of the
cases are German and French. Dutch, English or American cases cannot
have been collected very systematically by Neugebauer – as my own research
and other contemporary work on the history of hermaphrodites in America
clearly demonstrate.[7] I have, however, not tried to 'complete' Neugebauer's
collection by doing further research. Only a very few cases, found through
references in the sources, were added to Neugebauer's basic collection. My
study is therefore mainly based on French and German source material,
with sometimes a reference to a telling example in another language; only
towards the beginning of the twentieth century, when medical debates on
hermaphroditism became more international, do Dutch and English sources
play a more prominent role.

    Alongside the language restriction, two choices for handling source
material have fundamentally affected my analysis. First of all, Neugebauer
never tried to sort his material chronologically. Doing this allowed me to show
that what was referred to as 'hermaphroditism' changed fundamentally over
time. Secondly, I restricted myself to hermaphrodites who were alive at the
time their case histories were compiled. In that way, I left out pathological–
anatomical hermaphroditism based on the deceased which was the basis
for conceptualizing sex and hermaphroditism *scientifically* and *theoretically*.
Restricting myself to doubting sex in clinical practice produced a history

remarkably different from a history based on theories and concepts – such as Alice Dreger's *Hermaphrodites and the Medical Invention of Sex*.[8]

Neugebauer was *the* international expert on hermaphroditism at the time. Born in Poland in 1856, he became the director of the gynaecological department of the evangelical hospital in Warsaw, but was very much integrated into German scientific medical circles. He had contacts in Paris, London and Vienna, and belonged to several gynaecological societies, such as the New York Obstetrical Society. He published not only in Polish but also in German, and had his articles translated into French, English and Italian. Many physicians and gynaecologists turned to him to ask for advice in cases of doubtful sex. Interestingly, Neugebauer was also acquainted with the sexologist and pro-homosexual campaigner Magnus Hirschfeld. He was interested in Hirschfeld's journal *Jahrbuch für sexuelle Zwischenstufen* ('Yearbook of Sexual Intermediates') which was first published in 1899, and published several articles in it.[9] This relationship may account for his growing interests in the non-physical aspects of hermaphroditism, which can be seen in his own case histories as well as in the topics listed in the index to *Hermaphroditismus beim Menschen*. To the many medical categories he added categories such as 'Public bullying of pseudo-hermaphrodites' or 'Consciousness of sex not according to character of the sex glands'.[10] In Part III, Neugebauer's interest in the psychological aspects of doubting sex, as well as Hirschfeld's involvement with cases of hermaphroditism will be discussed in detail.

My confinement virtually to only one genre – nineteenth-century medical case histories[11] – allows me to locate very precisely the logics I am studying: there, in these case histories, in the practices they refer to, logics of sex categorization change. But to which extent can these be read, also, as a way of analyzing the parameters of the category of sex outside these specific examples and genre? The social historian in me wants to point at the interesting crossroads of social classes that can be found in these texts documenting the meeting between highly educated doctors and often rural and lower-class people.[12] The logics I am deriving from these texts are certainly not only those of the doctors; in particular the earlier case histories reveal a lot about the social circumstances and life course of hermaphrodites. Moreover, my turn to tacit logics rather than outspoken (medical) opinions is a way of retrieving an underlying mentality which seems to have been shared by most people involved and only moved very slowly through time and place. Finally, my sources do not offer by themselves the answer to the question why these changes happened; much of the explanation has to be sought in the larger context of individualization and modernization. But I do consider the emergence of medical techniques and routines isolating the body from its social context and its embodiment one of the essential conditions for the coming into being of a separate, autonomous, inner sexed self.

A PRAXEOGRAPHIC APPROACH TO THE HISTORY
OF SEX AND SELF

From 'hermaphroditism' to 'doubting sex'

The many different case histories collected from over more than a century give the impression that hermaphroditism could be almost anything: from a woman growing a beard to a highly sophisticated discussion between experts on the exact nature of cells in a malign tumour of the sexual glands; from speculations about the internal organs of a woman without vagina and breasts, to the extensive description of what could be felt by introducing a catheter into the urethra while penetrating the anus with one's index finger; from the shame of a boy who had started menstruating to a girl seducing all the other girls in the village; from thorny legal questions about the degree of sex difference required in order for a marriage to be valid, to descriptions of the content of erotic dreams.

Of crucial importance at this point in my research was the appearance of Annemarie Mol's *The Body Multiple* and the international furore it created. Mol systematically argues that bodies in (medical) practices are *always* multiple. Bodies, in her 'ontology in medical practice', never simply 'are' but have to be *enacted*: they appear, gain shape and are manifested through a whole range of different techniques, practices and routines. This variety of ways for enacting a body does not ultimately refer to one 'true' body, but produces different bodies, that are not necessarily aligned: a body multiple. So, by stressing the highly different *material* conditions under which a body is approached or engaged with, Mol demonstrates its very multiplicity.

This led me to acknowledge that there is no such artefact as 'hermaphroditism' or the 'hermaphrodite' to be clearly defined and subsequently retrieved from historical sources. What was called hermaphroditism over the nineteenth century could refer to many different things and many different situations. Moreover, these can also vary greatly within a single case history. Hermaphroditism was, in Mol's terms, enacted multiply. I therefore started to picture hermaphroditism as a verb: *doubting sex*. This doubting sex could happen in all sorts of circumstances (on the street, at birth, in bed, in hospital, during the public exhibition of hermaphrodites, in the laboratory, in published medical discussions or during medical meetings), it could be done by many different kinds of actors (parents, midwives, doctors, hermaphrodites themselves, neighbours, next of kin, lovers, spouses, friends, colleagues, the general public, teachers, nurses) and could be about numerous different objects (a woman's beard, the characteristics of the way ovaries feel in comparison to the way testicles feel, the genuineness of menstrual signs, the force of ejaculation, the relation between sexual desire and internal anatomy, the character of gonadal cells, the direction of urine). It turned out that, once someone's sex was doubted, doubt soon spilled over into many other situations, subjects and actors.

This way of looking at the wildly differing case histories prevented me from trying to classify the cases according to current medical classifications of hermaphroditism or any other categorization that seemed to be logical from my own viewpoint. For example, I did not try to group the case histories in terms of how hermaphrodites identified themselves in relation to medical diagnosis. Nor did I treat the historical case histories as backward medical accounts (guessing what the 'real' or 'true' syndrome behind the accounted phenomena would have been from a modern medical viewpoint), or as more or less sensible ways of dealing with the hermaphrodites' own experiences or identification. I kept my analysis very close to how contemporaries doubted sex and how they dealt with it. This enabled me to carefully historicize notions of physical sex, the sex of the self, and the social and legal order of sex.

Theoretical shifts based on the dissection of dead bodies could not readily be employed in practices in which living bodies were at stake. Studies into the history of medicine focusing on practices have demonstrated how techniques, routines, disciplines, institutions, know-how, and attitudes to the body and illness were involved in fundamental shifts in the way bodies were enacted.[13] These studies helped me to recognize, for example, that enacting bodily sex by penetrating a body with instruments and fingers not only required the doctor's techniques, but also the patient's willingness, the routine of temporarily overcoming shame, the isolation of the patient from the social environment, the know-how of comparing many different internal sexual organs by palpation, and so on.

On the basis of this *praxeographic approach* to the body and its history, I developed the main analytic framework with which I could sort out the huge variety all my case histories constituted; by *historicizing* the different ways in which sex and doubting sex were enacted in medical practices. The changing medical enactments of doubting sex in clinical practice over the nineteenth century became the framework for *Doubting Sex*. Soon this led to my first important conclusion: so many new medical techniques and routines had been introduced in the twentieth century compared with the nineteenth that the ways in which sex could be doubted medically had multiplied dramatically. Hermaphroditism was no longer confined to something lay people could observe or experience, but had also become something only medical experts were able to discern. This caused a fundamental change, not in the least in how hermaphrodites themselves were involved.

Sex and gender: from discourse to practice

This study was partly inspired by a reorientation towards the body in feminist and queer studies in the 1990s, in which the marked division between gender and sex was criticized. Physical sex could not be so easily distinguished from cultural and social or discursive notions of gender, the argument went, because bodies only gained significance in an already existing discursive and gendered framework. In *Bodies that Matter* Judith Butler argued that the only way we gain access and give meaning to bodies is through the discursive function of gender.[14] Thomas Laqueur's *Making Sex* showed how the concept of bodily sex and sex difference shifted radically over time, and how the way it was employed in justifying the order of gender changed fundamentally too.[15] According to him, medical science accentuated the *sameness* of the sexes rather than their incommensurable difference until the eighteenth century. It was only with the political changes of the Enlightenment and the French Revolution that sex differences came to be seen as absolute and dichotomous. Not scientific discoveries, according to Laqueur, but the emerging role of 'nature' as the basis for political rights caused this paradigm shift in the conceptualization of sex difference from the metaphysical to the physical, away from the one-sex system.[16]

Bodies indeed cannot gain significance outside discourse. That does not mean that bodies can be *reduced* to discourse. If a body cannot ejaculate sperm, it cannot ejaculate sperm – whatever the meaning attached to that phenomenon may be. But there is more: bodies may gain meaning through existing discourse, but they cannot be 'read' just like that. There are a lot of materialities, technicalities and practicalities involved in 'reading' bodies, or in making words, numbers, measures and meanings out of bodies. How does one know, for example, that a body ejaculates sperm? From what the person involved says? Or from statements by sexual partners? From investigating stains on the sheets? From assumptions on the basis of the palpation and observation of a full-grown testicle, a spermatic cord and a fully developed penis? By observing an accidental ejaculation during the manual examination of the genitals? Through the microscopic analysis of sperm after deliberate masturbation before or during a consultation? Routines, traditions, rules, discipline and habits are involved; knowledge, know-how, expertise and capacities play a role; instruments, techniques, locations and all sorts of practical provisions are required; these are in turn related to institutions varying from universities to marriage, from hospitals to the army, from schools to prostitution, from churches to courts; finally all these have to be financially, socially, culturally and politically upheld. All these aspects together define how bodily sex has been enacted or made available to be 'read' and what sorts of sex result from these readings, and all of them are historically and geographically specific. In addition to this, what medicine was capable of doing with bodies, for example whether it could help women who grew a beard to remove the hair from their faces, was of importance to how that body would be perceived discursively.

This book therefore does not foreground concepts, theories, definitions or discourses of sex and how these have changed over time, but employs a praxeographic approach. As a result, this history of bodily sex differs noticeably from Laqueur's account, in particular by showing major changes in the enactments of physical sex *within* what he has labelled a two-sex system. It is inspired by, and builds on, the work of other historians, primarily orientated towards the early modern period, who have focused on multiple practices and discourses in their histories of the (gendered) body, such as Barbara Duden, Laura Gowing and Jens Lachmund, as well as Evelyn Ackermanns work on the nineteenth century.[17]

But, the reader may now wonder, are case histories from the nineteenth century not primarily *texts*? Is the historical methodology involved, then, not by definition a form of discourse analysis? Can a historian using such textual sources actually employ a praxeographic approach? Being a historian trained in all sorts of methods of textual and literary analysis, emphatically having embraced such methods for the interpretation of referential historical sources in earlier work, I have deliberately decided to directly read certain parts of my sources referentially in this study.[18] Especially when it came to the way physicians carried out their examinations, the techniques they used, and the actual findings resulting from these practices, I have not focused my interpretation on the use of metaphors, style, narrative structures or symptomatic details, but have more or less taken the information provided for granted. If a physician, for example, described how he carefully palpated a testicle, epididymis and spermatic cord as well as measuring the penis in its non-erect and erect state, my analysis concentrated on the fact that he was able to use these techniques and interpret them, in terms of the extent to which patients were disciplined to undergo such an examination, rather than on the language used to describe the procedure. (This is, of course, not to say that such an analysis could not be useful in the context of another study). Such interpretations sometimes also called for counting – how often was such and such technique used during which period? – in order to be able to order techniques, routines and the practicalities of enacting sex chronologically. A praxeographic approach therefore entailed a focus on the reported practicalities and technicalities of physical examinations, an analysis of what kinds of sex resulted from these practices, and the chronological ordering of that type of information.

Both referential readings of data and counting are tricky methods, as I am fully aware. My referential readings are confined to the information reported on what people actually did or did not do – both within and outside medical contexts. That is, the bits and pieces of information available in the sources about the hermaphrodite's life outside the medical context have been taken as a basis for an analysis of social practices with regard to doubting sex.

Similarly, reports concerning medical techniques and practices and the resulting data have not been analyzed as discourse, but as practices. At the same
time however, labelling, naming, verbalizing bodily features and functions,
structuring case histories, and narrating life histories are *part* of the practices
involved. If, for example, a physician did not pay any attention to a hermaphrodite's own sense of sex, or if a medical scientist dwelt on the exact appearance
of certain glandular cells over a considerable number of pages, I have taken
that as practices to be analyzed. And when it comes to the way physicians
explained or justified their course of action or built up their case history,
discursive or narratological–analytic tools were certainly employed.

Counting is tricky in particular if this would implicitly stabilize the very
category under investigation. I have therefore emphatically resisted giving
numbers of 'hermaphrodites', as this would inadvertently affirm the category
as an existing artefact instead of contextualizing and historicizing it. But sometimes counting can be a quick way to present order in a large mass of material
and with regard to techniques and practices of disclosing 'doubtful sex' this
sometimes turned out to be highly useful, without fixing or generalizing the
categories I aimed to historicize.

Sex and self

But what does all of this teach us about the sex of the self? What does
the way bodies were enacted in medical practices have to do with what
hermaphrodites themselves had to say about the sex they were assigned,
or with the way in which physicians or others involved took the hermaphrodite's own sense of sex into account?

First of all, the conceptual framework for distinguishing gender identity,
sex and sexuality, including the many critical discussions of their mutual
relationships, has to be understood as historically specific in itself. As for
example Bernice Hausman argued, changing technicalities and practicalities
in medicine in the 1950s actually made it possible to conceive of 'gender
identity' as something separate from the body. In her view, the concept of
a core gender identity came into being at the precise historical moment
when bodies could be made to appear convincingly male or female through
medical techniques.[19] In order to be able to historicize the concept of gender
identity, I will carefully avoid the use of the word and instead use the term
'sex' as it was used at the time of my research period. *Doubting Sex* will
thereby critically elaborate on Hausman's hypothesis, illustrating that the
process of physical sex and sex of self falling apart started earlier than she
claimed, that is, as early as 1900.[20]

Furthermore, unearthing the role hermaphrodites themselves played
from the case histories was quite a challenge. Was the person in question
aware of her doubtful sex, and how would I know if the sources did not state

this explicitly? Would a girl who started to grow a small penis or a beard start to think of herself as a boy? If other lay people had started to doubt her sex, would that necessarily mean that she would do the same? And what would happen if not lay people, but doctors, discovered a sex to be doubtful, because they had found something during their palpation of the interior of the body, or during an operation? How would that have been related to the hermaphrodite's sense of sex? These questions multiply if we think of the role of the hermaphrodite not only in the initial discovery but also in the further medical examination and diagnosis, and in the decisions made on how to deal with the situation.

Conceptually, moreover, the problem in asking these questions lies in the notion of a 'sex of the self' itself. For in a modern Western society we may take it for granted that people have a 'self', an interiorly located psyche that defines our authentic being, and we may assume this is deeply gendered from very early on in life, but several ground-breaking historical studies have demonstrated this concept of self to be a modern invention. For example, in his famous philosophical history *Sources of the Self*, Charles Taylor argues that the idea of an interiorly located self, which has to be fully known and expressed, only became a 'constitutive good' in Western societies over the course of many centuries. That is, not only did a concept of an interior and authentic self come into being, it also became one of the pillars of Western morality to 'find oneself', to fully become oneself.[21] In a different way, the cultural historian Dror Wahrman persuasively describes the transition from what he calls an *'ancien régime* of self' to a 'modern *regime* of self' in late eighteenth-century England. According to him, notions of class, race and gender, which in pre-modern times primarily defined an individual's place in society through outward appearance, shifted into inalienable characteristics of the authentic self. All of a sudden, for example, masquerades were no longer perceived as transgressions of a social order, but as betrayal of one's true self.[22] Studies more focused on social history and based on ego documents from ordinary middle-class people, however, tend to question this periodization of the culturally, literarily and philosophically based histories of the self. They argue that even during the nineteenth century diaries, memoirs and autobiographies hardly displayed an interest in the inner self.[23]

Similarly, a debate on the exact period in which the concept of '(homo) sexual identity' emerged has taken place in the field of gay and lesbian history. Some studies point to the existence of early modern gay subcultures, labels for men and women preferring same-sex love, and explanations of their inclinations using the terms 'nature' or 'inborn', to show that the category of the homosexual – albeit with another label – already existed in the eighteenth century.[24] Others – including myself – have adhered more to Michel Foucault's original claim that homosexual identity came into being as a result of the involvement of medicine and more specifically the new branch, psychiatry, during the last quarter of the nineteenth century. Although Foucault himself clearly pointed to the importance of a mechanism of power forcing people to talk in meticulous detail about their sexual desires, he never described the important role same-sex lovers themselves had in defining homosexual identity. Later studies demonstrated how much male same-sex lovers actively participated in a dialogue with psychiatrists, thereby affecting the terms in which homosexual identity was understood to a large extent.[25]

Against the backdrop of these ground-breaking historicizations of the concept of the (sexual) self, this study will in the first place treat the absence of references to a hermaphrodite's own understanding or experience of sex as more than a simple omission of information or lacuna in the sources. Instead, *Doubting Sex* takes the lack of interest on the part of physicians for the sex of the self as a meaningful fact. However, that does not mean that hermaphrodites were not involved; if there was no discussion *about* their sense of sex, they still acted as subjects. Within the sources, traces and fragments of social practices, legal procedures and decisions can be found: keeping sexual ambiguity secret, attempting coitus with 'same-sex' friends, confessing doubts to a priest, being ridiculed, shaving beards, not being able to urinate in public, wearing veils, deliberately having one's sex reassigned, comparing one's sex to those of a bed-mate, continuing marriage despite the doubtful sex, etc. What do these social practices tell us about the way hermaphrodites themselves dealt with a sex that raised doubt? Tales about the hermaphrodite's way of dealing with a doubtful sex outside the clinical encounter abound in the earlier case histories, but seem to slowly disappear from physicians' reports over the course of the nineteenth century. At the same time, increasing attention was paid to the hermaphrodite's individual experiences, emotions and self-conception in clinical enactments of sex from the beginning of the twentieth century.

In this book I carefully try to make sense of how hermaphrodites themselves told physicians they dealt with their situation. Furthermore, in line with a praxeographic approach to the body, I will not just pay attention to the way case histories refer to a hermaphrodite's sense of her own sex and sexual preferences or activities, but also to the way these were enacted: to the techniques, practices and routines used – or not, as the case may be – to produce the self of the hermaphrodite. Moreover, I hope to further the discussion on the historical emergence of the phenomenon of sexual identity by filtering out the factor of urban gay or lesbian subcultures; the source material enables me to do so, as virtually no hermaphrodites were said to have contacts in such subcultures. Finally, two chapters will be devoted to a very specific technique of the self: two autobiographical writings by hermaphrodites. Here literary techniques of analysis will be fully employed to investigate an important and historically changing way of enacting the self through the narration of one's life history.

There is an interesting rift in the histories of hermaphroditism and intersex. Studies of hermaphroditism in the Renaissance and early modern period tend to concentrate on the wider, metaphorical meanings of hermaphroditism as both a spiritual ideal and a symbol of political and social ambiguity and instability.[26] In contrast, studies on late nineteenth-century hermaphroditism and twentieth-century intersex are much more inclined to question how the relation between a doubtful bodily sex and psychological sex was dealt with in individual cases, and how (individual) sexual ambiguity was repressed or 'resolved' in the process.[27] *Doubting Sex* turns out to bridge that remarkable difference in outlook on the history of ambiguous sexes. It shows how hermaphroditism itself underwent a metamorphosis: from something that mainly troubled the social and moral order of the communities of which the hermaphrodite was a part, to something that threatened to disturb a person's relationship to herself and her own body. This is also reflected in a general change within the case histories, which increasingly leave out the social circumstances and the hermaphrodite's course of life during the long nineteenth century.

This study thereby historicizes Stefan Hirschauer's interesting observation in his 1993 ethnographic study of practices surrounding transsexualism. Hirschauer shows how the phenomenon of transsexualism metamorphosed as it travelled through different contexts, and describes how an initially social conflict concerning gender roles in which a person adamantly claims another gender role and physical appearance than the one assigned to him at birth, in the course of the process of sex change is transformed into a medico-psychologically diagnosed conflict between an individual's physical sex and gender identity.[28] *Doubting Sex* shows this metamorphosis also to be a historical transformation.[29] In other words, I do not take for granted that hermaphroditism is always also about the possibly conflicting, confusing or oppressive relationship between an objectively diagnosed body and an authentic sense of self. I therefore do not follow the example of Alice Domurat Dreger who, in her pioneering history of hermaphrodites, severely criticized the fact that medicine did not take hermaphrodites' subjective experiences and inclinations into account in its diagnosis of sex. Because I do not start from the assumption that there self-evidently or naturally *is* such a thing as a sex of the self, that sort of criticism is not my objective.[30] Rather, I am suspicious of what Joan Scott called the 'evidence of experience', and historicize the concept of a sex of self or 'core gender identity'.[31] Therefore, this study is an attempt to understand how, when and why hermaphroditism started to be primarily understood as a problem of the suffering or well-being of an individual self. This is not to say that this particular way of understanding the problem of hermaphroditism did not also affect the entire 'sex-gender system', to use Gayle Rubin's famous concept, but to say that this system in itself fundamentally changed by making the 'proper' relation between objective sex and subjective sex of self into the core of its concerns.[32]

Studies of hermaphrodites and intersex – and more broadly of sexual ambiguity, cross-dressing and transsexuality – are often, and with good reason, critical of a system of only two dichotomous sex categories, a system which is, moreover, implicitly and thoroughly heterosexual. Such studies disapprove of the fact that in society and law there are only two options available, male or female, or of the fact that people have to be assigned a sex at all. They show how the law or medicine systematically rules out sexual ambiguity, whereas 'nature' at least provides a lot more variety.[33] More generally, it is argued that sexual ambiguity is – to use Judith Butler's terms – an 'unintelligible' and 'uninhabitable' position within the discursive formation of a 'heterosexual matrix'.[34] These studies try to destabilize normative sex by researching its crossed boundaries in many different ways – historical, medical and cultural. They have greatly inspired my thinking – witness my earlier work in which I sought to detail the historically changing (im)possibilities for women to embody masculinity through an analysis of the available narratives and social scripts.

But what has also become clear from most of these studies is how the outside of discourse, or the abnormal, always in the end sustains the inside, or the normative. Concepts such as 'third sex', 'ambiguous sex' and 'transgender' in principle simultaneously refer to the existing strict categories of male and female, as well as their transgression or undermining. Therefore it is to a certain extent a vicious circle to take 'the variety within nature' or the 'authentic subjective experiences' of people who do 'not fit into the sex-gender system' as a critical point of departure. After all, the stricter the sex-gender system is, the more people 'cross' or 'do not fit'. More fruitful, as several studies have already demonstrated, is not to take the normative and suppressive function of sex-gender systems at face value, but to study how these systems actually *function* in cases of ambiguous sex.[35] My study, therefore, follows this strategy and aims at destabilizing and defamiliariz- ing the category of sex *from within*: it *doubts* sex. It reads medical practices, to use Ann Laura Stoler's provocative phrase on colonial archives, '*along* the grain' in order to understand the rationales underlying the category of sex.[36] Consequently it shows these logics to shift over time, conflict internally and be inconsistent. For example, instead of repeating over and over again how the way hermaphrodites were dealt with shows the deeply heteronormative character of nineteenth-century conceptualization of sex difference, I will show how in practice 'heterosexuality' actually meant quite different and sometimes diametrically opposed things.[37] Neither sex nor heterosexuality turns out to be 'one'.

This is also the reason why I have chosen to *follow* the existing categorization of people into only men and women, and not to create new in-between or ambiguous ways of referring to hermaphrodites, such as 's/he' or 'hir'. I have chosen to shift 'he' and 'she' and 'her' and 'him' almost randomly, only slightly in line with the logic of the narrative, hopefully disturbing the expectations of the reader somewhat. Only if a hermaphrodite emphatically embraced a single category of sex have I wanted to respect that by referring to him or her accordingly.

The uses of history

The history presented in this book should help to illuminate how the current way of dealing with intersex has been built on foundations created in the nineteenth and early twentieth centuries. Some elements of this are quite concrete, such as the very first techniques used to create a vagina from the skin of a penis/enlarged clitoris, or the development of questionnaires to examine a person's identification as male or female. Others are more institutional, such as the shift of sex assignment from an essentially legal issue to a medical decision. Most important, however, is the change in the tacit rationales determining to which sex a person should belong, in which the rationale of sex as representation of a true self started to appear. That change in logics has become the core argument of this book.

At the same time, this study aims to *defamiliarize* the modern Western way of 'managing' intersex by mapping nineteenth-century ways of dealing with doubtful sexes, which are sometimes quite surprising to modern Western eyes. I hope this study will help to create some disassociating distance from what currently seems so self-evident or natural. This concerns both the fundamental assumptions on the basis of which medicine deals with inter-sexual newborns and the very grounds of LGBT and intersex politics, in particular their focus on gender identity and sexual identity. The function of history, in that case, is to ask new questions about the present.

Deriving three rationales from the recorded practices helped tame the extremely heterogeneous source material. Instead of trying to order the material according to all sorts of possible categories (national, regional, medical, social) it led to thinking through and explaining the logics behind practices involved in doubting sex. These are at once derived from very specifically located case histories and at the same time – because they are *logics* – not necessarily or fundamentally tied to a historical time, region, medical practice or background. Therefore they can be significant for current questions with regard to intersex, transsexualism, transgender and sex in its broad sense: similar logics may still be at work, reinforce each other or be in conflict.

So, questioning the rationales behind sex assignment practices in cases of doubt in the nineteenth century helps to relate meaningfully 'strange' histories to modern assumptions and practices with regard to the category of sex in general. They cannot simply be set aside as just awkward stories about unusual people and backward physicians in an old-fashioned society, but can be connected to current basic assumptions about the category of sex. It makes the histories look back.

I

INSCRIPTION

The first part of this book discusses a rationale of sex – sex as the category to which one belongs and is entitled – which is probably the least evident: the rationale of sex as inscription. The other two rationales, sex as the truthful representation of the body, or sex as the truth of the self, are much more familiar to modern Western readers. The argument in this part is therefore a partially negative one: it tries to make space for this more unexpected rationale of inscription by showing how, in many cases, neither the body nor the self determine how a doubtful sex is dealt with. This requires a reading of the sources against the grain of what seems so self-evident to contemporary Western readers.

The first chapter seeks to take seriously the fact that, in many cases of hermaphroditism until around the 1860s and 1870s, the initial response was *not* to disclose the sexual body to a physician in order to have it examined objectively. We cannot ascribe this secrecy simply to the feelings of shame felt by the hermaphrodites in question because, as we will see, others involved also often opted for a strategy of non-intervention. The first chapter aims to understand the logic of such practices of secrecy and non-intervention; practices of which only fragmentary evidence exists, as non-intervention logically leaves no traces in historical sources. The existing traces therefore only represent the tip of the iceberg. As the cases discussed all ended up in being disclosed to a physician who published about the case, the chapter ends by asking at what point secrecy and non-intervention were exchanged for disclosure – or, when the rationale of the body started to play a significant role. This question will not only be discussed for individual cases, but also in more general terms: when or where did the rationale of sex as inscription function, and in what contexts did it start to lose out against the rationale of sex as truthful representation of the body?

What is experienced as self-evident and natural does not need explanation. This is also true for the rationale of sex as inscription: it is not verbalized. We can only guess why people rather left hermaphrodites alone than directing them to a physician to sort things out. However, precisely when it was confronted with the rationale of sex as truthful representation of the body, more of the logics of the rationale of sex as inscription can be unearthed. What was the problem when hermaphrodites finally did visit physicians and possibly got their sex reassigned? The second chapter will discuss what happened with hermaphrodites who reassigned their sex during the first three-quarters of the nineteenth century. For the modern Western reader, it would not be surprising when the rationale of the body in some cases would turn out to conflict with a rationale of the self. When, for instance, a doctor would recognize a female-raised person as male at the age of twenty-one, we would not be surprised when the woman would react: 'Hey, wait a minute, but I don't *feel* like being a man'. Some historians of intersex have indeed shown to be quite indignant about the fact that physicians did not seem to take the sex of self into account.[1] I do not deny that this was indeed the case, but I will try to reinterpret the fact that in the medical case histories nobody seemed to care so much about the psychological consequences of an erroneous or reassigned sex. What I want to show is that the rationale of the body did not conflict with some sort of inner sexed self, but with a hermaphrodite's inscribed social and moral status. At the same time, it cannot be denied that people could suffer real distress and damage from having their sex doubted or reassigned. So, if sex is not conceived of as rooted in the inner self, how can we understand such experiences and emotions?

The last chapter analyzes the memoirs of Herculine Barbin in order to elaborate on the problem of the (absence of) the sexed self. These memoirs will be familiar to many readers through the reissue introduced by Michel Foucault and the consequent hot discussions from several theoretical points of view. My close reading of the memoirs will doubt Foucault's suggestion that at the time 'true sex' referred to both a physical *and* a psychological sex. After having explained how the biological opinion increasingly excluded the concept of hermaphroditism and forced people to have only one primary sexual identity, which had to be deciphered by physicians, Foucault points to the (still current) opinion that there is an essential relationship between truth and sex in psychiatry, psychoanalysis and psychology.[2] My point will be that such a relationship was *not yet* established in Herculine Barbin's memoirs. I will argue that, both for the physicians involved and for Barbin himself, sex was a social and moral *position* rather than an expression of individual identity. This is not to say that Barbin had no personal emotions or did not suffer from the situation – on the contrary. But the suffering is never expressed in terms of a damaged self, as we will see.

SECRECY AND DISCLOSURE:
THE POLITICS OF CONTAINMENT

Sex, as the category each of us is entitled to, should correspond to the sex of our body. There is no doubt this rationale for the category of sex is primordial. After all, its logic determines everybody's sex from birth, when the genitals are immediately checked and the baby is subsequently inscribed as either female or male. If there is doubt concerning someone's physical sex – at birth or later in life – the question arises to which sex the person in question belongs. In such cases, further inspection of the body seems in order to decide that question. Consider, however, the following three stories.

Anna Barbara Meier

In the summer of 1794, it was rumoured that the daughter of a solicitor in the German village of Göbrichen, called Christina Knoll, was pregnant. She finally confessed as much to the parish priest, but at first refused to reveal with whom she had engendered the child. However, on 30 July 1794 a message arrived from the parish of Wössingen that the 49-year-old Anna Barbara Meier, baptized as a girl and until then acknowledged as a woman, but with the reputation of being a hermaphrodite, had declared that Christina Knoll had become pregnant seven months earlier 'through her masculine intercourse'. According to her, there could be no doubt that she was the father. Therefore he humbly asked permission to marry the pregnant woman while adopting masculine attire and 'character'. Christina Knoll affirmed that Anna Barbara Meier had got her pregnant and wanted to marry him as a man.[1]

In tears, Anna Barbara Meier recounted that he had been the 'object of public laughter and mockery'. She had been considered a girl since her birth and had been baptized as such, through carelessness of her parents and lack of expertise on the part of the midwife. But during adolescence Meier had been able to thoroughly consider 'the various genitalia' and had observed her body's 'genuinely masculine characteristics'. Since then she had felt 'this manly energy'. The emergence of a beard had given her entire being an increasingly masculine appearance, and her playmates had started to mock her and to call her a *Zwitter* (German vernacular for hermaphrodite). He had become very shy and ashamed, and had decided never to show his 'private parts' to anybody.[2]

> . . . So she resolved, following the death of her parents, owing to an ever stronger sense of shame, never to let herself be found out, but rather, as she must live, to remain as she was, to keep her unusual, somewhat aberrant nature forever secret, and to take this secret with her to her grave, in order not to be a laughing stock throughout the world. Thus it has remained undisclosed till now, in the forty-ninth year of her life, and she would forever have been taken for a so-called *Zwitter*, although she herself is convinced she is a true man.[3]

Finon

Born in 1828, D. was registered at the registry office as 'sex: hermaphrodite, and under a double name, one male, the other female'. A year later, the crown prosecutor demanded a physical examination, after which the infant was declared male. Until the age of ten, he lived and was dressed as a boy. But he could not urinate without wetting his trousers and his parents, suspecting they had been mistaken about his sex, did not want him exposed to military service. For that reason, they decided to have him wear women's clothing. From that moment on 'he remained a man–woman' (*homme-femme*), until he entered the asylum at the age of seventy-two. They gave her a special name to indicate the sexual ambiguity: 'Following the rather widespread custom in Lorraine of calling masculine-looking women by diminutives ending with -on, D . . . was called Finon'. After she entered the women's ward of the lunatic asylum, her situation was disclosed as a medical case history by Ricoux and Aubry, both resident doctors at the asylum. They presented the case in 1899, not so much as an anatomic rarity, but because of 'the strange sort of life the patient led in his/her village'.[4]

Since she was feeble-minded, she did not attend school very long but worked as a swineherd instead. As a grown-up, he did men's work: forestry and raking hay. He specialized in extremely heavy labour like squaring, sinking wells and clearing out ditches. But when there was not enough men's work to do, she knitted and did the laundry. Despite her being dressed as a woman, her appearance was quite masculine. He shaved his beard every week, rode horseback, smoked, cursed, and got drunk. When he was too drunk, Ricoux and Aubry report, he sometimes assaulted women. It was said that they regularly had to defend themselves against his approaches. The two physicians did not think these attacks could have had 'great consequences', as Finon D. was not capable of having coitus. She was also said to have played 'the other part' in relations with the soldiers of a neighbouring garrison. She was an object of curiosity and was known in the area as the 'bearded woman'. Finon led an absolutely ambiguous life, the doctors summarized, 'combining field work and the habits of the stronger sex with totally female attire'.[5]

When she was brought to the asylum, she was dressed in old women's clothes, a black dress, a sleeveless blouse, and a white bonnet with frills, and she was freshly shaved. Her features and voice immediately alarmed the wardens, who started to examine her sex and concluded she was a hypospadiac male[6] with undescended testicles. When she was put in the women's department of the asylum, the doctors noticed that she did not feel out of place at all. But when he was declared male and sent to the men's department, he seemed very much surprised to find himself in that environment, and hugely embarrassed about his male costume. 'He freed himself a bit from the demands of his new clothing by tearing his trousers so as to continue urinating as in the past.'[7]

Elisabetha Holzheid

Elisabetha Holzheid was the only child of a wealthy farmer by the name of Köhler, from Ueschersdorf, in the district falling under the Hofheim rural court. She married at twenty but lived in perpetual disharmony with her spouse, who discussed her condition in the public house, which she got to hear about, and, as the people who informed me on the life of this unfortunate individual expressed it, he went elsewhere, but never slept with her. A drinker, her husband is said often to have made fun of his wife when inebriated, claiming her genitals greatly exceeded his own. . . . As for her external appearance, the woman was a virago, around 5′5″ tall, broad-shouldered and of a muscular build; the breasts on her corpse were under-developed but not withered or flaccid. Her facial hair, particularly her moustache, was highly developed.

According to everyone who knew her, Frau Holzheid was an enterprising, dauntless woman who managed and farmed her extremely large agricultural estate almost entirely without the help of her husband. I also heard that in school she had played more with the boys than with the girls. She died, aged seventy-seven, on 3 April 1852.[8]

If the body is indeed the decisive factor in establishing to which sex a person belongs, why could these people live for so long with obviously doubtful sexual characteristics without ever having been examined by a physician to establish their true sex once and for all? For fellow villagers knew the physical sex of Anna Barbara Meier, Finon D. and Elisabetha Holzheid to be ambiguous. And yet, they had to reach the ages of 49, 72 and 77 respectively before their sex was physically checked by a doctor. In the case of Finon, there was doubt from birth, which was the reason the crown prosecutor asked for a medical examination at the age of one. However, when his parents later decided to assign him to another sex, no authorities seem to have been involved, and neither did they become involved over the decades that followed, when Finon exhibited profound sexual ambiguity. If the rationale of sex as a representation of physical sex is indeed primordial, how should we understand the fact that in these cases, for such lengths of time, nobody – not the hermaphrodites, nor their (marriage) partners, nor their fellow villagers, nor the religious, legal or medical authorities – took action in order to get the hermaphrodite's physical sex thoroughly examined and to decide to which sex they effectively belonged?

And the stories of Meier, Finon and Holzheid are, as it turns out, not extraordinary exceptions to an otherwise clear rule. There are many other stories, embedded in nineteenth-century medical case histories, which show that sexual ambiguity was often covered up. Mostly these are short, fragmented, frustratingly incomplete stories preceding the description of a physical examination by a doctor. But by putting the bits and pieces together, it is possible to gain a perspective on a world where taking action in case of a doubtful sex (either one's own or someone else's) by asking for a medical examination, possibly followed by social and legal consequences, was not the primary response. What is more, the existing fragmentary evidence for such a world must be the tip of the iceberg because cases that were not revealed, or were let be, naturally escape the reach of the historian. It is only through the life stories finally disclosed to physicians and subsequently described and published, that I can find out about this hidden world. As Neugebauer stated in 1908, it was impossible to discover reliable statistics concerning hermaphroditism because presumably in many cases in which an 'error of sex' was discovered by parents or others, this was deliberately hushed up.[9]

As we will see later on in this book, *how* doctors interpreted the sex of the body changed fundamentally during the nineteenth century. Here, my point is *that* it was not as obvious as we might think to examine the physical sex in case of doubt. For the person concerned, it was quite understandable to be ashamed of an ambiguous-looking sex and to therefore hide it from others, but why would a husband refrain from making a complaint? Also, the fun of publicly ridiculing somebody might have been satisfying to fellow villagers, but should the priest, doctor or the local authorities not intervene? There must be another rationale, a logic that explains why, in cases of doubtful sex, secrecy and non-intervention were to a certain extent preferred to disclosure to a physician. This chapter is an attempt to define that rationale behind these policies of secrecy and non-intervention.

To this end, I will use the medical case histories as a window on to a social world that is otherwise hard to discern. I will not pay too much attention to the fact that this window was obviously constructed by physicians. Later chapters will pay ample attention to the specific ways in which physicians dealt with doubtful sex. For now, I will deliberately isolate those passages that report on the history of the hermaphrodites prior to their encounter with the medical profession, and try to 'feel out', so to speak, case histories in which doubtful sex was kept secret and let be. What do these case histories reveal about the parents and midwives who kept ambiguous sex secret? What about the people involved themselves? In what sort of situations did the social environment more or less leave a person with a doubtful sex alone? And what was the role of sexual partners, fiancé(e)s or spouses? Finally, what were the policies of the – religious, medical and legal – authorities? I will read the available fragments of information on secrecy and non-intervention as *symptoms* of an underlying rationale, a non-verbalized logic when dealing with doubtful sex, *other* than the logic that the sex of the body should determine the sex of the person. What do the sources reveal about such a logic behind the practice of secrecy and non-intervention? What do they tell us about the meaning of sex as a category, alongside its meaning as a reference to aspects of the body? I will end the analysis by asking why, in the cases I have described, there came a point where the strategies of secrecy and non-intervention no longer seemed to work. If covering up sexual ambiguity was such a regular and accepted practice, what made hermaphrodites disclose themselves to medical or other authorities, and what made others coerce or force them to do so?

Most of the stories revealing a relatively long period of secrecy and non-intervention took place between about 1750 and 1870. Some were only revealed later. Finon's story, for example, was published in 1899, but refers to a person who lived during the seven decades prior to that year. Certainly not *all* stories of secrecy and non-intervention happened before 1870, but roughly speaking this practice became increasingly rare during the last quarter of the nineteenth century. Parts II and III of this book will further elucidate how and why that happened. For now it suffices to note that the emergence of modern medicine *in practice* caused that development, which in turn was instrumental to and part of a larger historical development: the growing influence of the modern nation state.

Moreover, among the cases I have collected from before about 1870, almost all the stories occur in rural areas and remarkably few in urban or industrial environments. The rationale I will try to establish in this chapter might therefore not only be limited to a certain period, but also to a specific environment: rural communities. As Eugen Weber has argued, around 1870 many parishes in France were as yet untouched by the manifold forces of modernization.[10] The modern state attempted to control the anonymous masses through different institutions (schools, the military, hospitals, the police, civil administration, regulated medicine, etc.), but this did not affect rural communities as much as it did the cities – although, as we saw in the case of Finon, who was examined on request of the crown prosecutor, it sometimes did. Ackerman has persuasively demonstrated how long it took before 'modern medicine' took hold in the rural areas surrounding Paris during the nineteenth century.[11] In the light of this slow pace of modernization in the countryside, the stories analyzed here might seem remnants of an 'old time' or 'ancien régime', a world that existed simultaneously with the emergence of the modern state and its institutions in urban areas. But I do not wish to suggest that the rationale described in this chapter is definitively delineated in time, and I would rather label it 'rural' than 'pre-modern'.

SECRECY AND NON-INTERVENTION

Doubts about sex at birth and throughout childhood
If there was doubt about a baby's sex at birth, the parents were often ashamed. In many cases, the fact that there had been any doubt at the start was carefully hidden. For example, in 1819, Henning described a case in which a midwife could not make out the sex of the duke's groom's newborn, and reported: 'As *usual*, the situation was handled very secretly in the beginning . . .'.[12] More than three-quarters of a century later, the story of N. O. Body reveals that at his birth, his father and the midwife were inclined to think he was a girl, whereas his mother thought he was a boy. A doctor was consulted, who declared the child to be a girl on account of its outward appearance. The father then made the doctor promise to keep his mouth shut and paid off the midwife in order to make sure that 'this awfully offensive matter' did not become more widely known.[13] Malformation could therefore be experienced as a disgrace which needed to be hidden at any price.

If, later on, it became apparent that an error might have been made, the family's reputation sometimes weighed more than the duty duly to represent a body, as the case of Hanna O. illustrates. When Hanna O. was born, she was declared female by the midwife, but there must always have been doubts about her sex. Her mother, who had left the child with its grandparents during the first eight years of its life in order to work elsewhere, immediately checked the girl's body upon her return. Because she feared 'the clamour over this delicate question', she 'ordered her so-called daughter to keep the deepest silence concerning the state of her sex and urgently demanded that she very carefully evade any situation in which she could be compromised in this respect'.[14]

For similar reasons, many people decided to stick with the sex they had been assigned to, even if they knew that an error had been made, as in Anna Barbara Meier's case. Consider, for example, the case of Jules Gobet, who was only discovered to be female when he ended up in hospital after an accident in 1883:

. . . As the midwife had announced her to be a boy when she was born, she had always passed as such and was raised as such by her parents, who were very poor, ignorant peasants. Even when the phenomenon of menstruation made its appearance, and she experienced the sensations experienced by girls at puberty, feminine modesty, or the dread of exposure or being talked about in the village, prevented her from proclaiming the true nature of things, and she therefore went on playing the part of a man until she ended up in hospital.[15]

What does this way of dealing with doubtful sex at birth and during childhood show? First of all, that hermaphroditism was experienced as a disgrace, possibly on the basis of its age-old significance as 'monstrous' – a bad omen, something frightening and offensive.[16] This in itself was an important reason not to have this sex further examined by a doctor, but to keep it secret. Secondly, it should be noted that the family's reputation was to be protected, not just that of the individual hermaphrodite. The reputation of being a hermaphrodite could apparently also rub off on others. So, in Anna Barbara Meier's case, this might mean that her parents and the midwife had not been careless or ignorant, but had wanted to protect the entire family's name against the shame of such a 'monstrous' body.

Publicly visible sexual ambiguity

In the short biographies of hermaphrodites included in medical case histories, their initial sex assignment was mostly indicated as follows: 'X, baptized or registered as a girl, having worn female clothing and done female work since [. . .]'. These three elements are always present: the registration as male or female, the clothing and the occupation. They represent someone's sex in the public arena after the first (and normally only) inspection of the genitals at birth. It is through ambiguities in outward appearance and occupation that doubt might be instilled in a local community concerning the sex which somebody had initially been inscribed with. Both were related to the sex of the body as well as to certain social and cultural assumptions about sex: to a woman's physical strength and to the definition of men's work, for example, or to the growth of facial hair and the habit of shaving, or to the ability of being able to urinate standing up and the custom of men wearing trousers. The outward and sexual function of the *genitals* only became relevant again if the body became more intimately known by same-sex peers or sexual partners. I will return to such occasions in the next section, although, of course, sometimes such knowledge was also passed on to the community at large and became public knowledge. Generally speaking, however, outward appearance – whether a beard or one's urinating habits – was very important to hermaphrodites in how well they fared socially. In many cases, this might therefore have been more decisive than the precise appearance or functioning of the genitals.

This is reminiscent of Dror Wahrman's description of seventeenth-century culture, in which a person's social position was primarily indicated by clothing. However, according to him this changed during the eighteenth century, when garments came to express unique individuality.[17] But Wahrman also observes that such changes primarily took place in the rapidly growing major cities of England 'where the comfort of knowing who people were by how they looked and dressed had been replaced by the play of unreliable appearances'.[18] It might therefore well be that the 'comfort of knowing each other' from outward appearance was continued in the countryside which was where the majority of people still lived throughout much of the nineteenth century.

Even though hermaphrodites carefully tried to hide their doubtful sex, they often could not help displaying physical signs of ambiguity. As the case histories of Finon, Anna Barbara Meier and Elisabeth Holzheid have shown, this mostly had to do with people raised as women who developed beards, or with those inscribed as males who had problems urinating standing up. In women, a physically strong appearance and a tall frame also attracted attention. In view of the fact that so many hermaphrodites tried to hide their ambiguity, it is remarkable that quite a few people raised as females did not restrain themselves from using their physical strength and doing what was considered men's work. In this section I will first consider these publicly visible sexual ambiguities, and then discuss why these apparently did not lead to intervention by medical or legal authorities.

Her fellow villagers began mocking and harassing Anna Barbara Meier and calling her a hermaphrodite as soon as she started growing a beard. According to the medical report, the beard was clearly visible, even if she had just shaved. The sex of many other people raised as females also became doubtful only because of their beards.[19] In 1870, for example, Marie Chupin reported to the head of police in Beaupréau the fact that her brother and two nieces had spread 'insulting words likely to harm his honour'. These rumours 'so insulting, consisted of words from the girls who found it strange that their supposed [female: GM] cousin had a beard and shaved like a man'.[20] Another example concerns two sisters aged twenty-eight and thirty-two, still unmarried, which, according to the medical case history, was highly unusual in the region. The reason for this, it is suggested, was that:

> . . . it is common knowledge that these are bearded, extremely hirsute indi-
> viduals, looking every inch the virago, who look very vigorous which gives
> them a truly masculinized appearance. These particularities are known: but
> everyone agrees that their behaviour is absolutely irreproachable and their
> reputation unblemished.[21]

Apparently, none of the local communities demanded further disclosure of the bodies of these women and the possible subsequent reappraisal of their sex.

I do not know of any cases in which such a masculine appearance occasioned a medical examination of the body.

In many case histories of persons originally inscribed as female, mention is made of their ability to do heavy (men's) work. For example, Anna Barbara Meier, when describing his physical appearance to a physician, mentioned his capacity to perform men's work, and, amazingly, *not* his capacity to perform coitus. As we have seen in the introductory stories, much attention was paid to the sort of work Finon and Elisabetha Holzheid were engaged in. Both did men's jobs. What makes this so remarkable is that in all these cases these women were also *allowed* to do men's work. Without much trouble, they seemed to be able to shift into men's occupations. If the sort of work one did was such a primary marker of sex – as the brief introductions to the life histories indicate – why would women be allowed to step across the divide between women's and men's work so easily? I think the value of such labour should not be underestimated here. Before the general availability of mechanized power, the value of physical strength was such that women could quite easily cross the limits of female work. Below, we will see that even some husbands thought their wife's strength outweighed her incapacity to perform sexual intercourse or produce offspring.

As these examples and the histories in the introduction to this chapter show, cases of doubtful sex often were ignored, even if the ambiguity was publicly observable. 'Ignored' here refers to the fact that neither the church, local authorities nor medical experts were called upon to establish whether the sex attributed to the person in question was correct. No further examination of the body was demanded by the community through these authorities. In Finon's case, it was even accepted that she did not clearly belong to either sex. The odd combination of hard labour and feminine clothing, of assaulting women and being used by soldiers, for example, did not occasion any action against her or pressure on some authority to determine her sex. Anna Barbara Meier's and Finon D.'s communities even used general idiom to express their peculiar position; Meier, like many other people in Germany, had the reputation of being a *Zwitter* or hermaphrodite. Finon was called Finon because in the region of Lorraine masculine women were given the suffix 'on'. Other hermaphrodites raised as females were described as 'bearded' or 'viragos'. This indicates a structural space for people of ambiguous sex.

I have found evidence for such tolerance mostly in stories from rural areas, among farmers and in villages. One of the explanations for this tolerance can therefore be sought in the non-anonymous environment these people had been brought up in and continued to live in. Everybody *knew* Anna Barbara Meier, Finon D. and Elisabetha Holzheid from birth. They probably knew their parents and siblings as well. There might be something odd or idiosyncratic about them, but they were no threat to the social or moral order because they had more or less *grown into* the community in the way they had turned out to be.

However – and this is a big however – this does not mean to say some sort of rural paradise existed in which people could freely occupy a sexually ambivalent position. On the contrary, the stories also show that people with a sexually ambiguous appearance were under constant surveillance: they were noticed, watched, talked about and judged. Moreover, calling them 'hermaphrodites', 'viragos' or 'bearded' was a way of controlling the situation – they would not fool anybody about their sex – for everybody was forewarned. The two elderly unmarried sisters were apparently carefully monitored, and any possible moral slip would be noticed. Gossip, mockery and public scorn must have kept most of the hermaphrodites involved neatly in their place. This worked, I believe, as a containment policy; a strategy through which a dubious sex was barred from 'contaminating' other people. Shame, the fear of being mocked and scorned, kept many hermaphrodites away from other people; several were said to have become extremely shy and to have avoided all people, living alone on a farm or in a hovel.[22] Most importantly, many decided not to marry, as did the two sisters mentioned above. By keeping a close watch, acknowledging them to be 'masculinized', and praising them for their impeccable lives, they were contained in their isolated and unmarried state.

Another comment should be made. It seems likely that public signs of a *man's* physical dysfunction, more specifically, his way of urinating, were less tolerable. The urinating posture turns out to have been extremely important in assigning a sex to someone. If the sex of a newborn raised doubts, its parents often decided on one or the other sex after advice from a midwife. As many cases show, and as Neugebauer also stated, the way the baby urinated was usually decisive.[23] This might seem a bit silly, but there are indications we should take this seriously. As we have seen, Finon was treated as a girl after he could not manage to urinate like a boy without wetting his clothes. At the end of his life, he tore up the trousers he had been forced to wear. Could he not simply have taken off his trousers and squatted? This was obviously not an option. But why not? There is one case, described in 1856, that might provide the key to this.

After three years of regular sexual intercourse with the unmarried Johanna K., Maria Oh. was surprised to find herself pregnant. So was the village which had always thought that Maria Oh. was not particularly interested in men. Johanna K. herself had always thought that since the semen flowed along the outside there was no danger of getting anyone pregnant. The baby's genitals turned out to have the same malformation (hypospadias) as Johanna K.'s, which confirmed that she was the child's father. When Traxel, the forensic medical expert in the case, asked himself whether Johanna K.

should be made to wear men's clothing from now on, he seriously considered the following objection:

> Johanna K. has lived as a woman in society for thirty-seven years. She discharges urine like a woman and thus cannot wear the usual men's leg attire. If she changes this to fit the circumstances, it will advertise a deformity which is no fault of her own. Must she nevertheless be forced to wear men's clothes?[24]

So, even though Johanna K. had made a woman pregnant, the way she urinated was a serious consideration in the decision about the sex she should represent in society. Traxel ultimately decided she should wear men's clothing, because both 'the situation at hand' and 'morality' demanded a distinction between the sexes. But the quote clearly shows how important the urinating position (standing up or squatting) was as an indication for belonging to either the male or the female sex.[25] A brief remark in another case also shows the social importance of one's urinating position. Describing a person who changed his social sex at the age of twenty-six, it states that he kept to himself and never sought companionship, directly followed by: 'no one saw him urinate'.[26] In another case, of a person who was raised as a woman but who had been declared male, the physician doubted his capacity to live as a man and fulfil his military service because of his failure to urinate like a man.[27] Neugebauer asserts that many hermaphrodites raised as females who had a hypospadiac penis did not put on male attire because of their problems with urination, even if they were sexually involved with women.[28] Thus, several sources suggest that a man incapable of urinating standing up was unacceptable. No wonder, therefore, that the earliest surgery on hermaphrodites I have found was intended to enable a person to urinate standing up.[29] Towards the end of the nineteenth century, surgically creating the possibility to urinate 'like a man' was one of the operations most in demand among hermaphrodites.

Bodies: disclosure versus surveillance
In all these cases of publicly visible sexual ambiguity, the modern reader unfamiliar with medical history is surprised by the lack of urgency to have the body examined. We would expect such a person, her parents, her schoolmaster or the parish priest to want to know more about her physical sex and, to that end, to (make her) visit a general practitioner. Such an expectation contains many presuppositions as to how people see physicians, on which occasions they visited them and what doctors actually did on those occasions. A first look at the basic conditions of private medical practice in the first half of the nineteenth century will help to explain why 'our' logic was not logical to contemporaries.

One reason for Anna Barbara Meier not to disclose herself to a doctor was her resistance to show anyone her 'secret parts'. As chapter 4 will show, she persevered in this resistance even during the process of being reassigned to the opposite sex, by stubbornly refusing a visual examination by the physician who had to establish her sex – i.e. she did not want a doctor to *see* her genitals. Throughout the nineteenth century, physicians mention the strong feelings of shame about and resistance to physical examinations hermaphrodite patients often showed. For example, a person 'baptized and dressed' as a woman with quite remarkable male characteristics, could not be examined because she was far too 'religious, ashamed and secretive'.[30] An extreme example, to which I will return extensively in chapter 5, was the case of Justine Jumas. She had been married for more than two years when her husband made a complaint against her, claiming she was not a woman, which would make the marriage null and void. Although the court ordered a physical examination, and although she lost her appeal against that order, she maintained her resistance to being examined.

However, such resistance was not just individual and not only originates in having an unusual body. At least during the first half of the century, it appears not to have been self-evident for physicians to see a naked body – especially the body of a female person (even if this female sex was in doubt). As several historians have pointed out, in private practice physicians were generally very careful not to expose the naked female body to their eyes, and restricted themselves to touching the body under clothing, under sheets or in a dark room.[31] When, for example, Herculine Barbin was examined for the very first time by the local general practitioner, he speaks of the doctor's hand slipping under his sheets.[32] In this respect, hospitals constituted a completely different environment where the predominantly poor women who wound up there could be examined without much restraint.[33] I will return to this topic extensively in Part II.

When persons of doubtful sex and inscribed as females were legally forced to undergo a physical examination, midwives often had to carry out the actual examination under a doctor's supervision. Such an arrangement was also made in Justine Jumas' case.[34] The problem might therefore be the exposure of the naked female body to the male medical eye. The doctors involved often tried to persuade the courts that they needed to examine the body themselves.[35] The immense discussion among forensic doctors and lawyers in the Jumas case clearly shows, moreover, that a physical examination was considered a serious intrusion on the body, only to be allowed under very specific circumstances, if at all.[36] In other words, the presupposition that it would be natural to call for a doctor to determine someone's sex through careful examination of the genitals is incorrect. During the first part of the nineteenth century, it was a far from self-evident response to the problem.

However, this should not to suggest that bodies were not kept under surveillance. Historians of the body and medicine in the early modern period have demonstrated that, in the early modern period, interference with the body was by no means the monopoly of physicians. There were many more people who dealt with bodies – midwives, surgeons, barbers, herbalists, quacks, married women who had given birth and were therefore considered to 'know', neighbours, family members and servants. These were often more in touch with the naked body than physicians, as during the early modern period at least, medical doctors often explicitly refrained from dealing with the physical body since this was considered to be quackery.[37] When it came to women and their supposedly open or 'leaky' bodies, they were under the severe control of other women, especially experienced ones – i.e. married women with children.[38] It seems probable that interference with bodies was generally arranged according to sex; especially women's bodies were for the most part supervised by other women. Take for example Hanna O., who started to doubt her own sex after having been mocked by her girlfriends while bathing, which ultimately led to her disclosure. It is often brought up that a person shared her bed with other girls, or if a boy, with other boys.[39] In a world where so many people could interfere with the body, Anna Barbara Meier probably not only considered possible lovers, but might also have been protecting himself against physical exposure to peers, neighbours or family when deciding never to disclose his private parts. Men were also supposed to be quite intimate physically with each other, to share beds and to urinate together; they were not expected to be ashamed of being naked in front of each other. For example, one of the case histories tells the story of a farmer from Regensburg, who asked the army physician to allow his stepson to undress separately, because of the feminine appearance of his genitals and the fact that he had his period at the time of the medical examination.[40] But boys' and men's bodies could also be controlled by women, especially their mothers. There was certainly much less concern about women seeing male bodies than vice versa.

This way of dealing with bodies and keeping them under surveillance not just by medical doctors, but by a whole range of people from their community, seems to jeopardize my hypothesis that the correct representation of the body was not always the primary logic in sex assignment. After all, if I only have sources in which a medical doctor had disclosed the case (in an article, to his colleagues), how can I tell that hermaphrodites were not controlled physically by midwives or family members? I cannot. Perhaps most of the problems concerning doubtful sex were solved through the daily surveillance of bodies, which left no trace in the historical records. I will certainly not exclude that possibility, and some cases do indeed show that the disclosure of a doubtful sex to a medical doctor was instigated by physical contact between siblings, cousins or friends as was the case with Hanna O. However, in many cases ultimately disclosed by a doctor, the hermaphrodite in question seemed to have been let be until that very moment.

Moreover, and possibly even more fundamentally, the everyday control of bodies does not seem to have been directed at establishing someone's 'true' sex; rather, it was meant to ensure this ambiguous body was contained within certain moral and legal boundaries. The two bearded virago-type sisters, for example, were not forced to disclose their bodies to a doctor, but their behaviour was carefully monitored. As the labelling of certain people as 'hermaphrodites' or females as 'masculine' suggests, it could very well be that many people did not even *think* a physician could find out something like one 'true' or predominant sex, but took the fact of an ambiguous sex for granted. Neugebauer tells of a late example from the Russian countryside. A Russian farm woman was sent to him because the examining doctor suspected a wrongly established sex. Neugebauer wanted to show this interesting case to a medical society. She refused, however, saying: 'If God had created her just this way, no doctor was going to change that, so what point was there in her accompanying us to a medical society?'[41] Her dry comment that a doctor could not change her situation indicates an attitude of resignation which may well have characterized a more general attitude with regard to doubtful sexes. Within such a framework, a policy of containment was indeed more adequate than the demand for disclosure.

In conclusion, the resistance many hermaphrodites felt to a physical medical examination cannot only be ascribed to their individual fear of exposing a 'monstrous' condition. There was clearly a generally supported restraint in physically exposing a (female) body to a (male) physician. At least in the first half of the nineteenth century, the integrity of the body in relation to doctors might sometimes – possibly even often – have been more important than the imperative duly to represent one's physical sex, both for the individuals involved and for society at large. At the same time, bodies were under constant surveillance from family members, married women, midwives and peers, not so much in order to find out the truth about the body, but to ensure that it would not violate the community's moral and social rules. Several hermaphrodites and their families tried to escape this social scrutiny, as we have seen, by completely isolating themselves and avoiding any intimate physical contact.

Marriage and morals

The containment through close observation and gossip did not always work, however. That is, at a certain point in their lives, many hermaphrodites inscribed as females had sexual affairs with women. Hanna O. started to have affairs with several female peers in the village, resulting in rumours. None of the partners involved complained to the authorities, however. The same goes for the other forty-six cases of hermaphrodites registered as women who were reported to have been sexually involved with other women.[42] Sometimes, such sexual relations were involuntary. Even then, this did not automatically lead to a disclosure to the police or other authorities. Take for example the case of Eva Elisabeth S., who showed increasingly masculine traits during puberty:

> At the same time, it became evident from her sexual desires that things were not quite as they should be with the virgin Elise. She only wished to be close to women, much preferred to associate with them and sought to be alone in their company. Indeed it went so far that she dared to harass the maidservants at night, and not only did her parents receive bitter complaints about this, some maids actually gave up what was a good position in order to be rid of this individual! This issue remained a firm secret however, as Elisabethe S. lived on a farm at some distance from the village.[43]

It might have been difficult for the maidservants to make complaints or even to gossip, for after all their own honour was also at stake. The same problem possibly also arose in Anna Regina Märker's case, who allegedly abused her position as a midwife to commit sexual assaults on women. In 1858, after a woman had reported that she had been raped by her, a long history came to the light which shows that 'rumours that the midwife Märker was a hermaphrodite had been circulating for a long time'.[44] For years, she was said to have sexually assaulted many women. For more than twenty years Märker had set tongues wagging about her being a hermaphrodite, and yet nobody had pressed or forced her to disclose herself. Only after one woman had officially accused her of rape, did other women come forward with their (sometimes old) stories. Their own involvement might have been an obstacle to disclosure, for their own respectability could be affected.

The endangered reputations of the people *related* to a hermaphrodite may also have been a reason many hermaphrodites were left alone. This was true for parents and family, as we saw above, but it affected intimate friends and spouses even more. In a world where, outside marriage, physical intimacies were very much restricted to one's own sex, the discovery of an inappropriate or doubtful sex could – in hindsight – put all sorts of seemingly everyday situations in an immoral or indecent light. Disclosing someone else's sexual ambiguity to religious, legal or medical authorities could therefore severely affect one's own honour. Similarly, spouses who disclosed their partner's sex to be doubtful or inappropriate risked the shame of having had a sexual relationship with a hermaphrodite or a person of their own sex. Although I have not found explicit references to such fears in the sources, this might well be one of the reasons why spouses did not always come forward with doubts about their partner's sex. We should keep in mind that it is difficult to find evidence of such instances, as spouses *not* making a complaint normally do not leave any traces in the sources. The best evidence for their hesitation to disclose the situation to the authorities is the fact that it took almost all of them a long time before they reported the situation. One good example is a farm woman from the Breslau area who happened to marry three times. The first two marriages ended with the death of her husband: they lasted four and a half years and two and a half years respectively. The third husband, the farmer Kaluza, demanded to be divorced from his wife because of *dyspareunie* (difficult or painful coitus) after three years. After several medical procedures and legal proceedings she was declared male on the basis of, among other things, her ability to ejaculate semen. So why did the previous husbands not complain, and why did Kaluza wait three years? The husbands' own reputations may have been the main cause. But there may possibly have been other reasons as well.

Some marriages with hermaphrodites were annulled after legal proceedings, but there are also many examples of long-lasting marriages.[45] Elisabetha Holzheidt, of the third story in the introduction to this chapter, stayed married until the end and was only physically examined after her death. Apparently, *her* husband did not care so much about his reputation, at least not when he was drunk, for he himself joked about her in the pub. According to the village rumours, the marriage was barely consummated and the husband found sexual satisfaction elsewhere. Why then did he not seek annulment? The answer seems obvious: Elisabetha Holzheidt was the only daughter of a rich farmer. Moreover, she allegedly did all the work, i.e. managing and running a rather big farm. Even while she was ridiculed, marriage gave Elisabetha Holzheidt a much higher and better protected status than if she would have remained single; her husband seems simply to have profited from her wealth and labour.

Marriage was not only about love, sex and procreation, it was also about economic support, survival and social status. A couple of case histories in which a masculine woman was married indicate that, even though the couple's sex life may have been minimal, the woman's strength was very much appreciated. Take the case of Anastasia G., a 41-year-old Polish woman, married for sixteen years to a farmer. She had a huge frame, strong muscles, female breasts and a hairy body, including a moustache. Her genitals looked female when she was standing upright, but when she lay on her back with her legs apart, her clitoris looked like the penis of a 'Jewish boy of twelve years old'.[46] The spouses lived harmoniously together, despite the fact that coitus was almost impossible and painful to her. The widower already had several children from his previous marriage. '. . . He climbs into her bed no more than once a month; on the other hand he is highly satisfied to have a wife of such bodily strength, who performs hard, manly work in the fields, woods and at home.'[47]

A couple of other husbands were also very happy with the heavy work their wives were able to perform.[48] In these cases the value of their work apparently weighed more than the prevalent sexual division of work and sometimes even more than sexual satisfaction and procreation. In contexts where hard physical labour was very valuable, a body's physical strength could surpass its sexual function (and its social, economic and moral meanings). Marriage, indeed, was not only a contract promising love, sex and offspring, it was also about economic survival. If a marriage did not work sexually or if it turned out to be a marriage between two people more or less of the same sex, that was not always considered the predominant issue.

Sometimes, however, it *was*. A German case of a marriage annulment, described by Tourtual in 1856, detailed the troubles the spouses encountered before the lawsuit started. In this case, the impossibility of coitus clearly was the husband's main complaint. In 1847 the artisan F., a widower with four young children, married a 37-year-old maid, G. They had already had sex before the wedding but at that time F. had not noticed the constitution of her genitalia; it had not interfered with his attraction to and affection for her. However, during the wedding night he discovered that she could not fulfil her 'conjugal obligation' because her vagina was not deep enough; he was unable to penetrate her and his semen immediately ran off on the outside. After several fruitless attempts, he became convinced that she also had masculine parts, that she was both male and female or perhaps neither, or that she was even more male than female.[49] At first they managed to live together peacefully, but then they started quarrelling, also because his wife accused him of having an affair with another woman.

> The parson from whom F. sought counsel for his conscience declared that under these particular circumstances the marriage was invalid and that he was not permitted to sleep with this person. And so, when in the summer of 1848 the wife left the house for a few days to visit relatives, he removed her bed from their shared bedroom and in answer to her query answered that he had done it because she was not a woman and could not live with him as a wife.[50]

On and off they lived apart and together. After some years, he finally left her in the autumn of 1851, out of weariness.[51] For the next three years, F. kept asking guidance from several confessors, but could not get consistent and decisive advice.[52] Only after having consulted a lawyer who claimed that he could annul the marriage he decided to overcome the problem of the costs of a lawsuit, because 'he found it impossible to live in abstinence'.[53]

We might view F.'s case as proof that an unsatisfying sex life could be the main drive for having a marriage dissolved. However, we may doubt whether his sex life was unsatisfactory to him. After all, he kept having sex with his wife for years, thus infringing the first parson's order to abstain from sex with his wife. But he was clearly afraid to live in sin and finally left her. He then started to seek advice from several other clerical authorities. Did he, perhaps, hope that some priest would permit him to have sex with his wife? Or did he wait until somebody told him how he could annul his marriage? We do not know. What we do know, however, is that for him marriage was a sanctified union. He very much doubted whether his own marriage was valid and whether having sex did not violate Christian morality. His attempts at abstinence seem to have originated in this fear rather than in his sexual dissatisfaction. Therefore, in the first instance he did not seek advice from *doctors*, but from *priests*. For him, and for many others, a doubtful sex in the first place caused *moral* doubts.

There is evidence that other hermaphrodites or people closely involved with them also primarily sought out clerical officials. Christina Knoll and Anna Barbara Meier, for instance, confessed their problem in the 'parish'; the decision about Meier's sex reassignment and marriage was taken by a matrimonial court of the German *Evangelische Kirche* (the Protestant Church). Others first went to a priest before disclosing themselves to a physician, for instance Maria Katharina Ulmerin who in April 1794, at the age of forty, decided to first announce her desire 'to enjoy the political advantages of being a man' to her confessor.[54] From Herculine Barbin's autobiography – to which we will return in detail in chapter 3 – we know that she confessed her problem to a priest at least three times before the bishop sent her to a physician for further examination. What is more, the second time Barbin was emphatically advised to keep her secret to herself while he himself was already aware that he was (physically) a man. At the time, Barbin was having a love affair with the daughter of the headmistress of the girls' boarding school he worked at. This is what the priest, according to Barbin's text, told her:

> 'I shall not tell you', he said to me, 'what you know as well as I do, that is to say, you are here and now entitled to call yourself a man in society. Certainly you are, but how will you obtain the legal right to do so? At the price of the greatest scandals, perhaps. However, you cannot keep your present position, which is so full of danger. I therefore give you the following advice: withdraw from the world and become a nun; but be very careful not to repeat the confession that you have made to me, for a convent of women would not admit you. This is the only course that I have to offer you, and believe me, accept it.'[55]

Avoiding scandal, in this priest's view, would be better than gaining the position Barbin's body entitled him to. The *social* and *moral* consequences of a sex reassignment seemed to be more important than its *physical* suitability. Possibly, the priest hoped Barbin could turn away from worldly and particularly physical matters altogether by entering a convent, to escape a world in which sex mattered.

In addition, it becomes all the more clear that keeping one's doubtful or inappropriate sex secret must have been quite an ordinary strategy, not only practised by hermaphrodites, their parents and spouses, but also by an institution such as the Church. The example may also once again clarify why my evidence must be the tip of the iceberg. Anyone in Barbin's position who followed this priest's advice, would never have left a trace in the historical records.

DISCLOSURE

So far, I have deliberately and artificially left out the fact that all the cases I have mentioned *were* eventually disclosed to a physician (and subsequently published). Below I will discuss the reasons for disclosure in cases where lay people were aware of irregularities concerning someone's genitals or sexual function and (eventually) decided to consult a doctor. Why did they disclose their problem to a doctor or decide to request a physical examination? What does that add to the logic of the rationale of secrecy and non-intervention as assessed so far?

Disclosure by lay people

There are two main reasons why lay people – hermaphrodites themselves, or others directly involved – went to a doctor in order to get a doubtful sex physically examined, and both are related to sexual function. Firstly, people went to see a doctor when they had doubts about a (future) marriage because of one or more physical dysfunctions. This could be the hermaphrodite herself, her (future) spouse or the two of them together. One example is the artisan F., mentioned in the section above, who after years of trying to have satisfactory sex wanted his marriage annulled. What followed was an extensive physical examination, first by several midwives and subsequently by a doctor. We will find out more about this in chapter 4.

But it did not only happen after the marriage contract had been signed. Often people wanted medical advice beforehand. An example is Marie B., who doubted very much if she was fit for marriage. This case was described by Justin Benoit in 1840. Marie B., twenty-seven years old, came to consult him and told him that she had become acquainted with a young man who desired her, and whom she herself loved, but that she had become worried about her sex. She had already been to see a local doctor who had made an incision to open the vagina artificially, obviously thinking it was just a case of imperforation of the hymen. This had no result. But, Benoit writes:

> . . . Marie did not lose all hope of recovering female attributes. As her tastes and penchants were those of a woman, she convinced herself that she belonged to the female sex. Since the different pretexts she used to try to postpone the proposed union were not sufficient to put off the young lover, she decided to confide to him the secret of her sexual conformation. In vain. He, probably

not suspecting the whole truth, seemed to attach little importance to it and persisted in his pursuit. The marriage was about to be concluded when Marie, wiser and more sensible, asked for a few days to reflect on her position. Having doubts in her mind about the reality of her sex, she decided to resolve them and learn about the fate in store for her. To this end she came to Montpellier and came to ask my advice on 24 August 1840.[56]

Marie B. was very decisive in her doubts. Although she felt she belonged to the female sex, she was clearly aware that something might be seriously wrong. We do not know exactly what made her doubt her sex. The combination of her being engaged and the earlier attempt of the local physician to cut open the hymen might indicate a problem with having sexual intercourse. There may possibly have also been other signs troubling her mind. It is clear, however, that she was not sure, and that she hoped to get a definite answer from a physician in Montpellier. Obviously, she thereby exchanged a local physician for a more academically trained physician (Benoit would become the Deacon of the Faculty of Medicine at Montpellier some forty years later). So, she expected the physician to be able to find decisive characteristics of her sex which she could not definitively make out for herself.

From other cases it becomes clear that such visits to the doctor prior to a marriage were often instigated by parents, who apparently suspected something might be wrong. Sometimes the fear of disappointing the future family-in-law was an additional reason for having the body checked, as will be apparent from the following case:

> This marriage was desired equally by the two families; however, *Marie's* parents considered it, and recalled that she was not at all made like other people; they knew she did not have periods, and in order not to blame themselves after-wards, in order not to take advantage of the son of old friends, they decided to have their daughter examined.[57]

A second occasion for medical inspection of a hermaphrodite body was when relations between a person inscribed as female and other females started to become too overtly sexual. In the case of Anna Barbara Meier and Johanna K., that point was reached when they each made another woman pregnant; another similar case occurred at the same time as Meier's in Norway.[58] Often, such sexual relations were a consequence of the ease of physical contact between girls or women. This is probably one of the reasons they could easily be hushed up. Johanna K. slept with her lover for three years without arousing suspicion. During the first half of the century, it was mostly only if rumours started, that such relations forced hermaphrodites raised as women to disclose themselves to a physician. Later case histories also reveal that it was at the hermaphrodite's instigation that action was taken.

Take, for instance, Hanna O.'s case. Her mother had warned her not to show her private parts to anyone. But she had already started to brood about her sex, after her comrades mocked her while they were bathing. Over time, she started having erections and became attracted to the female sex. Finally, she also experienced ejaculations. At the age of fifteen she confided in one of her girlfriends who affirmed her belief that she belonged to the male sex. The two started to have intercourse with each other. Later on Hanna O. also had intercourse with other girlfriends. Rumours increased and the mother finally understood that it was going to be impossible to keep a lid on it. The daughter herself insisted on reporting the situation to the authorities in order to be able to 'finally enjoy male rights'.[59] In June 1834, the city government was informed and the medical investigation started.[60]

The fact that most reasons for disclosure to physicians were connected with sexual function makes it clear that *relations with others* or, more generally, with the entire social, moral and legal order, were always at stake. In some cases, the interests of (future) spouses or of the local community, were the driving forces behind an inspection of a hermaphrodite's body (if a marriage was annulled or if public decency was in jeopardy). In other cases, the wish to have a body medically inspected was mainly the hermaphrodite's (to resolve doubts, for instance or to be able to marry as a woman or a man). But in the first half of the century, mere *private* doubts about one's own sex (such as Anna Barbara Meier had experienced since puberty), with no reference to the interests of others, were not enough to make someone visit a doctor. People may have been scorned, uncertain, isolated or desperate, but they would not consult a doctor just for the sake of their own questions with regard to their sex. If such feelings were connected to sexual activities or marriage plans, they might consult a doctor. Only later on in the century did autonomous feelings of doubt about one's own sex cause disclosures to doctors.

What does this add to our understanding of the rationale behind secrecy and disclosure? As long as the trouble of doubtful sex remained a problem for the people concerned and did not affect other people's moral or legal status, it was rarely disclosed to a physician. Those with doubtful sexes may have had all sorts of intimate or sexual relations, but if these did not start gossip or lead to extramarital pregnancies, the social environment could – and often would – turn a blind eye. However, if such matters became publicly known to the detriment of public moral order, gossip could force hermaphrodites to have the uncertainties medically investigated. Or, if these relationships were the prelude to marriage and would therefore eventually involve the legal system, doubts sometimes led to the hermaphrodite, their family or the future spouse's request for further examination. Finally, if doubts were raised *within* an already existing marriage, this could lead the spouse to request the court to order a medical examination. Within this rationale, the trouble of doubtful sex was therefore never disclosed to solve personal, individual problems in the relationship between the body and the assigned sex. *Only* if such problems affected other people, *and* if this in turn affected the moral, social and legal order of the community, was the assistance of a physician requested to determine, on the basis of a physical examination, to which sex the person concerned rightfully belonged. What about the sexual drives and desires described in these cases, the reader might wonder, were they not an expression of the individual? We will return to this question in the following chapters.

A PROVISIONAL RATIONALE

Let me now try to understand the logic of the category of sex as it can be discerned from what has so far been found in the case histories up until around 1870. The rationale is not *necessarily tied* to a specific period of time, however, as we will see below. At birth, the rationale of sex as a category was defined on the basis of the appearance of the genitals. Subsequently, sex was the social, economic, moral and legal position in relation to others which is represented by name (registration in the baptismal register and/or civil administration), clothing (or appearance) and work (and education and other activities). This position was primarily defined by a heterosexual order in the sense that non-sexual physical intimacies were allowed among persons of the same sex, whereas sex was only permitted in heterosexual marriage. In some cases, outward appearance, performance or physical strength could outweigh the significance of this heterosexual order.

Outward appearance (clothing) and occupation were important signifiers of sex. In this respect, hermaphrodites could attract attention by their physical deviation from what was considered normal for women or men. Especially hermaphrodites raised as females with obvious masculine physical traits such as a beard or extraordinary physical strength acquired a reputation as such: they were talked about, ridiculed, called *Zwitter* (in Germany) or hermaphrodite, bearded or virago, and received the special suffix 'on' (in Lorraine). The sources suggest that people raised as males who failed to urinate standing up (and with their trousers on) had more difficulties living as men than women who did not conform to the stereotype.

Generally, it was far from self-evident to have a physician discover 'the truth' about such an ambiguous body, however. Firstly, an unusual constitution of genitals and an ambiguous appearance of sex were considered extremely shameful. Both the individuals and their relatives involved tried to keep the private parts secret, also before doctors. Moreover, physicians did not have a monopoly on the body. At the time, other persons professionally dealing with bodies or otherwise intimate with the hermaphrodites – midwives, married women who had given birth, quacks, family members (including servants), peers, lovers and spouses – could access the naked body much more easily than medical doctors. Same-sex intimacies (such as sleeping, bathing, urinating together (for men)) were quite ordinary and sometimes led to same-sex sexual acts. But their knowledge of a hermaphrodite's unusual sexual parts did not automatically lead to a request for further examination and the possible correction of her sex assignment. Even when someone suspected their spouse to have an ambiguous or incorrectly assessed sex, it was not self-evident for them to make a complaint in order to get their spouse's sex examined.

Doubts about someone's sex not only involved the person concerned, but the entire community surrounding this person: family, peers, lovers or spouses, colleagues, etc. They might be *contaminated* by the doubt – become just as morally suspect or involved in scandal as the hermaphrodite him- or herself – and increasingly so in the event the doubt was further disclosed. Many hermaphrodites or their partners sought help from *priests* or *vicars* rather than from doctors. For them, doubts about sex were a *moral* problem rather than a physical question, affecting others and morality in general. Therefore, the danger of an inconclusive, ambiguous sex disrupting the social and moral order, was controlled not by disclosure and (re)assignment, but by *containment*. Containment was implemented by the habit of keeping a close watch on each other's bodies and by gossip and social isolation, which forced the hermaphrodite to be extremely discreet about her ambiguous sex and sexual relations. As a result, many hermaphrodites were reported to be shy, socially isolated, living alone and clinging to their unmarried state.

However, when this containment practice failed, and the fabric of the community was jeopardized by irregular publicly known or legal sexual arrangements, chances were that either the hermaphrodite in question or an interested party would request a further inspection of the body. Only then would the rationale of sex as the rightful representation of the body reappear. Neither the policy of containment nor disclosure seem to have been purely individual choices; other people or the community as a whole were always involved.

Therefore, once established after birth, the rationale of sex was primarily its being *inscribed* in the social, economic, moral and ultimately legal fabric of the community. Doubts about physical sex affected not only the individual and her or his body, but the entire community. In the introduction to this chapter I hesitated to call this rationale 'pre-modern' and chose to label it 'rural' instead. Understanding the rationale as described above, I think it would be more precise to locate this rationale in an environment where people were known by name and had been involved in a community from early childhood on. This is also the reason why the period in which this rationale functioned cannot be clearly defined, and why, to a certain extent, this logic could continue to play a role. In environments in which people were relatively anonymous, such as urban areas or at larger institutions such as hospitals, this rationale of inscription was much less likely to function. In an anonymous context, a person's sex was no longer attached to a lifelong acquaintance, but came to mean something of and on its own. Parts II and III will detail the consequences of separating sex from such a 'knowing' of the whole person, as they describe how modern medicine arrived at deliberately separating bodies from their biographical, social and moral attachments.

2

EARLY SEX REASSIGNMENTS
AND THE ABSENCE OF A SEX OF SELF

SELF, SUBJECT AND IDENTITY

In the previous chapter, I tried to determine the rationale behind the category of sex in view of the fact that it was apparently not self-evident that a doctor should examine the body if someone's physical sex was in doubt. As the case histories show, after the initial sex assignment at birth, sex became so intricately interwoven into the social, moral and legal fabric, that doubts about an individual's sex affected the entire community. Policies of containment therefore seem to have prevailed in communities in which hermaphrodites were known from birth. In that rationale, bodies were under constant surveillance from all members of the community, not to discover a truth, but to keep them in check. Therefore, which sex a person belonged to was strongly determined by her or his already being *inscribed* as female or male within the social, moral and legal structures. In many cases, this rationale of the continuity of inscription overruled the logic of sex as the due representation of the body. Only if the community was already morally and socially affected or threatened, would the body, examined by a doctor, become decisive in determining the hermaphrodite's sex (and possibly annulling their marriage).

But what about the self? What was, in this rationale, the role of the hermaphrodites themselves or to change a few letters and the fundamental meaning, of their 'selves'? Was there a logic that linked their own understanding of their sex, their experiences and the observation of their own bodies, their emotions, sexual desires and pleasures to the sex that was assigned to them? The first problem in answering this question is that, so long as hermaphrodites were more or less allowed to get on with their lives without intervention, there was hardly any evidence of what they may have felt, experienced or thought. It is precisely at the point where the practice of non-intervention no longer worked that the sources allow us a glimpse of the personal aspects of a doubtful sex. This chapter will therefore concentrate on the self of hermaphrodites as it appears in cases of sex reassignment following medical examinations.

Before discussing the question of the self any further, an essential distinction has to be made between a self as a position *from* which a hermaphrodite
speaks, wants or acts and a self as an object *about* which people speak or which
is dealt with. The first is the hermaphrodite's *subject* position. To what extent
was a hermaphrodite able to make her own decisions? When, where or how
was this subjective power exercised or restricted? The second is the self as an
object, something that can be imagined and described, which is used to refer
to the entirety of a person's unique inner characteristics. In modern Western
understanding, this self – often referred to as identity – is located in someone's
psyche and is the object of reflection. It is profoundly sexed. I propose to
distinguish between the two by calling the first 'subject' or 'subjectivity' and
the second, provisionally, 'the self'. Subject positions may change over time
– a person can do, say or prefer something at one point and something else
at another – but the self is considered to be essentially consistent over time
– you cannot coercively or wilfully change it. Has the self, defined in this way,
been an important factor in the medical diagnosis of the predominant sex of
hermaphrodites during the first two-thirds of the nineteenth century? And
what were the available options for hermaphrodites as subjects?

Subject and self cannot be entirely separated of course. In psychology
and more specifically in psychoanalytic theory, the relationship between
subjectivity and identity has been discussed extensively. However, as will be
clarified below, it is very hazardous for a historical study to employ current
psychological insights or psychoanalytic theory to explain the connection
between these two concepts in the past. The concept of the self as an image
of the entirety of someone's personal, deeply anchored, inner characteristics
has increasingly drawn the attention of historians, as there is a growing
awareness among them that the current Western idea of a unique, inner and
gendered self is a relatively modern invention. Therefore, I will opt for the
more structuralist explanation of the relationship between subject and self,
which, in my view, is less tangled up in a historical or cultural context.
Louis Althusser pictured subjectivity as something that comes into being
through 'interpellation', that is, through being called and through responding to that call ('Hey you, woman!' 'Yes, what do you want?'). The summons
comes from the 'ideological state apparatus' (Althusser) or from 'disciplinary
power' (Foucault).[1] Primordially, it gives you a name, a position to speak
from. Endorsing the name by responding to the way you are 'called', makes
your subject position possible. A name is the briefest description of a
person's individuality; it is *about* and not *from* the person and is therefore an
elementary form of what I have defined as the 'self'. A name almost always
also denotes a sex. This primordial relation between subjectivity and the
(sexed) self enables me to historicize the concept of self, as it leaves open
what 'the self' consists of besides a name. The *concept* of subjectivity is not

historicized here, for the fact that people act, speak, desire and think does not change. But, as subjectivity is always effected through existing discourses and practices, its *content* is historically in flux.

The first section of this chapter will supply a short introduction to the historiography of sex and self up to this point and introduce historically divergent conceptions of the self. The next section will describe how the selves of hermaphrodites were envisioned in German and French medical case histories. As we have seen, all the case histories concluded with the physical disclosure of the body to a physician; hence, they all reveal a pivotal moment when the rationale of inscription was, at least temporarily, superseded by the rationale of the body. That is certainly not to say, however, that the logic of inscription disappeared altogether. From the physicians' descriptions of the changes in the hermaphrodite's life, the notion of sex as inscription of the person – as opposed to sex as a representation of the hermaphrodite's self – can be clearly discerned and further detailed.

The last section moves away from the physician's conception of the sex of self, and discusses the hermaphrodite's subjectivity in dealing with the outcome of the medical judgement. What were the consequences of a civil reassignment of their sex or of an annulment of their marriage? What if the physician's judgement ran counter to their own conception of their sex? As information about these consequences can only be gleaned from medical case histories, the evidence is once again quite fragmented and incomplete. Ultimately, I will return to my attempts to understand the rationale of sex prevailing in non-anonymous contexts until the last quarter of the nineteenth century, particularly in relation to the personal position of the hermaphrodite. I will propose the concept of 'person' instead of 'self' to understand how the hermaphrodite related to her social environment.

GENDER AND SELF IN HISTORIOGRAPHY

The historiography of the coming into being of the modern Western self was originally dominated by either philosophers or literary historians writing about the genre of the autobiography; it was the domain of the history of ideas. Many of these studies consider the eighteenth century pivotal in the transition to a 'modern' sense of self.[2] Over the past decade, social historians have begun to investigate so-called (often unpublished) ego documents, posing critical questions as to the extent to which these cultural and ideological shifts affected the way ordinary middle-class people conceived of their selves.[3] More recently, Dror Wahrman made a major contribution to the history of the self from a cultural perspective by describing a fundamental shift in the conception of the self in relation to gender, ethnicity and class in late eighteenth-century England. Last, but not least, the historiography of

same-sex relations is an important field of study in relation to the history of
sex and self: in fact it is one of the main points of departure for this study. In
this literature, two different periods are considered crucial for north-western
Europe: either the early eighteenth century is a turning point or the late
nineteenth century, with the emergence of the category of the 'sexual invert'
within psychiatry.[4] Here, I will concentrate on the transformation of the self
in the transition from the early modern to the modern period. Later on in
this book, I will return to developments in the late nineteenth century.

In a modern concept of the self, people have a sense of self as an inalienable
and consistent inner essence. Fully acknowledging, developing and expressing (finding) this idiosyncratic self during one's lifetime is one of the major
modern moral imperatives.[5] Moreover, central to this conception of self is
a 'core gender identity', a strong, inarticulate feeling of belonging to one of
the sexes, fixed in early childhood, which is quintessential for one's proper
social and psychological functioning, especially with respect to sexuality. To
this I would like to add something else. In a modern regime of self, people
started to learn how to scrutinize their selves in a modern way, which includes
autobiographical writing, therapeutic sessions and a certain kind of private
conversation. The modern self did not arrive by itself and neither can it
survive by itself; it is enacted through manifold institutions, techniques and
practices, which all have a history of their own.

What essential features of a *pre*-modern self does the literature on the
history of the self specify? Historians have generally been better at describing
the steps taken towards the modern self than at appreciating how the
ancien régime of the self functioned. The exceptions, Charles Taylor and
Dror Wahrman, have made excellent attempts to understand a conception
of the self that is fundamentally alien to modern Western people. Taylor
has made it clear why, although classical antiquity ('Know thyself'), early
Christianity (Augustine's *Confessiones*) and the medieval and early modern
periods employed various techniques of self-scrutiny, these were fundamentally different from modern forms of self-expression and self-examination.
According to him, pre-modern techniques of the self were aimed at purifying
the self and attuning it to a higher divine or cosmic order. They were, in other
words, not aimed at finding or expressing a unique individuality, but rather at
making the self suitable for a higher order or destiny, because the self *in itself*
does not constitute what Taylor has labelled a 'constitutive moral good'.

Dror Wahrman's *The Making of the Modern Self* is a very impressive, elegantly
argued and well-documented cultural history of the self. It is, moreover, the
first to radically historicize the concept of 'gender identity', or what I would
rather call the idea of a sexed self. Wahrman – adopting the term from Sarah
Knott – speaks of a 'socially turned self' as far as the eighteenth century is
concerned, a self that is not so much anchored in an inner authentic identity,

but rather shaped through *identicality*. In this way, the pre-modern self is related to gender, race and class: people belong to certain types, they do not have a unique identity. The self or 'identity' tells us a person's status in society and his appearance indicates this position rather than expressing inner individuality. As this status was no longer secured within a divine order (which was the case in the seventeenth century and before), the eighteenth-century self was flexible, unstable and relatively easy to change or transform, according to Wahrman. Such transformations were no longer seen as impermissible and not yet as implausible.

Wahrman's theory is very helpful in making a distinction between different ways in which the self has been conceptualized throughout history. But his periodization of these different forms of self does not fit my data very well. Moreover, I believe that an important aspect of the self, that is, one's own understanding of one's self, is missing from his description. In the next chapter – in relation to Barbin's autobiographic text – I will elaborate on the historical notion of the self by incorporating autobiographic writing into the discussion. Here, I will confine myself to the way the self is presented within medical case histories up to the 1860s, and how these relate to Wahrman's way of historicizing the gendered self.

According to Wahrman, the new, modern, concept of self developed in England around the beginning of the 1780s in combination with new notions of gender, race and class. Instead of a self that was turned outwards and was primarily dependent on how a person was perceived by others, an inner self came into being: an innate, inalienable, immutable interior identity. This identity, a person's essence, could already be found in childhood.[6] Before that time, that is, during the short 'eighteenth century', identities seem to have functioned more like masks: they could easily be put on and taken off by their wearer. Gender, class and race were not yet fixed in an immutable state, but were instead conceived of as flexible, easy to transgress, fuzzy at the edges. The change from an 'ancien régime of identity' to a 'modern regime of identity' anchored the characteristics of gender, class and race in a person's unique inner essence from early childhood on. This remarkably sudden shift coincided, according to Wahrman, with the identity confusion brought about by the American Revolution. The English of the time were generally confused as to whom they should consider to be in the category of 'us' and whom in the category of 'them'; the enemy was no longer a clear-cut other. Within this major political, social and cultural conflict, obsessions and anxieties about transgressive identity categories emerged; at a later stage of the war, categories became safely fixed.

More specifically with regard to gender, Wahrman shows a distinct shift in the appreciation of women playing men's roles. During the eighteenth century, that is, until the 1780s, gender inversion could be both condemned and praised, but it was certainly not rejected by common consent. On the contrary, gender inversion was often enjoyed, was very popular on the stage and was judged credible. From the early 1780s on however, gender was suddenly seen as part of a person's inherent nature, as innate and fixed, so that gender inversion was generally rejected as unnatural or simply impossible and implausible. At this point, Wahrman elaborates on Laqueur's *Making Sex*.[7] According to Laqueur, under the one-sex system gender difference was not conceived as based on physical difference, but as a metaphysical order only reflected by the gendered order in human society. As there was no sharp – only a gradual – distinction between female and male bodies, and female bodies were considered to be able to 'grow' into male ones, physical difference was flexible. Juridical, moral and social rules were therefore, according to Laqueur, all the more strict: these had to maintain the order of gender.[8] With the shift from a one-sex to a two-sex system from the end of the seventeenth century onwards, gender no longer derived its position from the divine order but from the physical sex difference (two-sex system). Wahrman, however, asserts that this was not *immediately* the case. Instead it took some time, the short eighteenth century, before nature or the body became the fixed seat of gender identity.[9] In the meantime, a relatively loose concept of gender allowed for play, masquerade, transgression and mutation. Something similar happened to the notions of race and class, according to Wahrman.

But the shift Wahrman describes is not confined to gender, race and class. It refers to a shift in the conception of the self, of identity, as a whole. 'Here was the crucial shift from identity as "identicality" – or the collective grouping highlighting whatever a person has in common with others – to identity as that quintessential uniqueness that separates a person from all others.'[10] Identity was no longer turned outwards, but inwards. This can, for instance, be seen in contemporary critiques of novels from the previous period, whose characters were now perceived to be shallow. From now on characters had to be 'original' and 'individual'. 'Identity became interiorized, essential, even innate. It was made synonymous with the self.'[11] Moreover, it became 'harder . . . to imagine identities as mutable, assumable, divisible or actively malleable', or 'that personhood, or the self, could roam away from the man'.[12] Here, Wahrman draws on earlier histories of the self, notably Charles Taylor's *Sources of the Self*, which argues that in recent centuries Western philosophy started to consider the exploration and expression of the unique, individual self a constitutive good.

Did this individualization coincide with the assumption that categories of class, gender and race were rigid and fixed in nature? Yes and no, Wahrman argues. On the one hand, individuality superseded categories applicable to the person (there were more varieties of humankind than those of gender, race or class). The *unique individuality* of every single person started to be appreciated as such. On the other hand, these categories became part of the inalienable self – so that cross-dressing did no longer cheat the order of gender but was conceived as a dissimulation of *your very self.* Wahrman concludes that the fixing of these categories in nature belonged to the same shift towards a modern regime of self, because this primarily contributed to someone's unique identity, and only secondarily to the identicality of a collective identity.[13]

Wahrman's thesis is based on an overwhelming variety of cultural sources. He refers to theatre reviews, plays, prologues and epilogues, actors and their roles as well as to the process of commodification, to religious changes as well as to the rise of a new type of physiognomy, the changing significance of dress (from representation of status to expression of unique personality) as well as changing modes in portraiture, the rise of the novel as well as philosophical discussions. He does not indicate a single prime mover, but considers these developments as mutually responsible for this sudden paradigm shift at the end of the eighteenth century.

Yet, it is clearly very much a *cultural* history and we might ask whether the shift Wahrman describes in such a short, well-defined time period has also happened in other sectors of society than culture, and whether it might be limited to a specifically English context. For instance, social historians dealing with ego documents such as Rudolf Dekker and Arianne Baggerman, have demonstrated that nineteenth-century middle-class diaries and autobiographical texts often cannot be characterized as private expressions of unique individuality. Instead, they were family chronicles to which often several family members consequently contributed. My own research on masculine women on the European Continent in the nineteenth century revealed that, all through this period, there was amazingly little interest in the inner life of 'passing women' in France and Germany. Nor does anything refer to the idea of a betrayal of the female self or a concept like a 'male soul in a female body'.[14] Wahrman's descriptions of two different regimes of self might therefore not belong to the *ancien régime* and the modern period respectively as strictly as he suggests. Yet I do consider them very helpful in making a distinction between different conceptions of the sex of self. Keywords to distinguish these different regimes of self are exteriority versus interiority, flexibility versus fixedness, and identicality versus authenticity. These are the elements on which I will focus in analyzing how the self appears in medical case histories until about the 1860s and 1870s.

HOW PHYSICIANS TOOK THE SELF INTO ACCOUNT

German cases

What references do we have to personal characteristics of the hermaphrodites in question and how are these related to sex or sexual function? In this respect,

Anna Barbara Meier's case (see previous chapter) does not seem to be very informative. The only remark in the extensively described case referring to her own feelings with regard to her sex is that 'she is quite convinced *that she is a real man*'.[15] No more information is provided about her personal characteristics than that she performed men's work and that she had 'a rather masculine boldness and great strength of mind'.[16] These remarks, moreover, were part of an enumeration of otherwise physical characteristics and were certainly not an attempt to describe a separate 'sex of self'. We know something about her position in the village since she told the doctor that she was mocked, and we know she felt very much ashamed. But not a word was wasted on the reassignment of her sex and what this might have meant for him psychologically.

Anna Barbara Meier's case history turns out to be no exception, for other German case histories do not offer any more personal information. For instance, Schallgruber provides a very short separate description of Juliane Neubauer's female 'emotional nature' (*Gemüthscharakter*), characterized by shamefulness, slyness, an inclination to tears and an unlimited desire for men.[17] This typology of a female character does not say much about her specific emotions, feelings or thoughts about herself. Or take for example Virchow's case history of Barbara Höhn, in which he writes: 'Her nature is mostly masculine, but sexually she is orientated towards men.'[18] Tourtual restricts his reference to the sex of the woman he was examining to just one remark – 'G states that she has always believed herself to be of the female sex' – and provides no information as to her personal characteristics.[19] Schäffler writes only: 'She seems to have more inclination towards masculine occupations, which is indeed also mostly what she engages in amongst the farmers.'[20] Jagemann's remark was hardly more informative: 'The usual occupation of the person described is crafting, just as she only moves in feminine circles.'[21] The most elaborate German case in this respect is Eva Elisabeth S.'s. About her life it says: 'With the riding tackle and in field work she plays the house farmhand, led and saddled the horses and other domestic animals and took on the heaviest jobs; in short, without complaint she undertook the hard manly work of a farmhand.'[22]

These sparse remarks about personal aspects with regard to the sex of hermaphrodites in German case histories describe what can be observed of the person from the outside. They do not refer to an inner psychological life at all. The physicians involved do not seem to be interested in the way sex was rooted in the inner self of their hermaphrodite patients. Mostly, their remarks concerning the person in question are restricted to certain typical female or male characteristics, such as shame, an inclination to tears, boldness or intellectual capacity and do not describe unique personalities. They also often refer not so much to personal characteristics as to occupations or to the 'social circles' in which the hermaphrodite lived. Closest to an idea of 'self' are remarks about how the hermaphrodite conceived of her or himself as a man or a woman. But any further description of what exactly that meant is lacking. The lack of a notion of sex as something firmly rooted in a person's sense of self is most telling when we look at the cases in which a change in sex assignment took place. In the extensively described cases of Anna Barbara Meier, Maria Katharina Ulmerin, Johanna K. and Hanna O., not one word is dedicated to the possible difficulty the reassignment of sex might pose to these people's sense or conception of self. Sometimes doctors paid attention to problems such as shame, gossip and scorn, urinating while standing up, or someone's education and occupations, but the way sex reassignment affected the self was of amazingly little concern. If any difficulties of a sex reassignment are mentioned, they are *not* about the problem of changing a sex deeply anchored in the inner self from early childhood on.

This does not mean that the persons described had no personality, though. They did have certain specific characteristics but these were 'turned socially', to use Wahrman's term. Their gendered character was not placed *within* the person of the hermaphrodite, but is primarily described in the way it functioned socially. They can all be observed from the outside. Towards the beginning of the twentieth century, the very same characteristics will 'turn inwards' and suddenly be described in much more detail as lifelong inclinations, preferences or aversions characterizing the unique inner person.

Moreover, as we will see in chapter 4, the hermaphrodites' statements about their sexual functioning, their sexual attraction, arousal and pleasure, constituted an essential part of physician's examinations until the 1860s. These were not conceived of as an aspect of the inner self, however, but of the physical sexual functioning. In short, the self was not conceived of as a distinct entity, but presented in its connection to either the outside world or to the body. Only if doctors mention the hermaphrodite's own understanding of sex does there seem to be something clearly individual.

French case histories

The French cases are mostly more elaborated in their description of the person and what happened to her from the moment her sex was in doubt. The case of Marie-Marguerite, or Marie for short, which was published by Worbe in 1815, is remarkable in its very detailed description of all the social events surrounding the ultimate reassignment of civil sex. It even pays considerable attention to what happened *after* Marie was assigned the male sex, which is really exceptional. Until the age of thirteen, nothing remarkable happened in Marie-Marguerite's life, Worbe writes: 'He shared the bed with a younger sister; he grew up among other young girls with whom he was associated – through education, exercise and the pleasures of childhood.'[23]

Implicitly, Marie's person is sexed here through social and spatial connections: sex is determined by the children with whom she shared her bed, with whom she went to school, exercised and played. She then started to suffer from groin hernias on both sides, Worbe recounts, and consulted a surgeon who prescribed a truss: to no avail. For the intended, contemporary medical readers this may have been an indication that this was not just a hernia, but a case of late-descending testicles. Meanwhile,

> Marie reached the age of sixteen: [being] blonde, lovely, [and] a good housekeeper, the son of a neighbouring tenant farmer fell in love with her. The marriage fell through for reasons of family interests. Another opportunity presented itself three years later; everything was broken off at the signing of the contract. But as Marie grew older (she was then nineteen), her charm disappeared; women's clothes no longer suited her; her walk was somewhat awkward; day after day her tastes changed, becoming more and more male; within the household she was less interested than before in taking care of the animals; she preferred sowing and harrowing to milking cows and nursing chickens. With a bit more daring, she would willingly have steered the plough.[24]

Worbe's narrative suggests that, with the descent of her testicles during puberty, the outward appearance of the whole body changed, and with it her occupations and locations.[25] This is said to be caused by changing tastes. Marie was spontaneously more attracted to working in the fields than to working indoors. Here, bodily sex – or, more precisely, the descent of testicles – seemed to work as an autonomous force which naturally prescribes a person's place in society, particularly in terms of occupation and clothes. This is what Laqueur and Wahrman have indicated: how in the course of the eighteenth century a person's status in society came to be prescribed by bodily sex rather than by cosmic destiny. But while Worbe refers to Marie's personal appetites and proclivities, he fails to ask further questions. He seems to take the synchronicity of the shift in her tastes and her capacity for work with the change in her body for granted, and does not enquire into her thoughts or feelings concerning this change. Despite the more extensive description of this change in a person, the description is *typical* (for female and male occupations in particular) rather than connected to the unique interiority of Marie's self.

More than in any other case history from the first half of the nineteenth century, Worbe describes how shocking it was for Marie to hear his conclusion that she was male: 'Marie shed copious tears. She probably had some reasons not to doubt my assertion. The exclamation most repeated was: "So I'll never be able to settle down!" It took several months for Marie to become completely used to the idea she was not a woman.'[26]

This is one of the most explicit and moving physician's descriptions from the first half of the nineteenth century of the shock of disruption of the self with regard to sex. Even in the second half of the century, most physicians revealed hardly any awareness of possible difficulties in having to change the conception of one's own sex. Yet, in twentieth-century eyes, the sense of self is pretty malleable if it only takes a few months to get accustomed to one's new sex. Moreover, the most important emotion is not elicited by the confused sense of self (Worbe even suggests that Marie herself already had serious doubts about her sex, for she did not doubt or contest his assertion at all); the primary emotion, according to Worbe, concerns her inability to marry. The self as an *autonomous* entity – the way one thinks, feels and conceptualizes oneself – receives no attention. The effects on the person himself are only described through exterior aspects, such as occupations or marriage. As we will see below, this is also true of Worbe's description of the difficulties experienced after having a different sex assigned to oneself.

Finally, Worbe refers to Marie-Marguerite's sexual feelings. These were not discussed in the context of physical sexual functioning, as in the German and some other French cases, but in the context of social relations. 'When asked – as tactfully as possible – about what he felt when he was in bed with girls, which happened often; . . . if curiosity didn't lead him to try to learn what the occasion allowed him so easily to observe, he answered – blushing – "*Sometimes, but I didn't dare.*" '[27]

Although Worbe was enquiring into Marie's intimate, private feelings here, he was not so much interested in these feelings themselves. His questions already presupposed that Marie would have been curious to 'observe' the girls on the basis of physical characteristics. But he does not get much of an answer. Rather, this paragraph turns Marie's 'wrong' sexual position among her bed mates into a topic of curiosity while the phrases 'as tactfully as possible' and 'blushing' add to the voyeuristic feel. Therefore, rather than detailing aspects of an inner sex of self, the sexual feelings described here spice up the social and moral confusion of doubtful sex.

Huette's story about Alexina X.'s youth forty years later is remarkably similar to Worbe's story about Marie. Here, too, a miraculous change of occupations took place, because of changing preferences:

> During early childhood, he showed nothing that could have raised suspicion about the error that had been made. But around the age of ten or twelve, Alexandrine clearly distanced herself from household activities; needlework repelled her; she only enjoyed being with horses and gladly took part in the heavy work performed by the labourers hired by her father . . . [Alexandrine] liked the games of boys her age & scorned her girl companions.[28]

The story continues by relating how Alexandrine's gestures and posture contrasted strangely to her feminine attire, stresses yet again how much he liked boys' games, and then goes into his pronounced erotic appetite for girls at the age of seventeen.

Here again, the sex of the person is described through his occupations and place among her peers. As in Worbe's case, the change in occupations and company is not explained by an elaborate investigation and description of Alexandrine's feelings. The reported sudden shift in her inclinations at the age of twelve, with the emergence of her repugnance for needle work, contempt for girls her age or love of boys' games seem to be caused naturally by a changing body. Nowhere in the text however are these related to a description of Alexandrine's own image of her or his inner self. And what is more: such sexed tastes are not perceived as fixed from early childhood on, as they may suddenly and radically change during one's lifetime. This, too, is very similar to Worbe's description of Marie's sudden change.

The idea of a natural, autonomous force putting Alexandrine in her proper place in society is expressed in more detail when it comes to his sexual drives:

> Towards the age of seventeen Alexandrine, who was still very keen on boys' games, was no less attentive to young girls, and her attentions, sometimes overflowing into loving gestures, then raised suspicions; in the neighbourhood, astonishment gave way to worry caused by Alexandrine's nightly excursions. For a while they restrained these instinctive tendencies, which daily grew more compromising. But when she was twenty, the voice of nature spoke even louder; and when her mother admitted that her authority was insufficient in containing the now imperious generative instinct, we were called upon to examine Alexandrine.[29]

As in Worbe's history, there is a strong sexual curiosity in this episode, which suggests a lot but hardly gives any information about what is going on in Alexandrine's inner life. Instead, the social and moral confusion caused by a 'voice of nature' or 'generative instinct' breaking through conventions is the central theme.

In both case histories, sex is an indication of someone's proper place in society. Possible indicators of the self, such as tastes, capacities and sexual drives were described rather superficially. Invoking them suggests the naturalness of the different positions of the sexes in society. Without being told, Marie and Alexandrine apparently sensed that they had to change occupations. Also, sexual instincts were supposed to 'adapt' to the changing body. In this way these stories clearly support the medical theories based on the two-sex system and the cultural discourses of the relation between two incommensurable sexes legitimating the socially and politically different statuses of men and women. Sex is a place, but a natural or naturally felt, not metaphysically prescribed, place. However, the sex of self is not yet a 'modern self' in the terms of Wahrman: it has hardly has any interiority to it, it is clearly not rooted in early childhood and it shifts from female to male relatively easily.

An exception: Benoit

A case history exceptional in many respects was published in 1840 by the future Deacon of the Faculty of Medicine at Montpellier, Justin Benoit, concerning Marie B. As we have seen in chapter 1, she insisted on performing a medical examination of her doubtful sex before her prospective marriage. Benoit performed the first bimanual exam I know of, and thereby enacted a sex which was quite distinct from what Marie B. herself could have observed or experienced. Thus, the results of Benoit's examination were more detached from her own understanding of her physical sex than in most other cases, as they were not primarily based on the outer anatomy and her own statements about sexual functioning (see chapter 4 for an extensive description of physical examinations at the time).

This is not to say that Benoit did not pay attention to Marie B.'s own descriptions of her sexual functioning and inclinations. In his description these were part of what he called her 'moral characteristics'. According to Benoit, a physician needed to pay attention to 'the moral dispositions, the inclinations and the aptitudes' of a hermaphrodite, because this was 'a precious means of shedding light on the primordial sexual type to which the subject of our observation belongs'.[30] In doing so, Benoit was one of the first physicians to differentiate between his own observations of physical sex and aspects of sex as experienced by the person in question.[31] These aspects were not confined to sexual functioning and appetite alone. Raised as a girl, Marie B.:

> . . . joined in girls' games, cultivated their habits and for five or six years went to the same schools with them, enjoyed associating with them in the same exercises and games. Having reached the age of reason, she gladly took up housekeeping and fulfilled the role to which a woman is destined in society. Her occupations were sedentary, her usual work was sewing, and she always made the garments she wore herself.[32]

This description does not deviate much from Worbe's and Huette's: once again, sex is not so much related to an inner self, but rather to one's place among peers and one's occupations. However, Benoit paid more attention to these aspects in relation to Marie B.'s own perception of her sex and her inner feelings. Despite doubts about her 'organization' that had surfaced during her engagement and after an inconclusive visit to a local doctor, Benoit reports how she, having read some books on the issue of hermaphroditism herself, convinced herself that she was female because of her feminine taste and inclinations.[33] Aptitudes also belonged to the discussed 'moral characteristics', but these were, in Benoit's eyes, definitely more masculine:

> It must be admitted that her intellectual capacities are rather those of the male; so, for example, although she only received an incomplete education, she nonetheless reasons correctly concerning matters ordinarily foreign to the

sex; she speaks and writes with much assurance; she profitably manages her
father's house and business; and, whenever necessary, knows how to protect
her interests energetically.[34]

Note how Benoit makes much more of describing her capacities in terms of
sex than Huette or Worbe did. He is also more extensive in his description
of her sexual inclinations, which is not only concerned with sexual instincts
but also refers to imagination and fantasies:

> But if one receives her confessions about her desires and her heart's needs,
> one learns that her thoughts have always been those of a woman; that in
> her frequent erotic dreams, it is always in a man's arms she feels she tastes her
> pleasures; that in everyday life the sight of a handsome man produces in her an
> indefinable impression from which she derives pleasure.[35]

To this, Benoit adds her vivid desire to become a wife and mother, a task
about which she talks enthusiastically. Finally, he relates that Marie B. is very
resolute about never discarding the clothes she had worn all her life.[36]

However, the 'moral being' and the 'material being' may not always
correspond, Benoit asserts.[37] Such was the case with Marie. After having concluded that Marie B. was a man whose sexual organs had suffered an arrest
in development, Benoit discussed which elements would contradict this
assertion. These characteristics were principally 'moral,' according to Benoit,
and therefore only had a secondary value, for they were not even incompat-
ible with uncontested masculinity (!). So, despite all the attention he gave to
Marie's 'moral being', he did not attribute much weight to it in his final conclusion on her sex. Let us not forget, he argued, the education this subject
has received; moreover '. . . we must beware of confusing habits resulting
from the individual's social position with propensities which are innate or
which depend on her organic constitution'.[38]

By discussing education, social position and innate dispositions as its
possible causes, Benoit is one of the first physicians to treat the 'moral being'
of a hermaphrodite as an entity in itself, with origins of its own, ultimately
separate from someone's physical sexual constitution. It is not that in earlier
cases someone's sexual appetite always corresponded to his or her (possible)
sexual functioning, but lack of correspondence was considered a form of
sexual dysfunction or hermaphroditism, not an (essential) part of a separately
described 'moral being' (see also chapter 4). In Benoit's text, sexual inclinations
considered female, such as desiring men and longing to have a family, are
clearly associated with feminine occupations like needlework and domestic
work, and opposed to masculine intellectual capacities. Moreover, these aspects
are linked to Marie's own sense of belonging to the female sex. In this text,
sex is not just the natural position of a person in society; it is also rooted in
an independently recognized inner – here called 'moral' – self. The stability

of this self is still questionable, however, for Benoit points out how the female position Marie B. had taken up until that moment might have caused her feminine inclinations and sense of self, which might explain why these did not correspond to her masculine physique and talents.

Sex as location

How does the sex of self appear in these case histories? In nearly all cases, sex is not represented as rooted in a deeply anchored, autonomous self. The hermaphrodites' awareness of the sex to which they felt they belonged is hardly an issue. This becomes especially clear in descriptions of sex reassignments in which remarkably little attention is paid to the self. When an 'error of sex' led to sex reassignment, it was not described as something traumatic to the self at all, neither in the sense of having to abandon a sex to which one had until then thought one belonged, nor as something that had been suppressed until the sex reassignment finally 'liberated' or acknowledged a subjective truth of sex.

Rather than rooted in an interior sense of self, sex appears to be a location: a literal location (at home or in the fields, with men or women in church), a social location (the people you work, play or sleep with), an economic location (within the context of a gendered division of labour), a sexual location (whom you desire and have sex with) and, finally, a legal position (a civil status which also defines whom you can marry). These locations are sometimes accompanied, as we have seen most clearly in the cases described by Worbe, Benoit and Huette, by remarks about tastes and capacities which seemingly naturally suit the changes of their sexual bodies during puberty. Body and location then seem to be naturally linked to one another. So, the naturalness of the category of sex is affirmed in some (French) cases, underpinning Wahrman's observation that 'gender' was perceived as naturally fixed in late eighteenth-century tales of gender inversion. However, these allegedly natural sexual characteristics are not strictly conceived of as innate or unchangeable. Worbe and Huette both describe a radical change during a lifetime, and Benoit points to external factors – upbringing, habits, social environment, education – that may have overruled nature.

With regard to the issue of the periodization of the history of the self, my sources clearly deviate from Wahrman's findings. In the former, 'gender' does not seem to have been fixed in early childhood, was mutable and did not have an interior nature. Contrary to Wahrman's assertion, these case histories show the sexed self to be predominantly 'turned socially' and characterized as a type rather than part of a unique identity. The naturalness of the category of sex – if at all expressed as such – does not necessarily anchor sex in the inner psyche of one unique individual. Or, in individual cases of doubt, physicians do not seem to be able to draw a straight line from the category of bodily sex to the inner self. Hardly any of them – though Benoit is a notable exception – were able to make a clear distinction between an objectively established sex and a subjectively experienced sex, for they all use the experiences and observations of hermaphrodites to make sense of the ambiguously sexed body. Moreover, any techniques, routines and even vocabulary or discourse to describe a hermaphrodite's individual, sexed inner self seem to have been almost entirely lacking. The naturalness of sex therefore indicates a place where a person naturally belongs rather than an intrinsically sexed self.

Is this lack of interest in the self not simply caused by the character of the sources: medical case histories? Did the doctors not self-evidently confine themselves to their own field, the body, and leave the subject of the self to other people or professions? Apart from the fact that body and self were not so neatly separated yet, I do not think that a lack of references to a self as an object in its own right is unique to medical discourse. Until about 1870, doctors were consulted primarily about such crucial questions as: Can I (can we) marry? Should I be reassigned to the other sex? Is our marriage legally valid? I expect that at such crucial crossroads in life the physician would want to gather all the information he thought relevant. Moreover the hermaphrodite (and other people involved) would, I assume, bring forward any aspect she or he considered important. So, if until deep into the nineteenth century most doctors did not pay much attention to the inner personal feelings and thoughts of hermaphrodites concerning which sex they belonged to, I take this as a sign that these aspects were not *valued* at the time. This might be interpreted as a sign that, more generally speaking, people did not consider the self of importance when it came to assigning sex. At least they were not *incited* to produce stories of the self at the crucial moment of establishing someone's sex. Physical appearance and experiences were important, as were clothing and occupations, but the inner self hardly seems to have counted.

PLACE AND FACE

Yet, the case histories clearly speak of individual and remarkable personalities: people who dared to go against the grain of social and sexual conventions. How can that be reconciled with my assertion that the self did not receive any attention in the case histories? They *do* describe people with clear drives, a will, thoughts and emotions in relation to their sex, its outward appearance and function. Some of these people started to perform work considered inappropriate for their sex or had sexual affairs with people of the 'same' sex at a time that this was severely condemned. Others stubbornly refused to wear the clothes or to take up the position of the sex a doctor had pronounced theirs. So how can I deny these people a *self*? Remember the distinction between subjectivity and the self as object of imagination and reflection here. What is lacking is the self as a separate entity, as an object to be described, imagined and discussed. What some case histories do show, however, is what hermaphrodites *did* under the specific circumstances of their lives: how they acted, what they revealed or concealed, how they dealt with doubt and reassignment concerning their sex. Of course, this subjectivity provides an impression of what sort of person they must have been. But, as in a play, all you know about the character is derived from what she says or does, not from a description of her inner motives, feelings or thoughts. My purpose here is not, however, to give an account of some remarkable individual persons with doubtful sex, on the basis of their actions. To me, the hermaphrodites' subjectivities displayed in these sources offer a clue as to the sort of *social scripts* available to them at the time. The subjective role of hermaphrodites in disclosing themselves to a physician was discussed in the previous chapter. This section will discuss what happened as a result of the doctor's diagnosis.

Worbe's case history relates that, some months after her visit to the physician, Marie-Marguerite took the decision 'to make a solemn proclamation' that she was a man and to that effect presented a request to a court. After the request was granted she finally presented himself as a man in his community:

> Making a masculine entrance in the village whose inhabitants had until then only seen him in woman's clothing was extremely embarrassing for Marie; but overcoming any false shame, he went to mass on Sunday, passed through to the choir of the church, and took his place among the men. After this bold and decisive act, protected by one who was not long ago his lover, Marie went to the places frequented by young men of his age, and shared in their entertainments. Marie soon abandoned all feminine habits: an excellent domestic worker, he became a good labourer in very little time.[39]

This account – rather a rare source, for most case histories end when the medical conclusion is reached and do not relate what happened afterwards – makes several things clear. First of all is the fact that Marie herself made the decision to have her sex reassigned officially and publicly. Apparently, she could also have decided otherwise. Secondly, sex may not have been considered as fixed in a sense of self, but this does not mean that sex reassignment was an easy matter. According to this account, sex was rooted in many (sexed) locations: in church, in social company, in entertainments, and in occupations. In short, sex is a *location* and reassigning sex *uproots* a person. Finally, it is embarrassing to change one's civil and social sex; the entire community is watching. A person assigned to the other sex not only lost her place, she also lost face. I will elaborate on these three points below.

As to the refusal of a sex reassignment after a physician had concluded someone's sex had been erroneously assigned, my database of 300 cases makes it absolutely clear that doctors could not force someone to have their sex reassigned. During the entire period covered by my research between 1790 and 1908, adults may have been forced to have their sex reassigned in only two cases. One example is Anna K. who made another woman pregnant, but even in that case we only know the physician's opinion. We cannot be sure she was actually forced to wear male clothing.[40] The other case was not caused by a physician's examination, but occurred after a police arrest.[41] During the above period, many hermaphrodites resolutely announced they would refuse sex reassignment. One of those to refuse was Marie B., who would not stop wearing the female clothes she had worn all her life and was accustomed to.[42] Although the case histories generally do not recount what happened after the hermaphrodite's examination, the chances are that hermaphrodites could refuse a sex reassignment if they wanted to do so. Many European countries had laws or rules prohibiting the wearing of clothing of the other sex. But, as one French physician made very clear in 1893, it was not the physician's role to maintain these rules. On the contrary:

> It is true that it is forbidden by law to wear the clothing of the other sex beyond the scope of carnival permits. But the surgeon is in no way obliged to ensure the execution of police measures; he cannot even contribute to them if he is held back by the formal rule of professional secrecy. Before the surgeon, more than before anyone else, the subject must remain free to make whatever decision he deems appropriate, and he must remain certain of that discretion.[43]

Other physicians expressed similar frustrations on the subject of their position with respect to the law.[44]

In Prussia, hermaphrodites (or, during childhood, their parents) were legally allowed to choose their own sex. Only if the interests of third parties were harmed, was it up to a physician to decide the predominant sex.[45] Such cases involved marriages, of course, but could also be related to inheritances or custody. However, even in cases where a marriage was annulled, the sex of the person necessitating this was not necessarily reassigned. Eva Elisabeth S., for instance, had her marriage annulled, but continued to live with her family as a woman with the reputation of being hermaphrodite.[46] Another case in which the law was involved also did not lead to an unambiguous sex reassignment. Elisabeth Moll, in 1863 accused of incest with her stepmother, was declared male and given a male name, Wilhelm. However, she was allowed to stick to her female clothing, and she was referred to as Elisabeth Wilhelm Moll.

All this does not mean that sex diagnosis by physicians was of no importance. The possibilities and impossibilities of marriage were dictated by their

judgement, they could exert pressure on their patients to have their sex reassigned, and their diagnosis could also lead to or prevent further treatment.
(The latter only really became important at the turn of the twentieth century.)
Furthermore, no one could have her or his sex reassigned officially without
a doctor's consent (however, some people did illegally change their social
sex without consent).[47] But an important aspect of the hermaphrodite's subjective power was to be able to at least *refuse* a sex reassignment.

As Marie-Marguerite's story shows, having a different sex assigned to you
included a change of status and location; while the sex of self received almost
no attention, the changes of place in church, of places of entertainment, of
work and other occupations were all related to sex and noted. A change of
name and clothing was also often mentioned. In cases of marriage annulment,
it was the civil status in particular which changed. As marriage was a very
important social institution which provided protection, (reciprocal) support,
honour and sometimes love or companionship, this must have been a radical
change of social position.

The difficulties of a change of civil and social sex can therefore be described
more adequately as the difficulty of *dislocation*, overturning one's ingrained
place in society. The literal dislocation was, however, often accompanied by
the embarrassing feeling of 'being out of place'. I believe that this aspect of
the change of civil and social sex affected the hermaphrodite deeply. In many
cases this embarrassment led to rather radical forms of rootlessness.

According to Worbe's account Marie managed to face the curious eyes
of her community. Her reputation had already been damaged by rumours
before she consulted him, because of 'the statement of the surgeon, who
had made public that Marie was damaged in such a way as never to be able
to marry'.[48] But one year after he had boldly taken up his new place in
church, Worbe claims, Marie was considered one of the best farmers of the
region. Moreover: 'The residents of Bu and its environs have got used to his
new condition: they rarely think about it and do no longer talk about it.'[49]
Some other sex reassignments also seem to have played out smoothly, such
as in the case of the twins Katharina/Karl and Anna Maria/Michael, who
exchanged their female clothes for male ones at their own initiative and
started to learn the trade of mason and day-labourer respectively.[50] For many
people however, the accompanying public rumours, gossip and mockery
apparently were unbearable.

As mentioned above, few case histories describe what happened after
a doctor established an 'error' of sex. We do not know whether Hanna O. or
Anna Barbara Meier experienced difficulties in their communities similar
to the ones Marie faced. However, if an autopsy report was accompanied by
a biography,[51] or if the hermaphrodite in question ended up in the hospital
or had started wandering around and exposing her- or himself to doctors and

the general public, we have a better picture of their lives after the medical examination which led to an acknowledgement of an erroneous sex. A remarkable number of cases tell stories of people who apparently could not face the dislocation and subsequent embarrassment *within* their communities, and left their places of birth. The number of such cases is certainly dispropor-tionate – especially with regard to hermaphrodites who ended up exhibiting themselves and as such often became part of medical case histories – but, even so, the stories are telling.

Maria Katharina Ulmerin, for example, who lived as a woman for forty-one years, decided in 1794 to disclose herself to a priest and subsequently to the physician Schäffler. To the latter, she explained that '. . . since she was being laughed at in her own home town, where her story was known, she was now firmly determined to leave the region in order to flaunt himself as a man somewhere else'.[52] In 1828, Angélique Courteois, born in Fruge in the north-east of France, moved all the way to Paris to have her sex examined by a famous surgeon because she felt that her clothes did not coincide with her 'outward appearance' and 'taste'.[53] Ursula/Georg Thomasicz ran away from a farm at the age of twenty-six to adopt male clothing and become a coachman. When he came back in his birthplace after a failed engagement, the bullying ultimately forced him to leave for Vienna.[54] Margaretha Bergold is reported to have become a cobbler in his male life, an occupation that allowed him to travel.[55]

Many others left their region of birth and started wandering around, exhibiting themselves as hermaphrodites. After having been 'discovered' in the Berlin Charité in 1801, Marie Dorothea Derrier travelled through Germany, France, Britain and the Netherlands; her sex was discussed by many doctors.[56] Other famous, oft discussed and described hermaphrodites were Marie-Madeleine Lefort[57] and Marie-Josine/Gottlieb Göttlich,[58] both of whom travelled around Western Europe and Britain. It seems that for some hermaphrodites, their dislocation enabled them to earn money from the curiosity, gossip and laughter they invoked. But this was possibly only the case outside their region of birth. Take for instance Katharina Hohmann who exhibited herself to medical professionals in dozens of cities in Germany from her late forties onwards.[59] After a couple of years, she started travelling in men's clothes, but, according to Virchow who saw her in 1872, she donned women's clothes when she was in her own region: 'At present she still appears dressed as a woman when she is at home; she divests herself of the man's clothing that she wears on her travels at the last stop on the way to her home town. There, she is socially and legally considered a woman.'[60] Only one person, Joseph/Josephine Badré, who reportedly made money using her ambiguous body – in this case, by prostituting himself to both women and men – did not leave her region of birth immediately when she ultimately

THE ABSENCE OF SEX OF SELF

took to wearing male attire; he kept 'amusing' women. However, he too ended up wandering. He was described by both a doctor at a Parisian hospital and – after his death – by a doctor from Toulon.[61]

In conclusion, after a physical examination had established an error of sex or had led to the annulment of a marriage, there were roughly four scripts available to a hermaphrodite. First, the option not to have one's sex reassigned and, consequently, not to marry. It seems that social isolation was often the result. Some of the people concerned had the reputation of being a hermaphrodite. This possibility has already been explored in chapter 1, where I described the rationale of secrecy and non-intervention. Second, hermaphrodites could have their sex reassigned, and change almost every possible ingrained position they had held within their community, facing gossip, bullying and/or public mockery. Sometimes, such a change seems to have been ultimately accepted by a community; other stories mention continuous badgering. Thirdly, some people decided to leave their region after a sex reassignment and live their new lives in an environment where people did not know them. As we will see in the next chapter, this could also be extremely difficult. Finally, some hermaphrodites crossed the line of shame, and made a living of exhibiting themselves.

These four options for hermaphrodite subjectivity all clearly show that a reassignment of sex or an annulment of marriage deeply affected the lives of the people involved. Subsequently, maintaining, as I did in the previous section, that in the physicians' accounts there is no concept of a sexed self, does not mean hermaphrodites could not be shocked, distressed and deeply confused. What the case histories described *do* tell, however, is how much the shock, distress and confusion was related to the hermaphrodites' being uprooted, their being 'out of place'. It was their connection to an outer world, sexed in many different ways, which was disrupted. To the extent they had conceived of themselves as being of one or the other sex from birth – the sex expressed in their name, clothing and occupations – this sense of the self was shocked as well. As explained in the introduction, this self-understanding is a rudimentary form of a self. But there is not a single case history in which that shock was central to the hermaphrodite's distress and confusion; instead, their loss of place and face was crucial.

CONCLUSION: FROM SELF TO PERSON

When Wahrman introduced the phrase 'socially' or 'outwardly turned self', he already called it a contradiction in terms.[62] And I agree: to my mind, the notion of a self refers to a certain intrinsic, true *inner* essence, which can only be known through some sort of *intro*spection. Moreover, the word self indicates an immutable essence which cannot be betrayed or changed

without damage to the psyche of the person concerned, whereas the terms
socially or outwardly turned stresses the fixation to an outside world. Because
the term 'outwardly directed self' entails such confusions, I suggest replac-
ing that phrase by the notion of *person*.

Person comes from persona, a mask worn in theatre. It still has the meaning
of a character or role in drama or real life. In current language, a person can
refer to an individual human being, an individual with specific characteristics,
occupations, preferences and appearance (both physical and with regard
to clothing and adornments). Person has a strong association with embodiment through the expression 'in person' – it is an individual in her physical
appearance. Another meaning of the word is an individual with rights and
duties before the law.[63] Role, position and inclination, characteristics, physical
appearance and legal position therefore come together in the word person.
It definitely does not, however, refer to an *inner* quality, or any reflection
or understanding of an individual human being just in relation to itself. Its
characteristics are indeed, *turned outwardly*.

The identity (sex, class, race) of a *person* is known through how she relates to
the outside world through name, occupations, physical appearance, clothing,
capacities and behaviour. As we have seen in the previous chapter, the sex
of this person is inscribed in the social, moral, legal and economic fabric of
which she is part. That is what guarantees stability and continuity. If, in
an exceptional situation, a person happens to reassign his sex, the social and
moral confusion draws most of the attention. In contrast, a modern *self*,
and the sex of self, is known through supposed indications of an inner truth
or essence, which defines the self from within. Here, the continuity lies in
the immutable and inalienable character of that inner essence: nobody can
force a self to change, or wilfully change his own self. It is (also) the way an
individual relates rationally and emotionally to himself – how he *identifies*.
In this model, a story of sex reassignment will primarily concentrate on the
(damaging) consequences for the individual in question.

When physicians in these case histories, which describe non-anonymous
environments during the first three-quarters of the nineteenth century, refer
to individual aspects of the hermaphrodite, they refer to the *person* and not
to a *self*. This person is clearly sexed: role, appearance, occupations, physical
qualities, (sexual) preferences and legal position are all considered to be either
female or male. Sex is therefore *inscribed on the person*, that is, precisely at
the point where the individual is attached to the social, economic, moral and
legal fabric of her community. Note that the concept of person does not
entirely exclude the physicality of sex, as it includes the body as it appears
and functions in the community. But the sexed characteristics of the person
are in no way located within a self, in the awareness, imagination or description of oneself as a unique inner space, or in one's deeply rooted emotional

attachment to such a sexed self. The only form of a 'self' I have found in the case histories is the reference to an individual's understanding of his or her person as being male or female – an understanding I consider a basic necessity for any subjective functioning within a system in which the prevailing cultural, social, discursive and linguistic system primarily divides people into male and female.

Merging the conclusions of the previous and this chapter, we can reformulate the rationale of the category of sex in cases of doubtful sex from non-anonymous environments until about the 1860s and 1870s as follows. After the initial labelling of a newborn child as either female or male on the basis of the physical appearance and urinary function of the genitals, the logic of sex assignment was primarily orientated towards this person's inscription in either category. By this inscription, a person's place in society, her occupations and outward appearance, and her (intimate and sexual) relations with other people were determined. Doubting sex therefore threatened to shake the whole social, moral and legal fabric of a community, which made secrecy, non-intervention and containment the preferred strategies in non-anonymous environments. However, if this fabric had *already* been affected by overt sexual relations between persons who were apparently of the same sex, or if others had become involved through engagement or marriage, it was often decided that the body in question should be examined by a physician. In such cases, at least temporarily, the rationale of sex as due representation of the body took over. Only such cases have left traces for the historian in the form of medical case histories.

Enquiring, consequently, into the question of how such medical (re)assessments of sex affected the individual in question, the rationale of sex as inscription turns out to be affirmed strongly. Sex proves to be inscribed on the *person* and *not* inscribed in any way in an authentic, unique, inner self. Most profoundly, this can be demonstrated by the way hermaphrodites dealt with the difficulties of sex reassignment as reported in the medical case histories. Surprisingly, none of these case histories convincingly verbalize the traumatic effects of a sex reassignment on the self. What the hermaphrodites in these histories *were* struggling with, instead, was *dislocation*: either being out of place within their communities, or moving away. In the next chapter we will see whether these findings hold true when we turn to the first published memoirs of a hermaphrodite, which date back to 1868.

3

HERCULINE BARBIN

Many readers will be familiar with the existence of the memoirs of Herculine Barbin in one form or another, re-edited as they were by Michel Foucault in 1978.[1] And they might have wondered how this autobiographical text, found in 1868 upon Barbin's death, relates to the rationale of sex as the inscription of a person in a social and moral order as deciphered from medical case histories. After all, Foucault clearly speaks in terms of 'identity' in introducing the memoirs in their English translation. He labels them as 'memoirs that were left by one of those individuals whom medicine and the law in the nineteenth century relentlessly questioned about their genuine sexual identity', and states that Barbin was incapable of 'adapting himself to a new identity'.[2] The term 'sexual identity' (or 'true sex') in Foucault's text confusingly conflates a biological and a psychological 'inner' truth of sex.[3] According to him, from the eighteenth century onwards the biological opinion increasingly excluded the concept of hermaphroditism and forced people to have only one primary sex which had to be deciphered by physicians. Although the biological opinion has since become more complex, he maintains: 'Nevertheless, the idea that one must indeed finally have a true sex is far from being completely dispelled. Whatever the opinion of biologists on this point, the idea that there exist complex, obscure, and essential relationships between sex and truth is to be found . . . not only in psychiatry, psychoanalysis, and psychology, but also in current opinion.'[4] Thus, biology might have lost its certainty with respect to one true sex, but psychologically this idea of a true sex *still* holds true. My point is, however, that such a relationship was *not yet* established at the time Herculine Barbin's memoirs were found and published. Significantly, the doctor who performed the autopsy more or less triumphantly stated that the decision of the physician who had declared Barbin male had been correct so that he had 'assigned [Barbin] to his *true place* in society'.[5] There is no mention of identity here. Paradoxically, as Foucault himself was one of the first to thoroughly historicize the notion of an inner and authentic sexual self and pointed to discourse as constitutive instead of expressive of the self, my critique is actually quite well aligned

with much of his other work and his overall critical attitude towards the
psycho-sciences.[6]

For those not familiar with the story I will provide a brief summary.
Herculine Barbin was born on 8 November 1838, was baptized and raised as
a girl and received her education at a convent school. Afterwards she started
working as a teacher at a girls' boarding school. During adolescence she had
already started to realize that her physical development was different from
her fellow schoolmates; her chest remained flat, menstruation failed to appear
and a flush of beard emerged. As a teacher at the girls' boarding school, she
made friends with Sara, the headmistress' daughter, and became increasingly
intimate with her. Finally they started being lovers and having sex. Barbin
had slowly come to understand she was (predominantly) a man; witness the
fact that – among other things – after a second confession to a priest, the latter
immediately acknowledged that Barbin was 'entitled to call [her]self a man in
society' (see chapter 1).[7] From that moment onwards Barbin could no longer
ignore the fact that he was, physically speaking, more like a man. He was torn
between two rationales or moral systems with regard to sex. Should he stick
to the sex inscribed on him since birth so as to not damage the reputation of
those women he loved? Or should he stop betraying their confidence and be
'honest' about his bodily sex? As we will see, his autobiographical text can
partly be read as an attempt to come to terms with these tormenting questions.
After a long period of doubt, she decided to confess her story for a third time,
to a bishop, who sent her to an academically trained physician, Chesnet. This
doctor declared her to be male; referring to her future civil change of sex, he
parted from her with the words: ' "Give me your hand, mademoiselle; before
long, I hope, we shall call you differently" '.[8] Barbin arranged the reassignment of his civil status before a court on 22 July 1860. He moved to Paris and
committed suicide eight years later in February 1868, leaving his memoirs
and his body. Goujon performed the autopsy; the famous forensic medical
professor Tardieu edited and published the memoirs in 1874.[9]

My intention in this chapter is to return to the text of Barbin's memoirs
with the knowledge of the rationale of sex as an inscription on a person and
the absence of the notion of sex as something ingrained in the self from early
childhood on. To what extent do Barbin's memoirs refer to sex as identity,
as something inalienable, intrinsic to one's authentic self? And, if they do
not refer to an inner self, how should we interpret the obviously traumatic
feelings and experiences before, during and after her sex reassignment? As
I will analyze Barbin's memoirs, and not the medical reports on her case, I
will not focus on the medical examinations. Of course, during these medical
examinations the rationale of sex as a truthful representation of the body
prevailed, and many historians have already pointed at this case as an example
of the contemporary medical opinion of what has become known as 'true

sex'. The doctors involved were convinced that people could only have one true sex, which was signified by the sexual glands. As I will discuss the enactment of physical sex in medical practice during the long nineteenth century in Part II, I will not discuss this aspect of the case in this chapter. I do mention it here briefly, firstly, because Barbin somehow has come to represent the poor nineteenth-century hermaphrodite who was forced to change her sex because a physician decided that her sex was male without consulting her as to how she felt, which is simply not true. More significant, however, is the fact that the rationale of sex as a representation of the body, or even more strongly, of a 'true sex', *does not exclude* a rationale of sex as a person's inscription. Dror Wahrman, in his discussion of Thomas Laqueur's work, has demonstrated that the emergence of the concept of only one 'true sex' did not mean that this 'true sex' was also immediately 'fixed' as an internal gender identity. According to him, only 'the firm grounding of sex in nature made possible the conceptualization of masculinity and femininity as social and cultural attributes', which left a certain 'place to play' during the eighteenth century. This changed, Wahrman asserts, into the modern notion of gender identity mirroring sex at the end of the eighteenth century.[10] However, Barbin turns out to be a perfect example for showing that even around 1870 'true sex' was not yet necessarily linked to a notion of 'true self'.

'I am twenty-five years old, and, although I am still young, I am beyond any doubt approaching the hour of my death', the memoirs start.[11] From the very beginning the reader – who through Tardieu's (and Foucault's) introduction is currently already informed about the outcome – was warned that a dramatic story would unfold leading to suicide. What was at stake? 'I have suffered alone! Alone! Forsaken by everyone! My place was not marked out in this world that shunned me, that had cursed me.'[12] There is no place for Barbin but isolation, nothing to *mark* her place but a curse. Halfway through the text, Barbin briefly characterizes the changes that had happened during his life:

> My arrival in Paris marks the beginning of a new phase of my double and bizarre existence. Brought up for twenty years among girls, I was at first and for two years at the most a *lady's maid*. When I was sixteen and a half I entered the normal school of . . . as a student-teacher. When I was nineteen I obtained my teaching certificate. A few months later I was directing a rather well-known boarding school in the arrondissement of . . . I left it when I was twenty-one. That was in the month of April. At the end of the same year I was in Paris, with the railroad of . . .[13]

This brief story about changing places and occupations is immediately followed by a dramatic exclamation (a typical stylistic flourish in Barbin's text which I will discuss later on):

Go, accursed one, pursue your fate! The world that you invoke was not made
for you. You were not made for it. In this vast universe, where every grief has
its place, you shall search in vain for a corner where you may shelter your
own, for it would be a blemish there. It overturns all the laws of nature and
humanity. The family's hearth is shut to you.[14]

In this chapter, I would like to argue that place, being in the wrong place,
changing occupations and places, having no place, is central to Barbin's text.
It is what Barbin's text is essentially about: where to belong in the social and
moral order? How to deal with being in the wrong place experiencing literal
and moral dislocation? The text is a defence against being judged to have
been in the wrong place, and expresses the pain of having no place at all. In
many ways, I hope to demonstrate that what sex means to Barbin echoes the
logics of sex not as a truth of self (or one's own sexual desires and pleasures),
but as a moral, social and legal inscription. Nowhere does Barbin refer to an
intrinsic truth of an inner sex – be it female, male or something more ambiguous
– that has been damaged by the course of events. This is not to say that she
had no emotions, or that he was not confused and desperate, towards the end.
The dramatic statements larding the text easily prove the contrary. But, to
paraphrase Charles Taylor, the self as a moral good, as an inner truth everybody has the right and obligation to be, to find and to express, is failing.[15] In
other words, I do not deny Barbin subjectivity (which is obviously exercised
through his writing) – but I doubt whether the text in any sense refers to sex
as an interior quality of self that can be described, reflected upon, suppressed,
found out, damaged or defended. Barbin does not discuss or recount the
difficulty of his life history *in these terms*. Her memoirs do, however, shed a
unique light on the subjective experience of a sex which was not primarily
understood as either a physical or a psychological truth.

It cannot be denied that the fact *that* Barbin wrote these memoirs and
probably had thought of publicizing them,[16] indicates a growing public interest
in such extraordinary personal experiences. That was undeniably an interest
different to that of the long tradition of curiosity about hermaphrodites who
were 'exhibited'. Even if these shows were probably sometimes accompanied
by short biographies, as was the case with a lot of 'freaks' in the nineteenth
century, they did not provide the reader with insight into the private emotions
of someone who had her sex reassigned. Moreover, the fact of the writing
itself points to the generally increasing capacity of middle-class people to
write these memoirs down or to new practices in which personality or self
was produced. Therefore, the *content* of Barbin's writing might not have linked
sex to a modern sense of self, but its form certainly opened a passageway to
a more personalized understanding of sex.

Therefore, before turning to the memoirs themselves, I will take a little
detour in order to list the many different characteristics of what is referred to

as modern autobiography, as described in the literature. These characteristics are often used to describe how a modern sense of self came into being from the eighteenth century onwards. As the nineteenth century is known to be the period in which the search for a self became democratized through, among other things, the massive interest in and practice of autobiographic writing, we may ask ourselves to which extent Barbin's text can be characterized by these features of the modern scripting and expression of the self.

There have been many heated discussions about Barbin's text as well as about Foucault's introduction to it.[17] These all assume quite facilely that an 'anatomic truth' was in one way or another imposed on Herculine Barbin, thereby forcing her to unambiguously embody the position of a man or her 'true sex'. Much of the discussion pertained to the question whether she (her sexuality, her ambiguous body or her ambiguous reference to himself in the memoirs) had taken a sort of polymorphous, perverse pre-discursive position – a natural resistance against a discourse imposing the unity and coherence of one true sex. To my mind, the question has become quite a-historical as it actually discussed the relation between power, discourse and the formation of (sexed) subjectivity – and the question as to whether a subject can 'escape' discourse or whether 'the body' or 'natural pleasures' can be pre-discursive. Foucault – and many others after him – in their criticism of the term 'true sex' referred to both an anatomical and a psychological truth.[18] But the question of what the category of sex actually meant to Barbin – of how, exactly, sex and self are connected (or not connected) in his memoirs – has never been properly explored.

MODERN SELF AND AUTOBIOGRAPHICAL WRITINGS

The history of shaping a self through writing has been based on many different forms of autobiographical texts or ego documents from the past: published or unpublished diaries, chronicles, memoirs, and autobiographies, or ego documents related to court cases or originating in a psychiatric context. The differences between these sources have yielded very different results as to the periodization and exact character of the rise of the modern self in Western culture. Related to these differences, and probably even more important, are the differences in social status of the writer in terms of gender, class (with its many different cultures), ethnicity, religion and geographical environment (metropolis, city, countryside). This variety can make a major difference in the concept of the self found in the sources, to such an extent that what has been characterized as typical for the late eighteenth century might also be found in the early twentieth century.

This is one of the reasons why I have my doubts with regard to Wahrman's bold thesis that the transformation into a modern self happened at a very specific point in time, at least in England. My source material is so obviously at odds with his periodization that I have come to believe the history of the emergence of a modern self to be far more complicated, more layered, than Wahrman suggests. Therefore, I will discuss the existing historiography more extensively in order to gain a greater perspective on the issue. Within this literature, I will try to identify more characteristics for distinguishing between pre-modern and modern (sexual) selves, without ascribing these to a specific time frame. Moreover, I will be as interested in *ideas* about and (implicit) *concepts* of the self, as in *practices* of the self.

To understand the rise of modern notions of the self (the plural indicating the manifold aspects of such a transition) they must be studied much more precisely in terms of practices. What does a specific practice contribute to the way the self is expressed or shaped? Within the history of autobiography, which is of course most relevant here, most attention has been focused on the eighteenth century as the era in which a modern narrative of self emerged; the nineteenth century is known for its democratization of this interest in autobiography.[19] In the history of autobiographical writing it is not the philosophy or the concept of self that is the central focus, but the way in which the narrator presents or moulds him- or herself, and whether this can be called a 'modern self'. How is the modern self actually enacted by narrative?

According to one of the classical historians of autobiography, Roy Pascal, autobiography provides 'a coherent shaping of the past' whose central interest is 'the discovery of the self'. Recognizing one's dynamic inborn quality or innermost personality and presenting one's life history as 'its unfolding through all encounters with the outer world' is a classical characteristic of autobiography.[20] Ideally autobiography displays the characteristics of the novel, with dramatic narration, with the paradoxical 'finding of the self by losing this self', in Jerome Buckley's terms. 'The ideal autobiography presents a retrospective of some length on the writer's life and character . . . a voyage of self discovery, a life-journey confused by frequent misdirections, and even crisis of identity but reaching at last a sense of perspective and integration.'[21] According to these classic interpretations, such autobiographical forms emerged in the eighteenth century.

Other studies point out how the canonization of a 'true autobiography' has structurally neglected other forms of autobiographic writing, especially the ego documents written by women and lower-class people. Including these writings in the analysis of the history of autobiography reveals the fissures and discontinuities in the closed narrative of the discovery of one's integral personality or self, revealing this self to indeed be a gendered and ideological construction.[22] However, a theory of how women's autobiographies might differ from men's as far as style, scripting, plot or writing practice is concerned has not been fully developed yet. In this respect, theories of how women's characters in novels differ from men's will prove to be helpful, as we shall see below.[23]

Recent research by social historians into (mostly unpublished) ego documents confirms the many layers of historicity of concepts such as the self, individuality and identity. For example, nineteenth-century Dutch bourgeois autobiographical writings turn out not to concentrate on personal identity so much as on family identity. They were often written more as an 'ethical will' for the children than as a way of expressing individual and intimate emotions. The narrative is more moral, more a typical example, than the disclosure of a unique personality. Sometimes, spouses or children continued the diary after the death of the initial writer. Often, these writings were also intended as inventories for the family archive; messages from later generations can be found in the documents.[24] These studies have shown that, despite the rise of the modern self in philosophy and autobiography, well into the nineteenth century, middle-class people often saw themselves more as a part of a collective (family) identity. Their life histories were part of a collective identity rather than the unique expression of a separate individual's search for an inner truth. The morality that was expressed was linked more to the well-being of this larger entity than to the right to an idiosyncratic existence. These are crucial notions to keep in mind when reading Barbin's life story.

In order to analyze Barbin's autobiography within the context of the historical question of the emergence of a 'modern self' in ego documents, I suggest that it might be helpful not to tie the characteristics to a certain time, class or gender, but to assemble the main features distinguishing a 'modern self' from other ways of narrating an 'I'. I have been able to gather a list of important characteristics of the emerging genre of autobiography in the eighteenth and nineteenth centuries from the literature.[25] These are, more or less in order of historical appearance:

- the transition from a 'typical' story (in which the first-person hero is compared to biblical types and sets an example for others) to an original, idiosyncratic story;
- the shift from a soul separated from the body to a self integrated with the body;
- the idea of an individuality different from humankind in general;
- the quest of finding oneself as the central quest of a life history;
- the truth of a unique self as a moral good (instead of it being (re)directed towards God);
- the idea of an inborn quality, the unity and continuity of 'personality';
- the idea of the self as a (hidden) inner space that has to be explored;
- the disclosure and expression of one's 'dark' instincts, motives and desires as a key to oneself;
- remembering early childhood memories and adolescent experiences, dreams and fantasies as a path to one's innermost self.

Oosterhuis points to the importance of new techniques which only appeared in the late nineteenth century and which were employed to reveal those dark instincts and motives as well as to unearth early childhood memories and dreams. Certain practices connected to the 'modern self' therefore seem to have developed only with the emergence of psychiatry.[26] In my reading of Barbin, I will both be alert to all of these indications of a modern concept of the self, as well as to elements of the rationale of sex as the inscription of a person in a moral, social and legal structure.

Erotic attractions

Does Barbin, throughout the turbulence of his life history, refer to the continuity of the sex of her personality in one way or another? To begin with, Barbin's narrative does not try explicitly to gender her characteristics as a child, nor her erotic inclinations for other girls. For example, Barbin mentions the talents and inaptness of Camille (the name he gave to himself as a child) during her childhood at the nunnery without gendering them explicitly:

> Gifted as I was with a true aptitude for serious studies, I soon profited from them greatly. My progress was rapid, and more than once it aroused the astonishment of my excellent teachers. It was not the same for handicrafts, for which I showed the deepest aversion and the greatest incapacity.[27]

A talent for 'serious studies' was certainly seen as masculine at the time. I assume handicrafts (*travaux manuels*) at a nunnery refers to needlework and knitting, and such references to the incapacity for these activities is clearly a trope in tales of women's masculinity.[28] It might well be that these references to early masculine talents and aversions to female work indicate already his 'wrong place' as a girl at the time. But Barbin does not elaborate on the fact any further to demonstrate her innate masculine disposition – he does not even explicitly call it a masculine trait. As we will see in chapter 9, this is in marked contrast to a very similar autobiography written forty years later by N. O. Body, who referred to a whole range of boyish characteristics during his childhood as a girl and does not fail to interpret these explicitly as indicators of her true male being.

The many passages in the text in which she describes her intimacies with other girls seem much more promising in this respect. He describes his ardent kisses and intimate embraces with girls rather extensively and in the first part of the book suspense is built up by the increasing intensity of Barbin's feelings. The future sexual relationship with Sara is announced by pointing to prior physical closeness with girls, so that at this point continuity of the personality certainly is built up throughout the story. However, looking more closely at the sub-plots structuring the episodes of intimacies with other girls, reveals that the main concern of these episodes is *not* to show Barbin's inborn sexual attraction to women.

There is, to begin with, the passage describing Camille's love for an older pupil at the nunnery, about whom Barbin writes in exalted tones:

> I lavished upon her a devotion that was ideal and passionate at the same time . . . I could have wept for joy when I saw her lower toward me those long, perfectly formed eyelashes, with an expression as soft as a caress. How proud I was when she chose to lean on me in the garden! . . . Her beautiful blond head bent down toward me, and I thanked her with a kiss that was full of warmth. 'Lea', I would say to her then, 'Lea, I love you!'[29]

During the night, she would approach her friend's bed to kiss her goodnight; one time she was caught by one of the nuns and was sent to Mother Eléonore. Nowhere is there an explicit comment suggesting eroticism was at play here or one revealing inborn masculine desire. Instead, what Barbin tries to show is how well Mother Eléonore reproached her justly, but mildly: 'Then began for me one of those pious exhortations that revealed all the greatness of that truly pure and generous soul.'[30]

Later in life, at the primary school when Camille was already worried about her physical development and had been struck by Ovid's *Metamorphoses*, Barbin's tale about another very intimate friendship is still remarkably 'innocent' – with no explicit reference to sexuality or masculinity:

> We were always called the inseparables, and in fact we did not lose sight of each other for a single instant. In the summer, studies were held in the garden; we used to sit next to each other there, hand in hand, holding the book between us. From time to time my teacher would fix her look upon me at the moment I would lean toward Thecla to kiss her, sometimes on her brow and – would you *believe* it of me? – sometimes on her lips . . .[31]

There is certainly already more of a tone of possible immodesty here, which is also affirmed by the remainder of the story, in which Barbin recounts her escapades to her friend's bed at night. Sometimes, Barbin writes, she was caught by her teacher who would teach her a lesson in modesty and morality the next morning. 'So inspired could she become with that tone of voice, which had nothing human about it, that I never listened to her without weeping. I have lived enough to be able to say that it is impossible to find anything comparable to that superior nature.'[32]

Why would these episodes end with the almost angelic piousness of the nuns in charge?

The incidence, awareness and force of the erotic attraction to the girls surrounding Camille increased from adolescence onwards. The eroticism is not acknowledged explicitly, although the descriptions become increasingly suggestive. One of the first clear sexually charged moments – a turning point in the story, after which Barbin refers to himself much more as masculine – is during a thunderstorm. The pupils and the nuns were awake in the dormitory in the middle of the night because of this storm. After a terrifying flash and loud clap of thunder, Camille was so frightened that he leapt over the bed next to him, right into the arms of the beloved sister Marie-des-Anges:

> She put her arms around my neck, while I pressed my head hard against her breast, which was covered only by a nightgown. When my first moment of terror had been allayed, Sister Marie-des-Anges gently called to my attention the fact that I happened to be naked. Indeed, I was not thinking of it, but I understood her without hearing her. An *incredible sensation* dominated me completely and overwhelmed me with shame. My predicament cannot be expressed. Some students were standing around the bed and watching this scene, unable to attribute the nervous trembling that shook me to anything but my feeling of fear . . . I did not dare now either to get up again or confront the looks that were fixed upon me. My distorted face was covered with a livid pallor. My legs gave way beneath me.[33]

First and foremostly, this event invoked guilt:

> A total confusion reigned in my thoughts. My imagination was ceaselessly troubled by the memory of the *sensations* that had been awakened in me, and I came to the point of blaming myself for them like a crime . . . That is understandable; at this time I was completely ignorant of the facts of life. I had no suspicion at all of the passions that shake mankind.[34]

Retrospectively, Barbin forgives Camille her 'crime' by explaining these feelings as 'facts of life' Camille was not yet aware of. Barbin considered his feelings as a young man – or, as someone medically declared to be a man later in life – for young women to be natural. This naturalness is used as a *moral excuse*, and not to prove an innate masculine being. Similarly, guilt and excuses structure a description of a school trip during which the girls slept together:

> Half-dressed and stretched out side by side upon our improvised beds, we presented an appearance that might have tempted a painter . . . Beneath this charmingly scanty dress, one could distinguish here and there admirable figures that a casual movement exposed to view from time to time. When I look back to that already vanished past, I believe that I must have been dreaming! ! ![35]

Such scenes are described as naturally erotic to Camille.[36] Reflecting on these memories, Barbin claims she could write a novel, but – turning to his readers – then writes:

> Remember that I am writing my personal story, a series of adventures involving names that are far too honorable for me to dare to reveal the involuntary roles that they played in it. What a destiny was mine, O my God! And what

judgements shall be passed upon my life by those who follow me step by step
in this incredible journey, which no other living creature before me has taken![37]

What really concerns Barbin here is the moral judgement of her readers.
First of all, he asks them not to judge the girls who were involuntarily involved
in this compromising situation. Again, the innocence of the girls and women
involved in his life history is very important to him. Then she expresses her
fear of future readers' condemnation and blames 'destiny'.

The utmost moral confusion is expressed when Barbin describes the period
after Camille had started her affair with Sara, living with her and her mother
while directing the boarding school together. Sara is introduced as 'truly pious';
in her eyes Camille read 'the ingenuousness of an angel who is unaware of
herself'.[38] Camille was passionate about her from the very beginning, kissing
and hugging her so ardently and passionately that it sometimes surprised
Sara. One night, Camille, who was suffering from intolerable pains, asked Sara
to share her bed, to which Sara agreed with pleasure:

> It would be impossible to express the happiness I felt from her presence at my
> side! I was wild with joy! We talked for a long time before going to sleep, I
> with my arms encircling her waist, she with her face resting near my own! My
> God! Was I guilty? And must I accuse myself here of a crime? No, no! . . . That
> fault was not mine; it was the fault of an unexampled fatality, which I could
> not resist!!! Henceforth, Sara *belonged to me! ! . . . She was mine! ! ! . . .* What, in
> the natural order of things, ought to have separated us in the world had united
> us! ! ! Try to imagine, if that is possible, what our predicament was for us both![39]

The 'fate' he could not 'resist' of course refers to a heteronormative idea of
sexual instincts – but she invokes them, again, in order to excuse herself for
a moral fault.

So, although Barbin built up a story of increasingly intense, erotic and
sexual relations with women, there is no indication that these episodes are
used to build up a 'case' to reveal an inborn, innate personality, whether in
terms of sexual inclinations or in terms of masculinity. Nowhere in the text
has Barbin concluded something like: 'look, this was the real me breaking
through the misleading clothing and upbringing as a girl and woman'. What,
instead, constantly concerns him is his moral position. With hindsight, he
had embroiled other women in utterly dishonourable situations; could he be
blamed for this? Could they be blamed? *These* are the questions that trouble
Barbin, and which he tries to answer by writing this text. And in this context
only Barbin invokes the 'facts of life', 'fatality' or 'destiny'.

Moral troubles and angelic innocence

Entering into a sexual relationship with Sara is not described as finding out
some final truth about himself. Even if it was the most joyous experience he

ever had, it only led to more and deeper moral confusion. This was, more-over, not confusion about his own identity, but about his 'place' and 'title' in the world:

Sooner or later I would have to break with a kind of life that was no longer mine. But, alas! how was I to get out of that frightful maze? Where would I find the strength to declare to the world that I was usurping a place, a title, that human and divine laws forbade me?[40]

Whereas Camille's and Sara's behaviour evoked suspicion at least in some older students and two of Sara's sisters, her mother, Madame P., did not suspect a thing. That they shared the same bed in her house 'had not entered the admonition of Madame P., who was unaware of it', Barbin writes. 'And furthermore, she was not about to suspect us. The excellent woman was too sincerely virtuous and trusted us too blindly to fix her thought on such ideas.'[41] In Barbin's narrative, all the girls and women she lived with were pure, innocent, pious and beyond reproach, especially those who were in charge such as sister Marie-des-Anges or Madame P. Barbin goes to great pains to prove that these women could not be blamed for a situation that might have compromised them retroactively. This also applies to Sara:

. . . My poor Sara, who was crushed beneath the weight of shame! Dear and ingenuous child! Does her behavior need an excuse? . . . Could she refuse the lover that tenderness of feeling she had devoted to the *girlfriend*, to the *sister*? And if that naive love became passion, what was to be blamed if not fate?[42]

The innocence, ignorance and piousness of other women involved are often contrasted to his betrayal, his fouling of pureness and sacredness. Thus, Barbin describes her position in the house with Sara as follows:

In that family, the most respectable in the locality, I occupied an excessively delicate post, one of trust. I had a total, an absolute authority; in addition, all the members of the family had given me their sincere affection, of which I received new proof every day! And yet I was betraying them.[43]

During the first summer holiday, he decided to go to the primary school's annual retreat. On entering the building, Barbin writes: 'How many things seemed to forbid me to enter that house in which innocence and chastity lived!'[44] In her description of his saying goodbye to her beloved teacher Sister Marie-des-Anges, there is the same contradiction between his guilty knowledge and the other's pure ignorance: 'I can still see her angelic gaze fixed upon mine, while my hands clasped hers! ! ! My God! What if she had been able to read into my soul!!'[45] Barbin was in a state of utter confusion – intoxicated by happiness, as she writes, and frightfully tormented:

My poor mind was a chaos in which I could distinguish nothing. Confide in my mother? But it was enough to kill her! No! I could not initiate her in such

a discovery! Prolong the situation indefinitely? If I did so, I would inevitably
expose myself to the greatest misfortunes! I would outrage the most inviolable,
the most sacred moral principles! And could I not be called to account later for
my guilty silence . . . ?[46]

So far, Barbin's text has primarily been concerned with the way she might
harm others or severely compromise them – constantly seeking a way out of
the guilt this entails. Her erotic inclinations for girls and women which she
had experienced from early childhood on, and which she presented as the
'facts of life' and 'fate' had made him guilty involuntarily. His text is primarily
meant to ask forgiveness for himself and to exonerate those who might have
been compromised by the course of events. Compared with what characterizes
the modern self in autobiography, sexual drives in Barbin's text quite clearly
do *not* serve as the hidden, dark forces of the self that have to be revealed
in order to find an ultimate inner truth. Although they break through the
conventional moral codes and thus are presented as an autonomous force –
in a manner quite similar to that of, for example, Alexina X.'s and Marie B.'s
case histories described in the previous chapter – they do not serve as an
ultimate indicator of the self, but as excuse for the violation of 'the most
sacred moral principles'.

According to Barbin's story, such an excuse was very much needed after
her sex was reassigned and rumours started to spread like a wildfire. After
having started the whole process of her legal sex change, to which she had
felt increasingly morally obliged, Barbin still genuinely doubted the rightness
of her decision:

> Perhaps I had been wrong. Didn't this abrupt change, which was going to reveal
> me in such an unexpected way, offend all the laws of conventional behavior?
> Was it likely that society, which is so severe, so blind in its judgments, would
> give me credit for an impulse that might pass for honesty? Wouldn't people try
> to falsify it instead and treat it as if it were a crime on my part?[47]

Barbin's text offers a unique glimpse into the private considerations concerning the disclosure of a doubtful sex to a physician and the subsequent
sex reassignment in a context in which the rationale of sex as inscription
was very strong. Apparently, 'honesty' – perhaps this could be translated
into 'the rationale of a truthful representation of the body' – could lose out
against adhering to 'the laws of conventional behaviour'. Coming out was
not necessarily the best thing to do, morally – even if it led to a correction
of what was considered an error of sex. Barbin's story could therefore also
be read as a story in which these two different rationales of sex conflicted.
The first part of the story demonstrates Barbin's moral doubts because he
felt himself to betray her environment; in the second part, as we will see, the
moral disruption of all his previous social relations tormented his conscience.

Barbin was torn between two different rationales: should he obey the stability rule, and not upset the entire social network around him or should he be true to what he had come to think of as his physical sex? She was inescapably trapped in an immoral situation, because whatever she did, she would always infringe one of the rules.

In any case, his sex reassignment did not open up a new, happy life in which he could finally 'be himself' and openly or even legitimately love Sara. It did not offer happy closure to the story. On the contrary. First of all, the dishonour he brought on Sara and her family was not brought to an end by his sex change; it only *started* with it. 'As I had feared, hateful rumours circulated among the public concerning the intimacy of my relations with Mademoiselle Sara. According to some, she was really dishonoured. Oh! I confess it, I felt that blow most of all.'[48] When, retrospectively, writing about the lost prospect of marrying her and becoming Madame P.'s son-in-law, Barbin reproaches himself for ever having aspired to that status. He then goes on to argue that for Madame P., her daughter's reputation and that of her school were her dearest interests, which were both severely impaired by his sex change:[49]

> People were whispering all around her. The present explained the past, which was already so equivocal. The superintendents of the academy could not restrain themselves from broaching this very delicate subject with her. They knew about all the vicissitudes of this drama, in which the role that I had played stood out in a blazing light for everybody to see. To remind her of it in any way at all was to put her through all the torments of shame and fright, it was to cast doubt upon the respectability of her sensitively proud character.[50]

But not only Sara and her mother were contaminated with the dishonour and shame of Barbin's sex reassignment. The same was true for the teachers at the primary school, of which the chaplain reported in a letter to Barbin:

> When I gave her the news about your transformation, Sister Marie-des-Anges covered her face with her hands, thinking of the close intimacy that once bound you to her. 'My God!' cried the chaste creature. 'I kissed him so heartily when he was staying here recently for the retreat, which I had invited him to attend! And when he left me, he kissed my hands without any scruple.'[51]

Barbin hastens to deny any of the 'suppositions that were made about his earlier relations with those angels on earth'. Again, his primary aim was to stop the suspicions 'about creatures whose souls are above all else worthy of the attention of God'. Silence on the subject would foster such suspicions, Barbin feared.[52] He had therefore decided to write about what had happened.

A restoration of innocence

Barbin's text contains certain elements which align it with modern autobiography. This is primarily the fact that Barbin does not present his narrative as typical, but as idiosyncratic: it is a unique story, about an unprecedented situation. However, his text does not bear most of the other characteristics of modern autobiography. There is no indication that Barbin considered his soul to be integrated into his body; he does not invoke the medical truth of his body in order to point to the truth of his male self. Moreover, as we will see below, he tried to separate his being from his bodily existence. Barbin directly addresses God at several points in the text and constantly measures his own and others' alignment with Catholic morality. I cannot find indications that discovering his individual (sexual) 'truth' contains any intrinsic moral good. Although Barbin demonstrates a certain continuity in his personality – especially when it comes to his fondness for and erotic attraction to women – she does not explicitly point to this in order to demonstrate an essential truth about the self.

What does this autobiographic text aim to say, if not to reveal the truth of self? In my opinion, the text is first and foremost an attempt to recover from the moral dislocation his reassignment of sex had provoked. It is, at the same time, a confession and bid for absolution. But it is also – and perhaps even more so – an attempt to exonerate all others who were closely involved and whom he loved. As we have seen, *both* the situation before and the situation after the sex reassignment were described as immoral, and Barbin's text attempted to ask forgiveness for both situations while exonerating the others involved. The many discussions of Foucault's description of the 'pleasures' between Barbin and the other girls and women as a 'happy limbo of non-identity'[53] should therefore take into account what Barbin is trying to do much more, namely, trying to ensure that those he loved would not bear the brunt of even more scandal than they had already been subjected to. Presenting their intimacies as innocent is not a reference to 'reality' in which nobody was aware that these feelings were erotic: it is a narrative strategy designed to save them from any moral blame.

One question that might puzzle modern Western readers is what, exactly, was Barbin to blame for in her intimate and sexual relations with other women: was it lesbianism, or was it premarital heterosexual sex? Nowhere does Barbin address these topics explicitly; probably because the terms do not fit his discourse and concerns very well. To her, consciousness and conscience are crucial. Was Camille unaware of being physically male, overwhelmed by 'natural' feelings she did not understand and consequently, 'driven' into the arms of women? Or did he know he was 'actually' male and abuse the situation of trust, adding betrayal to the sin of premarital sex? The text strongly suggests a slow shift in Camille's consciousness, triggered by the apparent sexual feelings and acts. This was also expressed in the transition of adverbs linked to the 'I' in the text, which shift from mainly female to mainly male exactly at the time Camille started to become aware of his strong

HERCULINE BARBIN   81

sexual feelings.[54] The lesbianism might have been 'insignificant' in the sense
Valerie Traub described as applying in Renaissance and early modern England,
and therefore not a major problem.[55] As soon as Barbin became aware of
his position as a man in a world of women however, the situation became
extremely immoral. While suggesting that Camille was slowly becoming
aware of the sexual character of his feelings and acts, the narrative excludes
all the women involved from any such consciousness and this includes Sara,
at least initially.

The enormous moral weight Barbin ascribed to his sex reassignment
adds an important aspect to the rationale of sex as inscription. It shows how,
without being anchored in an innate, interior self, sex can be deeply related
to a person as a *morally conscious* being. This is in line with the more general
history of the self which described how the first techniques of the self are
not meant to *find* oneself, but to clean one's conscience (confession) and
to redirect the self to a divine or cosmic order. To a certain extent, Barbin's
text can be characterized as a Christian typological tale, as the story of suffering and leaving the world invokes many parallels to the passion of Christ.
However, since Barbin does not present himself as exemplary, but as unique,
there is a more modern, more distinctive individual tone to it.

Barbin's text shows sex and sex reassignment not to be something that
only touches the individual in question; as has already been argued in the previous chapters the moral reputation of many others is also at stake. The same
goes for Barbin's physical closeness to other women. The question of how to
deal with this (bathing, sharing beds, undressing) is a recurrent theme. Sex
is not just about one individual's physical characteristics and sexual drives
– it constantly involves other people. The first part of Barbin's narrative
desperately tries to cope with all these different moral aspects of her initial
inscription as a female, his physical, social and moral relation to other girls and
women, and the (retrospective) consequences of his sex reassignment.

Uprooted

When Goujon, the physician who performed the autopsy on Barbin's body,
introduced the case, he pointed to the importance of the fact that Barbin
had left 'long memoirs' and could be followed 'so to speak, from his birth
until his death'.[56] Actually, however, Goujon hardly refers to these narrated
experiences except for a brief mention of the fact that Barbin was brought up
as a girl and had to request a rectification of his civil status because of 'physical
modifications', and also a single quotation. This is the paragraph quoted at
the beginning of this chapter, in which Barbin briefly recounts the extreme
changes that happened in his life by referring to the company he kept (girls),

occupations (a lady's maid, student-teacher, director of a boarding school, working for the railway) and geographic place (small provincial town, Paris). Apparently, to Goujon, this radical shift in positions was the most surprising part of the memoirs. It demonstrates, in yet another way, how much sex was conceived of as being attached to positions people held rather than to some sort of inner sense of self. This section will focus on what dislocation meant to Barbin in a quite concrete manner.

In her place of birth, her sex change came as an enormous shock. Like Marie in the case described by Worbe, the public announcement took place in a church. The local newspaper recounted the event as follows:

> For some days they have been talking in La Rochelle about nothing else but a singular metamorphosis that has just been undergone by a twenty-one-year-old schoolmistress. This girl, who has a reputation for her talents no less than for her modesty, last week suddenly appeared dressed as a man in the church of Saint-Jean, between her mother and one of the town's most respectable ladies. Some people who had come to attend the mass, surprised by such a travesty in such a place and in such company, and being even less able to explain it on the part of persons who are known for their piety, could not restrain themselves from leaving the church in order to spread the news. Soon the whole quarter was in a flurry; groups were formed; all of them, looking in vain for the key to the enigma, gave themselves up to the most bizarre conjectures; the most preposterous stories circulated throughout the town, but the flower of the gossip blossomed above all right in the middle of the Saint-Jean quarter, where, as it is known, the soil could not be more favorable for it.[57]

Much like Marie in Worbe's case, a sex reassignment entailed a very concrete shift of locations and caused a public stir. As shown in previous chapters, many hermaphrodites who came to reassign their sex, or whose ambiguous sex was acknowledged by a physician, moved away from their region of birth to avoid the embarrassment provoked by this social dislocation. Barbin was no exception. The prefect, who wanted to see Barbin, advised him as to how to deal with the turmoil:

> You know what a storm you've raised and the many misdeeds that you are accused of. Don't pay any attention to all that. Walk with your head up; you have the right to do so. It will be difficult for you, perhaps. That's understandable. Also, and this is a good piece of advice that I'm giving you, resign yourself to leaving this region for a while. I'm going to take care of that.[58]

Barbin whole-heartedly embraced that advice: 'To the prospect of a journey to Paris was added the hope of promptly leaving a region that I had come to abhor, and of finally escaping from that kind of ridiculous inquisition of which I saw myself the object'.[59] After having arranged things in Paris, he returned to his town of birth B. to await an appointment with the railway company in

Paris. In the meantime, as in the case of Worbe's Marie, things had already calmed down a bit: 'The time that I spent at B. was not disturbed by any serious incident. I went out every day and always alone. The stir caused by my adventure was beginning to die down. The situation was better appreciated now that it stood out in broad daylight.'[60]

The doctor, talking to Barbin about his new situation, made it clear to him that he did not believe the bishop would allow him to return to L.: 'I don't know what Monseigneur will decide, but I doubt that he will permit you to return to L. There, your position is lost; it is not tolerable.'[61] So, the sex reassignment concretely resulted in a displacement from house, job and lover, in order to avoid social and moral disorder. This turned out to be very destructive, as we will see; but first let us examine a more subtle dislocation of social relations.

The bishop permitted Barbin to go to L. to take care of his replacement, so he went back and saw Sara and her mother again. In the light of the new situation, nothing was the same. The confusion all three of them experienced is described by Barbin as a theatre in which each of them played a perfect role. Although Barbin had been living there for two years, only now, after having made his decision (but not yet wearing men's attire), did he feel ashamed with hindsight: 'The shame that I felt because of my present position would alone have sufficed to make me break with a past for which I blushed.'[62] Barbin's knowledge of being a man makes the whole past different and shameful; from that perspective her earlier position appears to have been completely *out of place*. Also, the idea that she had given Sara in the latter's 'innocent ignorance' only 'incomplete joys' makes Barbin decide to break with the past.[63] Moving away and breaking the ties with the past (Barbin no longer corresponded with Sara's mother and finally also stopped writing to Sara) seemed to be the only way for Barbin to deal with the embarrassment the reassignment of his sex had caused.

So, despite the fact that in his home town the turmoil had cooled down a bit, he persisted in moving to Paris. From this point onwards, the story becomes very fragmented. It is difficult to find out what exactly happened among all the dramatic statements. But some aspects of what the loss of work, house and love meant are overly clear. First of all, Barbin had great difficulties acquiring and retaining jobs. For some reason, he must have left the railway company. But when he looked for a new job, his past worked against him. He begged some prominent people who knew him (possibly relations of the people in his home town who had arranged the sex reassignment) for help, but to no avail. He then tried to hire himself out as a valet. After a long time, he got an introduction to a lady: 'I had never been a servant, that was always the insurmountable obstacle. I could very well have said to her, "I have been a *lady's maid*." But how could I answer with such an outrageous remark?'

Barbin had lost his employment record by reassigning his sex. He acquired
an administrative job which he lost again and became increasingly desperate.
He was weak and in poor health. Hunger was an enormous threat: '. . . I had
come to the point of wondering how I would be able to have breakfast the
next day. May you, my readers, never know all the horror that is contained
in this remark.'[64] He had to ask his mother for financial assistance, which
made him deeply ashamed. 'Let it be clearly understood how painful such a
course of action is on the part of a son who knows what privations this assistance will involve . . . I can very well declare that this is the most desperate
extreme to which I could be condemned.'[65] Plans to enlist on a ship never
seemed to have been carried out.

Sex reassignments lead to a radical shift of positions in society, often
including work, social relations and love life or marriage. The embarrassment it invoked made a lot of hermaphrodites decide to escape their home
town. Such was also the case with Barbin. His memoirs show how crushing
the practical consequences of such a dislocation were.

Scripting masculinity

Another more subtle obstacle was Barbin's incapacity to adopt fully the
social script for masculinity which was new to him. Discerning male from
female social and biographical scripts is, of course, a perilous undertaking,
for ideas and practices of masculinity differ greatly in different classes, groups
and contexts and change over time. However, the moral double standard
with regard to sexuality generally represents a demarcation between honour-
able masculinity and femininity. Roughly speaking, according to this double
standard, men were encouraged to penetrate the (sexual) spaces of women
as a proof of their masculinity, whereas women could only allow men
in their intimate sphere under very restrictive circumstances, which their
honour and even their lives depended on. I believe a difference between
male and female social and narrative scripts can be deduced from this double
standard. Of course, other differences might interfere with these scripts
as well. It is quite imaginable that the way men proved their masculinity
differed considerably among different classes or between urban and rural
areas in France at the time.[66] I will come back to this briefly, but for now I
want to discuss the difficulties Barbin encountered inscribing himself in this
general masculine script.

As we have seen, Barbin strongly empathized with the position of the
women whose sacred spaces he had penetrated involuntarily; he understood
their shame, their feeling of being defiled. He reassures the reader that the
gossip about him being a true Don Juan conquering many of the women
he happened to live with leaves him cold.[67] He finds no male pride nor an
affirmation of the correctness of his new sex in having been Sara's lover, only

guilt. Moreover, he is afraid of having given her 'incomplete joys'. The fear of bringing Sara and her mother even further dishonour, as well as his belief that he was physically deficient closed the prospect of marriage to him.[68]

In the last part of his memories, Barbin alternately professes in an increasingly ecstatic style his own hopeless desire for love and his enraged contempt for men who fulfil these desires. He denies himself a family's hearth, for he thought his life to be scandalous to any 'young virgin' and did not doubt that the 'degraded' women who sometimes smiled at him and had kissed him would have 'shrunk back in shame under the pressure of my embraces, as from the touch of a reptile'.[69] He then starts to express his loathing of men: 'Men! I have not soiled my lips with your false oaths, nor my body with your hideous copulations.'[70] This theme recurs on the next page.[71]

These and other exclamations about the sexual life of men and women stem from his observations of Paris' erotic life in theatres, bars and restaurants. Clearly, Barbin longed for a relationship with a woman and was jealous of the 'electric currents' he observed around him, but could not identify with men who found pride in conquering women. Incidentally, he equally abhorred the immodest and unfaithful behaviour of women. Barbin's impossibility of scripting his new life with the scripts available for masculinity might have had to make do with the social scripts for masculinity available in Paris life *specifically*;[72] he might have found his way much more easily in more religious, middle-class and rural scripts for masculinity. However interesting and relevant, this cannot but remain merely speculation.

There are other paragraphs in which Barbin suggests that he did not feel at ease with the masculine role of penetrating female space, for instance in the section in which he refers to the way other males have tried to unveil female secrets, such as the writer Alexander Dumas. But Dumas, according to Barbin, '. . . lacked the password for penetrating the sanctuary'.[73] This is not something to be deplored, she continues, for:

> . . . there is a limit beyond which it would be dangerous for a man to go . . . I, who am called a man, have been granted the intimate, deep understanding of all the facets, all the secrets, of a woman's character. I can read her heart like an open book. I could count every beat of it. In a word, I have the secret of her strength and the measure of her weakness, and so I would make a detestable husband for that reason. I also feel that all my joys would be poisoned in marriage and that I would cruelly abuse, perhaps, the immense advantage that would be mine, an advantage that would turn against me.[74]

Although I do not exactly understand what Barbin had in mind when he wrote that his knowledge would poison any possible marriage or why exactly that would make him a detestable husband, I can see that he does not share the male pleasure of discovering the unknowable female secret, of 'penetrating the sanctuary', for he *already* knows. Whereas masculinity is constituted by attempts to infringe the borders of female space, to Barbin this is no longer a challenge as there are no obstacles to overcome. It is difficult for her to conceive of herself as a penetrating subject towards women without feeling guilty or vile, and she shows much more empathy with the female position.

Barbin's difficulty of inscribing in the present social script of maleness – especially with regard to male roles vis-à-vis women – made him someone without a sexed position, someone who could not be placed within the sexual order. However, Barbin nowhere concludes that he actually is not a (real) man. The troubles are not narrated in terms of being unable to be 'himself' or of the damage done to his true self. The self is not the main point of reference, the relation to others is. For Barbin, the sufferings are caused by being an outlaw, by having no moral position and hence no place in society. At several points in the text, Barbin refers emotionally to his having no place in the human world, to her isolation and loneliness, to his being cursed and forsaken. Towards the end, Barbin starts to express her death wish: 'Death is there, oblivion. There, without any doubt, the poor wretch, exiled from the world, shall at last find a homeland, brothers, friends. And there, too, shall the outlaw find a place.'[75]

As Barbin cannot inscribe himself to the available male script and moral order, he writes himself *out* of humankind's script altogether; he solves the impossibility of his position by placing himself outside and above humanity, by moving away again. In nineteenth-century narratives, being sacred or angelic is often linked to not being clearly gendered or to androgyny. Barbin finally inserts himself into that discourse, distancing himself morally from other people and detaching himself from earthly life: 'I soar above all your innumerable miseries, partaking of the nature of the angels; for, as you have said, my place is not in your narrow sphere. You have the earth, I have boundless space.'[76]

In Barbin's autobiographic writing, I would conclude, sex is a social, economic and moral position. A person is attached to sex through relations. When sex changes or when it becomes doubtful, these relations are disturbed, causing disruptions of the social, economic and moral position of the hermaphrodite and those closely involved. These disruptions include one's position within the family or in marriage, one's position within the social community, one's profession and livelihood, one's moral reputation and often, as a consequence, one's place of residence. These all affect and trouble the person in many ways. What can be learned from Barbin's text is that such strong, personal emotions do not necessarily point to a damaged or confused sense of one's sex of self, however. Even while invoking a lifelong history of erotic attraction to women, such a concept of sex as an intrinsic part of the self cannot be found in his memoirs.

Although a concept of a modern self cannot be found, Barbin's text is certainly modern in one respect: she *expressed* herself by writing her life history. Autobiography, can also be seen as a *practice* through which a modern self can be constituted. Acknowledging 'dark' parts of the self, reading child and adolescent memories as indications for the essence of one's individuality, constructing a plot of self-discovery from the misleading and confusing events of the past, can all be performed by the act of writing. The last section of this chapter will therefore discuss to which extent the *act of writing* itself constituted a pathway to Barbin's (sexed) self.

THE ACT OF WRITING

I find Barbin's text moving: partly because of the autobiographical pact which means we know Barbin really lived and committed suicide. But there is more to it, which has to do with what Barbin brings about through the act of writing. Many recent studies that refer to Barbin's text at some point dismissively describe the text as overwrought, melodramatic and sentimental prose.[77] But I think it is more interesting than just that.

The more difficult it became for Barbin to script her life, the more the text becomes *discourse* instead of *histoire*, as defined by Benviste. *Histoire* is a story told in retrospect about a first-person character from the past and is written in the past tense. The first-person narrator and the first-person character do not act simultaneously. The text aims to describe the life of the first-person character up to the point in time of the narrator's writing. Time passes in the past, not in the present of writing. *Histoire* is commonly used in autobiographies. In *discourse*, the first-person character and the first-person narrator act almost simultaneously; discourse is written in the present tense and focuses on the act of writing itself. *Discourse* aims to describe the psychological condition of the narrator while he or she is writing. Therefore, time goes by while the narrator writes. Diaries mostly use *discourse*.

In practice, these two writing methods often alternate. This is also true for Barbin's text. The first part of the text mainly consists of *histoire*. Until the sex change the story is clearly divided into different phases. There is a sort of control of and distance from the narrated history, for it leads to a clearly finished and defined point in time. Now and then, however, the history is interrupted by passages that can be characterized as discourse. They remind the reader of the unbearable present, for example in the exclamation: 'My God! You had given me an immense amount of happiness! Ought I to complain if, in the midst of the deep night that surrounds me, only dreams of the luminous past bring me a little solace in my long misfortune!'[78]

Towards the end of the text, the life history is increasingly replaced by *discourse*. The reader can only try to put bits and pieces of it together, but the story's course has been lost. The aim of writing has also changed, as the text does no longer tries to provide an overview of a whole life, but attempts to reflect the condition of the soul: the horrible solitude, the hunger, the unemployment, the feelings of having no place in the world and the desire for death. This shift from *histoire* to *discourse* fundamentally changes the text's effect. Firstly, the writing itself has become more important as well as the subjectivity directly produced by it. Secondly, the meaning of time has changed as time passes during the act of writing. Both these aspects will be explored below.

In the *discourse* parts of the text, Barbin often uses the figure of speech 'apostrophe', in which the speaker or writer directly addresses a person, usually a non-present person or personification. According to Jonathan Culler this often embarrasses critics; they would rather ignore it, consider it pure convention or completely outdated. I was indeed inclined to dismiss Barbin's many 'ahs' and 'ohs' and exclamation marks as nineteenth-century sentimentalism. However, it is exactly the apostrophe which can clarify why towards the end the text engages the reader so strongly. 'The apostrophe', Culler writes, 'makes its point not by troping on the meaning of a word but on the circuit or situation of communication itself'.[79] Barbin therefore uses a figure of speech in which communication *itself* is achieved against her isolation. The effect is poignant: while describing his extreme loneliness he directly addresses God, the people around him, his readers or the doctors he expects to find his body:

> Lord! Lord! The cup of my sorrows, is it not empty, then? . . . Can my isolation been more complete? Can my abandonment be more painful? Oh! pity, my God![80]
>
> I tell you this, I, whom you have trod beneath your feet – that I dominate you with the full height of my immaterial, virginal nature, with my long sufferings.[81]

With the apostrophe, Barbin creates a subject, a 'you' and therefore a relationship between two subjects. According to Culler it is possible to do this even if the subject addressed is described as having no subjectivity, no soul. Similarly, Barbin is able to address exactly those people who reject and avoid him, whom he could not address in real life. Addressing an object as 'you' not only makes the object into a subject, it also presupposes that this 'you' in turn will address the 'I' as 'you', that is, as a subject. By using the apostrophe, Barbin makes himself a subject in front of precisely those people who never address him as a subject:

> And it is upon *me* that you will cast your insulting disdain, as upon a disinherited creature, a being without a name? And you have the right to do so? You, degraded men, debased a thousand times over and forever useless . . . Do you, I say, cast sarcasm and outrage in my face?[82]

By addressing an imaginary 'you', Barbin constitutes his subjectivity directly. As Culler expresses it, when using 'apostrophe' nothing happens because what is happening is the addressing itself: 'Nothing need happen because the poem itself is to be the happening.'[83] Barbin becomes the immediate subject of the text, not by finding a name, a place or a script, not by referring to an inner self, but by using the apostrophe. The apostrophe creates, as Culler explains, not a timeless present but a temporariness of writing: 'Apostrophe resists narrative because its *now* is not a moment in a temporal sequence but a *now* of discourse, of writing.'[84]

With this, we have arrived at the second effect of the shift from *histoire* to *discourse*. The apostrophic discourse fixes the reader's attention on the now of the writing, thereby reminding her of the ominous future to which the text has pointed from the start. The plot of the text is no longer embedded in a logic of narrative order, but in a now that threatens to stop. In the reading/writing, time goes by like a ticking bomb. While reading the *histoire* the reader is hardly aware of this, for the time passes in the past. Moreover, we know the reassuring end of the story: a first person narrator writing down the story. But during the reading of discourse, there is no plot directing our reading, no acting subject trying to reach his goal. There is only a subject that constitutes herself as long as he is writing . . . as long as I am reading.

No techniques are employed to reveal or discover dark instincts or motives or to reminisce about hidden and forgotten memories. His writing is not what is sometimes called 'memory work'. It is not this quest for self-discovery which engages the reader. Barbin ultimately engages the reader by fulminating, whining, cursing, complaining, scolding, beseeching a non-present, imaginative other as in a theatrical monologue. And therefore, although the text reflects the new democratized bourgeois search for the self by means of autobiographical writing, this does not mean Barbin is looking for his true self through the act of writing. The importance of Barbin's engagement of the reader should not be underestimated. The text *does* creatively engage readers, and physicians at the time *were* obviously moved by her story; both Goujon and Tardieu express their compassion at Barbin's sad fate. Later physicians often mentioned suicide as a possible consequence of an 'error of sex', even if Barbin was only a rare example. Despite the fact that Barbin did not refer to sex as something attached to his interior self, it drew the *attention* of physicians to the more emotional aspects of an ambiguous sex. Barbin's text created the first truly 'humanitarian narrative', as Thomas Laqueur labelled it, about the troubles of an ambiguous sex.[85] The interest in and compassion for Barbin's self narrated 'poor fate' may therefore have been one of the grounds on which later, more 'humanitarian' discussions of sex assignment among doctors started to develop.

II

BODY

The historical development of a rationale of physical sex as the basis for sex assignment, unravelled in this part, will turn out not to be a straightforward history in which physicians became increasingly good at diagnosing people's physical sex. First of all, as has been asserted time and again in gender and queer studies, a body does not gain significance from itself. As Judith Butler has persuasively argued, a body only begins to 'matter' as soon as it is 'read' by a discourse. This pre-existing discourse, with its binary categories and hierarchies, and with its system of inclusion and exclusion, determines the meaning of a body. Outside discourse, a body is just matter without significance. Hence, physical sex is a notion that cannot be separated from the cultural and social organization in which it appears.

Historically, a comparable argument has been taken up by Thomas Laqueur, who in his famous *Making Sex* revealed that physical sex was not the same thing over the centuries. Even such a seemingly a-historical object as the sexed body surprisingly gained a history. Laqueur demonstrated a fundamental shift in the medical conceptualization of difference between the sexes which occurred towards the end of the eighteenth century. Until the second half of the eighteenth century, anatomically the sexes had been perceived as similar, according to Laqueur; only men's genitals were viewed as further developed than women's. Legal and social sex differences were derived from an already existing cosmological order, which was based on metaphysics instead of the physical body. Within this conceptualization of physical sex difference as a gradual and hierarchic difference, hermaphroditism was only a logical intermediate state of development. Yet this did not give hermaphrodites the right to take on a social and legal position in between men and women, for the fluidity and flexibility of physical sex differences were compensated for by the strict legal categories of male and female.[1]

This one-sex system, as Laqueur labelled it, was replaced by a fundamentally different two-sex system by the end of the eighteenth century. Physical sex differences were suddenly perceived as absolute and irreducible, the sexes being incommensurably, diametrically opposed. Just as natural rights had become the basis for political equality in Enlightenment thinking, natural differences – such as sexual and racial difference – became the justification for social and legal differences. Within this conceptualization of sex difference hermaphrodites could not exist. One was either female or male, and it became the physician's task to determine not the 'dominant', but the 'true sex'.[2] Alice Domurat Dreger further nuanced the latter argument by showing how, over the course of the nineteenth century, the criterion for 'true hermaphroditism' became ever narrower, so that in the end only microscopic proof of the coexistence of ovular and testicular tissue could count as 'hermaphrodite'. As she argued, this practically excluded everyone from being a hermaphrodite, so that everyone indeed had to have a 'true sex'.[3] Both Laqueur and Dreger point to the many discrepancies between the scientific findings (Laqueur) or the clinical problems related to establishing gonads (Dreger) and the dominant medical opinion they describe. However, these authors argue that conceptualizations of sex are often stronger than the empirical findings that could have undermined them.

There is a second complication. Trying to work out the rationale of the category of sex as based on physical sex is not restricted to medical opinions, perceptions or theories about sex. It is an attempt to understand the logic of how the body played a role in the way people *dealt with* cases of doubtful sex *in practice*. This does not so much contradict the notion that a body gains significance through existing discourses, but it considerably expands and complicates the history of physical sex. For, inasmuch as a body does not gain significance without being 'read' through the lens of a certain discourse, there is no reading of a body without a whole series of different practices being involved. Routines, rules, money, institutions, instruments, skills, techniques, knowledge, disciplines, habits – these are all involved in *enacting* a body before it even can be read, and all have their own history. The questions central to Part II concern these practices. How, by what means, and where were the bodies of hermaphrodites examined? And how did the routines, practicalities and techniques involved change over time?

The idea of not simply considering a body to 'be', but always to be *enacted* in a specific way, stems from Annemarie Mol's highly influential *The Body Multiple*. In this book, she has made a radical turn to the body in practice. Her focus is no longer on conceptions, theories and knowledge about the body, but on the ways in which the body becomes present in medical practice through different enactments. Rather than criticizing medicine for its monopolizing knowledge of the body by contrasting that knowledge with other, subjective, cultural or social significances of the body, Mol shows how modern medical practices *themselves* produce a 'multiple body'.[4] Similarly, in medical practice many different enactments of (doubting) sex coexist.

How this approach differs from those mainly concerned with conceptualizations and opinions can be illustrated quite easily by returning to
nineteenth-century hermaphrodites. Both Laqueur and Dreger concentrate
on the medical criteria for telling a male from a female. The outer appearance
of the genitals (as under the one-sex system) did not count, but the essential
different male and female functions in procreation. Sexual function, procreative heterosexual function, was therefore decisive. However, if we look
at the way in which this sexual function was enacted within the clinical context, there is a huge difference between the start of the nineteenth and the
start of the twentieth century. Whereas the capacity for 'proper' coitus in
a female or male, including not only anatomical aptness, but also sufficient
lust, was decisive during the first half of the nineteenth century, the existence
of ovular or testicular tissue determined physical sex from the end of that
century onwards. However, as we will see, even such a seemingly clear-cut
criterion was enacted in multiple ways: by palpating inner organs, by establishing the presence of sperm in the ejaculate, by extirpating sexual glands
or putting slices of glandular tissue under the microscope.[5] And even then,
other aspects of the sexual physique, such as hair growth or the anatomy of
the genitals, were not entirely excluded from a physician's establishment of a
person's sex. In other words, the clinical establishment of physical sex was
not so much improved as complicated by the end of the nineteenth century,
as the enactments of sexual function had multiplied.

Finally, while concentrating on the practicalities of the clinical assessment
of physical sex during the nineteenth century, one topic seemed to present
itself with ever-increasing urgency. Quite early in my research, I was struck
by the importance of shame. Overcoming the patient's shame in order to
carry out a thorough physical examination turned out to be a real problem
for the doctors involved. At first, I related the theme mainly to the shame
involved in exposing something experienced as a monstrosity or deformity.
But a more precise historicization of all the issues involved in gaining access
to the physical bodies of hermaphrodites proved that it was a much more
general issue.

One of the reasons for my rather slow recognition of the importance of
the theme has to do, I believe, with the casualness with which present-day
Western people can temporarily detach their person from their bodies in a
clinical context. Most people do not give the fact that they undress themselves
for complete strangers in such circumstances a second thought, and they know
how to separate a pelvic exam from intimate manipulations of their genitals
– however unpleasant they may find it. Moreover, they are accustomed to
techniques reading their bodies in ways that have nothing to do with their
own physical experiences and observations, such as X-rays or blood tests or
exploratory surgery. For the sake of medical examinations, the person can

be *dislodged* from the body. Hence, they are accustomed to the existence of a body-object to be read by experts. Of course, that body-object enacted in a consulting room, hospital or laboratory is somehow related (through a discussion with a physician, for example) to the person involved. But it has become quite normal to have an autonomous body, with a significance of its own, detached from subjective experience.

In order to understand the crucial transformation in the logic behind sex assignments as well as the role of the body therein, it is necessary to defamiliarize this modern self-evident, autonomous body-object. During at least the first part of the nineteenth century, the body could hardly be detached from the person or from the social context of which it was part, even in a clinical encounter. Physicians only saw the outer shape of the body and had to rely on patient statements when it came to sexual experiences and functions. Bodies were understood within their social and moral context, as inalienable parts of the person. How then, did medicine manage to cut the body loose from the person and her environment? Which obstacles did it find on its path? And which consequences did such a detachment have for the sex enacted in a clinical encounter? These are the central questions I will address in Part II.

Chapter 4 explores the ways in which sex was examined in the early case histories. Until around the 1860s most case histories can be labelled 'bedside medicine', in which lay experiences and observations were still very close to the physician's. How were sex and sexual function enacted under such circumstances? The following chapter focuses on the issue of access. It discusses the case of Justine Jumas in 1869, whose husband claimed – after two years of marriage – that she was not a woman at all. It will show the enormous tension between the medical insistence on baring the physical 'truth' and personal, social and legal strategies aimed at keeping a doubtful sex private. Finally, chapter 6 will show how, at the turn of the twentieth century, many routines and techniques had come into being enabling the (temporary) separation of the person from the body examined. Even under these circumstances and with a single scientific criterion for sex, clinical practice produced a 'sex multiple'.

4

HOW TO GET THE SEMEN TO
THE NECK OF THE WOMB

Anna Barbara Meier decided to disclose himself to his physician because he
wanted to marry the woman he had made pregnant 'out of genuine affection'.
She had accepted 'that she would have to make her masculine nature public
and declare it in court'.[1] To that end, she had asked the physician to visit
her house.

> Thus she called on me, as a doctor, as her medical confessor, to examine her
> discreetly as far as her peculiar constitution allowed, in order that I would
> provide a testament which would disclose and attest to her true masculine
> constitution. She declared her absolute trust in me, that I would not reveal her
> somewhat deviant sexual constitution anywhere except at this particular court
> of law. In the same way, she also begged me, that I would not force her to bare
> her genitalia – for the love of God![2]

Meier wanted to account for the truth and veracity of her statement before
the omniscient God, and asked the physician to believe her and to testify to
her masculine constitution before court. Thus, Meier's disclosure consisted
merely of his own words describing his sex. He said:

> 1) that she possessed a genuine, clearly protruding masculine rod, with an
> opening in its head, through which she always passed water;
> 2) under her masculine member hung a scrotum, in the right side of which a
> testicle was to be found, around the size of a pigeon's egg, but on the left side
> only a small protuberance the size of a bean;
> 3) the right side of the scrotum was thus drawn noticeably downwards, the left
> side was drawn upwards;
> 4) further to this, neither within the scrotum nor in the perineum did she
> possess an opening resembling a vulva;
> 5) since her fourteenth year she had had a beard and since then had shaved it a
> few times a week;
> 6) as could be ascertained within the village and throughout the area, she
> undertook men's work such as ploughing, carpentry and woodturning.[3]

In Meier's conception, his masculinity was proven by his physical appearance and masculine occupations: the presence of a penis, a scrotal sac with one full-grown testicle, the absence of a vaginal opening, a beard and masculine work. Remarkably, he does not refer to his capacity to have sexual inter-course and impregnate – possibly he was too shy to talk about it in detail. The physician was not satisfied by this statement and tried to persuade Anna Barbara Meier to expose his genitals:

> Given the nature of the situation, I sought other means to encourage Barbara Meier to abandon her false modesty and allow me to become an eyewitness to her sexual nature, thus able to present a truthful testimony. Yet all my endeavours and remonstrances were in vain![4]

Instead, he interrogated her, in particular about the functioning of her sex, and summarized the results. Furthermore, he examined her outer appearance and felt her exterior body (not the genital area, however). According to the physician, the results of the confession and interrogation all pointed to the same 'cause and effect', that is, 'all prove the real masculine constitution of Anna Barbara Meier, who had hitherto been considered as a hermaphrodite'.[5] After some theoretical remarks, the physician concluded in his official statement to the court that there was no doubt about Anna Barbara Meier being a man, provided her statements were truthful.

The court, however, was not satisfied with this verbal examination and demanded a visual examination. Another examination followed, again per-formed by G. Although Meier had consented to this second examination, she still did not cooperate fully:

> Even during this process much effort and persuasion was required before the aforementioned person – who retained her wilful opposition, born of genuine modesty, right up to the last moment – could be examined adequately. Via the intervention of the local priest, Meier finally capitulated to the extent that she consented to a *digital* examination, but not to one *per oculum*.[6]

G.'s second report was submitted to Schweickhard and the head midwife Zandt, who concluded that a proper medico-surgical examination, includ-ing a visual inspection, was needed before anything could be decided on the sex and procreative function of Anna Barbara Meier. A physician (D. G.) and a surgeon (H.) carried out this examination. The report on the third examination does not contain one word about Meier's resistance, but gives the results of the visual examination; finally, she had surrendered to the legal pressure.

As Anna Barbara Meier wanted to reassign her sex and get married, she had to overcome her deep shame at exposing her genitals because this was ordered by the court. However the physicians did not penetrate her body with fingers or instruments, nor was there any thorough palpation attempting to feel the interior organs of the body or of the scrotal sac. After the 'examination by touch' only the magnitude of the testicle was reported, without any details about how the tissue within the sack felt or whether an epididymus or a seminal duct could be palpated. The only more invasive aspect of the examination was the palpation of the left inguinal canal where a small, testicle-like organ could be felt sometimes inside, sometimes outside the body.[7]

Medical entrance to the (female) body
The body – in particular the female body – has been a contested site of mystery, secrecy, power and knowledge for centuries. Because the female body hid the secrets of procreation, knowledge about what happened within her body was often of crucial importance: in matters of generation and inheritance (which could be hotly contested legal issues), in criminal matters of rape, infanticide or fornication, and, from the nineteenth century onwards, in matters of public health and reproduction. In the seventeenth century, the power of knowing the female body was primarily in the possession of married or widowed women who had borne children themselves. On the basis of their experience they were thought to be able to decide in matters of pregnancy – a very difficult matter, hardly to be determined before the child started moving – procreation and childbirth. These women and midwives were allowed to touch and penetrate other female bodies.[8]

But there is more to it. In the seventeenth and early eighteenth centuries bodies were conceived of as open, fluid, vulnerable, and this was even more the case with the female body. The flux of humours through the body, their transformation from one fluid into the other, the openings through which they could enter or leave, were all central in the imagination of the body. In this way, the body was not a closed entity, but something connected to the outer world, to the cosmos. This made the female body in particular a site to protect, to keep private, to 'enclose'. The walls of the house protected her dangerous openness; making the female genitals into 'privates' made them shameful and demanded chastity. Gowing has shown how sensitive women in seventeenth-century England were to different sorts of touching, to rules as to whom you could and could not bare the body for.[9]

As early as in the seventeenth century, married women's power of knowledge was contested by another body of knowledge: medicine based on anatomical knowledge of the organs of generation.[10] The access of physicians to the physical bodies of living women was very problematic, however. Barbara Duden, in her book on the female patients of the German physician Storch in early eighteenth-century Eisenach, has described how very rarely these women allowed the physician to approach them in person, let alone touch them. Most of the requests were handed to him as messages through mediators; he only built up a relationship with a few women who were trusting enough to allow a more intimate contact.[11] Such a physical distance between a medical doctor and a patient is not confined to female patients. Jens Lachmund has described how doctors under bedside medicine usually confined their physical examination of patients to parts of the body that were already bare (hands, face) and to the secretions. Touching the body was associated with non-academic healers and quacks or surgeons – an association medical doctors tried to avoid. They were therefore to a high degree dependent on the patient's narrative concerning the disease. In practice there was therefore no major difference between the doctor's conceptualization of the body and its disease, and those of the patient (and all the others present at the bedside).[12] In the case of female patients, an examination by touch was preferably carried out by midwives or other (married) women. In some cases of doubtful sex in the nineteenth century, the first examination was also carried out by a midwife. Whether in certain cases such examinations were considered sufficient and how often this was the case is unknown. All the cases I have been able to trace were published by physicians – midwives obviously did not publish about these cases.

Although midwives' power of knowledge in relation to matters concerning the female body and generation was already contested in the seventeenth century and even more so from the end of the eighteenth century, in practice the actual transference of this power to medicine (both science and clinical medicine) only took place in the second half of the nineteenth century. The resistance against this transformation is not unique to female bodies or more specifically gynaecology, but fits into a larger picture of the transformation of 'bedside medicine' into 'hospital medicine'.[13] Jens Lachmund has meticulously described this transformation, concentrating on the introduction of auscultation and percussion. He analyzed how the change in medical paradigm towards a pathology-based medicine at the turn of the nineteenth century as described by Foucault in *The Birth of the Clinic* depended on related fundamental changes in the *practicalities* of the clinical encounter.

To understand how outer symptoms related to lesions in the tissue of the future dead body, major shifts in medical practice had to take place. Such shifts demanded radical transformations in the relationship between doctors and patients: in the patient's expectations concerning a consultation, in the concrete and social environment of the exam, in the routines of doctors and discipline of patients, and in the possibility of doctors penetrating the patient's bodily integrity. Lachmund demonstrates how such a transformation could take place in the Paris hospitals, where poor people had no choice but to surrender to the power physicians had over them and could therefore be disciplined into undergoing the new experimental medical examinations. Moreover, these hospitals offered the ideal circumstances for comparing the symptoms of the living with anatomical findings of the dead, for all the dead bodies from the hospitals were used for autopsies. Certain sounds of the lungs could thus be linked to certain lesions in these organs after death. Previously, it was almost only criminals who had been subject to dissection after death; now the bodies of all poor people could be opened. This made France, and in particular Paris, the centre of modern medicine in the first decades of the nineteenth century. Under the new regime of hospital medicine, patients were no longer examined in their own environment in the presence of family and neighbours, but isolated, amid other ill people; their history of the disease no longer defined what was wrong, this was now determined by signs extracted from the body (by auscultation or percussion) only understood by the doctor; the patient had to submit to the hospital regime, and to what the doctor demanded him or her to do with the body (to bare the breast, to inhale deeply, to bend over, etc.); finally, prognosis and treatment were no longer central, diagnosis was. The doctor's language about the body and its diseases started to differ fundamentally from the patient's observations and experiences. For the first time in history, a doctor could declare someone ill without the patient experiencing illness.[14]

However, Lachmund's and Ackerman's studies both convincingly reveal how bedside and folk medicine survived outside these specific locations – in private practices – until at least the second half of the nineteenth century. In Germany, there was an articulated resistance among physicians to the new medical paradigm and its accompanying practices.[15] Ackermann has described how the peasantry around Paris dealt with health and illness during the long nineteenth century.[16] She concluded that most farmers were reluctant to consult doctors during the first half of the nineteenth century. Only very slowly, did medical officialdom gain access to rural households, while peasants continued to make use of healers who were not medically trained (midwives, folk healers, purveyors of drugs, priests or nuns). Generally, peasants were suspicious about vaccination and hygiene programmes as well as reluctant to visit hospitals. The peasants proved to be quite pragmatic. They could pick and choose, and as soon as a medical treatment clearly offered good results, they turned out to be quite willing to change. Ackerman mentions many different reasons why it took so long before medically trained physicians became predominant in dealing with sick bodies: a general suspicion of change among the peasantry, irregular (eating) habits versus the medical regimes of order and discipline, the difference between the peasant's attitude and the doctor's elite culture, the high cost of medical consultations, and the poor distribution of physicians across the countryside (for many farmers, the nearest physician was several villages away).

Furthermore, shame and resistance from patients against medical techniques intruding into the patient's body hampered the new medical techniques. As did Foucault, Lachmund reminds us to be cautious with the term 'shame', as it is directly connected to a medical practice attempting to bare and penetrate bodies. Shame was not much of an issue in medical practice as long as there was no medical need to undress and intrude upon the body. The problem arose with the need to know the inside of the body.[17] Thus, disciplining patients into a willingness to undergo physical exams which demanded baring, touching and penetrating the body was a major task for modern medicine. This was especially so with regard to female patients. Not only was there the problem of physicians being of the other sex, but also the fact that modern medicine increasingly considered the female's organs to be crucial to understanding procreation made the need to penetrate her body more urgent than was the case with men.

The rise of gynaecology therefore seems to have met even more resistance than the transformation to hospital medicine in the nineteenth century in general. The male appropriation of what had hitherto primarily been a female domain of knowledge, and the new practicalities that were felt to be an offence against female decency, presented extra objections against medical modernization. Especially with relation to baring the female body to a male doctor, the introduction of instruments for difficult deliveries and examination techniques that penetrated the female body were problematic. There were major arguments about the emergence of male midwives (or obstetricians), about the use of the speculum and about the use of anaesthetics during childbirth over the course of the nineteenth century.[18] The only way gynaecologists could try out modern techniques on living female bodies ('clinical material') for education, experience and research, was at special birth clinics which usually only catered to poor women, prostitutes and single mothers.[19] In America, the famous 'father of gynecology', Sims earned his fame by experimenting on female slaves.[20] Birth clinics were avoided by the middle and higher classes. In private practice, doctors covered the genitals while they were examining them, or darkened the room; examples of this can be found until well into the nineteenth century.[21]

Palpation, penetration and the search for internal organs of generation
We have to consider Meier's shame, her resistance against the subsequent examinations, the pressure executed by the court, and the ultimately rather superficial examination of her genitals (which did not even ask about menstruation) within this wider historical context. Her sex could only be established by means of an examination that had to maintain a precarious balance between what needed to be known and the culturally and socially respected bodily integrity. What sorts of techniques were employed in cases of hermaphroditism under these conditions in the first half of the nineteenth century?

The bedside medicine practices described above, which probably remained in place outside hospitals during the first half of the century, explain why only if the person in question or people involved with this person had serious doubts and an interest in bringing these to the fore, would they eventually visit a doctor. Besides such situations, physicians hardly ever saw hermaphrodites, or did not notice when they did, because they generally did not examine their bare bodies. It therefore turns out that almost all the extensively described medical case histories from this period were cases in which important legal matters were at stake: requests for sex reassignments, demands for the examination of sex before an intended marriage, or marriage annulments. Only a few cases were discovered at hospitals or after a request for an operation. Moreover, in a couple of other detailed case histories from this time, a hermaphrodite exhibited him- or herself to several doctors in exchange for money. I will not deal with these cases here nor with the specific opportunities they offered for medical scientific research. The consequence of the particular legal circumstances concerning medical exams was that patients underwent invasive examinations more often than usual – Anna Barbara Meier being an explicit example of the legal pressure aimed at such transgressive practices. In other words, the following descriptions of cases of hermaphroditism will relate physical examinations which were probably more invasive than those administered during a private consultation.

Visual examination of the outer genitals was considered very important and the most accurate. In Meier's case, the pressure to overcome her shame in order to enable the physicians to carry out a visual examination is telling in this respect. While the physicians and the court were insistent that she should make her genitals visible to the examining eyes, there was hardly any impulse to try to find signs of sexual organs under the surface of the skin. This was generally true for the first half of the century. Both palpation as a technique for feeling under the surface of the skin and more penetra- tive techniques (using fingers, instruments and sound) were not very well developed yet and did not seem to constitute the essence of the exam. The extent to which palpation was restricted to the exterior of the body or was used as a means for feeling what was under the surface differs from case to case, however. Again, shame on the one hand, and urgency on the other, determined how far an examination could go.

Generally, the medical fraternity only seemed to develop their skills in palpating internal sexual organs very slowly during the first decades of the century. There were several stages of increasingly penetrating techniques: feeling the testicles, separating the labia or split scrotum to have a better look at what lay in between, feeling the inguinal canal, introducing a finger into the opening between the labia or the split scrotum (in order to find a possible vagina and uterus), introducing a finger into the urethra (if possible),

introducing a finger into the anus (to feel the uterus), introducing a catheter
into the urethra, and, finally, the so-called bimanual technique: a combination of a finger in the anus and one in the vagina or a catheter in the urethra,
to feel which organs lay in between (uterus, ovaries, prostate, undescended
testicles). Although all the penetrating techniques were used separately by
1860, I only found examples of actual bimanual examinations in two French
cases dating from 1840 and 1856.

   What physicians attempted to feel – if at all – through either the anus or a
vagina or a vagina-like opening, was the uterus, or sometimes more vaguely
the inner 'organs of generation' (Geburthstheile). There is usually not much
more information other than whether they could feel something or not.
This constitutes a sharp contrast to the often meticulous descriptions of the
outer genital apparatus and sometimes the inner construction of the vagina
or vagina-like opening; often, the location of the outer part or the opening of
the split urethra in relation to the penis and vagina was described in detail.
I will return to this below.

   More significant even is that none of the invasive examinations explicitly
aimed to try to find ovaries. The most telling example in this respect is the
earliest bimanual palpation I found, performed by Benoit in 1840, which is
also relatively detailed in its description. 'If after introducing a men's catheter
into the bladder one puts a finger into the rectum one finds only a thin layer
of soft parts separating the two cavities, and it is impossible to grasp anything
indicating the existence of a prostate, a vagina or a uterus.'[22]

   There is no mention of ovaries at all, even though the most advanced
palpation techniques were employed. So, even if some influential German
anatomists, such as, for example, Johann Christian Stark and Johann Müller,
had announced that only the sexual glands could decide someone's sex,
in practice there was neither the option nor even an urge to find ovaries.[23]
Testicles were of course often easier to find, but even so the entire male
apparatus was taken into account if a person's sex had to be assigned.

SEXUAL FUNCTIONING UNDER BEDSIDE MEDICINE

Anna Barbara Meier

What sort of sexual functionality was established given these practicalities
and technicalities? Let us once again first examine how sex and sexual function were assessed during Anna Barbara Meier's subsequent examinations.
After having given evidence of her maleness by describing her physical
appearance and commenting on the masculine work she was able to do
(the numbers 1-6 quoted above), Dr G. asked her some additional questions.
These questions focused on her sexual functioning and G. drew the following
conclusions from them:

7) that she [Barbara Meier] has an image of masculine semen corresponding to general knowledge, including its colour and consistency;
8) that she was aware of the presence of semen in herself since her eighteenth year;
9) that she required sexual intercourse lasting only a minute before it was released from her masculine appendage;
10) and that at its release during the sexual intercourse she experienced a feeling approaching the greatest possible pleasure;
11) and ultimately, as throughout the animal kingdom, for her it was also true that, *omne animal post coitum triste*.[24]

After this interrogation, the physician examined her (covered) outer appearance and felt her exterior body. He measured her height (six feet) and described her facial features and voice as masculine. He noticed the prominent Adam's apple, the manly proportions of shoulders and pelvis, the breasts with a 'volume not uncommon to fleshy men' and covered with hair, the just shaved parts of the face, her 'masculine boldness and greater intellectual strength', and finally the strong limbs and remarkably large hands.[25] On the basis of these results, the physician G. declared Anna Barbara Meier to be male. The second examination, before which Meier had been persuaded to allow the palpation of the genitals, resulted in a description of the anatomical structure of the outer genitals: the two-inch penis, the single full-grown testicle and the absence of a vagina or any vagina-like opening. G. added a remark about Meier's sexual functioning; he thought it not impossible for him to have procreative capacities, despite the strong, thick foreskin curving the penis downwards. He suggested that Meier might have to help himself by using a different sexual position.[26]

The physician D. G. and the surgeon H. executed the third visual examination. They saw that the top of the penis was not perforated by the urethra; there was only a furrow reminiscent of the urethra. Actually, urine emerged from an opening at the root of the penis. They asked Meier to urinate and saw the urine flow horizontally, parallel to the penis being held up. Based on these observations, the physician and surgeon drew up an extended argumentation to defend Meier's capacity for procreation. Firstly, they argued against the opinion that men who had the opening of the urethra at the base of the penis would never be able to procreate because the semen would never reach the neck of the womb. According to them, semen had to reach the ovaries at least. But not all the semen – all the 'coarse material' (*gröbere Materiale*) – had to wander through the vagina; probably the power of generation had to be found in a much finer and volatile substance, something contained within the essence of the semen, the *aura seminalis*. This was proved by the fact that throughout the course of history women had been fertilized without the penis even entering the vagina.[27] What follows is a quite concrete and mechanistic reasoning about the way in which, in the given situation, sperm could reach the neck of the womb.

> . . . As . . . the masculine appendage does not have the peripheral circumference which would otherwise be normal, a gap must remain in an otherwise normal vagina between its lower cavity and the inserted masculine appendage, . . . and as moreover . . . the mouth of the urethra is aligned entirely horizontally, the ejaculated semen would flow in the direction taken by the erect appendage and for this reason could easily be transported into the vagina.
>
> When ejaculation is finally achieved – following a process conforming to the highest laws of nature, in other words following pleasurable arousal of the nerves, stimulated by a previous build-up of semen, in other words with a high degree of potency allowing erection and the enhancement of all energies required – the cervix should especially be slightly lower than normal, the ejaculated semen could and would even touch the entrance to the womb, and thus all the primary, relevant conditions for fruitful intercourse would be met.[28]

But, the next question was, did Meier really *have* sufficient potency for an erection and real semen? D. G. and H. explicitly denied themselves 'all experiments insulting to common decency' – if necessary, they would have used electricity to test the capacity for erection in order not to disturb morality too much.[29] But they did not do so and therefore remained dependent on what Meier himself had told them about his capacity for erection and ejaculation. With regard to the presence of semen, they argued that the presence of at least one normal and healthy testicle, which was the real organ for the secretion of semen, made it plausible that semen was actually produced. Their final conclusion was that there were sufficient grounds to prove that it was not impossible for Meier to procreate.[30]

In his response to this last report, Schweickhard expressed several objections. He doubted very much whether the force of the ejaculation in this malformed male would be strong enough to have a horizontal direction. He questioned the presence of a proper outlet for the semen produced within the testicle. He also doubted whether Meier with his curved penis would have been able to beget a child from a virgin (both Christina Knoll and Anna Barbara Meier had stated Christina Knoll had been a virgin); even his physical capacity of defloration seemed questionable to Schweickhard.[31] He concluded that Meier would probably never reach 'the first goal of marriage' by copulation in the 'normal natural position'; the other sexual positions, however, were against human decency. At least, enquiring into these forms of intercourse would be as indecent as the methods required to confirm the capacity for erection and the presence of semen, Schweickhard asserted.[32]

Schweickhard, so sceptical of Meier's capacity to impregnate his lover, had to give in at last. The matrimonial court in Karlsruhe had allowed Anna Barbara Meier to receive full rights as a male, to use a man's first name, to dress in male attire, and to marry Christina Knoll, a decision which *Markgraf* Karl Friedrich approved afterwards.[33] After the first child (who died within a year) two other girls were born, who – eight years after the marriage and at the time of Schweickhard's publication – were still alive and raised no doubts concerning their sex.[34] Schweickhard published the case to show that most theories of conception so far – including his own – had been wrong.[35]

Actual and manifest capacitiy to procreate
Central to the argumentation in the final report on Anna Barbara Meier was the following statement on fertility: 'The fertility of the masculine semen must be such that it can reach the ovaries, and join with the feminine part (whatever this might be), in order to engender the ensuing fruit and set the beginnings of life in motion.'[36] As we have seen in this case, procreative capacity was not taken as some abstract hidden foundation of the functional division between male and female. It was about the actual and manifest capacity to get the 'procreative power of semen' to the neck of the womb, in which the functioning of the whole genital apparatus was involved and of which sexual lust and copulation formed an integral part.

This appears to be in many ways representative of the manner in which the sexual function of people with a doubtful sex was examined during the first half of the nineteenth century. The question of whether (and how) sperm could reach the neck of the womb was also central in most other case histories during the first half of the century, as the following examples will show.[37] Fronmüller, in his description of the sexual functioning of Hanna O., partly based it on the history she told him:

> Erections and attraction to the female sex gradually started to occur; finally genuine ejaculations of semen were achieved. In the fifteenth year she confided in this matter to one of her girlfriends, who now fully convinced her that she belonged to the male sex and with whom she finally had sexual intercourse, which she also repeated with other [girl]friends.[38]

After the physical examination, Fronmüller drew conclusions as to Hanna O.'s procreative capacity. As in Meier's case, the flow of the urine is described in detail as a way of understanding how the semen could possibly be secreted. Apparently he trusted her declarations, yet he doubted whether she would be able to impregnate a woman:

> The urine flows out in a stream which can be changed at will, smaller or larger, and when the member is held horizontally, flows along the aforementioned groove to the tip of the *glans penis* so that it appears as if the urine flows from the *glans* itself . . . O. is capable of achieving coitus several times in succession and in any situation. However it seems very doubtful to me whether O. actually has the ability to fertilize, as the opening of the urethra is not really

near enough to the penis for the semen to reach the vagina, which seems also
to be confirmed by O.'s own statements.[39]

The French physician Worbe ended his report on Marie-Marguerite with
a commentary on the reproductive capacity of such 'imperfect males' in
general:

> But can we be sure that these individuals, truncated in their virility, can never
> become fathers? I used to solve this question by affirming we can; but today,
> after deep reflection on this delicate point, my opinion is that there may be a
> host of circumstances (I do not deem it necessary to itemize them), in which
> this imperfect copulation may be fecund; and I would not hesitate to declare
> legitimate the children borne by a woman to a husband thus formed.[40]

The case of Anna Barbara Meier had not been published yet in Worbe's time,
and the possibility such a hypospadiac male could impregnate a woman was
still considered doubtful. His question was considered very relevant with
respect to judicial decisions as well. In a German forensic medical treatise on
the legal position of hermaphrodites from 1809, the German doctor Schneider
made procreative ability, as the basis of the capacity for marriage, into one of
the most urgent questions to be answered. He referred to his English colleague
Hunter at length in order to show that penetration was not absolutely necessary for conception, describing an experiment with a man whose semen was
not ejaculated from the top, but from the root of the penis. Also note the
role ascribed to the female organs in accepting sperm, enabled by the act of
copulation:

> The husband had to be equipped with a specially prepared syringe, warmed in
> advance, and immediately following ejaculation the semen had to be drawn into
> the syringe and injected into the vagina, while the female genital apparatus was
> still under the influence of the coitus and in an appropriate condition to receive
> semen. The experiment was carried out, and the woman became pregnant. I
> am well aware, Hunter says, that observations of this kind are a delicate matter.
> But neither Hunter nor the husband believe that other circumstances were the
> cause; the pregnancy could only be a result of the experiment.[41]

Despite such experiments, and despite case histories such as Schweickhard's
concerning Anna Barbara Meier, a hermaphrodite's capacity to father a child
was often estimated solely on the basis of the exterior shape of the penis,
especially its length, its straightness and the position of the urethra. The ability
to ejaculate in the vagina was obviously regarded to be the first and foremost
condition for generation. Hence, to estimate procreative capacity, knowledge
of exterior anatomical characteristics was considered crucial in order to make
a reasonable estimation of the ability to have intercourse and the chances of
actually procreating. Thus, the size of the testicles, the circumference of the

penis, the shape of the penis (erect), the position of the urethra, the direction of the urinal and seminal discharge, and, in the case of female fertility, the width of the vagina and its connection to the uterus were described in detail. In 1801 Schäffler wrote:

> Although the penis looks unpleasant and malformed, similar cases have been seen before on more than one occasion. The member, which is otherwise thick enough, could be prevented from extension by the skin which tightens it downwards. This unpleasant deformation thus makes this person unsuitable for marriage . . .[42]

And in 1856 the French doctor Huette concluded, after having affirmed the stains on the laundry of the hermaphrodite under inspection to indeed be caused by sperm: 'The direction of the urethral canal makes it possible to think ejaculation is effected by a horizontal spurt as is the case for urine, a favourable circumstance that in no way excludes an aptitude for procreation and therefore marriage in this hypospadiac.'[43]

At about the same time, the physician Traxel described the exterior appearance of the genitals of Johanna K. in detail: she had a split scrotum, the opening of the urethra was situated at the bottom of the penis, the penis was relatively short and had a groove from the bottom to the top, indicating the split urethra. Traxel stated that it was generally impossible for such a person to procreate, even though Johanna K. allegedly impregnated a woman. The fact that the son born from this impregnation had the very same peculiar build of genitals made the assumption that Johanna K. had indeed impregnated the boy's mother virtually inevitable. Traxel therefore tried to explain this exceptional fact using various hypotheses, for example, 'is it not possible that during sexual intercourse Johanna K.'s split urethral canal was sealed by the rear wall of Maria Oh.'s vagina in such a way that during ejaculation the male semen was able to reach the cervix via it?'[44] As for female fertility, information from the hermaphrodite about her sexual appetite and her menstruation was of great importance. Hunter's experiment refered to above had already shown that female lust was considered important for successful conception.

The physicality of lust

Within the central question concerning male procreative capacity, the strength of the ejaculation was considered crucial. As we have seen, the direction of the ejaculation was often calculated from the direction of the urine, as well as from the anatomical make-up of the penis and the urethra. In Meier's case, its strength was connected to lust, to the production and filling up of semen which would stimulate the nerves producing a strong erection. Others also clearly linked lust to the capacity to have intercourse and to procreate. Lust was, finally, taken very seriously as a *physical* phenomenon; it was part of the whole chain of mechanisms that transported semen to the ovaries.[45]

Lust being an integral part of this chain, a hermaphrodite's experiences were directly linked to her or his capacity for generation. The hermaphrodite's sexual feelings were therefore examined in a very concrete, physical way. Such information could hardly be obtained without interrogating hermaphrodites, although doctors would also estimate the possibility of arousal and satisfaction from the outer shape of the genitals.[46] Only the capacity for erection was sometimes established from direct physical examination, albeit often not on purpose, but as a side effect.[47]

A simple example of such an examination of sexual lust and satisfaction is the way Benoit interrogated Marie B. about her sexual experiences such as erection and ejaculation. Pleasure simply and self-evidently was part of the physicality involved:

> The member is capable of erection . . . and this erection is brought on by tickling it. Marie having sometimes indulged in solitary pleasures, remarked that tickling the urethral canal by introducing a foreign body produced no pleasure, but that touching the member after bringing about its turgescence, was followed by a very strong voluptuous sensation during which two or three drops of a serous and transparent liquid dripped from the urethral meatus. I provoked repeated explanations on this point and have come to the certainty that there was nothing milky or resembling sperm in this secretion; it was always like very clear water and never came out in greater quantity.[48]

In a publication on the annulment of a marriage in 1848 in Germany, the medical expert involved, Tourtual, dwelt on the wife's estimated capacity for coitus for several pages, a discourse in which lust and satisfaction were given serious consideration. On her capacity to have coitus with a man, it says that the penis could only penetrate to a depth of one and a half inches, an act which could lead to the ejaculation of semen caused by the stimulus of friction. However, according to Tourtual this would not entirely satisfy the man's sexual drive; it would even make him averse to intercourse, as the husband had informed him. For the semen would not find enough space within the short cul-de-sac, and would therefore push the penis back immediately while the semen would flow outwards.[49] Coitus with a woman would be equally difficult, Tourtual imagined:

> Even though the end of the stunted penis could be inserted into the entrance of the vagina, it would still not adequately fill the width of the latter, and thus the physical coital stimulation which causes the ejaculation of semen would not reach the necessary level. Should this however succeed after all, the excretion would then occur via the urethra, and as the latter's entrance lies in the hollow between the side mounds of the vulva, below the root of the

swollen member, it would not even reach the interior of the vagina, much less the cervix. Ultimately it is to be expected that the semen secreted by such under-developed testes is likely to be meagre in quantity, and unsuitable in quality for impregnation.[50]

From this imaginative exercise Tourtual concluded that only a penis introduced into her vagina could physically arouse her sexual feelings.

A last, extensively described, case which can shed more light on the way in which medicine examined sexual functioning, especially in relation to pleasure and satisfaction, can be found in an article written by J. Martini in 1861 concerning the midwife Anna Märker who had been accused of sexual assaults on several women. There had been rumours for years that the accused midwife was a *Zwitter*. There were two different sexual examinations in this case, the first of which clearly showed the characteristics of bedside medicine, whereas the second was definitely more advanced in its invasive examination techniques. It becomes quite clear from the second forensic examination that the examining doctor supposed a relation between the outer anatomy of the genitals and Anna Märker's sexual desires:

> The person Märker is not capable of procreation, because she lacks any excretory exit for the otherwise ready male semen, or a member, in order to transmit it into the female genitalia. Neither is she however capable of carrying out sexual intercourse either actively and passively – not as man nor as woman. For the latter the ostensible vagina is much too small and narrow, for the former she lacks the masculine member or a formation of corresponding length and width. The rudiment of the penis is, as mentioned simply a small, fixed, unperforated *glans penis*, without a *corpora cavernosa*, lacking any ability to extend or for the stimulation of pleasurable feelings in the presence of a woman. Obviously it can therefore also never be used by Märker for this purpose and she conceded to me, without my asking, that for the relief of her lustful feelings she used her finger. *That however a feeling similar to that felt by a fully formed man is felt by the person Märker towards female persons is not only believable and probable but also, for anatomical reasons, easily explained.*[51]

The fact that sexual desires and drives were self-evidently the subject of the forensic physical examination is striking. Moreover, as in the earlier German cases on hermaphroditism, this is very much linked to the anatomy of the outer genitals.

During the court case against Anna Märker, the defence doubted whether the accusation of 'unnatural sexual acts' could be applied to this case. Unfortunately, I have no details on the defence; probably it questioned the femininity of the midwife (and with it, the unnaturalness of the act) and/or the character of the sexual acts that may not have included penetration. The lawyer apparently appealed to the compassion 'a person must earn, whom nature has provided with sexual drives, yet failed to provide with the means to satisfy them'.[52]

This compassion is expressed in the relatively mild sentence (one month's detention).[53] Thus the physicians' discourse on the naturalness of her drives, combined with the impossibility of copulating in any way, were accepted as mitigating circumstances in court.

In sum, during the first half of the century visual inspection combined with superficial palpation, simple penetration and interrogation of the hermaphrodite were the main examination techniques. Medical judgements on someone's capacity for procreation were therefore clearly linked to aspects of the sexual body hermaphrodites could themselves have seen, felt or experienced. Moreover, patient statements carried much weight. In other words, 'sexual function' was concrete, manifest and close to the hermaphrodite's own (and other lay) experiences and observations of sexual functioning.

The question how or if semen could actually reach the neck of the womb was central to the examination of sexual functioning – and therefore sex – of hermaphrodites. Sexual functioning and someone's possible sexual role were considered very much dependent on the actual functioning of all the manifest organs involved in that process. The medical imagination of how procreation worked was very concrete and mechanistic, and so were the leading questions, argumentations and judgements of the medical examinations. There is – contrary to what the cultural and scientific discourses labelled by Laqueur as the two-sex system suggest – not a single decisive organ for making a distinction between male and female sexual functioning, no synecdochical relation between one such organ and the entire categorization of a person as male or female.[54] Instead, there was a chain of causes and effects, a contiguous relation of all the elements involved in bringing semen into the neck of the womb. Thus, a healthy testicle is considered to produce semen, which is subsequently linked to the accumulation of semen and the titillation of the nerves and voluptuous feelings which are linked to the vigorousness of erections and therefore the strength of ejaculations; the size of the penis is connected to its capacity to be rubbed within the vagina and ejaculate inside; the length and width of the vagina is measured to judge whether an erect penis would be able to enter it and to gain satisfaction; it is examined whether the vagina leads to the neck of the womb; it is estimated whether a penis which curved down could penetrate the vagina and which direction the semen would then take; and, finally, the morphology of the genitals was believed to indicate the direction of sexual desires. No wonder physicians put so much effort into describing the external genitals, whereas the attempts to palpate inner organs of generation were quite weak.

Such enactments of sexual function in clinical case histories of hermaphroditism during the first half of the nineteenth century seem very similar to what Thomas Laqueur described concerning theories of generation in the early modern period. As heat was considered to transform blood and semen into the right substance for procreation, orgasm was necessary for both partners. Therefore a lot of attention went to the right rubbing and chafing of the genitals to produce the required heat. Also, a good coital rhythm between partners was considered crucial.[55] The practicalities of intercourse, the pleasure, heat, orgasm and flow were central in these cases of hermaphroditism. This is a clear indication that we have to be cautious with presuppositions about the relation between medical and cultural *opinions* with regard to the sexed body and the way sex was enacted in medical *practice*. It also undermines the idea of a totalizing model of either a one- or a two-sex system, because elements of both systems can easily coexist.

Dreger has already shown how, within the two-sex system, the definition of what defined 'true sex' narrowed down to the gonadal criterion during the nineteenth century in France and England.[56] Reis however mistakes Laqueur's 'two-sex system' for Dreger's description of the 'age of gonads', when she claims that in America, as against Dreger's study of France and England, the 'two-sex system' already existed early in the nineteenth century, 'although the system used different criteria to establish maleness or femaleness'.[57] Then she goes on to say that, because of the lack of modern medical technologies, the establishement of sex was based on outer criteria and on a person's mannerisms, clothing and (sexual?) 'tastes'.[58] Of course such a sex distinction also existed in Europe much before Dreger's 'age of gonads'. But my point is to show how crucially the way of establishing sex in the first half of the century differs from turn-of-the-twentieth-century technologies of sex diagnosis, in particular with regard to the role the hermaphrodites themselves – or their selves – played in the medical establishment of their sex. *In practice*, the very same (heterosexually defined) two-sex system can turn out fundamentally different.

Direction of lust

After having dismissed the idea that 'true hermaphrodites' – 'i.e. people possessing the complete, fully formed genitalia of both sexes, who can make use of both within sexual intercourse' – had ever existed,[59] the physician examining Anna Barbara Meier stated that the predominance of someone's sex was not just defined by the anatomy and functioning of the genitals, but also expressed by the desire for and practising of a specifically female or male role in sexual intercourse: 'Depending on which sex predominates, the hermaphrodite will exhibit the sexual function either of the first or of the second kind, in other words they will either feel sexual attraction towards the female sex or towards the male . . .'[60] In general, during the first part of the nineteenth century lust and sexual attraction were taken into account as a part of the chain of mechanisms through which semen could be brought to the ovaries. After all, physicians seemed to have thought, sexual appetite triggered the whole sequence of mechanisms leading to propagation. However, there were cases in which the sexual appetite did *not* lead to possible generation, because the rest of the organs of generation, as far as they were thought to function, was (more) apt to the role of the other sex.

Sometimes, this is simply noted without much comment, as in the case of Wilhelmina H. described by the Berlin physician Jagemann in 1845. She demanded an operation to remove the two hernias that could hamper her forthcoming marital life. Having established the existence of pretty well developed testes on both sides and of a small but well-developed and erectile penis and the absence of a uterus, Jagemann concluded that the presence of ovaries would be unlikely.[61] Consequently, he discussed possible '*Molimina mensium*' and menstruation. These never occurred.

> . . . however the person certainly does claim to have felt a powerful turgescence of the genitals and a strongly increased sexual drive, periodically recurring, perhaps at the times when a regularly formed female menstruates, for which reason at this time she usually engages in coitus with her lover, resulting in an immense relief of her lustful feelings.[62]

The description does not betray any idea that these aspects of sexual function might be contradictory; they are neither impossible nor morally suspect. What the consequences of this examination were – if he operated on her, advised her not to marry, or told her to be a man – is unknown. The case closes with a remark about an aunt who had a similar anatomy and was married but had no children.

Often, a 'contradiction' between sexual drive and capacity is seen as part of the ambiguity that made someone into an androgyne or hermaphrodite. In 1823, Schallgruber, for instance, noted in Juliane Neubauer's case the existence of testicles as well as a penis, which erected easily after being touched or even only at 'the sight of a man' and continues: 'The nature of the soul is feminine. Modesty, shrewdness, a tendency to weep and a vigorous desire for men *characterize her as an androgyne*. She often has lustful dreams, without ejaculation, and is not unfamiliar with the games of Venus.'[63] To Schallgruber, the combination of the patient's penis and testicles with her female character and sexual appetite made her an androgyne. Similarly, Froriep claimed Marie Rosine Göttlich was a hermaphrodite, because her body was male while her sexual inclinations were female.[64] Others considered also sexual drive an aspect to be taken seriously in weighing female and male characteristics.

The French surgeon Coste, for example, decided in 1835 to amputate the well-developed penis and to cut open the vagina of a woman in order to make intercourse and marriage possible, even though he had also found a single testicle. Her female appearance, her account of regular menstruation since the age of thirteen, her female character and inclinations, her loving devotion to a single man, and her assurance that she had never masturbated or experienced an erection (ejaculation was not asked about) apparently convinced him to do so. Not the non-erectile penis, nor the easily palpable testicle, but the way she said she actually functioned sexually was decisive: the menstruation and love for a man.[65]

Tourtual concluded virility was dominant in the wife he was examining; her sexual inclinations towards men he considered a possible counter-indication. However, his imaginative assessment of her ability to have coitus as either a man or a woman convinced the physician that only a penis could physically arouse the woman's sexual feelings intensely. This might have explained her alleged sexual inclination towards men, according to Tourtual, undermining the direction of her lust's significance as a counter-argument to his conclusion that virility was predominant.[66] In other words, her sexual inclinations might have been 'erroneous' because they were 'merely' the result of an anatomy that, contrary to all other anatomical evidence, provided lust only in relation to men. In his final assessment, the anatomy of sexual pleasure lost out against the anatomy of coitus and generation. The marriage was nullified on the basis of Tourtual's report. Whether the woman changed her civil sex is however unclear. It is possible that she did not, as in a similar German case.[67]

In these – predominantly German – cases of doubtful sex, the chain of mechanisms bringing semen into the neck of the womb could be broken at any time: if erections were not forceful enough, sperm did not take the right route, if the vagina was too small or did not end in the neck of the womb, if not enough friction could be produced to gain satisfaction, etc. One of the places where the chain could be broken was if a hermaphrodite experienced lust or sexual attraction in the 'wrong' direction, if this was not in line with the rest of the functioning genitals. This seems to have been considered a dysfunction rather than something that referred to an abnormal sexual self or something to be dismissed morally. It was part of the hermaphrodite's sexual malfunction. It is unclear what was dominant in deciding someone's sex; in Tourtual's case the woman's sexual pleasure was ultimately dismissed as an error, whereas in the Coste case the declaration of the woman about her loving feelings towards her husband seems to have been given the most weight.

As we have seen in chapter 2 which discussed the question of the self, in most French cases sexual drives were often more strongly related to a person's moral and social position than to her physical sexual function. French physicians were often more concerned with the socially disrupting effects a mistaken sex could have and the corresponding confusion about someone's sexual role. In French case histories, the details of physical sexual lust and satisfaction give way to the spicy stories of sexual error – almost as if it were about unveiling a masquerade in a novel or a play. There is only one German case in which I found a similar reference to the socially disruptive effect of an error of sex. This was in Schneider's description of the deceased Eva Elisabeth S., who, after developing quite masculine characteristics during adolescence, could not keep her hands to herself when she was around the farm girls who lived at her parent's farm. In these cases, it seems, sexual attraction is not only related to sexual function as a way of getting semen into the womb; it is also an autonomous force which breaks through the convention of someone's sex assignment, outward appearance and education, a hidden nature indicating one's proper place in society. All the other German cases hardly pay attention to these aspects of lust and mainly connected them with physical sexual (dys)function.

CONCLUSION

Part I clearly revealed that until about 1870 in an environment of non-anonymity a policy of silence and containment predominated when someone's sex was doubted. A physical examination by a medical doctor in cases of doubtful sex was only demanded if legalized sexual relations or public decency were at stake. Moreover, knowledge about the body and controlling an unruly body turned out to be not the monopoly of physicians, but a much more diffusely divided, daily task for several members of the community. The problem of an ambiguous sex was then contained by surveillance, gossip and possibly social isolation. If these policies of silence and containment no longer worked, and the social, moral and legal fabric was seriously affected, I argued, physicians would be ordered to provide their judgement on someone's physical sex. Often, this happened voluntarily just before marriage or, in cases of annulment of a marriage, by means of a court order. In other cases, the hermaphrodite in question had jeopardized public morality by enjoying 'same'-sex sexual relations too openly. If, as a consequence, sex reassignment was demanded, the physical examination was also ordered by the court.

This chapter has shown that during the first half of the nineteenth century, until approximately 1860, medical examinations of sexual function and sex were primarily based on the outward appearance of the genitals and their functioning according to the hermaphrodites' statements. Central to a physician's enquiry was the question of how (in which role) a person could function in procreation. This was conceived of quite concretely and mechanistically, as a chain of functions starting with arousal and ending with semen at the neck of the womb, or in short with successfully performed coitus. Within this sexual function (or, sometimes, malfunction) sexual lust and arousal played an important role; they were considered physical aspects of sexual function rather than psychological ones. When sexual drives did not correspond with the genital apparatus, this was not considered a moral defect. It was more likely to be considered an element that had to be weighed in the physician's assessment of the hermaphrodite's sex. All in all, there did not seem to be a clear distinction between the way in which sexual function was enacted among lay people – including the hermaphrodite – or in a clinical situation. Even a physical examination by a doctor did not separate the body neatly from the person or from the social and moral community in which it functioned. It turns out that when the rationale of sex as inscription in this period was taken over by a rationale of sex as representation of the sexual body, the body was not enacted as a medically separated and objectified thing. It was animated and connected to other bodies. Or, the sexual body enacted as part of bedside medicine was part of the whole *person* of the hermaphrodite.

However, there is an important difference between a lay person's and a physician's enactments of sexual function. This is not so much a difference in the *content of what* was enacted, but in *the context in which* it was enacted. As we have seen, the problem of gaining access to the body was a major one during the first half of the century. What doctors achieved by examining hermaphrodites was perhaps not so much a distinct medical enactment of sexual function, but much more the intrusion of medical *authority* into the private and intimate body. This authority could – and sometimes did – make decisions against the hermaphrodite's will despite taking her statements into account. The next chapter will discuss the topic of medical authorities' invasion of individual bodies in detail on the basis of the case of Justine Jumas.

JUSTINE JUMAS:
CONFLICTING BODY POLITICS

Gendarmes doing violence to a woman, forcing her to allow herself to be examined by men of the profession! We believed that torture had been abolished![1]

ACCESS TO BODIES

This chapter is about a woman, Justine Jumas, who refused to subject herself to a forensic assessment of her sex. Her husband Antoine Darbousse had instituted a lawsuit against her because he claimed, after two years of marriage, that she was not a woman. Justine Jumas appealed against the court of Alès' order to have her sex medically examined and the order was reversed by the court of Nîmes. Then her husband appealed. All in all, the lawsuit and appeals which were dealt with in three different courts in the south of France lasted from 1868 to 1873. Several forensic medical experts including Ambroise Tardieu indulged in page-long discussions about Justine Jumas's possible sex on the basis of the scant knowledge available which came from the statements of her husband and the midwife, and a very brief report by a certain Doctor L. Carcassonne. Both these experts and the court of Alès put considerable pressure on Jumas to have her body medically examined. However, when after a long and complicated process of several appeals and judicial decisions, the very same order was upheld, she simply let the visiting medical experts know that she refused to undergo the examination.

Important legal questions with regard to hermaphroditism were reviewed: on what basis could a marriage be nullified? Should a neutral or doubtful sex be acknowledged medically and legally? To which extent could a person be legally forced to have her body medically examined? These discussions were embedded within a wider discussion in France of how to deal with the sex on the birth certificates of children born with a doubtful sex, how to proceed in cases of 'erroneous sex', and what role the state should play in this. Generally, academic medicine advocated a much more important role for professional physicians in controlling doubtful sex and establishing sex in cases of doubt, claiming they should have much more access to bodies than had been the case up until that point.

As Lynn Hunt has recently argued, human rights could not have emerged as 'self-evident' if two essential conditions had not been met first. These were the capacity for empathy, on the one hand, and the individuation of the body from the collective body, on the other.[2] According to Hunt, from the second half of the eighteenth century onwards, people increasingly started to experience the body as an individual, autonomous entity entitled to integrity. Before then, the torture, exposure and dissection of bodies had been common forms of punishment. However, public corporal punishment and the exposure of bodies was not directed against individuals, but was viewed as a collective purgation. By the end of the eighteenth century, torture, public executions and public dissections were increasingly viewed as disgusting and insupportable (empathy), as well as infringing the integrity of the individual body.[3] It is in that same context that the abolition of so-called impotency trials, in which spouses demanded divorces on the basis of impotence, can be understood. From 1550 onwards, 'trial by congress', during which the (im)potency was physically tested before witnesses, had led to major public scandals. After the French Revolution, French courts were extremely cautious never to expose spouses to the public scrutiny of their potency.[4] In summary, after the French revolution the individuality and integrity of the body became an important concern within legal discourse.

However, such a history of the body fails to acknowledge another history which is almost diametrically opposed to the former. As the discussions surrounding the Jumas case will clearly demonstrate, another discourse of the body emerged in the nineteenth century which demanded that the body be exposed, penetrated and monitored: modern medical discourse. While (private) medical practice in the eighteenth and first half of the nineteenth century was usually extremely cautious about seeing, touching and penetrating bodies, academic physicians and 'hospital medicine' increasingly demanded bodies to be the willing, docile objects of observation and experimentation.

Tardieu commented extensively on the Jumas case in the very same publication in which he published Herculine Barbin's memoirs. Alongside some other, less elaborate case histories, these two cases are meant to underscore his main argument: 'there is always, whatever the appearance of the exterior genitalia, one or the other system of internal organs that truly constitute the sex, testicles or ovaries'.[5] This sex should be decisive in defining someone's civil sex or aptness for marriage; this is the 'true sex' Foucault mentioned in his introduction to Barbin's memoirs.[6] The main difference between this new scientific determination of physical sex and the enactment described in the previous chapter is the shift from the concept of a 'predominant' to a 'true' sex, and from outward appearance and function to inner constitution. No longer a combination of several associated aspects of coital function, primarily based on outward appearance and declarations of the hermaphrodite in question, but the invisible, internal 'system' – to be established by a 'modern' physician – should be decisive. In practice, however, such new scientific criteria were not so easily applicable.

Therefore, in this chapter I will read the tension surrounding the access to Jumas's body not just as a rare incident, but as the exponent of a much larger tension between traditional policies of containment of doubtful sexes supported by the (new) legal protection of the privacy of the body, and a policy of exploring and exposing bodies in order to bare the 'truth' and consequently restore the (moral) order.

THE CASE OF JUSTINE JUMAS

On 18 March 1869, Antoine Darbousse, landowner in Cruviers et Laseours in the French *département* of Gard lodged a complaint against his wife, Anna Justine Jumas, claiming that she was not a woman at all and demanding their marriage be nullified.[7] The wedding had taken place more than two years before, on 20 December 1866. The demand was made on the basis of the husband's assertion as well as the declaration of a midwife, who stated that Justine Jumas had no organs representing the female sex, no breasts, no ovaries, no uterus, no vagina, that her pelvis was small like the pelvis of a man, and that she had never experienced menstruation or periodic abdominal pains.

The court of first instance in Alès (*Tribunal de première instance*) passed sentence on 29 April 1869. The considerations accompanying the sentence already indicate some of the important legal questions at stake. In the first place, the court had to clarify that this was not a case of divorce on the grounds of impotency, because any similarity to the 'trials by congress' from the era before the French Revolution had to be avoided. The physical proof of potency during these trials had been the subject of many excited public discussions. Therefore, nineteenth-century French courts were extremely cautious not to let this happen again and carefully precluded any litigation on the basis of impotency.[8] In the words of the court, Darbousse did not contest his marriage, but claimed that it 'never legally existed as a marriage, owing to a radical defect that contaminated it from the start'.[9]

Secondly, the court had no problem stating that the marriage was fundamentally a contract between a man and a woman, but it had to decide when exactly this was not the case so that annulment was justified. It thereby chose not to demand what was called 'identity of the spouses' sexes' – in this case meaning that there had to be positive proof that Jumas was male – as a ground for annulment of a marriage, but to also accept the following conditions: 'that one of them absolutely lacks the natural organs constituent of their sex, even different from those of the sex other than the one to which he claims to belong'.[10]

Finally, the court extensively defended its decision to command forensic expertise in order to check the husband and midwife's claims. Their allegations, the court argued, could only be really appreciated by a medical expert, 'whatever repulsion one might feel at having recourse to the use of that means of investigation'. Because, in contrast to the verification of a hypothetical natural impotency, alleged by one of the spouses, this was a:

> . . . demonstration of the purely material fact of verifying if the defendant is or is not deprived of all of the distinctive female organs, some external and apparent, the others internal, it is true, the existence or non-existence of which, will be no less easy to certify for people in the profession . . .[11]

Note that the fact that there has to be an internal examination is specifically mentioned and defended. The court thereby took care not to force Jumas to undergo physical examination administered by a man. It created an elaborate method to avoid any physical contact between the medical expert and Justine Jumas. It ordered Anna Puéjac, chief midwife at the *Maternité* of Montpellier, to examine Jumas and to report whether she was deprived of all female organs and had indeed never menstruated or felt periodic abdominal pains. She would thereby be instructed by a doctor who would be in a separate room and would also report back to him.[12] The court proved to be very aware of the difficulty of having a male physician violate a woman's physical integrity.

Despite the court's precautions, Justine Jumas refused the physical examination and appealed to the imperial court (*Cour impériale*) in Nîmes. She produced new evidence by handing over a report from a Doctor L. Carcassonne from 'a visit made at the request of the Jumas family'.[13] Carcassonne's complete report (Nîmes, 5 November 1869) reads as follows:

> Madame JUSTINE JUMAS has every appearance of a person of the female sex, the external reproductive organs, the mons veneris, labia majora and minora, clitoris and urinary meatus. Everything is formed as in a woman, but there is no vagina, or at least this canal, if it exists, is not perforated. It follows from there that the act of copulation is impossible as well as, consequently, impregnation. The breasts are not very developed, the pelvis is not very wide; but nothing, however, recalls the male sex nor any of its attributes.[14]

It is quite apparent that this report is characteristic of bedside medicine as it describes the outward appearance of sex as well as its functioning within coitus, and stays quite close to possible lay observations. Compared with some German reports submitted to court, it is remarkable however that no attention is paid to Justine Jumas's own statements concerning her sexual functioning. On the basis of this new evidence, the imperial court of Nîmes declared the earlier decision by the court of Alès null and void on 29 November 1869. There was insufficient proof, according to this court, that Jumas was not just a female with a congenital deformation of the reproductive organs.[15] It was actually a demand for annulment of a marriage on the basis of impotency, which the court of Nîmes did not accept.

The case subsequently went to the supreme court (*Cour suprême*), I assume because of an appeal on the part of Antoine Darbousse.[16] It was around this time that several legal-medical experts became involved. Darbousse brought in as expert witness Ambroise Tardieu, one of the most prominent forensic experts in France at the time and Amédée Courty, Professor of Medicine at Montpellier, was brought in by the court. The legal expert Philippe Jalabert, Deacon of the Faculty of Law at Nancy, also joined the debate. They all published lengthy discussions of the case, the legal problems involved, and Justine Jumas's probable sex.

Forensic medical discussion of the case

Up to which point would a marriage still count as a marriage and when should it be nullified? Tardieu, Courty and Jalabert all expressed different opinions on that central question. Yet, there were also fundamental similarities between them. They all agreed that a marriage between persons of the same sex was no marriage at all and should be radically nullified. On the other hand, they were also all concerned not to affect marriages that might well not be perfect (for example in cases of impotency) but should still be considered natural or legally proper.

Tardieu strictly adhered to what he called 'identity (or sameness) of sexes' between the persons married as the only grounds for nullifying a marriage. It was not sufficient to establish, he wrote, that marriage could not be consummated because of the malformation of the sexual organs of one of the spouses. 'It is absolutely necessary to obtain proof and certitude about the similarity of the sex of the persons who believed they have entered into marriage.'[17] Tardieu's fear of same-sex marriages was the fundamental motivation for his reasoning. Even in cases of people with a double sex, which Tardieu considered to be an absolute exception, he reasoned that marrying such a person would entail the perilous situation described above because there would still exist similarity of sex between the two.[18] Tardieu did not comment on the possible legal problems that might occur in cases in which the sex of the person in question was neutral or indifferent (or where sex was altogether absent), because he did not believe that such persons could exist, for the 'system of internal organs' always indicated one or the other sex (or, in rare cases, a double sex).

It took Tardieu a long and complicated course of reasoning from these principles to arrive at a concrete judgement in Justine Jumas's case. He used a rather sloppy argument, borrowed from the authors of a contemporary French forensic medicine manual, that in the event no female internal organs could be found, the sex would automatically be (atrophied) male.[19] He subsequently argued that the outward appearance of Justine Jumas as described by the midwife and Carcassonne were no guarantee at all that she had the essential characteristics of a woman.

> Everything, on the contrary, . . . coincides to demonstrate that this person is not a woman affected by some congenital malformation of the sexual organs, but that, in terms of general constitution as well as the peculiar deviation of the sexual conformation, the individual belongs, in reality, to the male sex; that between Jumas and Mr. D. . . . there is not only an impossibility of sexual congress, but also a similarity of sex.[20]

Courty drew the line much more rigorously than Tardieu. According to him, there was no way in which he could prove that Justine Jumas had the essential organs of a male. The only thing he was able to prove on the basis of the existing evidence was the absence of the essential female organs or at least their 'barely rudimentary' state. Consequently he impetuously announced in the concluding remarks of his forensic medical report for the court of Montpellier: 'The person in question must therefore be classified in the category of those teratological subjects who do not, strictly speaking, have a sex, and who cannot, as a result, be united in marriage to any normally organized individual, whatever the sex of the latter.'[21] Jalabert strongly opposed Courty's reasoning and primarily based himself on a legal argument. According to him, identity of sex in a marriage and the latter's subsequent annulment could only be permitted after one of the spouses' sex had been officially rectified.

> We nevertheless believe that the declaration of a sex other than the one established by the birth certificate is absolutely necessary for the marriage to be recognized as nonexistent . . . In other words, the birth certificate cannot be negative, and it is not with an a contrary argument that it can be rectified, so a positive and categorical affirmation in the opposite direction is required.[22]

As there was no legal possibility of having no sex, such a concept could never play a role in the legal radical annulment of a marriage, Jalabert argued. There first had to be a legal change of sex, which could only be based on the positive proof of the essential characteristics of the other sex and not, as he added in an implicit attack on Tardieu, 'by way of induction' or by 'suppositions' and 'conjectures'.[23] In Jumas's case, Jalabert therefore argued that she pay damages as long as she refused to be examined by an expert; that was, according to him, the only legally justifiable path to have her sex rectified and to nullify the marriage.

Conclusion of the case

On 15 January 1872, the decision of the Nîmes court was annulled and the case was sent back to the court of Montpellier, which passed judgement on 8 May of the same year.[24] It ordered that the court of Alès' very first sentence to have her medically examined be put into operation. The earlier sentence offered sufficient 'desirable guarantees' and would only entrust her to experts designated by the court. Moreover, this court argued, it did not believe Jumas would violate the law and disobey the court's authority any more, as she 'had already voluntarily submitted to a visit from Doctor Carcassonne'.[25]

The pressure on Jumas to give in must have been enormous. Earlier in the process her family had already pressurized her to allow Carcassonne, apparently someone the family knew and trusted, to examine her. Jalabert imagined several sorts of pressures on a person who hesitated to undergo a physical examination ordered by court. Such a person would:

> . . . ceding to friendly advice, to respectable intercessions, feel that there is a duty, a moral obligation to comply with the justice of her country, not to appear to want to claim for herself a state contrary to reality when she carries in herself the undeniable evidence of her right to retain it. Whatever the conclusions of the examination, they will not be more unpleasant to her than inductions drawn by public malice from her refusal. If all of these considerations are without influence, she might be impressed by the sole fear of forced compliance, and will find, in what she will call a moral violence, an excuse in her own eyes and in the eyes of public opinion in the necessity that she submit.[26]

Courty provides evidence of yet another form of pressure by subtly suggesting that she might have won by allowing for the expert examination:

> It is regrettable that Mme Jumas refused to submit to an examination; because science today possesses, and this only recently, quite precise diagnostic means allowing for the recognition, particularly in the pelvis of a thin woman (as we are assured Mme Jumas is), of the ovaries, oviducts, and above all the womb.[27]

This would have been the only way for Jumas to provide positive proof of femininity, Courty implied, for in the absence of these 'positive signs' he could not presume them to be there; on the contrary, from the scarce information he had derived the conclusion that Jumas had none of the essential internal female organs.

However, Justine Jumas was adamant in her refusal to undergo another physical examination; as Jalabert recounts: 'This absolute refusal was noted on 18 November by the two experts who successively presented themselves at the domicile of the father and at the current residence of J. J. . . . and collected it, from her very mouth, in their second approach.'[28] And so, the last sentence passed in this case, by the court of first instance of Alès on 28 January 1873, assessed initially Justine Jumas's 'formal disobedience' of the prescription of the law. Medical experts, the court argued, were perfectly able to establish the inner organs of generation in a person as slender as Jumas was. But, because she refused the examination, the court 'finds itself reduced to only being able to deduct the probable absence of those two organs in the person from the presumptions drawn from already established facts'.[29] This was her own fault, the court decided, because it did not accept chastity as the true reason for her refusal. By leaving the actual physical examination to a midwife, the court had sufficiently guaranteed her modesty. The court could no longer take her 'alleged sense of modesty' seriously since 'on 5 November 1869, she was not yet afraid for the presumed necessity of her cause, voluntarily to be examined by a man, Doctor Carcassonne, after having previously been so by the midwife from Tamaris'.[30]

The court partly grounded the final decision on the refusal itself, claiming that her 'formal disobedience' underscored the deductions made on the basis of the scarce facts known. For, the court argued, the refusal did not seem to be anything other than a calculated attempt on her part not to provide her husband with further ammunition, whereas she had enjoyed full advantage from the report of Carcassonne. The court could not permit Jumas to employ its instructions voluntarily whenever she thought this to be in her advantage, while refusing them as soon as she thought they would damage her interest. Although the court admitted it could not interpret the refusal as a direct or indirect confession, this certainly had to be weighed with regard to the proof the husband had been able to provide.[31] So, in the end, her refusal no longer made any difference, as it was read as an extra argument against her case.

On the grounds of a small pelvis and the absence of breasts, menstruation and periodic abdominal complaints it was decided that – leaving aside the question of whether a neutral sex could exist – it was certain that she had none of the essential female organs. The court of Alès consequently accepted Courty's argument that a person with no sex could not marry, for it stated that it had been sufficient to have acquired the conviction that 'she truly lacks the . . . essential constituent organs of the sex, even different from that of Darbousse'.[32] It argued that the two fundamental objectives of marriage – procreation and the regulation of the sexual drives – could not possibly be reached in this case and declared the marriage 'radically null and void'.

MEDICAL INTERVENTIONS

Forensic medical responses to the judgement of the court of Nîmes

To understand what was going on in the legal–medical debate surrounding Justine Jumas's case, we should bear in mind that it was not so much a conflict about the characteristics of her sex per se. The major clash was about the question of whether the court could order a medical expert to examine

her sex. While the court of Alès had ordered such an exam, the court of
Nîmes expressly rejected a request aimed at proving that one of the spouses
was impotent. This court, as we have seen, considered Jumas to be a woman
with a sexual deformity and, consequently, the case to be one of divorce on
the basis of impotency. Tardieu, Courty and Jalabert completely disagreed
with the court of Nîmes, however. In the eyes of these forensic medical
specialists the court of Nîmes did not just make the wrong decision by accepting the brief report from Carcassonne as sufficient evidence of Jumas being
a woman. What was worse was the court simply dismissing their medical
expertise by not permitting a physical examination. By doing so, the court
of Nîmes completely disempowered the medical experts. It was the court's
indifference to medical expertise which bothered the medical experts the
most. We will see how they responded to it.

In this section I wish to argue that the pressure on Jumas to make her body
available for medical examination was not an isolated instance of pressure on
a disobedient woman. It was part of much wider medical pressure on legislators
and courts to involve academic or 'modern' medicine in legal decisions concerning sex and to give medical professionals the right to establish doubtful
sexes medically – coercively, if necessary. During the same period, but not
specifically related to the Jumas case, other medical professionals in France
were calling for the employment of modern medical expertise for the medical
surveillance of doubtful sexes from birth and in other cases of contested
marriages. In this discourse 'modern' medicine contrasted itself with superseded medical practices such as midwifery or bedside medicine. Practices
with regard to access to the body were highly gendered, as we have seen in
the previous chapter, because it was the contact between a male doctor and
a female patient which was most contested. It is therefore interesting to note
that Justine Jumas was treated as a woman in this respect until the very end,
even when the experts had come to believe that she was actually male. This
is true, I believe, for most hermaphrodites initially designated to be female.

In the Jumas case, the experts Tardieu and Courty tried to convince their
legal audience that just revealing the genitals was not enough to establish
a sex. They warned that the outward appearance of sex could be deceptive.
By explaining that the real markers of sex were inside the body they made
someone's sex a secret that could only be discovered by medical experts.
Courty in his introduction to Jumas's case, contrasted the ignorance of lay
people – even the most educated among them – and the recent knowledge
(medical) science had been able to discover. He described Justine Jumas as
one of these 'rare monstrosities who so deeply astonish the wisest and most
educated men if they are unfamiliar with the science of the natural development of our organs and of the deviations that that development undergoes
time and again in its course'.[33]

His contribution, he continued, aimed not so much to provide his personal opinion, but instead to explain scientific knowledge about reproductive anatomy, 'which was once so obscure, but which has become so clear in our time, however confused it still remains for the common herd and however sensitive it may appear to the jurist in its social applications'.[34]

Using Enlightenment metaphors Courty made a clear distinction between those who were ignorant of scientific knowledge concerning the development of sexual organs, and those who knew, that is, medical professionals. In a lengthy didactic survey of the characteristics of the sexes and their development before birth, he argued that the internal organs were the true signifiers of sex: they were the producers of eggs and sperm whereas the external organs only transported the former two. Moreover, he explained, the embryological development of the external genitals showed these to be different only in scale, whereas internal organ development was absolutely distinct. Therefore, he concluded, 'even if Mrs Jumas possessed the external appearance of the female sex, we would still have to ask ourselves whether she exhibits positive signs of the existence of the internal organs of that sex'.[35]

Tardieu was more ardent and direct in his attack on both the court of Nîmes and Carcassonne's report. The court's claim that Justine Jumas was without doubt female was, according to him, 'a pure hypothesis, a prejudice which nothing justifies'.[36] Medical expertise could very well have proven exactly the opposite of the court's statement, he claimed. The court, Tardieu continued, based itself on Carcassonne's report which was 'on all counts incomplete and insufficient'.[37] After having quoted the complete report, he commented:

> Without one more word, it is in these few lines that M. Carcassonne summarizes the results of the examination he had to carry out, and upon these facts, so manifestly insufficient, he believes he has the right to formulate his opinion about the sex of the person he examined.[38]

How could Carcassonne possibly have concluded that she was female without commenting altogether on the absence of the vagina, the barely developed breasts and the narrow pelvis, Tardieu asked. And how could he not comment on the presence or absence of a uterus and ovaries? 'Has the doctor forgotten that it is only their properly observed existence that allows for a finding in such a case?'[39]

Whereas Courty and Tardieu took pains to show the court of Nîmes to be utterly ignorant medically, they hardly paid any attention to the court's moral objections against the forced examination of someone's sexual potency. They simply argued it was not about potency at all, but about being male or female, which actually restricted the examination to objective facts. Jalabert, however, was much more conscious of the possible legal and moral objections. For example, Jalabert wrote that:

> The Minister of Justice, consulted about the necessity to rectify the birth
> certificate of a hermaphrodite individual who had been declared to be of the
> female sex and been dressed accordingly since childhood despite the fact that
> she appeared to belong to the male sex according to her constitution, responded
> that the errors of nature, fortunately rare, must not be excessively deepened
> when they present themselves, and that it is up to the individuals concerned,
> or their parents, to choose the sex that seems to suit them.[40]

It would take Jalabert some elasticity of interpretation to conclude that
this statement did not necessarily exclude medical examinations, as we will
see. Jalabert also mentioned another defender of personal integrity – female
integrity in particular – against forced medical examinations, the famous
contemporary Belgian legal expert François Laurent, who had exclaimed:
'Gendarmes doing violence to a woman, to force her to allow herself to
be examined by men of the profession! We believed that torture had been
abolished'![41]

The objections were therefore very much related to the protection of
personal integrity, revealing a preference for keeping doubtful sexes private
rather than making them (publicly) visible through forensic medical examinations. There are clearly resonances, too, with the extreme care doctors at
the time generally had to take when physically examining women's genitals
in order not to violate their modesty, as described in the previous chapter.
Morally speaking, the physical examination of a woman by a doctor was still
tricky and raised a lot of controversy and debate. This clarifies how the tension
surrounding Jumas's refusal can be understood as a tension between a policy
of containment of ambiguous sexes and a policy of exploring, exposing and
regulating them.

Jalabert launched a sort of counter attack against the (moral) objections
mentioned by warning against the severe moral consequences of *not* performing a thorough medical examination, and by contrasting the restrictions
of civil law to the much lower protection of physical integrity by criminal law.
According to him, it was not only ignorant and unscientific to avoid speaking about cases of hermaphroditism and errors of sex, it also constituted 'a
systematic scorn for the moral suffering that certain situations can entail':[42]

> We could never contest, for example, that the habitual wearing of clothing
> of another sex can present grave moral dangers if it occurs in establishments
> bringing together adults of the same sex for education, work, or charity.[43]

He finished his argument by confronting the reader with the rhetorical
question:

> Could a married man with the birth certificate of a woman maintain, by refusing
> examination, and despite all opposition, contrary to the laws of nature, morals,
> law, and the orders of the court, his so-called marriage with another man?[44]

It is from this that Jalabert drew the conclusion that, precisely in order to find out if this was indeed the case with Jumas, an exam was indispensable. After having shown concealed errors of sex to be a severe moral danger at same-sex institutions and in marriage, Jalabert's argument concentrated on the question of whether the state (*Ministère publique*) could initiate a sex change procedure if an error of sex was suspected. In his opinion, the question had been the subject of a 'lively controversy'.[45] There had been a precedent during the Napoleonic Wars, when people had tried to escape conscription by giving boys female birth certificates. In such cases, the state had been allowed to initiate a medical examination in the interest of the execution of the law of recruitment. Similarly, Jalabert argued, in other cases where public order was at stake, the state had to be granted the same right, as cases of doubtful sex presented a serious threat to the moral public order.[46] However, Jalabert continued, should people be forced to undergo a medical examination? Often the state had been denied such a right in civil law, he writes:

> To resist the use of force one invokes the individual freedom, dignity and modesty which would be breached to the highest degree by a brutal execution contrary to accepted standards of behaviour and which would revolt the public. In the civil courts, physical examinations are declared arbitrary and illegal by many legal advisers . . .[47]

But in criminal law the 'inviolability of the person' had its restrictions with regard to crimes in which physical examinations were indispensable for acquiring proof as, for example, in cases of injury, abortion and rape. Not only the accused could be forced to undergo an examination, even the victims could. Thus, Jalabert argued, the interest of the public order could legitimize the use of coercion; why, then, was there such a difference between criminal and civil cases?[48] In Justine Jumas's case, Jalabert therefore supported coercive examination and suggested that Jumas should pay a fine as long as she did not give in.[49]

From rectifying occasional disorder to regular surveillance
Jalabert therefore argued that the interests of the state outweighed the moral objections against a coercive medical examination which were based on personal integrity and modesty. Around the same time, several French forensic medical experts followed a similar path and warned courts and legislators against hermaphroditism's moral and social threat if it were not monitored by the medical establishment.

In 1846, the surgeon Joseph-Napoléon Loir proposed changing article 57 of the civil code to introduce the possibility of a third sex category at birth, that is, *sexe douteux* or doubtful sex. He revised the proposal in 1854 in a lecture before the *Académie des sciences morales et politiques*. He critiqued the insufficient way in which French law had regulated 'the distinction and observation of sex with regard to birth registration'.[50] In his opinion, modern medicine with its knowledge of embryology had to shed its light on cases of contested sex, just as it was the legislator's duty to avoid the 'sad results of errors'. Briefly, Loir pleaded for the possibility of classifying newborns as of 'doubtful sex' on their birth certificates in certain exceptional cases, in the interest of morality and the security of families.[51]

In a clearly structured argument, Loir first explained the medical condition of hermaphroditism as known at the time. He gave several examples of cases in which sex had been erroneously established at birth, and claimed that it was not only the persons themselves who became victims of such errors. Society at large, and morality in particular, could also be harmed. Under contemporary French law incorrect determination of sex led to the following results, according to Loir:

> 1. The wrong education and the unfortunate position left to child victims of this type of error;
> 2. Marriages against nature, recognized only after they have been performed;
> 3. The damage done to the morality and well-being of the young lady or young man whose marriage, only just entered into, is rendered null and void or followed by separation.[52]

As errors of sex affected the interests of both the individual in question and society at large, Loir thought a law reform was necessary. He proposed three additions to the existing regulations: first, the obligatory presence of a physician to establish the sex of each newborn; second, the possibility of indicating doubtful sex on birth certificates, and, finally, a compulsory physical examination of such persons before marriage. The objective of these measures was to thwart 'the guilty conduct, full of dissimulation and bad faith, of this exceptional class of individuals, who have no scruples in knowingly deceiving both individuals and their families'.[53] In this phrase Loir suddenly betrays his aggression and fears concerning people with an erroneous sex.

Thirty years later, P. Garnier and the Professor of Anatomy Charles Debierre from the University of Lille extended the dangers of doubtful sexes beyond 'unnatural' marriages when they argued in favour of the institution of the category *sexe douteux*. At birth, Garnier explained, it was very easy to make a mistake in the establishment of sex, for:

> . . . The external reproductive organs of the two sexes are generally irritated, red, edematous . . . One must look very closely and with attention to recognize the true sex. In the event that first-time parents, an ignorant matron, a prudish midwife or a myopic doctor be charged with that task the slightest congenital malformation can lead to error.[54]

Just a split scrotum or a hypertrophic clitoris often led to a wrong decision. Such errors could have severe moral consequences, Garnier maintains:

> That one or another of these wrongly sexed individuals enters religious or teaching orders, and morality will be gravely compromised. If it is a man–woman admitted to seminary, what will become of the young Levites in contact with her, or in any other congregation or monastery? It would be even more dangerous if it is a woman–man . . . ; straight away there would be fire in the convent consuming all the nuns! It would be worse yet in schools, boarding schools, secondary schools. What would it be in the barracks if the examination prior to recruitment did not now guarantee against similar mistakes?[55]

Also, there was the danger of a 'monstrous' marriage. Garnier claims that if there were however a suspensive restriction on the birth certificate, indicating 'indeterminate or uncertain sex', 'this monstrous marriage between two men could never be scandalously consecrated by law'.[56] Demanding a medical examination every time the birth certificate was used would prevent 'so many men from passing as women and so many women from passing as men, in defiance of morality, law and truth'.[57]

> You would preclude many of the indictments of unnatural relations, affronts to morals and public morality frequently incurred by these wrongly sexed individuals, neither men nor women, dressed contrary to their true sex and who indifferently abandon themselves to or attack both . . . Husbands and wives would no longer run the risk of being fooled about the true sex of their spouse . . .[58]

Charles Debierre described the moral dangers resulting from the French civil code in almost exactly the same terms, without, however, mentioning Garnier.[59] He too warned that it was very difficult to establish sex at birth. There was also little originality in his proposal to prescribe a medical examination of sex at each birth, and to register uncertain cases as 'doubtful sex' which would demand a later examination, for this was exactly what Loir had proposed.[60] New in Debierre's proposal was to prescribe, in the case of doubtful sex, a medical examination at some point between the ages of fifteen and eighteen performed by a forensic medical commission, after which the person's sex could be established and inscribed in the register of births and deaths.

As to the annulment of the marriages of hermaphrodites, Debierre similarly criticized contemporary court decisions. In the Jumas case the court considered the satisfaction of sexual needs and the reproduction of children to be marriage's main goal. The final sentence in the Jumas case contained the consideration that marriage:

has both a social and a moral goal: the first, to perpetuate the family, the basis of every society, through the procreation of children; and the second, to encourage moderation of the instincts of nature, thus to prevent the deviations of passion and to guarantee the joys and prosperity of the home . . .[61]

The same argument was used in another French case in 1881 heard by the court of Domfort, Hubert versus Hubert, in which it was medically established that the wife had no vagina, no uterus and no ovaries. After having stated that the main objective of marriage was procreation and the legitimate satisfaction of natural desires, the plaintiff argued that therefore each spouse should have a sex and that this sex should be different from the sex of the other spouse. If one of the spouses did not have sex organs, there could therefore be no marriage.[62] Moreover, the plaintiff referred to 'old French, ecclesiastical and physiological law' and to 'natural and moral rights' which would protest 'coupling that can only result in unnatural acts'.[63]

The appeal case was heard by the court of Caen which rejected these arguments, arguing that marriage was in the first place 'a union between two intelligent and moral persons'.[64] Marriage was, according to this court, indeed a contract between a man and a woman, but:

> . . . The woman cannot be belittled to the point of only being considered a sexual system, and to see in her only an organization good for making children and satisfying the passions of a husband; that the possibility of producing children and carnal cohabitation is not absolutely essential to the existence of marriage; that this possibility is often lacking, in deathbed unions for example, and in those of the very elderly . . .[65]

These quite different takes on the ultimate aim of marriage by different French courts reflect the traditional distinction between Roman Catholic and Protestant definitions; in the Catholic perception, procreation was the main goal, whereas Protestants declared the union between the spouses the highest objective. The sentence by the court of Caen caused a furious reaction from Debierre, who exclaimed melodramatically:

> . . . Is it not against nature to condemn a young man in the plenitude of his physical force, he who wanted, through marriage, to share his life with the person of his choice, to start a family, and to satisfy his legitimate passions, to suffer an indissoluble union with an incomplete creature, with whom any congress is impossible or in whom the organism lends itself only to relations too shameful to mention; like of the woman in the case before the court of Caen (1882) for example, a woman who has no vagina whatsoever![66]

Debierre claimed he understood that the law had wanted to prevent the scandalous impotency lawsuits so frequent under old French law, but considered such codifications to be subordinated to the natural law of marriage and he simultaneously linked this to the national interest:

What is the purpose of marriage, the highest purpose, if not family? That is indeed a primordial law if ever there was one on earth; it is even more, it is a social necessity that, especially today, is essential to every Frenchman. [At the time, France was very worried about its rapid depopulation: GM.] If then some incorrect organic condition opposes the realization of that purpose, with the aggravating circumstance that it was unknown to the spouse, is it just that the marriage be valid? Is there not, if not an error of birth certificate, at the very least an error of human anatomy, and is the voice of nature not always the one that must decide and pass before all others? . . . Now, the union of the sexes, natural and primordial law, or rather necessity of nature, is well prior to all of our codifications.[67]

An interesting shift of argument has taken place here. The classic difference between the Roman Catholic and Protestant Churches concerning the goal of marriage is turned into an opposition between human law and natural law. Marriage in terms of a 'natural necessity', as something obeying primordial natural laws is contrasted to marriage as a contract and right. The first one essentially belonged to the field of competence of medicine; the latter to that of the competence of legal experts. By invoking nature as the ultimate standard for marriage, Debierre appointed the medical profession the best judge.[68]

In France, from the second half of the nineteenth century onwards, academically trained physicians therefore argued in favour of the strict medical monitoring of sex in order to avoid what they conceived of as all sorts of outrageous moral violations. Their point of view entailed a fundamental shift in the rationale of the category of sex. Rather than maintaining the status quo unless serious moral disorder was caused – the logic of sex as inscription – bodies in *any* circumstance ought to dictate to which sex a person was entitled. Sexually ambiguous bodies should not be checked only in cases of obvious public moral disorder, but should be kept under regular medical control. Moreover, instead of sharing the control of bodies with the community to which it was connected, these medical experts claimed the doctors' monopoly on properly establishing sex characteristics.

Legal versus medical bodies
Within the context of a modern nation state which acknowledged individual rights and guaranteed bodily integrity in contrast to a 'barbaric' pre-modern society, examining bodies was a contested area. To which extent could the state impose physical examinations on individuals if the moral and social order of society was at stake? Within the context of medical discourse, however, modernity was defined very differently. Here, superficial physical examinations and subjective declarations from the patient were viewed as

outmoded, whereas penetrating a body in search of the essential, defining, internal organs was seen as the modern, scientific approach. In the Jumas case, as well as in a more general forensic medical discussion of doubtful sexes, the conflict between these opinions can be derived from the ardency with which professional academic physicians advocated their case.

The discussion of the Jumas case in the forensic medical and legal literature at the time clearly demonstrates that the right to establish a person's sex by means of coercing them into an invasive medical examination was by no means self-evident. Academically trained medical professionals had to convince the courts of the necessity of such examinations by rhetorically distinguish-ing themselves from backward doctors and midwives, and calling upon Enlightenment metaphors to prove their monopoly of the scientific truth of sex. Moreover, they had to expose the moral dangers of indifference and ignorance to make sure the courts were convinced that only such examinations could prevent major moral disorder.

Loir, Garnier and Debierre stressed the dangers of the frequent but hidden presence of misleading and dangerous sexes in society, thereby urging legis-lators to take action. They pointed out the unnatural and immoral practices caused by a legal attitude that would either rather not interfere in the private question of sex or prioritized human regulations over 'natural law'. Only medicine, these authors implied, could see through the outward appearance of sex and define its essential characteristics in order to avoid moral disorder and 'unspeakable' sins. They were the best judges if natural laws had to be applied. Thus warned against the moral threat of deceitful sexes, the state could not but desire modern medicine's expertise and demand its monitoring of sex from birth.

In the case of hermaphrodites, legislators did not take up the challenge posed by these physicians to ordain the more strict regulation of sex assign-ments by involving doctors. I know of no important change in this direction in the laws of any of the major European countries at the time. The only major legal change took place in Germany, where the introduction of a new national *Bürgerliches Gesetzbuch* (civil code) in 1900 involved the complete abolition of any regulation vis-à-vis hermaphrodites. The legislator argued that modern science did not acknowledge 'true hermaphroditism' and left the difficulty of establishing someone's 'true sex' to medical experts. In practice, as we will see in Part III, decisions concerning sex assignment and marriage were increasingly made by physicians. For several reasons, they gained ever-increasing access to bodies and after 1900, they had much better operating techniques at their disposal. From the turn of the twentieth century onwards, the role of the courts was therefore mostly reduced to the legal affirmation of what had already been established in the consulting room or operating theatre.

The question as to why legislators allowed such important social and moral issues to escape their authority, leaving them to medical competence, is very important, in particular if we realize that the question of the assignment of someone's sex became an almost entirely clinical – not legal – problem in the twentieth century. Interestingly, only recently have intersex activists tried to return the issue of the sex assignment (and the accompanying medical and psychological treatment) of intersex babies from a medical context to a (human) rights discourse.[69] Within the larger context of the development of human rights in general, it could be very interesting to see which topics have been removed from the domain of human rights as they were (re)defined as medical or biological issues.

HAVING OR BEING A SECRET

It is intriguing that Justine Jumas continued to refuse to be examined until the very end even though she was put under extreme pressure. What can we make of her refusal? What possible meanings can be attached to her decision not to disclose her genitals to an expert and to keep her sex private? Like the forensic experts at the time, I am inclined to fill in the blanks. However, they were only interested in her interior anatomical sex and did not dwell on the reasons for her refusal. My curiosity and deduction have much more to do with what might have going on in her mind, in her social environment, in her life.

In Part I of this book an extensive argument was constructed to demonstrate that keeping a doubtful sex secret and leaving it be was a widely practised strategy at least until Jumas's time. This might also explain why Justine Jumas tried to continue her marriage and therefore resisted further examination of her sex. The fear of losing her (married) status, social position, house, livelihood and, possibly, lover or companion gave her very good reasons to fight for her marriage. Total social, economic and moral dislocation was a price she apparently was not willing to pay for exposing herself to doctors who claimed to be able to establish her true sex.

Chapter 4 allows us to deduce more reasons why Jumas might have refused any further physical examination. Can her resistance against the internal physical examination indeed be understood in the light of a generally felt resistance against medical intrusions upon the (female) body? However, by first having herself examined by a midwife and later, after pressure from her family, also by a family doctor, the question remains why she resisted so much to the examination ordered by the court of Alès *in particular*. The court certainly had a point when it stated that modesty could not be the argument in the light of the prior examinations. As the midwife had already started to gossip (two witnesses were called in court to declare what she had told them),

Jumas's reputation was probably already ruined. Also, the court's decision to leave the physical examination to a midwife actually rules out the argument based on shame and chastity. The court suspected that she thought that her refusal would work to her advantage. However, the midwife actually declared Jumas to be devoid of all female characteristics and the final judgement was mainly based on deductions on the basis of *her* testimony; in other words, the existing statements were certainly not unambiguously advantageous for Jumas's case. Let us therefore look at the reasons why she allowed for the earlier exams, but resisted the latter in more detail. What could have made the crucial difference?

Both the statements by the midwife and Carcassonne point out medical enactments of sex that hardly took the internal anatomy of sex into account. They summed up what they saw on the outside and what Jumas told them about her sexual functioning (that is, the absence of menstruation and menstrual pains). At the time the midwife examined her, a couple of years before the trial, Jumas had not unwillingly related that she did not menstruate nor did she provide a story of monthly abdominal pains (this she would only desperately claim later). So she did not purposefully withhold information that could be used against her. To a certain extent, Jumas at that time must have felt in control of what she revealed about her sex to the midwife and to Carcassonne.

What might have seemed threatening to her, therefore, is an examination led by a professional medical scientist whose enactment of her sex was completely beyond her control. Palpating her internal organs would detach her sex from her own observations and experiences, even if a midwife would perform the examination. We cannot be sure whether Jumas was aware of this difference between traditional and modern medicine. But we do know that, by refusing to expose her body, she retained control of her sex. She stubbornly maintained the position of someone *having* a secret by not letting anyone else decipher her body *as* a secret. The tragedy is that the physicians started to decipher her body anyway, by reinterpreting the midwife's and Carcassonne's statements, and that her refusal itself was read as a confession of guilt.

Jumas's case exemplifies, in my view, a more general tension between different perspectives on the regulation of sex in nineteenth-century society: the wish to explore sex, to expose it, to know it, to bring it into the light, to define its 'truth' and then to (re)organize and regulate it, on the one hand, and, on the other, that to keep doubtful sex secret, silent, hidden, to sustain the sexual status quo and to avoid major dislocations caused by sex reassignments. Different forces are at work, different drives, different perspectives on what might solve or at least best manage the trouble of a doubtful sex. Modern legal ideals aimed at protecting the body's integrity merged with a more traditional rationale of sex as inscription. Together these conflicted with a scientific medicine that had begun to define sex solely in terms of the 'internal system' and demanded coerced access to the internal body in the event of doubt. As modern medicine increasingly claimed a monopoly on knowledge about sex and took over the authority to make decisions in cases of doubt, hermaphrodites generally shifted from a position of *having* a secret that they could or could not reveal, to a position of *being* a secret over which they had no control whatsoever. However, contrary to what has been suggested in other histories of hermaphroditism, this did not cause the subjectivity of hermaphrodites simply to disappear. How this simultaneously reappeared in the new shape of a sexed self will be demonstrated in the next chapter and discussed in more detail in Part III.

6

THE DISLODGEMENT OF THE PERSON

ENACTING CLINICAL BODIES

As we have seen, until about the 1860s, a regime of 'bedside medicine' dominated the primarily private clinical practices that dealt with cases of doubtful sex. Within these practices, sexual function was established by observing the outward appearance of the genitals and the body in general, calculating the physical aptness for coitus, and questioning hermaphrodites about their sex lives and drives. Doctors only made scarce, superficial attempts to establish the character of the internal organs of generation. The everyday understanding of sexual function therefore must have been quite close to its clinical establishment. In published medical case histories, such examples of bedside medicine started to disappear during the last third of the century. Theoretically, as the previous chapter has shown, a gonadal or at least 'internal' criterion for establishing sex took over; however, this was not easy to apply in clinical practice. The legal–medical fight concerning the coerced examination of Justine Jumas has revealed that violating a body's integrity in the name of medical truth could meet with considerable individual and institutional resistance. Scientific research into the functioning of gonads on the basis of extensive and repeated palpation and penetration of the internal body as well as observation of menstruation and ejaculation could only be performed in the context of hermaphrodites on show.[1]

From about the 1860s and 1870s, and even more so from the turn of the twentieth century onwards, a transformation in clinical practices took place, making bodies more available to physicians than ever before. People had started to trust physicians more, and were increasingly inclined to consult a doctor for complaints that were not considered life-threatening.[2] The increased willingness of hermaphrodite patients to have their naked bodies inspected, to stand in specific poses, to be drawn or photographed, to be penetrated by fingers and instruments, and to produce semen for examination is one aspect of the growing access to bodies. But from about 1890 onwards, new techniques for overcoming patient resistance, in particular anaesthesia and surgery, had also started to be routinely employed which had revolutionary consequences. For the first time in history, doctors were able to examine tissue inside the body of a *living* person. The enactment of sex and sexual function in the context of autopsies and dissections of dead bodies could now be more or less transferred to an enactment of sex in a living, anaesthetized, person who was operated upon, from whom tissue was removed and examined under the microscope. Thus, the developments described by Roberta McGrath with regard to the medical microscopic and photographic vision on *dead* female bodies (reduced to the reproductive function represented in the ovaries since the 1840s), started to affect *clinical* case histories from the 1890s.[3] This chapter aims to describe some distinctive examples of these developments in order to show how much the enactments of doubting sex and sexual function under bedside medicine differed from those under this new medical regime.

The German sociologist Stefan Hirschauer has made a beautiful ethnographic 'thick description' of bodies in surgery. Among other things, he has described the ritualistic transformation of a patient's body into an object-body during the preparation for and administration of anaesthetics by which the person of the patient disappears behind a surgical screen step by step. But not only anaesthetics bring about such transformations. Sociological descriptions have been written of how this process unfurled in gynaecological practices. One early example is Henslin and Biggs's description of how a woman comes to accept a pelvic exam (and how a doctor comes to examine a pelvis rather than a woman) after going through a script of standardized phases of depersonalization. They describe the complex role-play that allows modern physicians to dislodge the person from the body during their exams. Terry Kapsalis critically evaluated their description of such a clinical role-playing as pervaded with standards of what is considered proper female behaviour, but kept to an analysis of the pelvic exam as a theatrical script. To historians who are aware of the fact that there were times when the shame and resistance of patients against physical exams could not be overcome quite so easily, these studies clarify that at some point in time, in some way, a whole set of roles within a series of standardized scenes must have been developed in order to overcome these objections. This chapter will address the many routines and techniques used to detach the person from the process of medically establishing sex after about the 1860s and 1870s. But the examples also point to the many internal differences of the enactment of (doubting) sex *within* such a regime.

It seems reasonable to expect that under conditions in which a person could be dislodged from the body, establishing someone's sex could be settled much more easily and precisely. After all, the techniques for establishing gonadal sex could now be applied in clinical practice. If people were willing to have their bodies palpated and penetrated, if doctors could offer anaesthetics in order to overcome possible shame and pain, or if bodies could be cut open and sections of gonadal tissue examined under the microscope in case of

continuing doubt, doctors could finally apply their theoretical notions concerning sex differences in clinical practice. Would this be the point in time
that the gonadal criterion for sex finally took over in clinical practice? This
chapter will show that this is not the case. As Annemarie Mol has claimed, it
is incorrect to assume that in modern Western medical practice one enactment
of the body (particularly, the internal anatomy) overrules all others. Instead,
in the new clinical practices, physical sex will turn out to have become an
ever more layered and complex phenomenon. In Part III this argument will
be further elaborated, detailing how these developments in clinical medicine
entailed new hermaphrodite subject positions, as well as the emergence of
notions of an autonomous, internally anchored sexed self. In this chapter
I will constrain my focus to the many new clinical enactments of the sexed
body, in particular to the establishment of male sexual glands.

   First, a general overview of how and by whom hermaphroditism was
disclosed will clearly show a fundamental shift in medical practice which
entailed a completely different enactment of hermaphroditism itself. Not
a lay person's doubt and a community's sense of social and moral disorder,
but scientifically defined characteristics of sex, could lead to someone's sex
being declared doubtful or erroneous. The next section discusses the dislodgement of the person in clinical encounters. It describes a case in which the
examination of a testicle is performed meticulously, showing the willingness
of a hermaphrodite to undergo all sorts of examinations. Subsequently, the
emergence of what I label as 'clinical masturbation' will be discussed. In the
last section, the issue of temporarily silencing the body through anaesthesia,
surgery and dissection is raised. In cases of hermaphroditism anaesthesia was
often used as a way not so much to overcome pain, but mainly to suppress
the hermaphrodite's feelings of shame and resistance against an internal exam.
One further step of disembodiment is when this led to operations allowing
for the extirpation of gonadal tissue and its subsequent examination under
a microscope.

WHO STARTS DOUBTING SEX? MEDICINE'S INCREASING ROLE

The general developments in medicine at the end of the nineteenth century
are clearly reflected in the way hermaphrodites were disclosed. An overview of
the reasons for or occasions of disclosure of a doubtful sex to either physicians
or the authorities over the course of the nineteenth century presented in
figures 1–2 and table 1, shows medicine's role increasing. In my source material,
I have tried to pinpoint the initial moment at which someone was labelled
as having a doubtful or erroneous sex, not through private knowledge or
gossip, but by a medical or other authority. I have hereby made a distinction
between those who disclosed themselves to doctors or other authorities

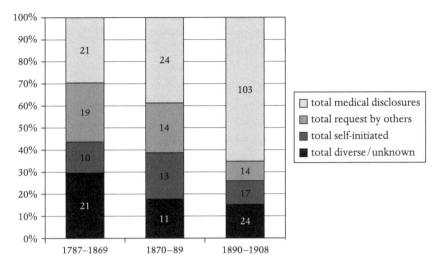

FIGURE I. REASON FOR DISCLOSURES IN ABSOLUTE AND RELATIVE NUMBERS

as having a doubtful or erroneous sex, those who were sent to doctors by others (lay persons, institutions, authorities), and what I will label as 'medical disclosures': discoveries of doubtful sex made in the consulting room or operating theatre without their sex having been doubted in everyday life already. This would be the case, for example, if a woman, of whom there was no doubt concerning her sex, almost fainted from pain in the left of the groin and was found to have testicles during the subsequent consultation. Figure 1 shows a major shift in the category of subjects – hermaphrodites themselves, other lay people, physicians – who started to doubt someone's sex. There was a dramatic increase in the relative numbers of medical disclosures after 1870, and this became even more pronounced after 1890. Until 1870, medical disclosures made up only a quarter of all disclosures; between 1890 and 1908 this had risen to two-thirds.

Figure 2 and table 1 provide a more detailed view of medical disclosures. They show not only that the number of cases disclosed through medical encounters – without the patient or other lay people being aware of the possibility of a doubtful sex – had risen significantly, but that the occasion of the disclosures also changed considerably. The first category, in which people consulted a physician because they were worried about the functioning or appearance of their sex, is closest to people being aware that something might be seriously wrong about their sex assignment. Some of these cases have been described in Part I, for example if people doubted whether they could marry. The relative number of these cases clearly drops over the century.

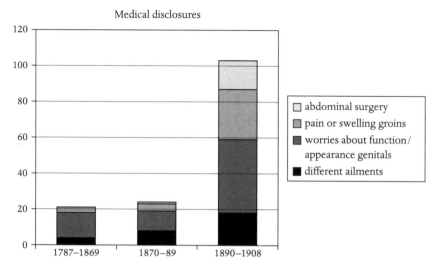

FIGURE 2. DIFFERENT MEDICAL DISCLOSURES IN ABSOLUTE NUMBERS

TABLE I. DIFFERENT MEDICAL DISCLOSURES IN ABSOLUTE AND RELATIVE NUMBERS

Medical disclosures	1787–1869	%	1870–89	%	1890–1908	%	TOTAL
Worries about function/appearance of sexual organs	14	66.7	11	45.8	41	39.8	66
Pain or swelling in the groin	3	14.3	4	16.7	28	27.2	35
Abdominal surgery	0	0	1	4.2	16	15.5	17
Miscellaneous ailments	4	19.0	8	33.3	18	17.5	30
TOTAL	21	100	24	100	103	100	148

In the second category, pain or swelling in the groin (which generally turned out to be descending testicles in people born as females), people were even less aware that something might be wrong with their sex. It is amazing that before 1870 people hardly consulted physicians if they had this often extremely painful condition, an indication that people were generally less inclined to visit a doctor during the first half of the century. The third category, abdominal surgery, produced even more surprising disclosures of hermaphroditism, as mostly nothing was suspected before the operation. Testicles were found in women, and ovaries or a uterus in men. The relative numbers of these two categories did rise considerably at the turn of the twentieth century.

Finally, the category of 'miscellaneous ailments' first shows a rise and then a fall in relative numbers. The rise certainly has to do with the rise of hospitals where people were systematically subjected to more comprehensive physical exams than at private practices. Some of these disclosures raise questions as to why no one else had noticed the unusual sex before, others were only discovered after more technically advanced examinations. Why these numbers fall again around 1900 is not entirely clear. It might be the case that, because people had become more inclined to consult doctors with worries about their sex or pain in their groin during the last part of the nineteenth century, the number of discoveries entirely unrelated to a problem with the appearance or functioning of one's sex decreased.

All in all, the number of medical disclosures in which lay people probably might have had some notion that there was something unusual about their genitals, genital area, or sexual functioning or characteristics drops relatively. The number of cases in which lay people did not suspect anything at all rises dramatically from the turn of the twentieth century onwards. So, not only did the proportion of medical disclosures rise significantly over the century, in a relatively increasing number of these cases people had no suspicion at all as to the doubtfulness of their sex.

In a nutshell, these graphics show a major shift in what hermaphroditism actually *was*. Hermaphroditism fundamentally changed over time. Until about 1860–70, hermaphroditism in living people was almost only disclosed as such if lay people could somehow perceive their sex as doubtful. From that time onwards, it increasingly occurred that doubting sex happened *exclusively* in a clinical or laboratory context. In general the person in question was increasingly separated from the enactment of hermaphroditism, as will be shown below.

THE DISCIPLINED PATIENT

Exposure, palpation and penetration
A brief description of a meticulously described, but otherwise quite representative, example of a hermaphrodite's physical examination from the 1890s will suffice to show how disciplined patients had apparently become in the last quarter of the nineteenth century. In 1893, a woman called Louise-Julia-Anna was sent to the French surgeon Guermonprez to be cured of a massive hernia that had already caused a constriction. The doctor who had sent her to Guermonprez had already concluded this woman was male. Guermonprez extensively examined her sex before considering the operation she had requested. The case has been discussed extensively elsewhere by Dreger and myself with regard to the 'gonadal standard', but here I will restrict myself to the topic of doctor–patient routines.[4] As the case is so scrupulously

detailed and no resistance whatsoever is mentioned against the observation and physical manipulation described, I interpret the proceedings to have become an accepted routine in France at the time. It is very likely that the surgeon would have mentioned any resistance, for he *did* complain about the lack of cooperation during the interview on her life history.

Guermonprez provided an extensive, painstaking description of Louise-Julia-Anna's naked body, in particular of the genital area, which was many pages long. Several measurements were taken. Just to give an impression of the sort of descriptions these observations produced, I will quote a small section of Guermonprez's description of the hernia,

> ... which presents an elongated configuration, and descends quite far ... ; the hernia is seven to seven and one-half inches in length, measuring from the inguinal orifice to the extremity of the lowest bulge. The shape is almost perfectly cylindrical with a transverse diameter varying from one and one-half to three inches, up to three and three-eighths with a coughing effort. The protruding portion forms a veritable pouch, almost four inches in length, even more in the standing position.[5]

Apart from the astounding level of detail, the excerpt shows the many manipulations of the body involved. He had Louise-Julia-Anna make 'a coughing effort' and adopt different poses (lying down and standing).

Guermonprez provided the reader with three different engravings of the genital area as well as two of her whole naked body in various poses. The engravings show the physician manipulating the clitoris / penis, as well as Louise-Julia-Anna posing in quite specific positions. Not only do these engravings show her to have accepted the physician's touch and her compliance in adopting certain poses, she must also have been willing to have herself drawn in these positions. She therefore exposed herself to the gaze and the measuring activities of at least two (but probably more) observers for quite a long time.

Next to this sustained exposure of her naked body, Guermonprez demanded her willingness to undergo several different techniques of palpation, auscultation and penetration. He extensively palpated the hernia in an attempt to discern its content, for example, mentioning in two different instances the intense pain these palpations caused. An auscultation – listening to the sound of percussion – of the hernia followed. The surgeon entered the cavity between the labia and the hernia (vagina) with his fingers describing its feel as well as its depth. A bimanual examination followed: inserting a catheter into the urethra and a finger deep into the anus, he tried to palpate the internal organs of generation. Judging from the scrupulous descriptions of the results of this bimanual examination, it must have taken considerable time or repeated attempts.

This case history provides evidence of a huge change in the routine of a physical examination during a medical consultation compared with those conducted up until around the 1860s. Temporarily and within the context of the consulting room, the usual shame or prudishness involved in protecting what Goffman labelled the 'boundaries of the self' was removed. Also, the physician had to put aside his sense of decency for a while and treat the body being examined not as the body of a person, but as a disembodied object. The routines (or 'role-playing') necessary for the temporary dislodgement of a person from the body must have been developed over the course of the nineteenth century. In the case of hermaphrodites, these new routines enabled new enactments of (doubting) sex which hitherto had only been possible in the case of hermaphrodites on show.[6] It is not easy to attach a precise chronology to these developments, as they are quite unevenly distributed across various doctors, patients, countries, and occasions, but there is a clear rise in numbers of such more penetrating and demanding techniques to be found in my source material after the 1860s.

The new enactments of sex in cases of hermaphroditism caused a (further) detachment from lay enactments of sex as the palpation of internal organs had little to do with the outward appearance of someone's sex. However, a consultation was not *restricted* to a physical examination, and the hermaphrodite's personality was not altogether absent from the case histories. Guermonprez not only described Louise-Julia-Anna's naked physique, for instance. The case history also contains descriptions of her appearance, clothes, pose, attitude towards him, emotional responses, life history, occupation, family circumstances, etc. We have to keep in mind that a single clinical case history usually records *several* enactments of (doubting) sex. In clinical encounters from the last quarter of the nineteenth century, however, a growing discrepancy can be discerned between enactments that include and those that exclude lay observations and experiences, because many more routines and techniques had become available in which the person could be dislodged from the body. This chapter will focus on the latter development, but in Part III I will return to this *tension* between the various enactments of sex.

Clinical masturbation

It is striking within the context of such a meticulous examination as Guermonprez', that he did not examine the alleged sperm stains on her nightclothes, nor asked her to produce sperm for examination. Many case histories contain indications that doctors considered it indecent to ask patients to produce sperm. Only old stains on night or bed clothes were sometimes examined. However, accounts of patients delivering sperm for examination after masturbation in or nearby the consulting room or hospital appear increasingly in case histories after 1880, without mentioning possible objections in the name of modesty.[7] What I will refer to as 'clinical masturbation' mainly occurred in cases in which it was the hermaphrodite's wish to change his sex from female to male. In a context in which 'true masculinity' increasingly required microscopic proof of testicular tissue or spermatozoa, the pressure on them to produce semen in order to get permission to change sex grew. Practically speaking, producing semen was a far easier way of providing evidence of functioning testicles than giving proof of testicular tissue inside the body. So it was clearly in the interest of such a hermaphrodite to overcome his shame and produce semen within circumstances controlled by the physician.

The case of Marie Raab (1883) was the first instance of a hermaphrodite asked to produce the sperm-like secretion he allegedly ejaculated during coitus and spontaneous seminal discharges, in quite considerable quantities during his stay in hospital.[8] Raab had been gossiped about in her village for the peculiar build of her genitals and her sexual encounters with women, which was why she had been made a ward of the court. Her brother abused the situation and maltreated her. Her complaints against him led to the examination by a doctor who subsequently sent the 'unfortunate individual' to his colleague Marchand for further inspection. She urgently wanted to be acknowledged as a man. The examination of the secretion would be crucial in order for him to support this request in his report, Marchand claimed. Under this pressure, Raab was apparently willing to cooperate but failed: 'During Raab's two-day stay in the clinic it proved impossible to obtain any of the secretion in question. Two drops of a watery fluid, presented to us furthermore in a dried state, contained none of the typical elements.'[9] Despite this failure and the – according to current medical criteria – quite inadequate other evidence of his masculinity, Raab was declared male.

Several French cases report an analysis of ejaculate, without being clear under which circumstances this ejaculate had been produced. We cannot be entirely sure that ejaculation took place during the consultation or the stay in hospital. The addition 'recently emitted' is in one case an indication that the ejaculate was not produced at home and brought in afterwards.[10] Only one French case is explicit about the way in which the ejaculate had been acquired, namely, by the excitement his examination provoked: 'I found myself to be assisting an erection of the clitoris . . . and of the emission of a secretion similar to that of a man's prostate liquid'.[11]

Apparently, in French case histories an accidental emission of semen could be described, but intentional masturbation to acquire semen had to be concealed. German case histories were a little more explicit, although they could not hide some embarrassment concerning masturbation. Kösters, for example, reporting on a case in which the person in question finally happily had her sex reassigned as male, wrote: 'A twice repeated microscopic analysis

of the secretion – obtained not, it must be added, via sexual intercourse –
revealed no spermatozoa'.[12] In another case it was subtly suggested that
the sperm was obtained during intercourse.[13] Two other German physicians
were happy to leave the explicit report on the examination of the semen
to their colleagues, who had examined the sperm gained by 'rubbing' and
'auto-masturbation' respectively.[14] Neugebauer, reporting on two cases in
which hermaphrodites born as women desperately wanted to change their
sex, was the most explicit about the ejaculation having taken place at his clinic
and even of having observed it himself. In the first case he wrote: '. . . a microscopic analysis of a fluid, released *sub masturbatione*, revealed entirely normal
sperm with over 200 spermatozoa in one field of view, sperm crystals, etc. and
even vigorous movement on the part of the spermatozoa a whole hour *post
ejaculationem*'.[15] In the other case, Neugebauer had already mentioned the
examination of the ejaculate but (accidentally?) also observed the ejaculation
itself.[16] However, the best recorded observation of ejaculation is the case
described by Magnus Hirschfeld and Ernst Burchard, and published by the
former in 1912.[17] It concerned a person born as a female with completely
ordinary-looking female genitals as well as a palpated uterus. During adolescence, she did not start to menstruate, her voice broke and some down
appeared on her chin. She increasingly felt like a man, fell in love with a
woman and performed 'an act approaching normal intercourse as closely
as possible'. She claimed to produce a slimy-milky fluid from the urethra.
According to Hirschfeld, this could be crucial for the judgement about the
case; she was asked to bring some of the fluid, in which spermatozoa were
found. This did not entirely satisfy Hirschfeld, however, so he asked her to
produce the sperm by masturbation during a consultation:

> For reasons of obvious decency, and in view of Miss M.'s highly credible and
> understandable statement that in the presence of another person, who was
> not involved, orgasm would be impossible, we clearly had to leave her alone
> in the room. The ejaculate she handed to us around ten minutes later was at
> body temperature and, according to the analysis conducted two hours later,
> contained still *living* spermatozoa.[18]

Hirschfeld could apparently hardly believe his eyes, so he wanted to provide proof excluding every possibility of fraud. To this end, he invited *five*
colleagues to check the procedure and guarantee the results together with
himself and Burchard.

> Once Miss M. had removed all her clothing, and it had been established by
> Dr Stabel and the two signatories via a detailed inspection that she had not
> concealed anything on her body, she was shut in a room she could not previ-
> ously have entered and in which we had placed a sterilized test tube in readiness
> without a single item of her own clothing. After close to fifteen minutes she called

us back in. The test tube contained around 1.5 cubic centimetres of a milky, mucoid liquid; on the floor, in front of the chair on which she had sat, lay a few sprinkled drops, dispersed characteristically. Miss M. appeared somewhat aroused; her pulse had increased to 116 beats per minute. Despite her self-control a certain touchiness and irritability in her manner was unmistakable, as is typical following masturbatory acts. Her clitoris had reddened; it was possible to determine traces of the liquid at the opening of the urethra.[19]

Hirschfeld thought the case to be really exceptional; he claimed it to be the first and only case in which the ejaculation of sperm containing live spermatozoa had been observed from completely normal-looking female genitals.[20] The first two instances of producing semen for medical research in this case are probably exemplary, but the last observation with seven expert witnesses must be considered exceptional. Even so, it provides a detailed impression of the way in which physicians at the time could make the ejaculation of sperm the object of medical investigation.

First of all, Hirschfeld's request to bring sperm from home does not seem to have been too embarrassing, for the problem of decency only appears in the text in relation to producing semen during the consultation. Apparently, masturbation in order to produce liquid for medical examination was no longer felt to be indecent. In this context masturbation had apparently become a medical procedure, detached from possible emotions, fantasies and moral judgements. If we follow Thomas Laqueur's hypothesis that one of the major objections to masturbation was related to the unbridled passions it allowed, unrestrained by relations to others, masturbation aimed at acquiring sperm for medical inspection may have been considered less sinful.[21]

During the first consultation both decency and the capacity to have an orgasm in the presence of 'uninvolved others' generated a problem. This hampered the examination, for the doctors had to retreat and leave the patient alone in the room which meant they could not observe the ejaculation. They observed the temperature of the ejaculate, an indication that it had just been produced, and found living spermatozoa (another indication that the sperm was fresh). Within two hours Hirschfeld got the results of the microscopic examination. Given the time span reported in some of the other case histories mentioned, it now seems plausible that these ejaculations also took place during a consultation.

The detailed description of the second time sperm was emitted during the consultation shows some additional ways in which physicians assured themselves that they were not being cheated: they saw 'squirted droplets', they checked her pulse, they observed the clitoris to be reddish and they noticed her somewhat agitated state, both excited and irritable. Although other physicians requesting the production of semen during a consultation or at a clinic did not describe these observations so meticulously, they probably made them all the same. It is a clinical gaze which transforms a personal sexual act into sperm emission evinced by certain physical and emotional clues.

The dislodged person

In summary, from around the 1870s onwards new clinical routines became available allowing for the extensive palpation of the internal organs of generation and in certain cases for the ejaculation of sperm for the purpose of microscopic study. These options became available as a result of the institutionalization of a new relationship between the doctor and the patient. Within this relationship the patient is able deliberately to dislodge her person from her body during the physical examination. Everyday feelings of shame and embarrassment with regard to exposing one's naked body and allowing one's genitals to be touched and penetrated by a relative stranger, as well as masturbating at the request of (non-intimate) others, had to be deliberately and temporarily overcome. The patients therefore put their bodies at the disposal of the examining physician as an object for the duration of the examination. This enabled masturbation to become 'clinical' in the sense of 'detached'; within the clinical context it was (temporarily) deprived of its personal and moral significance.

The sociological descriptions mentioned in the introduction to this chapter, demonstrated how the clinical context (rituals of (un)dressing, organization of space) made this possible. Apparently from about the 1860 and 1870s onwards, doctors had rapidly begun to develop the necessary routines and rituals, while patients were disciplined to be able to submit themselves to such procedures. Terri Kapsalis has argued that the enactment of a pelvic exam does not just arrange roles for a patient and a doctor, but that this relation is highly *gendered* as well. The pelvis is culturally defined as a zone to be ashamed of and the passivity required from the female patient, the incitement to act as if her vagina is detached from herself and her own experiences, enacts, according to Kapsalis, a typically passive, powerless female sex. She fiercely rejects the cultural and social norms Henslin and Bigs reproduce by showing a case of a woman who did not cooperate properly in terms of passively undergoing the exam.[22] However, I do not believe that this dislodgement of the person in front of the doctor is *in itself* typically female, it only fits the extant passive and prudish female role better. My historical cases show that the same mechanisms occurred when examining sperm. I do think Kapsalis is right in pointing out the gender inequality of pelvic exams however in relation to male control over (female) reproduction and sexuality in general, and the comparatively much higher number of female genital exams carried out.

ANAESTHESIA, OPERATION, DISSECTION

Anaesthesia

One of the techniques that became available at the end of the nineteenth century to overcome a patient's shame and pain was anaesthesia. Although the technique had already been used in 1846 in the United States when William Morton used ether during an operation, it took several decades before it was in general use for surgery. In the first decades, there was a real danger of anaesthetic poisoning owing to insufficient dosage regulation. However, Martin S. Pernick has shown that the selectiveness of the initial introduction of anaesthesia did not only have to do with its safety.[23] Opponents claimed that pain was not solely bad by stressing the importance of pain for the healing process. Or they assumed that different types of people responded differently to pain and therefore various groups were given anaesthesia (women, children and whites as well as highly educated people) whereas others were less likely to be allowed to receive it (men, working-class people and blacks).

Another objection against anaesthesia had to do with the doctor–patient relationship. Some doctors complained that they missed the assistance of the patient during surgery, such as their help picking pieces of bone out of a wound. Others were convinced that patients wanted to know what was being done to their bodies, or wanted to be conscious when facing death. The French physiologist Magendie, for example, thought it to be 'brutally dehumanizing to deprive someone of consciousness at such a critical hour; to carve a human being like so much meat'.[24] But most of all, there was a fear of abuse of power by the doctors. Patients under anaesthesia no longer had control over what happened; they could no longer protect themselves against medical carelessness, for example by indicating which tooth or which limb had to be removed. Doctors could abuse their power to perform unnecessary or experimental operations, while patients were no longer able to refuse. With regard to the anaesthetization of women, there was a widespread fear of voyeuristic behaviour, indecent assault or even rape by surgeons.[25]

The very same arguments against the use of ether or chloroform were however also used to argue in favour of their use. Of course, its proponents saw the prevention of pain as an advantage. Moreover, despite the danger of abuse, the power over their patients was warmly welcomed by a lot of surgeons. Anaesthesias produced 'tranquilly pliant' patients, subduing noisy, unruly, uncooperative or timid patients.[26] Thus, anaesthesia was not simply a handy new technique, it brought about a revolutionary new relationship between the surgeon, the patient and his or her body. As Stefan Hirschauer put it, the patient's person does not seem relevant any more, because the anaesthesia 'moves the patient's person out of his/her body and leaves it in front of the closing doors of the operating theatre'.[27] Apart from some prior cases of people who appeared dead, but were not, this was the first time doctors could treat a living body without a person inhabiting it.[28] Its introduction into medical practice, and its general use from 1880 onwards, literally gave physicians the opportunity to silence their patients and to treat their bodies temporarily *as if they were dead*. The ideal of revealing the anatomical–pathological truth of the dead body was now a real possibility during a patient's lifetime.

Anaesthesia turned out not only to be helpful for surgery, but also for internal examination. Pernick does not refer to the question of the use of narcosis only for the sake of examination, probably because his book only deals with the first decades after the introduction of anaesthesia, but my cases reveal that this happened from the 1880s onwards. In her discussion of the bimanual physical examinations of hermaphrodites, Dreger described anaesthesia as a rather common way of performing such an examination, either for pain relief or for modesty. She mentions a general French textbook of gynaecology which suggested chloroform anaesthesia during such examinations 'when needed'.[29]

In my database, the first instance of the use of anaesthesia solely for the purpose of bimanual examination appears in 1883 in a case described by Marchand. He did not comment at all on the question why he used anaesthesia for his examination, but simply stated: 'The examination *per anum*, performed under chloroform narcosis, produced the following results . . .'[30] Five years later, discussion of a case demonstrated with the help of photographs to the British Gynaecological Society led to the following suggestion from one of the participants: 'If the patient were put under an anaesthetic and the bimanual examination made, *per rectum* and through the abdomen, they might succeed in finding ovaries or testes.'[31] The report on the demonstration mentions that this suggestion had indeed been adopted. Thirteen more cases could be found mentioning the use of narcosis only for the sake of diagnosis, whereas in five other cases it is reported that the hermaphrodite refused anaesthesia while being examined.[32] Although not all physicians reported on why they used or wanted to use narcosis during the examination, it is clear that this was often related to shame or resistance on the part of the hermaphrodite. Sometimes this concerned showing their outward appearance; mostly it was about resisting an internal examination.

Pernick mentions the use of narcosis to 'suspend human volition and to control people's behaviour' in the case of 'unruly' or patients that resisted, especially children, the insane or retarded people, and sometimes women.[33] In the case of a little girl, for example, Neugebauer insisted on narcosis. This was refused by the mother, who was shocked by his 'rude treatment' and threatened never to appear again with her child. Neugebauer noticed:

I therefore had to treat her and the child very gently, in order not to sacrifice these interesting observations. Naturally this meant providing travel and other expenses, etc., several times over the years indeed, but in this way I was able to continually observe the child and its further development.[34]

When chloroform was refused, the 'old-fashioned' method of paying off an interesting case apparently could still do the trick.

The physician Schneller from the village of Waldmünchen had to use anaesthesia to make a twelve-year-old bearded girl reveal her body. 'As the child vigorously resisted all further examination, a gentle chloroform narcosis was applied and thus it was determined that the chest was covered with dense hair . . . .'[35] A similar example is the case of the 23-year-old Franziska B., who entered hospital suffering from nausea and heavy pains in the abdomen. She had undergone major changes in her body from her twentieth year onwards, her voice had dropped and her body was covered with hair:

> Having begun to develop a heavy beard, she became shy of human company, and ceased to go out by day. She shaved her moustache almost daily and hid the lower part of her face with a shawl (ostensibly owing to facial pain), so that even her own father was unaware of his daughter's beard.[36]

An 'internal examination' had already taken place, but she covered her face with a shawl and 'asked the nurse accompanying her not to remove the shawl before the narcosis'.[37] Thus only the narcosis allowed for 'a more precise inspection of the whole body, which gave the firm impression of a strong, manly physique'.[38]

Narcosis was also sometimes used to overcome the hermaphrodite's resistance to being photographed.[39] The most striking example is the case history reported by Alberti from Potsdam, for here narcosis was used to bypass the necessary patient consent. Narcosis was used in order to perform surgery, but it also allowed for a better physical examination and, Alberti wrote:

> As the patient's shyness regarding any kind of exposure rendered permission for a photographic record impossible to acquire, this was quickly undertaken during the narcosis. The first image shows the patient as an eighteen-year-old girl, the second shows her after the operation, still under the narcosis.[40]

Finally, an internal physical examination under narcosis could apparently be performed more easily and better than without. Another Neugebauer case, in which there is no evidence of patient resistance against any internal examination, shows that Neugebauer would have preferred another examination under narcosis, for he asked the patient for it. She refused this, as well as a diagnostic laparotomy which had apparently also been proposed.[41]

Certainly shame and resistance on the part of the hermaphrodite were important reasons to use anaesthesia for diagnostic purposes. It shows that anaesthesia was not only about alleviating pain, but it also rendered the body a passive object of medical research without the patient being able to intervene. The objections mentioned above against the use of narcosis during the first decades after its introduction to medical practice indicate how, at the time, the objectification of the body through narcosis could be seen as a disadvantage. The case histories of hermaphrodites around 1900 quoted above no longer reveal traces of such a critique; the use of narcosis to overcome shame and resistance shows that silencing the subject was often even the *main objective* of anaesthetization. The sex enacted within these internal examinations entailed the feeling of internal organs by means of various penetration techniques involving fingers, speculum and catheter, as signifiers of the presence of testicles, ovaries, a uterus or prostate.

Cutting off the person: scientific discussions of gonadal hermaphroditism
From about 1890 onwards, the number of cases in which hermaphroditism was discovered 'by the knife' to use Neugebauer's expression, increased significantly. During these operations the gonads were often, as Dreger has also suggested, completely removed. The reasons for doing so differed, but were mostly related to the hermaphrodite's health. Gonads in the inguinal canal were often removed to relieve patients from extreme pain, fainting and nausea; undescended testicles that had remained in the abdomen had become known as a dangerous risk for malign growth and were often removed for that reason;[42] abdominal surgery was performed in cases of (malign) tumours or appendicitis. According to Dreger, English doctors also performed surgery with the sole *intention* of desexing a person to save the patient from a sex change; I have not found evidence of this in my case histories.[43] Whatever the reasons may have been, the fact remains that from around 1890 these operations were performed in rapidly increasing numbers. Neugebauer's statistics on 'surgical surprises' in the field of hermaphroditism clearly indicate this.

Neugebauer tallied operations on hermaphrodites and published the results in various years. More cases appeared in every new publication; some of these cases could be old cases that Neugebauer had not known about until then, but most of them must have been new cases. Table 2 shows the increase of numbers to be significant: from only 38 in 1898 to 182 ten years later: 144 operations on hermaphrodites in ten years.[44] Laparotomy (abdominal surgery) and herniotomy (hernia surgery) led to disclosures of doubtful sex; 'diverse' operations mostly refer to plastic surgery at the hermaphrodite's request (see Part III).

In all these cases narcosis was used primarily to make the patients insensible to pain, but at the same time the hermaphrodite was rendered unconscious. What physicians and surgeons found out during surgery about the internal sexual organs and their 'sexual functioning' was therefore completely detached

TABLE 2. NUMBERS OF OPERATIONS ON HERMAPHRODITES AND DISCOVERIES OF
ERRONEOUS SEX

	Laparotomy[a]	Herniotomy[b]	Divers[c]	Total	Total cumulative	Disclosure 'erreur de sexe'[d]
1898[e]				38	100%	
1900[f]	13	41	18	72	189%	44
1903[g]	45	55	35	135	355%	55
1908[h]	45	69	68	182	479%	68

[a] Surgery of the abdomen.
[b] Surgery of (a hernia) in the groins.
[c] By 'divers operations' Neugebauer in particular meant plastic operations on the outside of the genitals to improve the appearance or the function of them, like operations to straighten a curbed down hypospadiac penis, operations to make men able to urinate standing upright, operations to widen the vagina or to remove large clitorises. Before 1890, these were the operations most frequently performed. See also chapter 7.
[d] These were cases in which was revealed that the person operated upon hitherto was assigned a sex different from the gonads (cut out and often also microscopically examined). How much doubt there already was beforehand on the part of this person is not entirely clear, but the term suggests these were rather 'surprising' results.
[e] Solowij, A., 1899, 'Ein Beitrag zum Hermaphroditismus', *Monatsschrift für Geburtshülfe und Gynäkologie*, Bnd IX, 210–11, mentions this number on the basis of an article published in 1898 (*Centralblat für Gynäkologie*, 1898, No. 15) by Sänger, who based himself on Neugebauer.
[f] Neugebauer, Franz Ludwig von, 1900b, 'Quarante-quatre erreurs de sexe révelées par l'opération. Soixante-douze opérations chirurgicales d'urgence, de complaisance ou de complicité pratiquées chez des pseudo-hermaphrodites et personnes . . .', *Revue de gynécologie et de chirurgie abdominale*, tome IV:4, 457–518, see 459, 478, 483, 485.
[g] Neugebauer, Franz-Ludwig von, 1903, 'Chirurgische Überraschungen auf dem Gebiete des Scheinzwittertums', *Jahrbuch für sexuelle Zwischenstufen*, V:1, 205–424.
[h] Neugebauer Franz-Ludwig von, 1908, *Hermaphroditismus beim Menschen* (Leipzig: Werner Klinkhardt), 712–24.

from any subjective observations, feelings or experiences on the part of the hermaphrodite. After narcosis and surgery other techniques such as the macroscopic analysis of tissue samples or microscopic pictures of sliced and stained tissue could reveal the gonads' characteristics – representing, according to the medical view at the time, the hermaphrodite's quintessential sexual function. To the hermaphrodite, this would show nothing, however, for even if they could have seen what was excised it would not have meant anything to them.

Like photographs, whether or not taken under narcosis, these artefacts could subsequently be shown, transferred and discussed without the hermaphrodite being present.[45] Thus, the *scientific* discussion about the sexual function of a hermaphrodite – as opposed to the *clinical* discussion – did not necessarily any longer take place in the presence of the exposed hermaphrodite. Live exhibition was scientifically no longer interesting and so the problems of shame and decency stopped troubling scientists in these cases.

In my database, I have collected twenty-seven cases of people who had undergone an operation and whose gonadal tissue had been cut out and examined under a microscope.[46] In the accompanying case histories the increasing specialization within medicine can be easily recognized: most case histories contain both a general anamnesis and examination, written by the surgeon, as well as an anatomical–pathological and/or histological analysis written respectively by a pathologist or a histologist. In most cases, the histological analysis stands entirely on its own and counts as the final word that speaks the anatomical truth about sex, frequently supported by photographs of the tissue removed and the gonadal cells under a microscope. In many cases, the extirpated gonads as well as the microscopic sections were shown during medical demonstrations. Often, the case history does not mention if and how the outcome was translated back into the clinical encounter, let alone into the hermaphrodite's social, moral or legal situation. Some case histories explicitly doubt whether the outcome should be communicated to the patient in question at all.[47]

A representative example of such a case stems from the Parisian surgeon Marion. He was consulted by a woman, Jeanne G., thirty-six years old and married for sixteen years, who had a tumour in the abdomen. She said she had never menstruated. At first sight, she was an ordinary-looking woman, but during the internal examination a speculum was employed and it became clear that the vagina was a cul-de-sac. The surgeon thought the tumour was possibly connected to the uterus as a consequence of the fact that the vagina was not perforated. Another, smaller tumour was found on the right of the groin. During the operation it became clear that there were neither uterus nor ovaries. Both tumours were removed and the patient went home 'completely recovered'. The surgeon was struck by the cord which attached the smaller tumour to the inguinal canal, which seemed very similar to a sperm duct. To his further surprise, the little tumour looked very similar to a rather well-developed testicle. The tumours removed were sent to the laboratory. The head of the laboratory thought the tumour was so evidently a testicle that he asked what he was supposed to do with the testicle. Nevertheless, both a macroscopic and a microscopic analysis were made of the tumour and the testicle. The former did not contain any testicular tissue; the latter was a full-grown testicle without signs of physiological activity.

In the case history, the story of the patient (pain in the abdomen, tumour found, tumour removed, returned home healed) has already ended when the laboratory story has yet to start. Although that story is about the same patient, about bodily tissue from the same patient, it seems to be completely detached, to live a life of its own. In some cases, the microscopic results *did* indeed start another life, that is, they became the subject of further discussion in implicit or explicit comparison to other pictures of other slices of dissected and stained gonadal tissue under the microscope. For looking through a microscope at such tissue does not automatically reveal a sex. It takes a lot of training and comparison to other pictures of gonadal cell structures to be able to interpret what is seen.[48] With hermaphrodites during this era, gonadal tissue that had been removed was often atrophied or fused with tumour tissue, which made it even more difficult to recognize ovarian or testicular cells. Pictures of slices of stained gonadal tissue were therefore shown during medical demonstrations and discussed in medical journals, often detached from the original general case history in which there was at least still a person (and her story) linked to the tissue.[49]

This happened in particular when physicians or histologists thought they had found gonadal tissue that contained cells of *both* ovaries and testicles: ovotestis. As Dreger has argued, from the end of the nineteenth century onwards, the search for the 'true hermaphrodite' started to concentrate on the proof of the existence of ovotestis.[50] In 1896, Blacker and Lawrence published an article in which they critically reviewed earlier claims of 'true hermaphroditism' using the criterion of microscopic proof of ovular and testicular tissue. Only three of the earlier cases in history passed this test, including their own case of one instance of ovotestis and one ovary in a stillborn foetus. This publication was soon critically analyzed by the Dutch professor Siegenbeek van Heukelom, in which none of the cases Blacker and Lawrence had labelled as 'true hermaphroditism' were acknowledged as such. He thought their own microscopic section was ovarian tissue, their subject was therefore a case of female pseudo-hermaphroditism. In 1899, a year later, Professor Nagel from Berlin provided his opinion on the Blacker and Lawrence case and thought exactly the opposite: both gonads were male. Karl Meixner followed in 1905 with, again, a very critical review of the cases Blacker and Lawrence had presented as 'true hermaphroditism' and introduced his own case of ovotestis. Pick and Salén also produced evidence of ovotestis by publishing pictures of microscopic sections and discussing them meticulously.[51] In these discussions, the details of the hermaphrodite's life, his appearance, her sexual inclinations, pleasures or habits, and the functioning of his genitals disappeared. What remained of sexual functioning was a slice of tissue stained and viewed through the lens of a microscope.

How were 'ovotestes' recognized in practice? Let us describe one of these cases, the Pick case. In 1905 Pick published a lengthy article in the *Berliner klinischer Wochenschrift*, the text of his lecture that the *Berliner Medizinische Gesellschaft* heard on 5 April of that year.[52] First he reminded his audience of the demonstration provided of an earlier case, Unger's case of a male pseudo-hermaphrodite. His summary of the case left out the life history and other personal details, immediately focusing on the (excised) testicles. There had been something special about these testicles, having 'multiple, yellow, opaque, nodular bodies of round or elliptical form', and Pick showed pictures of them again: 'Here we see another piece of the testicle, with a bean-sized, yellow, solid body (demonstration)'.[53] Unger understood this to be the tissue of peculiarly built, benign glandular tumour (adenoma), and asked Pick to do further research.

Pick initially established the peculiarities of cryptorchic atrophied testicles by comparing the tissue with that of an adolescent boy and with other atrophied testicles. He then described in detail, and showed in pictures, how the cells of the adenoma were exactly related to the canal-like cells typical for testicles and how the same condition had been described by others. Subsequently another, new case was introduced with a very short description of the general case history. A 24-year-old woman, who had had two children and an abortion, had entered hospital because of continuous bleedings from the uterus. The examination showed no peculiarities with regard to her sex. There was a tumour in one of the ovaries, which was removed by laparotomy. The patient healed and soon left hospital. Pick again concentrates his demonstration on the microscopic analysis of the ovarian tumour removed. He demonstrated several examples of different types of tumours typical for the ovaries, which are all meticulously described. His conclusion is that none of these matches the characteristics of the adenoma in the ovary of his case. However, the characteristics of the adenoma in the atrophied testicular tissue demonstrated shows 'a quite astounding anatomical conformity' with this alleged ovarian tumour. Pick shows the picture of the slices of stained tissue of both glandular tumours under the microscope and concludes that this must be an adenoma developed on the testicular part of an ovotestis: 'Here you can see a case of genuine hermaphrodism exhibiting adenomatous mutation to the male part of the hermaphrodite gland.'[54] 'Here', in this case, means: here, on this *Mikrophotogramm*, you find true hermaphroditism.[55] The hermaphrodite who is both 'lover and beloved' is far removed.

First of all, this chapter has shown how the clinical enactment of hermaphroditism fundamentally changed from about the 1860s and 1870s onwards; doubting sex was something ever more separated from the experiences and observations of lay people. In a rapidly increasing number of cases, hermaphroditism was disclosed not by lay people, but as a result of medical control, examination, surgery or dissection. This development can be explained by the gradually changing medical practices, techniques and routines, in which patients could be increasingly dislodged from their bodies. Physicians routinely gained access to their internal bodies through palpation, auscultation and the insertion of instruments and fingers into bodily openings, where anaesthetics proved to be of great help in overcoming the accompanying shame and pain. Other new techniques and practices were clinical masturbation, anaesthetization and cutting bodies open, dissecting extracted bodily tissue and examining this under the microscope.

Second, despite these developments and the fact that in medicine there was quite general agreement on sexual glands being decisive for sex, the enactment of sex differed considerably from case to case, and even within individual cases. Even gonads turn out not to be 'one', but enacted multiple: through getting proof of spermatozoa in semen, through palpating sexual glands and other internal sexual organs, through observing glandular tissue macroscopically, through observing sliced and stained glandular cells through a microscope. New discrepancies between these different enactments could arise, and new ways of 'doubting sex' emerged. One example is the discussion about the exact character of certain gonadal cells in a scientific search for ovotestis which could be seen in slices of tissue under a microscope.

A crucial difference can be discerned between sex enacted in the context of a clinical encounter and that enacted in a scientific or laboratory context. What was enacted in a clinical encounter was to a certain extent always also related to the person the examining doctor encountered. What was enacted outside the clinic, under the microscope, or during a demonstration of a picture to a medical society, could be completely detached from the person. Discussions about the character of gonadal tissue were held as if this had no relation whatsoever to the life of a person. In a scientific context, doubting sex had become an almost abstract discussion among scientists about certain pictures on a screen, which were not connected to other (clinical or everyday) enactments of sex.

However, within a clinical encounter, at a certain point in time a physician had to link his findings to the person sitting in front of him, even if the hermaphrodite had been temporarily detached from his body. The clinical physician was therefore confronted with the question of how to translate a very specific enactment of sex, for example restricted to the character of gonadal tissue, to the person in question i.e. to someone with a name, an appearance, a life history, social and sexual relations, and work, who was inscribed in the moral, legal, social and economic order. Part III will discuss this translation from the many different enactments of gonadal sex to the situation of the hermaphrodite in question at length. It will show, paradoxically, that the dislodgement of the person from the body in the enactments of gonadal sex described in this chapter provoked the emergence of sex as something autonomous and deeply ingrained in the inner self.

III

SELF

As the modern Western world has grown accustomed to the phenomenon of transsexualism and – certainly in Western Europe – has institutionalized the physical, social and legal transformation of men into women, or women into men, the idea of sex being fundamentally anchored in the self has become a quite dominant rationale. The sex of self, then, ultimately legitimizes the infringement of the other rationales, of sex as a representation of the body and sex as someone's inscription in society. The last part of this book is about the emergence of the first signs of a rationale of sex as a representation of the self in hermaphrodites' medical case histories.

As I pointed out in Part I, self is not the same as person, nor is it the same as subject or subjectivity. The concept person, I maintain, refers to many (sex-specific) aspects of an individual, such as their name, appearance, typical characteristics, functioning and rights, but *not* to a (sexed) unique inner, immutable essence. It places an individual in his social, moral and legal relationship with the outside world, not in a relationship with an interiorly located, psychological entity. I have reserved the concept of the self for unique individual qualities located and firmly anchored in an individual's inner psyche. It can be imagined, described, reflected upon and treated as a separate object. In the modern Western understanding, this self is mostly referred to as identity. It is considered profoundly and constantly sexed from early childhood on.

When and where did the idea that sex was fixed to an inner self appear? Under which circumstances was someone's belonging to one or the other sex legitimized by references to a truth of an interior, inalienable and authentic self? How could such a logic of sex as ingrained in the self start to surpass the other rationales in cases of hermaphroditism? As we have seen in the previous two parts, the rationale of sex as inscription could be overruled by the rationale of sex as a representation of bodily sex as soon as the moral, social or legal order was too obviously or publicly infringed. The balance between these two rationales dominated dealings with doubtful sexes in non-anonymous environments until around the 1860s and 1870s and partly continued beyond that time. Contrary to the suggestions of other authors that, from that time on, only gonads defined a person's true sex (and we have already seen how complex such a criterion was in practice), I want to argue that within my source material the sex of self emerged at the *exact* same time when clinical practice enabled gonadal tissue to be excised and microscopically examined thanks to anaesthesia and surgery. From the 1900s onwards, the rationale of the gonadal body started to conflict with a rationale of sex as something deeply rooted in the self.

The sociologist Stefan Hirschauer has noticed a similar, but slightly different transformation which pertains to transexuals and not primarily to hermaphrodites. In his book *Die soziale Konstruktion der Transsexualität* ('The Social Construction of Transsexuality') he describes how social conflict concerning sex, when a person revokes her or his sex of birth, becomes a medical problem concerning the relationship between physical sex and psychological sex.[1] This transformation takes place in the contemporary Western world when someone in conflict with her or his gender role enters a treatment programme for transsexuals, he argues, but is also the result of a historical development. His historical analysis of this transformation was based on his reading of the secondary histories of 'sexual inversion', hermaphroditism and transvestism.[2] Here I hope to present a more profound analysis of that very transformation based on hermaphrodite case histories. I hope to demonstrate, that what was once a social, moral and sometimes legal conflict concerning a person inscribed as male or female whose physical sex started to be doubted, began to transform into a clinical problem in which the relationship between the bodily sex of the hermaphrodite and her individual well-being and own sense of sex became of central importance. This is not to say that social and moral concerns completely disappeared from view, but to show that a fundamental relocation of the core problem of a doubtful sex started to take place. Only in the 1950s, with the birth of the notion of 'core gender identity' and the introduction of the Johns Hopkins Intersex protocols in the USA, a full shift to a rationale of sex as self had taken place. To be sure, this does not mean that from then on the sex of self was fully respected – rather the contrary. But the logics behind the protocols refer to the well-being and (future) sense of self of the intersexual – even when, as many authors including Hirschauer have shown, in fact societal norms about sex, gender and sexuality were at stake.[3] The question central to the last part of this book is how we can explain this fundamental shift, from a conflict between social inscription and bodily features, to a conflict between body and self. In other words, why did a rationale of sex as a representation of the self emerge around 1900? Along with Bernice Hausman, I am convinced that (new) medical technologies are part of the explanation and not just the *results* of what she calls 'gender ideologies': 'To argue that technology suffers from being an inevitable effect of gender ideologies is to ignore its internal

differences and diverse local circulations . . . Rather, developments in technology make new discursive situations possible, open up new subject positions'.[4]
In contrast to Hausman, I do think changing technologies at the turn of the
twentieth century already enabled new subject positions. Thus, new techniques of plastic surgery introduced around 1900, making hermaphrodite
bodies look more univocally male or female were not only the result of a
dichotomous gender ideology. They also provoked new ways of thinking
about the objective of the medical treatment of hermaphrodites in which
their 'sex of self' started to be taken into account.

Alice Dreger, among others, has suggested that in the period in which the
gonadal criterion for sex dominated scientific medical opinion (1870–1920),
hermaphrodites were defined male or female only according to their gonads,
without taking their own feelings, outward appearance or sexual desires into
account.[5] According to Dreger an objectively diagnosed medical sex ('anatomical
sex') overruled both the hermaphrodite's gender ('a category of self and
social identification') and sexuality ('sexual desires and/or acts').[6] Dreger
confined her analysis mainly to medical diagnoses and hardly discussed what
the actual consequences were of such diagnoses in clinical encounters with
hermaphrodites. She noticed that not everyone was also socially designated
the sex of their gonads, but kept stressing that, 'until 1915 when William Blair
Bell did so, apparently no medical man dared to openly question the gonadal
definition of true sex'.[7]

Apart from the fact that I have found many other, earlier examples of
physicians doubting the gonadal criterion, my analysis will take quite another
direction. My point is not whether physicians were diagnosing their patients
with due respect to the hermaphrodite's own feelings and experiences.
Neither am I all that interested in how medicine could theoretically adhere
to a dichotomous conceptualization of two different sexes in the face of so
much intermediateness. My questions concern the coming into being of the
notion of sex as something located in the inner self, something independent
from someone's body or inscription in society, something quintessential to
any individual. Instead of taking 'gender' and 'sexuality' for granted as natural
and a-historic aspects of the self not yet properly recognized and acknowledged
by medicine at that time, I will take up Joan Scott's call to *historicize* these
categories which so self-evidently seem to be based on 'experience'.[8]

By doing so, I resist a criticism in which the self of hermaphrodites is
presumably 'suppressed' by an authoritarian medical discourse. Michel
Foucault's analysis of power allows for a much more complex and, in my
view, helpful analysis of the power relations here. Foucault distinguishes
between a legally based sovereign power on the one hand, and a 'disciplinary
power', aimed at normalization and maximization of (re)production, based
on surveillance on the other hand. The term 'suppression' seems to refer to

sovereign power only: who has the right to decide over whom? But it actually
also presupposes an authentic self to be already present. With Foucault, I see
the emergence of such a concept of an authentic 'sex of self' *itself* as an effect of
disciplinary power.[9] A call for the hermaphrodite's sovereign right to 'choose'
her or his own sex covers up these less obvious disciplinary mechanisms of
power by suggesting there is a free, true self 'out there' which is the victim
of suppression.

Before laying out my own argument on the coming into being of a sex
of self, one last remark on a much discussed issue: the heterosexual norms
lingering behind all the discussions and decisions of hermaphroditism. The
nineteenth century and the first half of the twentieth century were no doubt
predominantly and fundamentally heteronormative. Both Dreger and Reis
have discussed this in their books on the history of hermaphroditism in
France and England and America respectively, and in particular point to
the homophobic anxieties of the turn of the twentieth century. They rightly
show how the issue was much discussed in precisely that era, and in general
discourse often linked to (the moral threats of) hermaphroditism. However,
they both also argue that doctors had profound difficulties in defining the
true sex – even if, as Dreger pointed out, the gonadal *standard* was clearly
set – without noticing how that very difficulty actually completely undermined the heterosexual standard.[10] Dreger very precisely defined the fear of
homosexuality in France at the turn of the century as a fear for love and
sex between two people with the same gonads, whereas Reis refers mainly
to the outer genitals and the possibility for performing coitus as the heterosexual norm.[11] In cases of hermaphroditism, as we will see in the following
chapter, this is *exactly* what doctors at the time discussed so fervently: should
they comply with a hermaphrodite's ('heterosexual', according to Reis) wish
to facilitate coitus and marriage through surgery, or would that amount to
'complicity' with gonadal homosexuality? Both among doctors and among
their hermaphrodites patients, heterosexual norms indeed went uncontested,
but there was disagreement and doubt about what these norms implied from
the very start. Even though I agree that these norms, especially when they
led to 'corrective' surgery, could be truly harmful for the patients involved,
I think this is a period in which the doctor's role shifted from diagnostic
judge to a provider of medical advice and treatment, with profound *structural*
consequences for the way in which hermaphrodites themselves were involved.
In that resperct, whether heterosexual norms were based on the patient's
own declaratations and observations of the outer body, or on microscopic
evidence of gonadal cell structure, makes a lot of difference.

The emergence of a rationale of sex as a representation of an inalienable
part of the self can partly be understood on the basis of developments with
regard to the interest in and the general appreciation of the 'inner self' in
nineteenth-century Western culture (see also chapter 3). The coming into being

of psychiatry as autonomous discipline in the last quarter of the nineteenth century, and in particular the emergence of psychoanalysis at the end of that century, not only offered new techniques of exploring the hidden, inner self, but also created a general new awareness of the value and importance of that self. Also, the increasing interest in cases of 'sexual inversion' in medicine and the nascent discipline of sexology played an important role, as we will see. But it can be shown that in hermaphrodite case histories the medical developments *themselves* gave occasion to the emergence of the notion of an inner sexed psyche at the start of the twentieth century. Paradoxically, the first notions of sex as ingrained in the self emerged precisely at the point when – and often in the very same cases in which – physical sex could be detached from the person and the social body of which this person was a part. In clinical case histories of hermaphroditism, a sex of self appeared as a separately discussed, autonomous entity, appreciated in its own right at exactly the same time as the emergence of anaesthesia and surgery. Below I will briefly address the two most important developments in medicine in their relation to the emergence of a sex of self.

Firstly, the function of physicians in cases of doubtful sex became increasingly confusing from the last quarter of the nineteenth century onwards. Until around the 1860s, and more particularly in non-anonymous contexts, medicine's main role had been one of a more or less formal expert witness when a person's sex caused social, moral or legal doubt and disorder. Part I demonstrated that hermaphrodite bodies almost solely were medically examined after such disorder could no longer be kept under control in any other way. Medicine's role, in such situations, was not legal in its purest sense – after all, physicians could not make definitive decisions about marriages or sex assignments – but can be seen as an extension of the law or at least of the moral order. Doctors provided a *diagnostic judgement*. Even if no judge was involved, people may have refrained from marriage after advice from a doctor on the basis of such a judgement.

As we saw in the previous chapter however, people were increasingly found to have a doubtful or erroneous sex during clinical encounters, *without* their sex assignment having been a problem, either for themselves or for others. In a growing number of cases doctors were not consulted in order to provide their diagnostic, expert opinion in a case of socially, morally or legally doubted sex. Instead, they *found out* that someone's sex was doubtful or erroneous, often quite accidentally. Several developments explain why this happened: the general public's increasing trust in physicians and growing willingness to consult them with less severe ailments, the increasing role of hospitals where routine checks took place on naked bodies, the growing acceptance of thorough physical examinations during private consultations, the introduction of anaesthesia during physical examinations which enabled more penetrative palpation methods, and, finally, the sudden increase in surgery after both anaesthesia and effective antiseptic measures had become more commonplace. These developments went hand-in-hand with the growing separation of the diagnosis of physical sex from the sex of the person. All the aspects of sexual functioning which, under bedside medicine, had been part of the assessment of sex – outward appearance, capacity for coitus or sexual desires – were then left out. However, in the consulting room these aspects had *not* disappeared, for the doctor was dealing with a patient *in person* after all.

So, while physicians were asked for medical help with regard to some sort of ailment, they could (more or less involuntarily) be confronted with a case of doubtful or erroneous sex. Because physical sex enacted within medical science could differ so much from the sex of the person represented in the consulting room, these discoveries could be quite surprising and embarrassing. For example, from the end of the nineteenth century onwards, physicians started discovering people who lived happily as females but had testicles in their abdomens. What were doctors supposed to say or do in such cases, with which they had not been confronted before? Should the physician feel responsible for the social, moral and legal order and somehow ensure that a person would not infringe the sexual mores of society? Should he offer the hermaphrodite medical or surgical help in dealing with a dysfunctional or ambiguous sex? Or should he just help the patient with the problem for which she consulted the doctor, without even mentioning what he had found? In clinical encounters physicians were increasingly challenged to bridge the gap between scientific sex diagnosis and their clinical treatment of doubtful sexes. This topic will be addressed in the first part of chapter 7.

Part of what happened can therefore be understood in the light of more general developments in medicine. At the end of the nineteenth century, a growing tension can be discerned between scientific or laboratory medicine on the one hand and clinical medicine on the other. Scientific and clinical careers were increasingly split.[12] It is therefore no surprise that clinical physicians started to differentiate their specific clinical professional criteria from scientific standards. With regard to hermaphrodites, caring for the well-being of the person answered to their own humanitarian professional profile. In discussions between physicians at the time, this conflict between 'theory' and 'practice' can clearly be discerned. This is, for example, how the Dutch gynaecologist A. Geijl described the distinction:

> This is why I can easily explain the *pathologist's* interest in the purely scientific matter of the nature of the sexual glands present in hermaphrodites. But it is far less comprehensible to me why the *clinician* concentrates solely on this side of the matter. He and his profession run the risk of being discredited and he often becomes the cause of great suffering and unhappiness in those unfortunates who seek his help and advice.[13]

As we will see, because of the increasing gap between medical enactments of sex and everyday ones, the issue of whether to *inform* the patient became crucial. Deciding whether or not a patient should be told his sex was erroneous or doubtful increasingly became an issue, in particular if a (future) marriage was at stake. It is still a major topic in critical discussions of current protocols for 'intersex management'.[14] The first half of chapter 8 will show how this problem led to more extensive discussions among clinicians about the impact of 'awareness' and 'consciousness' of one's belonging to a sex.

The second medical development of importance for the coming into being of a sex of self within the clinical context of hermaphroditism is the emergence of surgery as a routine treatment. From the 1890s onwards, a rapidly growing number of hermaphrodites, who were aware of the ambiguity or malfunction of their sex, consulted doctors in order to get surgical help. They mainly asked for plastic surgery, striving to hide their sexual ambiguity and/or to improve the functioning of their genitals. Instead of baring the truth of sex, the role Tardieu and Debierre had claimed so fervently for modern medicine, clinical medicine was asked to help out with the old strategy of silencing and hiding sexual ambiguity by making it invisible. In this new situation, doctors became *directly* and *solely* responsible for sex assignments, as they could irrevocably alter the sexual organs of their patients. No legal proceedings were needed. Medicine certainly did not suppress the hermaphrodite voice here, but rather invoked new forms of hermaphrodite subjectivity vis-à-vis physicians. As we will see in chapter 7, medicine's diagnostic task underpinning the social, moral or legal order conflicted with this new curative task if the subjective will of a hermaphrodite ran counter to the physician's diagnosis of his sex. The sometimes heated discussions between physicians about this conflict between diagnosis and requests for help caused some doctors to invoke the concept of a sex of self as an autonomous, internally fixed entity. Such a notion of a sex of self, something to be described and cared for by physicians or at least taken into account, enabled them to take the interests of the person of the hermaphrodite into account without simply giving in to purely subjective demands. My appreciation of the role of changing medical routines and techniques is therefore clearly different from Meyerowtz's.[15]

In conclusion, in clinical discourse, the person of the hermaphrodite – after having been dislodged from the scientific diagnosis – re-entered the stage through the back door. Diagnostic judgement turned into clinical care for the well-being of the person, and uncovering a true sex gave way to covering up ambiguity. A slight, but fundamental, difference thereby began to emerge: the sex of the person transformed into a sex of self.

However, just invoking the image of sex as an individual's mental framework, as something also psychologically anchored, something existing more or less independently from a scientifically established gonadal sex, did not automatically provide physicians with the techniques and routines necessary to examine the sex of an inner self. The few doctors who made a serious start in this field clearly borrowed their analytic concepts and interview techniques from the nascent science of sexology, to which the sexual identity of homosexuals and lesbians was of central concern. As homosexuality – until the first decade of the twentieth century – was conceptualized as 'sexual inversion', including same-sex sexual preferences, transvestism and psychological identification with the 'other' sex, sexology had developed many ways of establishing something like an autonomous, constant and deeply ingrained sense of belonging to, or identification with, the male or female sex. In that respect, cases of hermaphroditism did not generate original enactments of the sex of self, but just imported existing ones into a new context. The second part of chapter 8 will address those case histories in which the sex of self was made into a serious object of psychological–medical investigation for the first time in history.

The last chapter will analyze the autobiography of N. O. Body published in 1907, a history of a man's experience of being erroneously raised as a girl. Just like Barbin, he started to doubt his own birth sex and fell madly in love with a woman. As was the case with Barbin, he ultimately confessed his situation to a doctor who declared him to be male. How does this autobiography, of which the story is so very similar to that of Herculine Barbin, but which was written in Germany four decades later, differ from Barbin's?

SEX ASSIGNMENT AROUND 1900.
FROM A LEGAL TO A CLINICAL ISSUE

FROM DIAGNOSTIC JUDGEMENT TO CLINICAL ADJUSTMENT

Until the last quarter of the nineteenth century, the role of physicians in cases of doubtful sex mainly had to do with making decisions in cases in which a doubtful sex had caused social, moral or legal disorder. In such cases, the doctor primarily played a role as an expert witness in a conflict about rights. Even if no court was involved, a physician could play the role of an arbiter in moral or social conflicts. As we will see below, his power was restricted and his authority was not always obeyed, but even so his influence on the life of a hermaphrodite could be considerable. The subjectivity of hermaphrodites within such a system of sovereign power consisted of the option of secrecy and dis/obedience, as the example of Justine Jumas has clearly shown.

Owing to the developments described in Part II, however, medicine's role vis-à-vis hermaphroditism shifted fundamentally. Whereas the hermaphrodite person (including their appearance and the functioning of the body) had been the object of constant surveillance by the community while physicians only had to play the role of judge in the very last instance, during the last third of the century they started to monitor all bodies on a more regular basis. Moreover, physicians gained increasingly exclusive access to (internal) bodies and started to discover hermaphroditisms that had not even been noticed by others. They now tended to come across a case of doubtful sex more or less as a by-product of their general examination of a body. In such cases, they had not been demanded to provide a diagnostic judgement about sex, but to take care of the patient's health. Under such circumstances, several clinicians no longer aimed to establish scientific truth in order to define a person's rights ('true sex'), as much as to find the best solution for a confusing situation both for the hermaphrodite and society ('single sex').

The next section will discuss how physicians' relationships to the law had become troubled by the end of the nineteenth century. This was partly because of a change to the civil code in Germany, which provoked a great deal of discussion and criticism. However, these discussions also clearly show how concern for social and moral order had given way to caring for the well-being of the individual hermaphrodite. The conflict between legal purpose and a humanitarian perspective came to a head in discussions concerning plastic surgery on genitals and secondary sex characteristics, as the third section will show. In all these discussions, the 'sex of self' had, all of a sudden, become something seriously to be taken into account. Also this sex of self became an object of observation, discussion, care and clinical treatment. The obeying or disobeying subject called forth by legal discourse was thus transformed into someone who allowed her or his inner self to become the object of psychological–medical observation and care.

These shifts in the way doctors dealt with hermaphroditism can be understood in terms of Foucault's distinction between sovereign power on a basis of legal rights on the one hand and disciplinary power on the other.

AN EXTENSION OF THE LAW?

Regulations at birth: the new German civil code

As we have seen in the discussion of the Justine Jumas case, French physicians discussed the issue of sex assignment at birth extensively between the 1850s and 1880s. Legally, there were no regulations for the position of hermaphrodites in France at all. With the introduction of a new civil code in Germany in 1900, the old Prussian and Bavarian laws in which hermaphrodites (or, initially, their parents) were given the decision on sex, disappeared.[1] The argument was that modern medical science did not acknowledge the existence of neutral or double sexes, so that everyone had to have a medically established sex. From then on, the same situation existed as in France: in cases of doubt experts had to decide. This provoked another discussion of the issue, this time concentrated in Germany. Analogously with the French discussion, many German doctors argued for the option of assigning someone a doubtful sex at birth. However, their reasoning was markedly different.

Johannes Kösters, for example, warned against early sex assignments as these might prove to be wrong later on. He described a case in which the enlarged clitoris of one Wilhelmina K. was removed at the age of four. At the age of twenty-six, however, K. had his request for a civil sex change granted. This led Kösters to warn physicians to be very cautious in cases of doubt. To decide at such an early age was definitely more difficult than after puberty. 'If the sex had been determined correctly at the age of four, or at least left open to doubt, how much worry and pain would the person have been spared!'[2] The moral danger so evocatively described by Loir, Garnier and Debierre was not the reason for caution, the personal suffering of Wilhelm K. was: quite a radical shift of concern.

Kösters published his warnings just before German law changed. Physicians criticizing the new law used the same argument however, and referred to Kösters' case. Theodor Landau claimed it to be impossible to establish gonadal sex in many adult cases of doubtful sex, let alone in cases of newborn children. Deciding which sex 'prevailed' – as one of the main official commentators on the new law suggested – was equally impossible. What, Landau asked, was a prevalent sex? Did the commentator mean the secondary sex characteristics? These, Landau pointed out, were not yet visible in a child. Did he then mean the outward appearance of the genitals? They were precisely the reason for doubt in the first place. He therefore concluded that medical experts would often not be able to establish a predominant sex and advised:

> . . . that in such cases of hermaphroditism in which despite the means at our disposal a decision remains unfeasible, in the spirit of the Prussian legal code the choice of sex should be left, following the onset of puberty, to the individual, so that these unfortunate people can avoid a conflict with their own psyche or with the mores and laws of the land.[3]

The legal expert Eugen Wilhelm proposed an amendment to the German civil code in order to regulate better the legal status of hermaphrodites.[4] According to him, this was badly needed because the current regulation caused legal difficulties, severe abuse and damage to hermaphrodites and third parties.[5] Referring to the contemporary scientific opinions of Virchow and Neugebauer, among others, Wilhelm claimed it had been proven that neutral and double sexes did exist, and that gonadal sex could in practice often not be established immediately after birth.[6] His proposal suggested designating children with a considerable genital malformation 'hermaphrodite' on their birth certificate, to allow the parents of the child to decide which sex the child would be raised as, and to leave the decision to which sex he or she wanted to belong to the hermaphrodite upon reaching adulthood. By that time, physicians only had to be called in to perform an examination in order to verify whether the personal choice of the hermaphrodite was reasonable. I will deal with the latter later on.

Wilhelm not only referred to the many legal and medical difficulties that the absence of any regulations with regard to hermaphrodites provoked. He was also very concerned about the well-being of hermaphrodites. Most poignant is his plea in favour of designating *any* person with a malformation of the genitals a 'hermaphrodite', *even* if the nature of the gonads was known, in order to make sure that all these persons would have a choice later on in life. Many of these 'pseudo-hermaphrodites', he argued, looked more like someone from the opposite sex and 'often possess the sexual consciousness of the other sex and feel comfortable in this opposite sex'.[7]

The call to register 'doubtful sex' at birth if necessary, in order to be able to make a better decision with regard to sex assignment later on, was nothing new. But there is a crucial difference from the earlier French discussions of the matter: whereas the French physicians constantly and solely pointed to the moral threat to society brought about by the secrecy of hermaphrodites, the German discussion centred on the damage done to individual hermaphrodites. Kösters refers to Wilhelmina K.'s worries and pains, Landau speaks of possible 'conflicts with their own psyche' and Wilhelm of a hermaphrodite's 'sexual consciousness' and the avoidance of abuse and damage to him. Not the body, not the social and moral order, but the hermaphrodite's individual emotions or well-being, her psyche or consciousness were taken into account in these discussions of sex assignment at birth.

Erroneous or doubtful sexes in adults

Whereas the possible future suffering of a newborn hermaphrodite caused by an early sex assignment was in fact speculative, the problems facing adults with a doubtful or erroneous sex were only too real. Physicians were increasingly confronted with such cases, without the patients involved having asked for a diagnosis of sex. How did medical diagnosis in these cases relate to the law? First of all we will see that when doctors were not consulted within a legal context their diagnostic role was decidedly not the same as that of a judge. Secondly, some physicians had strong doubts as to whether the gonads alone should be decisive within a legal context.

The French surgeon Guermonprez had come to the conclusion that beyond any doubt Louise-Julia-Anna was male.[8] Moreover, he strongly suspected that she was actually aware of that fact and he was upset about her 'lie in the act'. However, at the same time he had to admit the restrictions his position as a surgeon entailed: 'On the matter of abandoning women's clothing in order to take on those of a man, I left the decision to the subject'.[9] Despite his fierce moral objections, he could not actually force her to change her civil sex because formal professional rules prevented him from doing so. A footnote discussed this remarkable pronouncement at length:

> One might wonder that there was not more pointed insistence about the change of clothing; but there is a certain principle of liberty that one must respect, even uphold, for the subject in question. Wearing women's clothing is probably, for him, a lie IN THE ACT; but it becomes a matter of conscience, which seems to go beyond surgical competence.[10]

As already shown in chapter 2, it was beyond his field of competence as a surgeon to execute police regulations or sumptuary laws. Physicians were not in the position to enforce legally the rationale of sex as a representation of the (gonadal) body. Professional codes prevented Guermonprez from revealing an 'erroneous' sex to the authorities. Even Guermonprez acknowledged that he had to secure discretion for his patient.

Neugebauer must have ground his teeth in a similar situation. In 1899 he was visited by a young woman and her father asking for an operation that would make marriage possible. Neugebauer soon came to the conclusion that there was no doubt about her being male. He therefore suggested a sex reassignment. However, neither the father nor the woman wanted to hear about it. They kept insisting on surgery. When Neugebauer explained that a marriage, in her situation, would amount to deceit and certainly not last very long (as it was actually null and void), the father declared he would find her a provincial husband who was unfamiliar with the constitution of female genitalia. Apparently upset about this case, Neugebauer asked for information from a legal expert.

> The lawyer whom I consulted regarding such persons told me that a change of status could only take place if the person affected themselves requested such a change; they could not be forced into it. That means in other words: the law allows a masculine pseudo-hermaphrodite, mistakenly raised a girl, to continue acting socially as someone belonging to the female sex, even if the error has been established. The law punishes any man who goes around in female clothing on the grounds of deliberate fraud, but in this case it tolerates such deception.[11]

These remarks about the physician's incapacity to interfere legally if an error of sex had been established are consistent with the three hundred cases in my database: legally forced sex changes of adult hermaphrodites initiated by physicians were virtually non-existent. The only exceptions concern children up to an age of about twelve or fourteen years old, in which case either the parents or physicians sometimes decided over their heads. This is not to say that Neugebauer and Guermonprez (and other doctors) in similar situations did not possess any power at all: both decided about requests for surgery, and both decided not to 'comply' with what they considered immoral. But as we will see in the section on surgery, the *sort* of power exercised by that refusal is very different.

Other physicians did not grudgingly accept the restriction of their power, but had started to doubt whether gonadal sex should be decisive at all. In a Swiss journal on criminal justice, Heinrich Zangger questioned the gonadal criterion without reservation after having microscopically established the male nature of the gonads in a young woman. At the time, he was an assistant at the pathological institute in Zurich. He published what was originally a lecture for a psychiatric–legal association when he was a professor of forensic medicine in Zurich some years later. Legal experts demanded that doctors decide on one or the other sex as they only accepted the existence of two sexes, Zangger began his lecture. He maintained that it was usually possible to establish a person's sex after puberty *in the scientific sense*. But does such a scientific labelling correspond with what would be the best *legally* and *socially* for both the individual and society?

Reporting both on what he labelled 'physical' and 'psychological' findings, he came to the conclusion that revealing the person the physical findings would not be a release, as it turned out to be in certain cases of hermaphroditism, but:

> a terrible psychological trauma, a complete confusion and disorientation in the world, for then she would lose her hard-won position, and her particular line of work altogether; as someone who is nothing if not a working woman, she would no longer be protected by the law. The state would place the same demands on her it places on a man. She would no longer be able to support herself and would have to turn to her relatives. To society on the other hand, which tolerates her as a girl, she is a harmless member, a useful one indeed.[12]

As a medical expert witness in this case, he therefore demanded permission to connect *all* findings on principle – and not just the scientifically established gonads – and also to assign a (sexually functionless) person a sex on the basis of her feelings with regard to her sex and her relationships with other people.[13]

Others also doubted whether only the sexual glands should be decisive in a legal context. Eugen Wilhelm, in his proposal for alternative provisions in the civil code in Germany, advocated having the adult hermaphrodite's choice checked by a physician; he intended this check to be mainly a guarantee against possible fraud. He, too, was sharply opposed to establishing sex by only considering the gonads:

> At the time of the verification, the physician should not have solely examined the hermaphrodite's sexual organs, but rather should have also considered the sexual features, secondary and tertiary, the direction of the sexual drives, tendencies, and the hermaphrodite's habits, as well as everything that would play a role in his future, such as relationships with others, etc. The physician can only refute the hermaphrodite's choice if this individual has very blatantly chosen an ill-fitting and for him, foreign sex . . .[14]

Even Neugebauer, who had been so indignant about the girl and her father who would not accept his diagnosis that she was a gonadal male, had started to doubt which criteria should be used for legal sex assignment. In a 1916 companion on hermaphroditism for physicians he complained about the lack of direction from legislators in this respect:

> What if, moreover, the individual patently ejaculates sperm but, raised a woman, feels psychosexually female and insists on remaining a woman? May the state in such specific cases enforce coercive measures against the wishes of the individual affected? May this individual be forced through legislative means to adopt masculine clothing, and to submit to a compulsory change of civil status? These are all questions which remain open and so far insufficiently acknowledged by the legislation.[15]

In summary: when the gonadal criterion started to be increasingly applicable in practice, this did not lead to easier legal decisions about adult hermaphrodites' civil sex assignments. On the contrary. For one, it confronted some physicians with the restriction of their role, which was definitely not a legal or policing one. Others were clearly embarrassed by the possible consequences of their diagnosis for the people involved, and came to stress the importance of the individual's position in society as well as her personal well-being. This was partly about the hermaphrodite's inscription as a sexed person within society. But physicians also started to use new phrases in the hermaphrodite case histories, in which the problems of the sex (re)assignment of a hermaphrodite were described as something in relation to her- or him*self*. This could be quite simply in terms like 'gratitude' or 'wish', but also in words more explicitly referring to sex as an issue of the inner self, such as 'terrible psychic traumas', 'conflict with their psyche', 'psychosexual feelings', 'drives, tendencies and habits', and 'sexual consciousness' (*Geschlechtsbewusstsein*). Within the clinical encounter, the sex of the person had not evaporated in the face of gonadal sex, it *emerged as a separate self* in the mutual confrontation.

SEX ASSIGNMENT THROUGH SURGERY

At the turn of the twentieth century, there was a rapidly growing awareness among people with a doubtful sex that there might be surgical and other medical solutions for the ambiguous appearance of their sex. All of a sudden many more hermaphrodites consulted doctors, not to have their sex diagnosed, but because they had a strong outspoken wish to have 'a growth' cut off or to be made 'apt' for marriage, to have a split urethra repaired, to straighten a curved down hypospadiac penis or to have breasts removed. Neugebauer's numbers reveal the number of 'diverse operations' i.e. plastic surgery on the outside of the genitals to improve their appearance or functioning. They grew from eighteen in 1900 to sixty-eight in 1908.[16] The request for, the offers of, and the actual performance of surgery or other treatments increased tremendously after 1900.

Doctors therefore became entangled in decisions on hermaphrodites' sex assignments through surgery from 1900 onwards in a way they never had been before. Before that time, physicians could *diagnose* someone's gonadal sex, but, as we have seen, without having any legal power to force hermaphrodites to assume that sex as their civil and social sex. However, as soon as they became able to perform surgeries that helped hermaphrodites to look more like and function better as one or the other sex, they became directly responsible for irreversible decisions about their future social and legal sex. So, individual surgeons as well as the medical profession as a whole had to face new dilemmas from that time on. They had to contemplate whether, under which circumstances, or to what extent they wanted to meet their patient's wishes through surgery.[17]

With the emergence of surgery, the hermaphrodite's old strategy of keeping their doubtful sex *secret* started to be exchanged for a strategy of making physical sexual ambiguity *invisible*. Julia Epstein has criticized 'modern medicine' for rendering 'the monstrous' invisible as just another way of suppressing sexual ambiguity: 'Suppression achieves its perfect form in "excision", and the potential of the monster-outsider for subversive social arrangements is eradicated altogether.'[18] She does not pay attention to the changing role of hermaphrodites in the process however, which seems essential to me both for calculating a possible 'subversive social arrangement' on the part of hermaphrodites and for explaining how medicine got the power to render sex ambiguity invisible. The new opportunities provided by plastic surgery put hermaphrodites in an entirely different position. Instead of trying to hide their secret parts or to continue living in their (semi-)known erroneous sex of birth in isolation, they now needed to call on the help of doctors and surgeons. They were no longer the obeying or disobeying subjects of a (medical) authority which assigned their sex through diagnosis, but patients requesting help and thus the object of medical disciplinary or normalizing power. As we have seen above, doctors had no legal authority over them in the end. But in this way they got the power to decide on surgery. Clinical standards were at stake here, not the law. How did this affect the hermaphrodite's subjectivity?

A heated international debate

After around 1900, there was a sudden rise in requests for, and actually performed, surgeries in which women with an ambiguous sex asked for surgery that would give them a more female appearance and would enable them to perform coitus (and marry). The request made to Neugebauer in 1899 has already been described at the beginning of this chapter. Other physicians were pressurized in similar ways by young women and their parents to perform such surgery, such as the American gynaecologist, J. G. Lynds. The patient, a school teacher aged twenty-six, came to see him because 'she has a growth on the external parts which she wishes removed'.[19] Lynds examined her under anaesthesia but was not able to establish an ovary or testicle with certainty. He was not entirely sure whether a rudimentary vagina existed either, and thought to have felt a virgin uterus. He then communicated his findings to the patient:

> After making the examination, I explained the condition to the patient and her mother, and advised that nothing be done as no operation could make her as she desired to be. They both insisted on having the enlarged clitoris removed and a vagina made. I explained the probable failure of any attempt to make and keep open a vagina under the existing conditions, but they still insisted on the attempt being made, and insisted so hard that I finally consented to make the experiment.[20]

The operation in which he removed 'the growth' and used its skin to line an artificially created vaginal opening went very well. Lynds recounts:

When she had been up a couple of days I accidentally heard she was contemplating marriage in the near future, and I plainly told her what the probable result would be should she carry out such intentions. She left the next day without my knowledge and went home. A few weeks later I saw a newspaper containing the announcement of her wedding. Again a few weeks ago I heard through a party who lives near them that she and her husband seemed to all outward appearance to be living together happy and contented.[21]

Clearly, something was nagging Lynds's conscience with regard to this operation. Not only had he already had his doubts as to its success, he also did not wish her to marry in her condition. She however managed to persuade him to operate on her and escaped his moral objections.

From the turn of the century onwards, an international debate developed around the topic of such surgeries on hermaphrodites which were practically tantamount to irreversible sex assignments. The discussion in France was triggered by a case history written by the French gynaecologist M. R. Blondel in 1899. He described the case of a married woman who sought help in order to improve her sex life. He suggested an operation to cut the thick hymen and create an artificial vagina, after having concluded that she had testicles and ejaculated sperm. He hesitated before he did so, and described his doubts in the case history. It was clear to him 'from a social point of view . . . the unfortunate's marriage was null and void. Were we, under these circumstances, authorized to perform an operation on her which would allow for more complete relations with her husband, as she had demanded?'[22] Blondel sought advice from his colleague Maygrier who also saw the patient. Together they became convinced 'that the doubt had to be interpreted in favour of the subject's intentions'.[23] For this Blondel was severely criticized by Xavier Delore.[24]

Internationally, the debate was launched in 1902 with Geijl's provocative article proudly defending surgery on a presumably male hermaphrodite. In 1902, he had been visited by a mother and her twenty-year-old daughter. The mother explained:

. . . that there was talk of her daughter's getting married, that she 'was completely smitten by the young man' but that so far she, the mother, had not dared to give her consent to the marriage because her daughter did not have a normal woman's body. The mother was afraid that there might be unpleasant consequences later on and wished to know whether there was any operation that could cure the existing 'deformity'.[25]

The daughter consented to a diagnostic examination under narcosis 'because she was ready to do anything that would make her fit for marriage', during which Geijl could not define her presumably male gonadal sex with certainty. He decided there was an 'indication for operation', incised the knitted labia, created a vagina and removed the penis. At first the 'aesthetic results' were not very appealing, but after three months: 'I could readily understand her delight. She skipped and danced for joy and kept repeating that I had performed a miracle because now she had become a real woman.'[26] Note the importance of the *girl's* appreciation of the operation here: her happiness seemed to be the definitive measure for the surgery's success. Geijl's case history does not stand alone in that respect. To be sure: this does not mean that the patient was *actually* happy, or that the operation was *really* such a success, but that Geijl and others had started to define their criteria for good treatment in *terms* of the patient's happiness and satisfaction. Geijl was the first physician I know emphatically and openly to reject the gonads as the only criterion for sex assignment. His lengthy discussion of the international literature in a sequence of articles dismissed the idea that only one aspect of sex could be decisive and he explicitly rejected gonadal tissue as the *only* signifier of 'true sex:'

> In a pseudo- or whatever other sort of hermaphrodite, there are male and female characteristics, real attributes of a real man and a real woman, differently and capriciously mixed together. One characteristic alone should *never* determine the question, to which sex such a deprived person is entitled. To that end, all [characteristics] should be reasonably estimated and weighed. Both from a social and from a scientific perspective it is desirable to weigh the nature of the feelings, the intellect and the sexual instinct as well as the condition of the copulating parts at least as much as the constitution of the sexual glands. As one will now understand, before I would incorporate the malformed into a particular category of sex, I would let him have a say, and a rather major one at that.[27]

The remarkable thing about Geijl is his frank admission of the role he allowed hermaphrodites to play in their sex assignment. Geijl's text was summarized in a German medical journal, in which it was incorrectly suggested Geijl had attacked Neugebauer for his strict application of the gonadal criterion. Neugebauer furiously rejected the criticism both in a comment on a similar case of surgery and in the introduction to his major work:

> I can assure you that all the male hermaphrodites who were raised as girls and whom I had enabled to rectify their erroneous registration as females, were always extremely grateful to me for this change. [. . .] In cases in which I establish the male character of a hermaphrodite raised as a female, I suggest (but do not by any means insist upon) a change in the birth register. These changes were only made at the special request of the individuals concerned.[28]

The words 'grateful' and 'request' stand out here: not gonadal truth counts as the ultimate clinical standard, but the desire and gratitude of the patient. They are in marked contrast to Neugebauer's outrage in the 1899 case of the young woman and her father described above. Below we will see how Neugebauer tried to combine both standards theoretically.

In 1903 and 1904, Neugebauer and the German physician Theodor Landau publicly disagreed on the same subject. Landau described a young widow who 'visited our clinic in order to be rid of her "growth"; she wishes to marry again and fears that the protuberance will be a hindrance to intercourse'.[29] Without having been able to establish the exact nature of the gonads, Landau complied with her request. Along the lines of Geijl, Landau extensively defended this decision. He explained in detail why physicians were often simply unable to define someone's sex if gonadal excretions or gonadal tissue were not available. He thereby declared himself to be opposed to diagnostic laparotomy because this was too dangerous to carry out just for the sake of establishing someone's sex. In such cases, he preferred to leave the choice to the hermaphrodite in question, exactly as the Prussian law had ordained until 1900. Neugebauer, after having triumphantly described the diagnostic laparotomy and subsequent plastic surgery on a maidservant, criticized Landau for not having first performed a diagnostic laparotomy on his patient. According to Neugebauer, Landau might have been right from a practical perspective, but he was wrong in theoretical respects.[30]

Dreger has suggested that diagnostic laparotomies did not become standard practice until the second decade of the twentieth century and biopsies were not carried out in Britain or France until 1910.[31] The latter is not correct, for the first diagnostic operations took place in France at the end of the nineteenth century. Both *laparotomies* (an incision made in the abdomen) and *herniotomies* (an incision made in the groin) for diagnostic reasons had already been performed several times by 1908 in France and Germany, although not all also included a biopsy (removal of a part of the gonad to be studied under the microscope); sometimes, the surgeon was satisfied with the macroscopic affirmation of the presence of testicles or ovaries.[32] Moreover, the question was hotly debated in both countries.[33]

Landau's humanitarian view on the options of modern surgery is clearly illuminated in his sharp rejection of Neugebauer's critique: 'It cannot be the physician's duty to do justice merely to the anatomical truth; his duty is first and foremost to extend help to the individual seeking help.'[34] Landau wanted surgery to be performed in order to help hermaphrodites. In his final justification of the decision to operate on the woman in question he stated:

When the genitals or their configuration represent a clear hindrance to the individual's own image of his or her sex, or to the enactment of conjugal relations, we must remove any excessive formations, such as a penis-like clitoris adjacent to a vagina, so that the unfortunate individual's psyche is not oppressed, at least not because of an external deformity . . . How would it help the patient merely to be medically certified a woman or permitted to marry?[35]

In opposition to Neugebauer's plea for diagnostic surgery, Landau claimed that surgery should contribute to the well-being of the hermaphrodite's psyche by ameliorating the physical *self-image* of sex and improving 'conjugal relations'. If the diagnostic, 'theoretical' *judgement* of a hermaphrodite's sex was exchanged for clinical, 'practical' *care* for the patient, her psyche could become an object of concern to a physician. A structural shift thereby took place, which is crucial to the history of hermaphroditism and intersex. For the initial subjective wish of a hermaphrodite (to get an annoying growth removed, to be able to urinate standing up, to have facial hair removed) was changed into something to be assessed by a physician: the psychological well-being of the hermaphrodite, his or her sexual drives and self-image of sex. This shift can be shown perfectly by a close reading of the discussion Goffe's case evoked.

Goffe's case[36]

In 1903, the New York professor of gynaecology J. Riddle Goffe performed surgery on his patient E. C. in order to remove the 'penis' and to construct a vagina. This patient had been raised a girl, definitely felt she was a woman and wished to get rid of her 'growth'.[37] After having examined her, Goffe asked whether she wanted to be made into a man or a woman. She decidedly wanted to be a woman, and 'according to her wish' Goffe operated her and was probably the first to use the skin of the enlarged clitoris/penis to form the inside of the vagina.[38] Three months later, she came to visit him and he reported that she was in a 'buoyant frame of mind over the success of the operation'.[39]

The discussion of the case started with Goffe's proud description of a new surgical procedure for creating a vagina. His article opens with a brief summary of state-of-the-art medical thinking on hermaphroditism at the time in which Goffe shows himself to be a true believer and supporter of the gonadal 'true sex' theory.[40] He mentions some examples of true hermaphroditism in animals and concludes his brief theoretical exercise by saying: 'But let us hope that man has reached such a stage of development in his ascent from his lower forms that no example of such degeneracy may ever be found.'[41] Thus, he shows his abhorrence of the idea of a truly ambivalent sex.

For Goffe, the relevance of the case lay in the renewal of the operative procedure with the total eradication of the sexual ambiguity he loathed as its goal. The subtitle of the article reads: 'Operation for removal of the penis [*sic*!] and the utilisation of the skin covering it for the formation of a vaginal canal' and he presented the case as 'of special interest on account of the operative procedure which I instituted and performed, and which effectually eradicated all semblance of duality of sex and placed the young patient safely in the ranks of womankind, *where she desired to be*'.[42] The illustrations which accompany the article underline this, showing as they do the success of the surgery. However, the reason his article became the subject of such a controversy was the nonchalantly formulated clause 'where she desired to be'. This is characteristic of the entire article: whereas the operation is described in detail, expressing a conscious pride at having found a new method of forming a vaginal canal, the part about the sex assignment and the decisive role he gave the patient, is commonsensical in a naive way.

Goffe's medical examination does not show a serious urge to find out the 'true' gonadal sex, in particular in the light of the knowledge and diagnostic techniques available at the time.[43] His description of her outward appearance, her gait and the general impression she gave him is clearly gendered and quite extensive. The bimanual internal examination did not result in finding proof of the presence of either testicles or ovaries. Goffe does not comment on this failure, nor does he discuss the possible perspectives on a sex assignment from a physiological viewpoint. Without presenting a conclusion concerning E. C.'s sex on the basis of his physical examination, Goffe continues his report on the case as follows:

> The patient insisted that 'the growth' was a great annoyance, that it made her different from other girls, and she wanted it taken off. When asked if she preferred to be made like a man or woman, said decidedly, 'a woman'. Accordingly she was sent to the Polyclinic Hospital, and the operation was done . . .[44]

Here the patient is not an object of observation, but the subject of a decision. She was operated on 'accordingly'. There is no indication at all that the doctor balanced the patient's wish against the results of his own physical findings. Neither is there any evidence that he tried to justify her wish by proving that her personality was definitely female, for he hardly made her (male or female) character into an object of observation. In other words, the strong subject position given to the patient here is not grounded in any medical or psychological justification. Her right to decide appears to be self-evident to him and the patient seems to define which goal has to be attained by the medical intervention. Up to this point, Goffe dealt with the situation in much the same way as his contemporaries Geijl, Lynds and Green who also performed comparable operations according to the wishes of their patients.[45]

With Goffe's relatively indifferent attitude towards finding the 'true gonadal sex' in mind, it seems that Goffe cared less about *which* sex E. C. chose than about eradicating sexual ambiguity. Finally, he defined the eradication of 'all semblance of duality of sex' as the goal of the operation. Thus, while paying lip service to the dominant medical theory on 'true' gonadal sex, Goffe proved to be much more concerned with hiding visible sexual ambiguity through medical surgery. The ideal of *true sex* is replaced here by the ideal of *single sex*. Whereas the ideal of a true sex adhered to a strict gonadal standard in decisions about sex assignments and surgery of hermaphrodites, the ideal of a single sex aimed at removing the confusion as much as possible, whatever the 'true sex' was. This difference in approach in the treatment of intersex is the essence of the basic discrepancies in the treatment of hermaphrodites and intersex patients during the entire first half of the twentieth century, which Alison Redick labelled the *Age of Idiosyncrasy*.[46]

Goffe continues his article by describing in detail how he managed to create a larger vagina by making two cuts along its length and then covering these cuts with the skin of the clitoris. The success of the operation is illustrated in part by photographs taken before and after the operation. But the article does not end with the healing of the wound and the patient's discharge from hospital. There is a final note:

> October 1, 1903. Patient reported at the office to-day [*sic*] . . . External genitalia were covered with new growth of hair, and the general glance presented perfectly normal appearance. The vagina took the usual bivalve speculum easily and without pain. The vagina walls were smooth and satisfactory in every way; the moisture of the vagina kept the skin-flaps soft and, to the touch, indistinguishable from the mucous membrane. *Patient was in buoyant frame of mind over the success of the operation, and left for her home the next day.*[47]

It is interesting to see what defines the success of the operation here. Clearly the general 'normal appearance' is important (the goal of 'eradication of all semblance of duality of sex'), as are the vagina's ability to accommodate a normal speculum without pain (doubtless to clear the way for a penis) and its softness and the indistinguishable difference between the mucous membrane and the newly attached skin. Not gonads, but the outer appearance and feel as well as capacity for coitus of the genitals, were normative. But the *final* measure of success is the patient's 'buoyant frame of mind'. As we have seen already, others such as Geijl, Neugebauer and Lynds also all refer to the happiness and gratitude of their patients.

Obviously Goffe was very proud of his success in this case of genital plastic surgery. By describing his innovation and the operation in detail, providing photographs taken before and after the operation, and describing the final physical results, he made himself the hero of the story. But that story was framed by the subjective demand from the patient and her final appreciation of the surgery.

Discussing the power to decide

Goffe was attacked the following year by several colleagues including Neugebauer and Fred J. Taussig.[48] In an article entitled 'Shall a pseudo-hermaphrodite be allowed to decide to which sex he or she shall belong?', Fred J. Taussig from St Louis severely criticized Goffe's treatment of E. C.[49]

His main argument was that Goffe did not invest sufficient effort into finding out E. C.'s gonadal sex, and then too easily accepted the patient's wish to be a woman. The second criticism is his main point as evinced by his description of Goffe's article as 'a case of a pseudo-hermaphroditism in which *at the patient's request* he performed a plastic operation'.[50] Taussig attacks the idea that a patient could determine '*our course* in regard to these plastic operations'.[51] The phrase 'our course' clearly addresses the medical professional readers, and suggests that doctors should not be their patients' tools. During the debate in the *Interstate Medical Journal* shortly afterwards, Taussig briefly summarized his standpoint on Goffe's case in an editorial: 'While we will not deny the possibility that the individual in this case may have *guessed* her true sex, the principle of allowing our patients to decide such questions is bound to lead to serious consequences.'[52] Taussig then referred to a German case in which, years after a plastic operation similar to Goffe's, the patient turned out to be a man. Actually, this was a case in which the clitoris was removed from a four-year-old girl who, much later in life, identified as male and wanted to change her sex officially.[53] Taussig suggested that Goffe legitimized 'his course' by referring to Landau's opinion (described above) who 'argues that the patient *ought* to decide his or her own sex in these cases'.[54] Goffe, however, did not seem to be aware of this international debate and simply denied that he had given his patient a choice.

Psychological sexuality as an object

The debate described so far was about who had the power to decide, not a debate about the reason why people would choose one or the other sex. Hermaphrodites were not obliged to legitimize their choices. They certainly did not have to prove that their 'self' was more male or more female. The reasons hermaphrodites had for choosing one or the other sex could be – and have been – for example income prospects, the ability to urinate standing up, planned marriages, education or job training, etc. However, in the remaining part of the discussion on E. C.'s case, the patient's 'self' itself was seen as an object of investigation.

Remarkably, this begins with Neugebauer's sharp criticism of Goffe's operation. Neugebauer approved strongly of Taussig's position. He joined the discussion by referring also to both Landau and Geijl, rejecting their positions fiercely: 'I would certainly refuse an operation if I should be able to ascertain the presence of testicles, and would in case of doubt insist upon an exploratory operation to ascertain the true nature of the sex before I would amputate a supposed clitoris, which, however, may be a penis.' According to Neugebauer, parents often asked for the removal of large clitorises 'at an age at which the child certainly does not know whether it feels it is male or female'. Others asked for surgery when they got engaged between the ages

of sixteen and twenty. 'The danger of a too ready compliance with such
requests', Neugebauer argued,

> . . . may be easily inferred from the experience that hermaphrodites raised as
> girls develop male sexual desires at a later date. It may be that retained testicles
> descend; it may be for other reasons. Some day pollutions will appear, and
> the sexual instinct will become distinctly male in character. This person then
> certainly wants to be a man. What shall become of him if a surgeon has pre-
> viously removed his penis under the assumption that it was a hypertrophied
> clitoris?[55]

Interestingly, Neugebauer does not base his criticism on the purely scientific
medical criterion for sex assignment. Although he seems to be in favour of
a strictly defined gonadal sex, arguing in favour of diagnostic surgery in cases
of doubt, his *argumentation* adopts the discourse of care for the individual
hermaphrodite's well-being. Landau and Geijl may *seem* to take better care
of the well-being of hermaphrodites in their approach, his criticism implies,
but they might turn out to be terribly wrong because they had not taken into
account possible future developments with regard to the hermaphrodite's
sexual feelings. Because Neugebauer assumed these feelings were linked
directly to either descending testicles or the ejaculation of sperm, only a good
medical assessment of the gonads could prevent such failures. That assumption
made him an expert not only on the body, but also on the hermaphrodite's
(future) sexual instincts. Ultimately, the medical expert had to decide for
the sake of the patient's own good. In this way, Neugebauer combined a
passionate demand for diagnosis – even surgically enabled – of the gonads
with the clinical standard dictating good care for the patient's well-being.

As we have seen, Goffe hardly provided any arguments to legitimize his
idea that in E. C. the female characteristics, whether physical or psychological,
predominated. Taussig, however, in his criticism of Goffe, discussed several
possible grounds on which such a conclusion could have been reached. Apart
from criticizing the physical examination, Taussig discussed the possibility of
a psychological argumentation. He did not understand how Goffe arrived at
the conclusion that the female characteristics predominated. All the characteristics described in the case, including the 'psychological-sexual feelings',
'might appear in either sex'. For Taussig argued:

> Von Neugebauer has shown how much the sexual feelings of an individual
> depend upon the conditions under which they have been raised. That the patient
> in this case has the sexual desires of a woman must, therefore, be looked upon,
> more as a result of education, of suggestion and imitation than as conclusive
> evidence of her true sex.[56]

It is important to notice that both Neugebauer and Taussig take the patient's
'sexual desires' as the marker of psychological sex. This indicates how sexual

preference, having lost its significance in a medical diagnosis of sex (as it had in bedside medicine), had regained importance as a signifier of the sex of self.[57] Only in his assumption that gonadal sex (ultimately or 'truly') defined one's sexual desires, Neugebauer upheld a relation between body and self. Further on in the article, again referring to the patient's wish to be male or female, Taussig argues:

> . . . such wishes are almost entirely governed by sexual feelings, and these in turn are largely the result of external conditions, such as education and surroundings. Moreover, the sexual feelings of a hermaphrodite frequently change from those of a man to those of a woman or vice versa, once, nay, even several times during the patient's life. Besides being therefore frequently at variance with the actual sex of the individual, we are here dealing with a very changeable quality.[58]

In his answer to Taussig, Goffe appears to have been more conscious of the grounds on which he made the decision concerning E. C.'s sex assignment than he showed in his initial article on the operation. After stating that it was impossible to carry out a diagnostic operation without unsexing the patient, he claims an even deeper competence in establishing someone's sex: 'So we must even go beyond what the microscope can reveal and study the individual mental and emotional attributes from a physio-psychological point of view.' Here he quotes an article by William Lee Howard, 'Sex perversion in America':

> 'A thorough understanding of the recent investigations in the anomalies of sex feeling, of sex perversion, and the fact that there is something more in sex and sexuality than physical organs is absolutely necessary if we wish to render justice to our fellow-men. [. . .] When, from the earliest recognition of self, the sexual instincts have been those of one sex and the anatomic organs are of the opposite sex we must, from a scientific standpoint, consider the sex determined by the mental factors.'[59]

Although Howard was obviously not discussing hermaphroditism, but sexual inversion, Goffe uses his argument to defend his conclusion on E. C.'s predominant female characteristics. In his response Taussig was not convinced and again based his argument mainly on Neugebauer.

> . . . We have many instances recorded in which, long after puberty, there was a change in the psychological sexuality of the individual . . . The possibility of change in such a mental attribute or inclination must be acknowledged, but no testicle has ever been known to change into an ovary.[60]

Arguing that physical sex is strongly connected to the power of reproduction, which is in turn connected to ova and sperm, and the gonads which produce them, he claimed that these elements have to be the determining factor, 'and not such a purely subjective element as sexual feeling or the psychological sexuality'.[61]

Although Goffe's initial article never suggested that he allowed E. C. to decide because he believed her 'psychological sexuality' to be more important or stable than other possible grounds for the decision on her sex, Taussig started arguing against him as if he did. His presupposition was that the decision to give E. C. the right to decide must have been based on Goffe's observation of her 'psychological sexuality'. Subsequently, he argued that in cases of hermaphroditism this psychological sex could not serve as a solid and stable ground for decisions concerning sex assignment. Only after Taussig started this discussion, did Goffe indeed affirm that his decision had been based on a psychological diagnosis of E. C.'s sex, defending himself by referring to another medical expert. Goffe even claimed that psychological knowledge was of higher value than 'what the microscope can reveal'.

The debate had clearly moved from the issue of power between doctor and patient, to a discussion *between* doctors about the question of what the best grounds were for a decision concerning a patient's sex. The sexual self suddenly had become an object of observation and discussion: whether it was stable, how it was related to sexual desire, how it was connected to gonadal sex and so on. It was about a self which was no longer a subject. Goffe's article became the object of such severe criticism, I contend, not so much because he had let E. C.'s 'psychological sex' prevail over her as yet unclear 'gonadal sex', but because he granted her a subject position in which she could decide for herself. Had Goffe tried to make her 'psychological sex' an object of investigation *from the start*, had he concluded that her psyche was predominantly female and that she should, therefore, be made into a female, *he*, the doctor, would still have been the one in charge of the decision. He would still have been able to claim the competence to decide. And that would have been much less provocative to his colleagues.

This difference – the difference between offering the hermaphrodite a choice between two medical options and the medical pondering of psychological and physical factors – is the crucial point where the rights and responsibilities of a sovereign subject are exchanged for a medico-psychological interest in someone's inner sexed self. Structurally, this meant the birth of a concept that only matured in the 1950s: gender identity.

CONCLUSION

This chapter has shown how, from the turn of the twentieth century onwards, the physician's function with regard to hermaphrodites' sex assignments started to shift from providing a diagnostic judgement of a 'dominant' or 'true' sex to providing clinical help in creating an unambiguous 'single sex'.

The position of hermaphrodites thereby underwent structural change: rather than either escaping or submitting to a moral, social and legal order ultimately sanctioned by a medical judgement, they became the object of clinical care whereby their 'psychological sex' started to count. As the work of Alison Redick proves, this was certainly not a total transformation effected within a decade; during the entire first half of the twentieth century medicine remained divided along these lines. However, there is no doubt an entire new rationale for determining a person's sex had emerged within medical practice: the rationale in which an individual's sex should correspond to her or his true sense of self. How did that happen?

First, physicians started to doubt their role as arbiters in uncertain cases. If they were not requested to provide their professional opinion in a *legal* case, but in a *clinical* situation, their role had always already been restricted because they could not force a person to live according to his gonadal sex. Because of the growing numbers of people consulting doctors and the progressing techniques of physical examination, doctors were increasingly confronted with such cases. The sex thereby enacted through penetrative palpation, anaesthesia and surgery could be very distinct from the everyday enactment of that person's sex. This discrepancy caused many physicians to doubt whether the gonadal criterion for sex should always be applied in clinical practice, as this would obviously cause psychological harm and social dysfunction. As we have seen, even in their function as expert witnesses at birth or in cases of erroneous sex, they started to doubt whether gonads should be decisive. The latter discussion was also triggered by the change in the German civil code, which suddenly left the entire decision about sex assignments to physicians in cases of doubt, instead of to the parents and the hermaphrodites who had been in charge before. Discussing the matter, many physicians started to appeal to notions of sex as 'consciousness', as part of the 'psyche', as a 'self-image', which could not be changed without causing harm, unhappiness or dysfunction. These physicians traded the protection of the social and moral order of sex for the care of the individual hermaphrodite's well-being.

Secondly, from the end of the nineteenth century onwards, doctors' surgical skills for hiding a hermaphrodite's physical ambiguity had improved considerably. Hermaphrodites started asking for medical help to erase their sexual ambiguity and solve coital dysfunction according to their wishes and regardless of their gonadal sex. As a result, doctors increasingly became directly responsible for the sex assignment of their patients through their decisions concerning sex surgery – without any legal institution being involved. Because the hermaphrodite's wishes did not always correspond to what the doctors knew or suspected to be their gonadal sex, these decisions led to an extensive and heated international debate *among physicians*. Their routines, standards, norms and ethics were at stake – without clear directions from legislators. So, in practice, sex assignments became predominantly medically discussed instead of legally regulated. The tension between clinical care and scientific diagnostic judgement gave rise to an extensive discussion of the hermaphrodite's sex of self.

This is not to say that all physicians suddenly thought that the sex of self ought to be decisive or even mattered for the final sex assignment. But even if physicians refused to acknowledge the importance of sexual consciousness, they at least claimed to be capable of professionally debating the subject. So, instead of offering the hermaphrodite the right to choose between various medical options, physicians had started to turn a patient's psychological sex into an object of medical investigation, something to be carefully observed, something possibly related to functioning gonads, something stable or not, a measurable identity the importance of which *they* could define. By discussing the subject professionally, they began to claim professional and exclusive competence to balance their judgement of someone's 'psychological sex' against that of their gonadal sex. In the next chapter we will see the first steps of doctors who diagnosed the self as a separate entity. But it would take several decades before professional psychological examinations could lend some sort of scientifically accepted objective proof of something like a sex of self – indeed before 'gender identity' was invented.[62]

8

THE TURN INWARDS

FROM PERSON TO SELF

If the category of sex refers to an inscription of/on a person, this implies a link to a sexed social body and to a sexed physical appearance. Physical appearance refers to a person's physical looks and clothing, to the way a person urinates, to their physical aptitude for certain types of work and last, but not least, to sexual performance. Of course, these are not 'just' the person's physical characteristics but are informed and structured by an existing gendered discourse. The reading of this outward appearance gives a person a place in the social, moral and legal fabric: it defines which places, occupations, social, intimate and sexual relations are proper, and which are not. This chapter will argue that, from the turn of the twentieth century onwards, these two links, to the bodily appearance and to the social body, were simultaneously cut off in medical practices. Sex turned inwards: it became linked to the interior of the body (see chapter 7), and to the interior of the self. This happened simultaneously: while medically established gonadal sex was cut off from other, outward, everyday enactments of (physical) sex which indicated a place in a social and moral order, physicians began to verbalize – discuss, describe, examine, question, analyze – sex as something deeply anchored in the self. The sex of self not only became an object of clinical concern – as also demonstrated in the previous chapter – but also became a separate object of examination and discussion. New techniques were employed, in particular verbal ones, to enact a sex of self.

The analysis in this chapter will initially concentrate on the issue of conscience versus consciousness. It will show how physicians confronted with an embarrassing discrepancy between the outward appearance of the person and their gonadal sex struggled with the question of whether or what to tell their patients. Some clearly wanted to make their patients morally responsible for future marital relations and considered telling the patient a matter of conscience. Others, however, referred to the traumatic effects such an announcement would have for the person involved and made the patient's consciousness of belonging to either sex their main concern. The next section will reveal how, in some physicians' case histories clothing and work started to transform from an outward index for someone's place in society into a key to a deeply ingrained sex of self. The influence of the nascent discipline of sexology is evident here, and even more so in the fourth section, which demonstrates how sexual fantasies, inclinations and habits became the object of investigation, neatly separated from the gonadal body. Here, the first traces of the influence of psychoanalysis can also be discerned. The last section will briefly show yet another way of separating the self from the body: Neugebauer's attempts to find statistical links between a person's own sense of sex and gonadal sex.

In demonstrating how hermaphroditism transformed from something troubling the social and moral order into something questioning the relation between the individual (gonadal) sex and his or her self, I do not want to suggest hermaphrodites stopped confusing or threatening the (heterosexual) sex-gender system. Rather, I want to show that the problem is managed at a new location and in a different way. In the closing section of this chapter, I will therefore address the question of how this transformation from sex as inscribed in a person to sex as ingrained in the self affected the sexual moral and social order. If (doubtful) sex was no longer constrained by social and moral (and eventually legal) control of the relationship between outward appearance and proper place, and individual well-being and sense of sex started to become such central notions, how, then, was the sexual moral and social order sustained? I will argue that the sex of self appeared as a *phantom limb*, as the projection of the severed moral and social order of sex on to the screen of an imagined self.

BETWEEN CONSCIENCE AND CONSCIOUSNESS

One of the major consequences of the newly practised medical routines and techniques was a rapidly growing number of female-looking people who were discovered to be masculine according to the gonadal standard. Of the total number of eighty-four cases of *erreur de sexe* among people raised as females (that is, cases in which the medical conclusion was that the person was had male gonads) between 1890 and 1908, twenty were definitely female-looking. In many other cases, the gonadal masculinity of the women concerned was not all too apparent in everyday life. Of these eighty-four cases, it is unclear in thirty-five of them what the physician said or what the consequences were of the discovery. On nine occasions a surgeon or physician emphatically decided not to disclose his findings to the person in question, so that she was able to continue living as a member of the sex assigned to her at birth. In the remaining forty cases, the physician or surgeon related his conclusion to the patient. Often, the physicians themselves proved to be embarrassed by their own findings and started to doubt whether they should disclose their findings to their patients, as the discussion on cases of hermaphroditism in the medical literature from the turn of the twentieth century onwards demonstrates. 'What to tell the patient?' in cases of doubtful sex thus became a clinical problem typical of 'modern' Western medicine from the time it started to employ all manners of techniques to dislodge the person from the body.[1] It is still a major topic in critical discussions of current protocols for 'intersex management'.[2]

Conscience and consciousness turn out to be key terms in this discussion. If a hermaphrodite was told what his gonadal sex was, the physician in question made him morally responsible for adopting his 'proper' position in society. Knowledge of one's gonadal sex, then, is related to conscience and defines one's relationship to the social and moral order. But knowledge also refers to consciousness: how did a person understand him or herself, as male or as female? And how would disturbing a person's own sense of sex affect her in her social functioning and psychological well-being? If marriage was involved, or if physicians were aware this might be the case in the future, the question of whether the welfare of the person or the moral and legal entitlement to one or the other sex should be central became all the more poignant.

Surprise and embarrassment

Discrepancies between what doctors naturally experienced as a person's sex and their findings with regard to gonadal sex might make them doubt whether to inform the patient at all. Some physicians only casually referred to the problem of disclosure. Consider for example the case described by Andrew Clark. A female-looking widow aged forty-two visited Middlesex Hospital complaining of acute pain in the left of her groin after having lifted some heavy furniture. She said she had menstruated since the age of twelve. After extirpation of the content of the groin, it was clear that it contained both 'an ordinary testicle and a spermatic cord'.[3] Clark commented:

> I have called the patient 'she', though as far as we were aware she had none of the essential generative organs of the female, but having always lived as a woman I did not think it necessary or even fair to inform her of what we had discovered, and when she left the hospital she believed, as far as I am aware, that she had been suffering from an ordinary rupture which had been cured.[4]

The Dutch surgeon C. W. J. Westerman had a more articulate view on the problem. In the introduction to a case he described from 1903, he mentioned the fact that in recent years hermaphrodites who previously never would have been noticed as such were now being disclosed through surgery. If hermaphrodites became aware of their true situation, Westerman noticed, they often become shy, misanthropic or depressed; this sometimes led to suicide. But a lot of masculine pseudo-hermaphrodites have lived and died in 'blissful ignorance' as women, of which his case was an example.[5] A twenty-year old girl came to him to be operated for appendicitis. She was carefully examined, and found out to have a hypospadiac penis and testicles in the groin. Westerman was absolutely sure that she was male: 'The person in question is of the male sex, since the nature of the gonads determines one's sex.'[6] But:

> ... This person was brought up as befits a well-mannered woman and has acquired a woman's outlook on the world. Furthermore, the secondary female sexual characteristics are most pronounced, such as lack of facial hair, a high voice (not broken), a marked development of the breasts, and a rudimentary vagina. Indeed, the outward manifestations of womanhood are so striking that a preliminary inspection would not arouse the slightest doubt as to the female nature of this individual, and the true state of affairs is only to be ascertained after a meticulous inspection.[7]

The female characteristics were so prominent that it would not be advisable to have this woman fulfil the role of the other sex, Westerman decided. Therefore there was no reason to examine the gonads microscopically. To this he added that the testicles were so atrophied that the person was actually sexless, and could be categorized as female 'as the appearance is entirely female'.[8] So, he rejected a diagnostic operation that would disclose the gonadal masculinity of this woman as he did not want to disturb her – and his own – understanding of her as a female and deliberately kept her in 'blissful ignorance'.[9]

Concerning their protection of these women's own sense of sex against the knowledge of their gonadal sex, neither Clark nor Westerman mentioned possible moral or legal consequences in the event they would (re)marry. The physicians seem to have acted solely in the interest of the well-being of the individual patient, and Westerman discussed extensively the social and psychological damage of disclosure. Others were much more concerned with balancing moral responsibilities with regard to others against a stable or true relationship with the sex of self.

Moral order versus individual well-being

As we have seen in the previous chapter, professional codes of conduct prevented Guermonprez from forcing Louise-Julia-Anna to change her sex. But there were other options for intervention, one of which was to tell 'the subject' his conclusions and recommendations.[10] And so he did. His article contains a fairly detailed description of what he told Louise-Julia-Anna, often literally quoting his own – rather aggressive – words. He told her she was no longer able to marry because both the Church and the law prohibited the marriage of 'subjects of your sort'.[11] 'You cannot marry as a woman', he told her, 'for you are not one'.[12] And if she would deceive a man, her husband would not even have to ask for a divorce, as there would be no marriage. 'With respect to you, you would have deceived him, and deceived *knowingly*, and in that case you would be condemned to pay damages.'[13] In other words, the fact that Guermonprez had told her the nature of her sex would make her guilty of deceit if she married a man. If she had remained 'ignorant', she could never be condemned for that reason. By forcing her to know, she became fully conscious of the fact and morally responsible, and Guermonprez deliberately chose to do so. Note that using this method, the moral and legal order was not protected by involving the law, but by emphatically making the hermaphrodite responsible for obeying that order.

In 1905 Zangger, for the very same reason deliberately decided *not* to tell a hermaphrodite raised as a female to be male. Zangger wanted to avoid the possibility that her consciousness of that fact would make her guilty of homosexuality or deceit, should she ever come to marry a man.[14] The marked difference between these two physicians must partly be understood on the basis of their appreciation of their patient's level of consciousness with regard to the doubtfulness of their sex. Guermonprez was strongly convinced – and determined to convince his readers by extensively describing her outward appearance – that Louise-Julia-Anna was clearly aware that she was not a woman.[15] He suggested that she could choose to change her category of sex and thus would be culpable if she did not do so. As we will see below, Zangger was, on the contrary, one of the first physicians dealing with hermaphrodites to treat a person's sense of sex as something subconscious; he understood sex as an inadvertent 'orientation' or 'outlook' on the world, so that a forceful change of category could cause 'terrible psychic trauma'.[16]

Some strictly argued that even if these people were not aware of the situation it was the physician's moral obligation to enable them to avoid harming possible future spouses. The New York Professor of Women's Diseases James N. West writes for instance: 'They [female hermaphrodites: GM] should be informed of their unfitness for the marital relation, of the outlook for sterility and advised to seek some useful occupation and give up all thoughts of matrimony.' Surgery to 'covert the uncertain sex into a female' was fiercely condemned as it would be 'bitterly unfair to the other party to be joined by holy wedlock to such a being'.[17]

Other physicians were struggling with the question of how to balance individual interests and consciousness against moral and legal accountability. In October 1907 for example, König asked Neugebauer for advice in a letter describing the case of Emma R. She was twenty-five years of age, had worked as a maidservant since her fourteenth year, and had been engaged for the past year and a half. In May of 1907, she had visited a gynaecologist because she never had menstruated. He told her that she should never marry. On October the nineteenth she developed violent pains on the right side of her groin and she was sent to hospital where König saw her.

Emma R. was a tall, strong person, with female secondary sexual traits and, in König's words: 'If you talk to her intensely you get the experience of meeting an unambiguous female being; all her thoughts and feelings are feminine.'[18] She had a small penis between her labia. König suspected the hernia to contain a testicle and gained certainty after removing it surgically. This was done partly because of the pain it caused Emma R. and partly because of his own curiosity. He mentioned the fact that Emma R. and her fiancé had tried to have coitus and that the fiancé had asked whether something could be done to improve her capacity for intercourse. König's question to Neugebauer concerned the extent to which he should disclose his knowledge to Emma R.[19]

> Nothing would be simpler than to say 'the female patient is a man and is forth-with to be categorized as such'. There are however significant considerations arguing against this. The person's feelings are without doubt feminine, not only because of the skirts she has worn her whole life; nature has endowed her, on the outside indeed, with so much that is feminine, that it can really be questioned whether in this case the genital organs alone (*sensu strictissimo*) determine the attribution of sex. She simply would not understand that she is not of the female sex; indeed she has not learned the slightest thing which would enable her to make her way as a man in the world, whereas she clearly fulfils her role as a woman very well.[20]

In order not to disturb Emma R.'s feminine feelings, her understanding of herself as a woman, and her social and economic functioning as a woman, König carefully avoided saying anything that might cause doubts about her feminine nature. He only warned her that she would never be able to have children, and said he was not able to improve her capacity for copulation. Yet he continued to worry about the possible legal and moral consequences of his silence:

> It is certainly possible that she will continue to have intercourse with the man; who knows, perhaps they will indeed get married? Am I then duty-bound to prevent this eventuality? Should coitus between the two be understood as intercourse between two men, and does the circumstance of her attraction to men constitute homosexuality? In my view it can be of no concern to the state, aside from the fact that perhaps a few less children will be born as a result, if the two people are joined as 'man and wife'.[21]

König's letter clearly shows the tension between sex as something defining social and moral relations, and sex as determined by one's sense of self (and the accompanying outlook on the world).

Neugebauer's answer is surprising. Even though in 1899 he had been so indignant about the girl and her father who wanted surgery to open up the vagina in order for the girl to be able to get married, and had been so opposed to operations that possibly contradicted gonadal sex in 1904, he now suddenly wrote:

> ... In such cases, in which the person concerned shows definite female sexual consciousness, the doctor acts more humanely if he does not inform the person about the *erreur de sexe* that has taken place. To the hermaphrodite his own sexual consciousness should be normative and more important than the anatomical character of his gonads.[22]

This is a very remarkable shift in Neugebauer's opinion on what should determine a person's sex, written in the appendix to his major work on hermaphroditism.[23] It strongly suggests that he had changed his mind under the influence of the discussion with Geijl, Landau and Zangger (see previous chapter). However, in a much later publication, he proved still to be upset by the lack of direction from legislators in such situations, pointing to the actual nullity of marriages in which the woman turned out during surgery to have testicles. I have the strong suspicion that Neugebauer remained very strict in his legal argumentation (equal treatment in equal cases, especially in comparison to transvestites and homosexuals), whereas in a clinical context he started to be much more inclined to what he called a 'humane' course of action, in which the individual's 'own sexual consciousness' would be normative.

Finally, Geijl too discussed the issue of disclosure to hermaphrodite patients. If a person 'thinks and feels' like the sex he was raised in and possesses the outward characteristics of that sex, Geijl has no doubt it would be damaging to announce without much ado that an error was made. This would in particular afflict those who unconditionally accepted the authority of the physician and believed that 'the first principles of morality demanded breaking with the past and sacrificing a future on which all their expectations had been founded'.[24] Those people, Geijl asserted, often became deeply unhappy or committed suicide. The less conscientious – morally and intellectually 'inferior' – simply ignore the doctor's advice. These two imagined reactions present the hermaphrodite as a person who (dis)obeys the moral prescriptions of a medical authority. But then another hermaphrodite appears in Geijl's imagination:

> Only a few would not believe the physician's announcement that they have been mistaken about their truest feelings from birth onwards. Despite the ban on marriage they marry, after having informed their future husband about the outcome of the medical consultation, and lead a happy married life. Even if the outcome of the medical examination had been correct, the entirety of her feelings and thoughts of past and present proved the conclusion derived from it wrong.[25]

This person is not disobedient, but *knows* better than the medical fraternity. The category of sex, Geijl seems to imply, should not be a moral prescription, but a truth of self.

Geijl suggested not providing too much information in such situations and only warning the hermaphrodite that copulation might be difficult and pro-creation impossible. Contrary to most other physicians, he thereby emphatically rejected the idea that a physician would be morally obliged to prevent such a person from marrying.

> I would consider it, without exception, utterly impermissible and frequently evidencing little tact to advise a person not to marry on the basis of their sexual organs and expectations for the future. If caution is required anywhere, then it is certainly needed here, if the doctor does not wish to be repudiated by the facts at a later date. Every prediction regarding the possibility of copulation, of a happy or unhappy marriage, etc., rests on shaky foundations. One should consider, above all, that people have different expectations concerning the psycho-logical and physical nature of their prospective partner or lawful spouse.[26]

In Geijl's opinion, it was not a medically defined gonadal standard that should decide what was morally right in the event of marriage, but the (future) psychological and physical satisfaction of both spouses.

In the discussion of the problem of whether physicians should disclose their findings of a doubtful or erroneous sex to someone who did not suspect anything, there seem to have been two opposing positions. The first con-sidered gonadal sex as a truth prescribing a person's sexed position in society: telling them would appeal to the person's conscience to take up his correct position or at least not to exercise rights connected to the wrong position. This was nothing new in itself, of course; only the circumstances under which such a logic was employed had changed dramatically, so that the discrepancy, between a hermaphrodite's outward appearance and understanding of her-self and the physician's moral prescription based on their gonads, became increasingly poignant. The other position was new: it held that sex was (involuntarily) ingrained in a person's own sense of sex and could not be changed without considerable damage to the person's psyche and social functioning. Therefore, the physician should not sow the seeds of doubt in the patient's mind about their sex. If there seemed to be a conflict or a contradiction between the gonadal sex and the patient's sense of sex, they maintained, it was the clinician's task to balance them carefully in the interest of the person's well-being – not in the interest of maintaining the social and moral order. With this standpoint, some physicians introduced a new rationale. Not the (gonadally defined) body, nor the original inscription in the social and moral fabric, but the individual's own consciousness became decisive. The logics of sex turned inwards. At first sight, it might seem as if this turn inwards – in which only the individual's understanding and feeling matter – caused sex to lose its relationship with morality altogether. However, I agree with Charles Taylor that a modern Western morality was implemented here: one in which knowing and expressing the inner self had become a basic moral good – if not obligation – in itself.

One remark should be made yet. The physician who emphatically and aggressively forced his patient to know the gonadal truth could not believe she thought she was a woman because *he* did not perceive her as such. All the physicians stressing the importance of their patients' own understanding of their sex mention the convincing impression they had of that sex themselves. This not only makes the hermaphrodite's 'ignorance' and therefore innocence plausible, but also shows that they actually projected their own everyday standards of what was convincing and proper sexual appearance and behaviour on to the 'self' of these hermaphrodites. This can be seen as a prelude to what Stefan Hirschauer has extensively analyzed in cases of transsexual diagnosis in which the impression the transsexual makes on the therapist is so crucial.[27] In a similar way, the next section will show how the basic, everyday indicators of a person's sexed position in society (clothing, work and sexual functioning) started to be projected on to the hermaphrodite's self.

THE PROJECTION OF SOCIAL AND MORAL POSITIONS ON TO THE SELF

Although the importance of a hermaphrodite's 'self-understanding' was certainly increasingly acknowledged, and physicians had started to take care of the psychological well-being of hermaphrodites at the expense of their role as arbiters of 'true' gonadal sex, there were only a few physicians actually employing new techniques in order to enact clinically a sex of self. It would still take a long time before they would use psychological tests to define a person's masculine or feminine identification, for example. However, the first 'psycho-biological questionnaire' (*psychobiologischer Fragebogen*) for an 'objective diagnosis of homosexuality' had already been developed and published by Magnus Hirschfeld, sexologist and fervent defender of the rights of what he called 'sexual intermediates' in 1899.[28] According to his theory, there existed an endless variety of sexes 'between' the ideal Male and Female. By that time, Hirschfeld had just started to differentiate within the category of 'sexual inversion' between homosexuality, transvestism and hermaphroditism, and his questionnaire extensively addressed questions with regard to a person's own (conscious and subconscious) sense of sex.

Physicians involved with hermaphrodites only started to employ the biographical and psychological examinations that were being developed in psychiatry and sexology with regard to cases of sexual inversion in a very minimal fashion.[29] However, the scant examples I have found do provide a good indication of what a shift from a logic of sex as the inscription of a person to a logic of the sex of self would entail. What hitherto had been primary indications of a person's place in the social and moral fabric – clothing, occupations, sexual capacities – were now inscribed in the self as authentic and inviolable characteristics.

Clothing

In 1898, Johannes Kösters wrote a dissertation on the story of Wilhelmina K., whose supposedly enlarged clitoris had been removed surgically at the age of four, and who after reaching adulthood opted for a sex reassignment on the basis of an erroneous sex assignment at birth. Kösters 'got' the case from Leopold Landau, Theodor Landau's brother. Kösters is the first author I know who gave an extensive description of the patient's 'psyche' in the main body of his case history 'on the basis of several interviews with the person'.[30] To be sure, this was different from an *anamnesis* in which the patient describes the complaints and problems leading to the consultation, because the interview was now part of the *diagnosis*. The patient's way of talking and its contents have become an object to be observed and analyzed. It was also very different from the way Guermonprez had interviewed Louise-Julia-Anna which was an interrogation aimed at establishing the extent of her guilt rather than an examination of a sexed inner self.[31] Actually, Kösters' case history was the first attempt to diagnose the sex of self through a series of interviews in a case of hermaphroditism.

Parts of Kösters' case history still resemble an anamnesis, as they sum up the most important events leading to the final consultation. But the description of K.'s life history has an extraordinary emphasis on the subject's own experiences, doubts and thoughts with regard to his sex, so that it was actually a way of describing his sex of self. This aspect was reinforced by the fact that Kösters did not treat Wilhelmina K. at all, but only used her as an object of study for his dissertation. The life story recounts how Wilhelmina did not have the faintest idea that something might be wrong with her sex assignment until her voice broke and she developed a black moustache, how she expressed her doubts to her parents who did not want to talk about it, and how she started experiencing lustful feelings and ejaculations in particular when she was seeing her best friend. He then increasingly became convinced he was male. Finally, having broken with her family and being mocked because of her beard, he had started to consider suicide. All in all, an extensive story to demonstrate the psychic harm done to him owing to the error of sex, with clear reminiscences of the story of Barbin.

Up to that point, Wilhelmina K. was the subject of the story and the perspective from which it was told. Then there is a rupture in the text, in which

Wilhelmina's way of talking suddenly becomes the object of focalization of the physician–narrator. To demonstrate how much Wilhelmina was occupied with her problem and wanted to gain clarity about her sex, Kösters noticed the vividness with which Wilhelmina described an episode in which she managed to wear men's clothes. She wrote a poem for a man's role for a bachelor's party which she recited in men's clothes:

> Never, the person declared with a look of radiant delight, had she felt as happy as the time when she was able to appear as a man, wearing men's clothes; never had she felt such joy and freedom as on that evening. The remarks of the assembled company, that she was so ideally suited to the masculine role, caused her great pleasure.[32]

The strong feelings of enthusiasm, joy, happiness, liberty and the sudden zest for living shown both in her way of telling the story and in its content made the episode into an important index of Wilhelmina's psychological relationship to his sex assignment. These were contrasted to an increasingly miserable life as a woman. The (temporary) change of clothes did not indicate her proper place in society: it revealed an inner truth.

Hirschfeld's diagnosis of the 'sex of self' similarly made clothing and ornaments into important indicators. Concerning Friederike S., for example, he wrote:

> In her dress she shows a preference for simple, close-fitting garments; the most comfortable garment for her being the English riding jacket or *façon*; she has an aversion to jewellery and a taste for high collars and men's hats . . . To her great delight she has been able to take part in masked balls several times dressed as a man. Earrings, which she also once wore, are anathema to her, along with bracelets, fans, perfume, powder and make-up.[33]

In Hirschfeld's analysis, a seemingly endless chain of types of clothing and ornaments were related to Friederike S.'s strong and apparently constant preferences and aversions. All of them are obvious but implicit outward markers of sex: to the onlooker at the time they indicated maleness or femaleness and would have positioned a person in a sexed moral and social structure. But in Hirschfeld's text, through the continuous connection to liking and loathing, they point to Friederike S.'s *inner* sex of self.

This was something new in hermaphrodite case histories. I found no 'inclinations' for clothing in earlier examples. According to Dror Wahrman, such a transformation of clothing's significance from an index of one's belonging to a certain category (gender, class, race) in society to an expression of an individual's inner authentic identity, had already happened in English culture at the end of the eighteenth century.[34] This study shows, however, how long it took before such a transformation gained a foothold in clinical practice with regard to hermaphrodites. It makes one wonder how such cultural and social histories relate.

Occupation

This was slightly different when it came to preferences and aversions with regard to work and other occupations. We have already seen in earlier case histories how some hermaphrodites allegedly miraculously changed their occupations from milking cows to ploughing, or how they suddenly started to hate housework or embroidery. They grew beards, they became strong, lost their feminine features and stopped looking after the chickens. These narratives showed how the people in question, who had mostly been raised as women, suddenly no longer fitted into the sex category to which they had been inscribed. Such stories underpinned the necessity of a – mostly also requested – sex reassignment. Most of the case histories from the turn of the twentieth century which express concern for the well-being of the person in question, such as Zangger's, Westerman's and König's, also refer to the importance of education and work, suggesting that the hermaphrodites in question cannot easily change their occupations. This does not so much refer to the incapacity for personal change, but to the impossibility of earning a living when occupying the other sex's role. Such stories underline the diffi-culty of a civil sex change as sex was strongly related to social and economic functioning.

Hirschfeld was an important exception to this pattern. He connected all sorts of childhood games, school subject matter, occupations and work to the *personal* preferences of the hermaphrodites, and strongly suggests that these are the constant characteristics of someone's personality. Once again, externally sexed phenomena became an intrinsic part of a person's inner self, thereby profoundly sexing that self. Examples of this abound in his case histories, so I will only provide some here. Of Friederieke S.'s childhood, for example, he wrote:

> Generally she preferred boy's games, above all climbing trees, but she also learned needlework and sewing.[35] She made good progress at school; her great loves were geography and science, and also arithmetic; she was less interested in religion.[36]

This provides a marked parallel with his description of her adult inclinations, suggesting a constant personality:

> She was interested in antiquity, but also in war and politics; what interested her most in the newspapers were the suicides. She showed no interest whatsoever in fashion and liked to read academic books, never novels. She can cook, understands housework and needlework, but she prefers masculine activities. She owns a revolver and bullets, likes to shoot and can ride and row too.[37]

Hirschfeld's description of Anna Laabs (alias N. O. Body: see next chapter) was very similar, and all his case histories of hermaphrodites reflected his systematic questionnaire developed for diagnosing homosexuality.[38] Thereby, there is a constant tension or ambiguity between letting the person tell her own story or express her feelings, and the attempt to observe, classify and objectify the characteristics of 'the self'.

Sexual desires

During the second half of the nineteenth century, the examination of what was incidentally labelled as 'of psychological interest' or as 'of moral interest' had been confined to the *direction* of one's sexual inclinations as expressed in voluptuous dreams, sexual excitement, attraction and acts.[39] These were mostly described as a part of the total description of someone's sex and physical sexual functioning. In Hirschfeld's case histories the nature of sexual desires became an object of investigation of its own for the first time, interesting in and of itself. His examinations and case histories are clearly indebted to Krafft-Ebing's immense collections of case histories of sexual inversion. One of the techniques that had been developed was a refined series of questions about someone's sexual life: their desires, obsessions, dreams, fantasies, appetites, experiences, pleasures and habits as well as personal history in this respect.[40] Hirschfeld himself started systematizing the research into this psychological aspect of sexuality by drawing up a diagnostic questionnaire. Using these techniques in cases of hermaphroditism was exceptional at the time, notwithstanding the general increase in interest in the psychology of sex and sexuality. Hirschfeld's approach can be beautifully illustrated by the following excerpt from the case history of Anna Laabs which dates back to 1906:

> The first sexual impulses started in her 25th year. They were spontaneously and instinctively directed towards women. Libidinous dreams referred to intercourse with women. On the street, in the theatre, etc., her eye was involuntarily drawn more to women. L. states that attractive female bodies, seen for instance when bathing, always aroused her admiration, so that initially she believed that this interest was a purely aesthetic one. Only very gradually did it become clear to her that this attraction might be attributable to her sexual drive. Conversely there was a very marked sexual aversion towards men. The idea of relating to them sexually awoke powerful disgust in her.[41]

To prove this, Laabs related that she had received marriage proposals from three men, one of whom was allegedly rich. After having asked her about her sexual drive and experiences – Laabs's sexual drive was quite strong and she claimed to feel 'strengthened and satisfied' after coitus – Hirschfeld continued the interrogation:

The type she is particularly attracted to are fully developed women between twenty and thirty years old, and since the awakening of her sexual drive this has remained unchanged. She likes brunettes with highly feminine figures in particular, whereas she finds women of a manly type with a trace of a beard or a deep voice repulsive. An attractive feminine alto or mezzo-soprano voice has an erotic effect on her. What she likes about women above all is their soft, surrendering nature.[42]

The very similar structure of the paragraph on 'sexual drive' in another case history, concerning Frederike Schmidt, clearly shows Hirschfeld's use of a systematic sequence of questions:

The first sexual impulses began in her 13th year. The orientation of the sexual drive has always been the same, namely that she has been drawn to the female sex from the start. Her amorous dreams have always related to women, she has dreamed of kissing a girl and pressing into her, during which 'erections' of her clitoris occurred. She also experienced this early on when touching or embracing her school friends. As regards sex she feels indifference towards men; aversion to the idea of 'coitus' with them. She has rejected four petitions for marriage made to her over the years; she twice gave in to the desires of men who wanted to have sexual intercourse with her, but felt highly unsatisfied after the act, performed *inter femora*. When asked what repulsed her about men, she replied, 'they hold no attraction'.

She has a particular proclivity for eighteen- to twenty-four-year old girls with full breasts and strong arms, especially more demure and educated individuals. She has a marked preference for beautiful hands. There have been no other fetishistic, sadistic or masochistic anomalies, nor proclivities for sexually immature individuals.[43]

Once again the experiences with women are mentioned, the strong sexual drive, the active role during intercourse and experiencing 'a health boost' afterwards.[44] Mentioning when she first experienced sexual excitement and at which sex this was directed, as well as the content of her sexual dreams, was nothing new. What was, was the attention paid to the way in which Schmidt and Laabs became conscious of their admiration for and sexual attraction to women. New, also, was the detailed way in which both Laabs's and Schmidt's sexual desires, imaginations and experiences in their life histories were examined. Hirschfeld revealed interest in the *type* of women they were attracted to, in which circumstances they felt attracted (in the streets, at the theatre, at a swimming pool, touching or embracing a friend) and what exactly attracted them (the timbre of the voice, the hair colour, the 'soft self-sacrificing nature', full breasts, strong arms or beautiful hands). Hirschfeld used scientific expressions such as 'have an erotic effect' or 'fetishism' to transform these feelings from mere subjective statements into objects of sexological enquiry.

The extensive way in which he described and proved that both Laabs and Schmidt felt abhorrence towards the idea of having sexual intercourse with men was without doubt borrowed from the casuistry on sexual inversion, as this had been one of the characteristic symptoms of inborn homosexuality.[45] Marriage proposals were rejected and even masculinity in women disgusted them. In Germany at the time, where homosexuality was high on the political agenda, this was one of the methods for proving that homosexuals and lesbians could not 'help' their sexual inclinations and certainly would not be able to 'overcome' these. By showing examples of hermaphroditism in which the person in question had herself 'sensed' her 'true sex' through her distinct attraction to feminine women and disgust for men and masculinity, as in the case of Anna Laabs, Hirschfeld intended to prove plausibly that homosexuals must similarly possess some as yet undiscovered physical characteristic which caused their sexual inclination.[46]

A quite different employment of new psychological insights into the sexual functioning of human beings, clearly inspired by psychoanalytic methods, can be found in the case history reported by Zangger. Compared with Hirschfeld's cases, he paid even more attention to the psychological life of his patient and thereby revealed his interest in seemingly unimportant details such as her gestures and manner of speaking. He, for example, reported:

> Then she said, laughing a little, that she had originally complained to her sisters that she wasn't getting periods; they then laughed at her and said she should count herself lucky. Then she laughed too and it became easier for her; she even teased her sisters from time to time about their 'curse'.[47]

Zangger, moreover, not only noticed which sex the woman was attracted to during libidinous dreams, but also reported the complete content of the dream:

> She also said (if very reluctantly and embarrassed) after particular hints which she immediately understood, that for many years she has very often had arousing dreams of a sexual nature in which a man wants to rape her, for instance in the woods or on a remote road she was on, or in which someone seeks to climb into bed with her. These dreams do not usually relate to a specific person she knows, but always concern men. She also said that she had a dream the previous night at the clinic, probably suggested by a conversation two fellow patients had held that day. She dreamed of giving birth, felt tension and pain in her belly, but could not give birth. Then the doctor who had recently operated on her arrived holding forceps, but she sought to defend herself and then woke up. On one previous occasion she had a dream in which she really did give birth; she watched as the child was taken from her belly and the umbilical cord was severed.[48]

The footnotes to the text refer to other literature on dreams, to the diagnostic value of dreams and to the relationship between the sexual imagination in the dream and during the sexual act. Zangger therefore employed an emerging approach to dreams and sexuality in an analysis of a hermaphrodite's case for the first time (without explicitly referring to Freud or Jung, however). His interpretation of the interview also differed considerably from earlier case histories as he lends much significance to the details of his patient's statements:

> In this case all statements seem consistent with a feminine sensibility. Pure sexuality does not occupy the foreground in women when awake, as it does with men. Psychology plays a central role in their desires; the need for a person who can mean something to them, for family, children. It is difficult to catch the purely sexual in her statements during conscious observation (particularly with a woman of her educational level) as it manifests itself almost exclusively in the gentle nuance of a slightly exaggerated movement, or a slightly embarrassed joke.[49]

Rather than, like Hirschfeld, using the hermaphrodite's conscious knowledge of his or her sexual desires, Zangger preferred to focus on subconscious signs of sexuality. These signs were expressed by unintended gestures, a shy laugh, and the content of dreams and daydreams. According to him, this method was in particular apt for women, for they would not be conscious of 'pure sexuality'. Zangger was no exception in attributing shame with regard to sexual functioning to women in particular; earlier physicians had also labelled shame on the part of the hermaphrodite as a particular sign of femininity. But he was the first to interpret that shame as a hidden signifier only he, as the expert, could read. Thus, analogously to the way the person had been dislodged from a microscopic analysis of gonads or their secretions in order to find a true physical marker of sex, here the truth of the sex of self could only be found in sexual desires of which the person was not conscious and which had to be analyzed objectively by an expert.

The difference between Zangger's and Hirschfeld's way of making the sex of self into an object of enquiry demonstrates a particular aspect of the crucial shift Freudian psychoanalysis entailed: while Kösters and Hirschfeld struggled with 'taming' their patients' subjective stories and statements into objective observations and classifications, the concept of the subconscious helped psychiatrists to enact a (sex of) self already detached from these.

STATISTIC RELATIONS

As Anne Fausto-Sterling and, more recently, Rebecca M. Jordan Young have demonstrated, intersex has played an enormous role in scientifically establishing the interrelation between what has come to be labelled as sex, gender and sexuality.[50] Since the late 1950s, numerous scientists have published a huge number of articles and books on this issue, in which intersexed people provided the much needed exceptions to find out the rule. This 'use and abuse', to quote Fausto-Sterling, of intersex in science by looking for statistical relationships between physical sex (and its many manifestations) and the sex of self (and its manifold indications) presupposes and reaffirms a neat separation of body and self.

As has been argued extensively in the last part of this book, however, neither the 'sex of self' nor 'sexuality' can be seen as given, natural, a-historical entities, but they must be considered the paradoxical products of separating 'physical sex' scientifically from everyday enactments of a person's sex. Therefore, I see the creation of the concept of a sex of self as a process of curdling, in which a seemingly harmonious unity – the sex of a person – came apart into different elements – physical sex, sex of self, and sexual identity. From the end of the nineteenth century onwards, when gonadal sex could be isolated from the person as a whole, the everyday manifestations of the sex of a person started to become part of a clinically observed, described and analyzed separate 'sex of self'. New techniques, varying from a straightforward observation of the clinician's own impressions, through systematic questionnaires, to a psychoanalytically inspired reading of subconscious signs, were employed to enact this sex of self clinically.

The last technique employed to curdle the sex of a person I want to discuss here, was to wonder explicitly how gonadal sex and the sex of self might or might not be related. As we have already seen in the preceding chapter, Neugebauer assumed a relationship between the direction of the sexual desires of someone raised a female, yet gonadally male, and the eventual descending of testicles or the ejaculation of sperm: it could change if the gonads started functioning. He therefore warned that such a young woman's own perception of her sex should not be normative for surgery or sex assignment. Others had expressed similar assumptions, such as Debierre and Guermonprez, although Mulder in 1844 explicitly rejected the idea that the descent of testicles would change anything in terms of sexual desires.[51] Such remarks often seem to have been based on incidental, unsystematic evidence; an intuitive guess rather than a seriously analyzed or precisely defined relation.

As Ulrike Klöppel has argued beautifully, it was the gonadal criterion for sex introduced by Klebs in 1876 which simultaneously and paradoxically sharpened the scientific question concerning the role of the gonads in the forming of other sexual characteristics and functions.[52] After all, the microscopic analysis of the gonads in an increasing number of cases revealed that there were cases in which the outward anatomical appearance did not correspond to the gonads. New scientific questions about this relationship arose and were scientifically addressed. The same happened, as Klöppel has also pointed out, to the relationship between gonads and 'sexual consciousness'.[53] Klöppel's argument focused on the scientific and theoretical debate, as opposed to my analysis of clinical practices.

Neugebauer was the first to investigate the relationship between gonads and 'sexual consciousness' statistically. Probably partly triggered by his own deeply ambiguous standpoint with regard to the criteria for sex assignment – first arguing for a strict gonadal norm, then claiming that person's own sexual consciousness should be left intact – he used his enormous collection of case histories to investigate the possible relationship between gonadal sex and 'consciousness' quantitatively. In the extended register of the 1257 cases described in his book, he sums up all the cases in which 'male pseudo-hermaphrodites, raised as girls, spontaneously recognize their male sex and want to change their sex assignment'.[54] He also listed all the cases in which the hermaphrodite refused to change the sex assigned to her at birth after an 'error of sex' had been established, and separately enumerated all the cases in which the 'consciousness of sex did not correspond to the character of the gonads'.[55] If anything, these numbers showed, as Neugebauer had already stated, that in cases of male pseudo-hermaphrodites raised as females 'heterosexual' (female-directed) feelings sometimes 'emerged violently', often leading to the establishment of an error of sex, while others retained their 'female', male-directed or 'homosexual' desires.[56] These first attempts to examine such a relationship between gonadal sex and the sex of self statistically were another indication of how the sex of self came into being as a separate object of medical concern *as a result of* reducing physical sex to gonadal signifiers. But it also shows how new ways of controlling the continuity and stability of the sexual order started to come into being.

PHANTOM LIMB

If the self of hermaphrodites was increasingly taken seriously as something of clinical concern, and physicians started to develop methods to take psychic issues into account, did that mean that the earlier moral and legal constraints had started to be removed? Did sex become something that was ultimately up to the individual hermaphrodite? This chapter has demonstrated how, with the emergence of a concept of the sex of self, entirely new ways of preserving the social and moral order of sex were introduced.

The scientific establishment of a hermaphrodite's sex on the basis of (extirpated) gonads cut sex off from the social and moral body in which it was inscribed, as well as from its everyday bodily enactment. However, the social, moral and legal constraints as well as the links between the category of sex and the many outer physical signs of sex, which had been separated from gonadal sex, were now imagined as something deeply anchored *within* the person. They started to be rearticulated as aspects of an inalienable, inner sex of self, a self that could not be changed at will and existed independently of gonadal sex. In other words: the sex of self appeared as a phantom limb in which the amputated links to a moral and social order, as well as to a person's physical appearance and visible sexual functioning, were still strongly felt. They reappeared as an imagined sex of self.

Far from wanting to suggest that this phantom limb – the sex of self – came into being immediately and everywhere sex was reduced to gonads in the laboratory, I have wanted to show how this rearticulation of the problem of doubtful sexes emerged at the exact time that gonadal sex could finally be diagnosed anatomically through biopsies from living people. In other words, the emergence of the sex of self as an object of concern and analysis in cases of hermaphroditism was incidental to the so-called 'objectification' of sex at the turn of the twentieth century. This could be initially demonstrated by the emergence of the topic of disclosure in cases in which a person's sex had not raised doubt among lay people, but only became doubtful after intense medical examination and sometimes surgery. In such cases, the hermaphrodite's own awareness of being male or female started to be presented as inviolable, whereas the public moral order was no longer always sacrosanct. At the same time, techniques for enacting a sex of self clinically were employed for the first time: appreciation of the hermaphrodite's own sense of sex, description of the physician's impressions, the diagnostic approach of clinical interviews, systematic diagnostic questionnaires, and psychoanalytic readings of involuntary and subconscious expressions of sex.

However, instead of creating a whole new, authentic, personal, idiosyncratic experience of sex, this chapter has shown that psychological sex was not much more than a projection of age-old sexed moral and social positions on to the screen of an inner self. By projecting the outer order of sex on to personal preferences, inclinations and aversions – as if these were entirely authentic, original, individual feelings instead of discursively pre-structured characteristics of sex – the stability of the sexual order could be maintained. After all, this sex of self was deeply anchored in the hermaphrodite's psyche from early childhood on and thus guaranteed stability. This is markedly different from what was described in chapter 2, where hermaphrodites could suddenly change their inclinations for work, clothing and sexuality as they grew up. Control now happened through observation and surveillance of the psyche by physicians. The new emphasis on the importance of the sex of self therefore started to displace the responsibility for maintaining the sexual order from the public social and moral (and eventual legal) body to the consulting room of a physician. Whereas judgements about their sex had made hermaphrodites into (dis)obeying subjects, this way of clinically disciplining and normalizing the sex of self *implicated* hermaphrodites through the affirmation of their sex of self. A criticism of physicians not paying due respect to the hermaphrodites' own sense of sex and sexuality misses that critical point entirely.

Finally, the creation of a scientific search for the relationship between physical sex and psychological sex was another new medical technique of control and discipline. In the future, it would increasingly define which psychological characteristics and sexual inclinations should be considered 'natural' or 'normal' or at least statistically predominant for women and men. Naturalizing and normalizing sex therefore began to replace legal and moral prescriptions.

Nevertheless, while the examples of concern for the hermaphrodite's psychological well-being abound, the examples of techniques *diagnosing* the sex of self were actually quite scarce and mostly far from original. The most developed technique – a systematic bio-psychological questionnaire – proves to originate in studies of sexual inversion by the sexologist Magnus Hirschfeld who, in turn, based himself on Krafft-Ebing's studies of sexuality. Therefore, in the case of hermaphrodites, not many physicians turned out to have initiated techniques necessary for mapping an interior sex of self. As twentieth-century developments with regard to intersex in the USA show, it took quite a long time before the sex of self could be enacted according to accepted clinical or scientific standards.[57] Only in the 1950s and 1960s, did the idea that, first and foremost, future damage to the sex of self in the shape of sex reassignment should be prevented, start to dominate clinical treatment.[58]

In contrast to hermaphrodites, most (male) homosexuals were part of sexual subcultures, in which at least from the end of the eighteenth century onwards notions of the inborn and 'natural' character of male-to-male desire started to circulate, and in which certain types of males and females were recognized as same-sex lovers. In response to Foucault's famous hypothesis of the invention of homosexuality at the end of the nineteenth century, some historians of homosexuality have therefore argued that homosexuals themselves had invented homosexual identity much earlier, not medical psychiatrists.[59] The fact that hardly any physicians who were not already involved with gays and lesbians introduced techniques to examine the hermaphrodite's sex of self beyond their own first-hand impression, offers perfect proof that (male) homosexuals and their urban subcultures must indeed have played an initiating, significant role in the conceptualization and clinical enactment of homosexuality as an inborn identity. I will return in more detail to this discussion of the emergence of the sexual self in the next and final chapter.

9

SCRIPTING THE SELF.
N. O. BODY'S AUTOBIOGRAPHY

IDENTITY AS A SCRIPT

Barbin and N. O. Body

The protagonists of N. O. Body's autobiography *Aus einem Mannes Mädchenjahren* (*Memoirs of a Man's Maiden Years*), published in 1907, and of Barbin's autobiographical writings have a lot in common.[1] Both were raised as girls and only discovered that they were male in their twenties. Both had already had a passionate love affair with a woman for quite some time before the medical discovery of the error of sex. For both the breakthrough came after a confession of their life story, which in both cases led to a medical examination. Both had been more or less aware that there had been a mistake with regard to their sex, although Barbin seemed to have been more clear about the exact nature of the mistake than N. O. Body. Both were relatively well educated and obviously modelled their narratives on fictional or (auto)biographical examples they themselves had read.

The *texts* also share characteristics. Both stories were published within the framework of a scientific discourse. Barbin's autobiography was part of a treatise by Tardieu on the identity of the sexes, in which the Jumas case was also extensively described. N. O. Body's book was provided with both a foreword by the contemporary German author Rudolf Presber and an epilogue by Magnus Hirschfeld (see the previous chapter, in particular the case history of Anna Laabs). Both were also rediscovered in the 1980s and 1990s, during which they were given yet another introductory frame. The introduction to Barbin was Foucault's famous essay (see chapter 3) and Hermann Simon wrote a short introduction to N. O. Body's autobiography, as well as a long piece, 'Who was N. O. Body?', on his attempts to trace the historical person of N. O. Body (Martha/Max Baer) before and after his sex reassignment.

There are, however, also fundamental differences between the two autobiographies. Important is the fact that Barbin's memoirs were found after his death and were edited and published by Tardieu, whereas N. O. Body's memoirs were published under his own control. Although Barbin refers to the future readers of his text several times, indicating that he intended it to be published, the last part of the text does not give the impression of being

ready for publication at all. As we have seen, towards the end it gets very
fragmented as a narrative and more diary-like, containing outbursts of rage
and desperation. In contrast, N. O. Body's autobiography must have been
very carefully constructed, given the fact that he completely and precisely
concealed the fact that he was a Jew. Hermann Simon has demonstrated
how he carefully changed every detail that could refer to his real person,
in particular his Jewishness. Sander Gilman has shown that this included
the description of his body which was the antithesis of what was considered
typically Jewish at the time.[2] Therefore, N. O. Body was very much more in
control of the message his narrative constructed than Barbin.

And there is more. Barbin's text is drowned in a pious and sentimental
Roman Catholicism; its style echoes romanticized narratives of saints or
other pious, moralist literature. N. O. Body's text is written in the context
of the women's and homosexual emancipation movement and betrays a
wide-ranging interest in medicine, social politics and science. Barbin confessed to a bishop while N. O. Body first confided his story to a doctor. The
most dramatic difference, however, concerns the conclusion of the history
told. In N. O. Body's text the episode of the discovery of his male physical sex
works as a catharsis. Just some days before, N. O. Body had bought poison
to commit suicide together with his lover Hanna; he was waiting for her
to come to Berlin. After his foot was seriously injured in an accident and a
physician visited him, he started to cry and finally told his whole life history
to this unknown doctor. The doctor examined his genitals and declared
him to be male. From then on, N. O. Body foresaw a bright future in which
he would/could marry his lover. In Barbin's text, as we have seen, the sex
reassignment was not at all the happy turning point in a difficult life. He
felt obliged to abandon his job, his lover and his place of birth and became
totally lost in his life as a man in Paris. His change of civil sex meant a total
dislocation which ultimately led to his isolation and suicide. How can we
explain this extreme difference in the stories' outcomes after what was basically
the same course of events?

The previous chapter presented some forms of enacting a sex of self: noting
the self-understanding of the person and the physician's own first impression,
analysis of personal characteristics and preferences as biographical constants,
psychoanalytic reading of subconscious gestures and expressions, objectify-
ing sexual desires. There is no doubt these were for the most part adopted
from psychiatrists and sexologists engaged in the subject of sexual inversion.
But the most important enactment of the sex of self, developed under the
strong influence of these case histories of sexual inversion, has not yet been
broached: the *scripting* of the self. In this chapter, I will first argue on the
basis of discussions in gay and lesbian history that precisely this scripting of
sexual *and* sexed selves as the discovery of a true identity was new to the late

nineteenth century. Then I will analyze the autobiographic narrative published in 1907 by N. O. Body, whose life history resembles Barbin's in so many ways, but whose scripting and writing of that story was so notably different. This difference indicates the ground-breaking emergence of the new rationale of sex as a representation of the self from the start of the twentieth century. It shows how the relationship with the self became prioritized above one's position vis-à-vis others, as the individual quest for an inner truth of sex started to replace the desperate search for a morally acceptable position in society.

THE HISTORICAL EMERGENCE OF (HOMO)SEXUAL IDENTITY

Homosexual identity after Foucault

Since Michel Foucault presented his revolutionary idea that late nineteenth-century medical psychiatry invented homosexual identity, this idea has been further elaborated, criticized and discussed by many historians of homosexuality and lesbianism.[3] The result, so far, of this discussion among historians – who all to a certain extent agree on the idea that homosexual identity was a historical construction – has led to a schism of opinion that can be roughly described as follows. Some argue that the major changes already took place in the early eighteenth century with the emergence of a third gender role, an accompanying urban subculture of men who could recognize each other, and the first indications of sodomites referring to themselves as a certain kind of people with inborn characteristics. Some commentators have cautiously left the matter of identity in this era out of their arguments, such as for instance Theo van der Meer.[4] Others, like for example Randolph Trumbach, have made full-blown attacks on Foucault 'and his followers' who situated the birth of the homosexual identity in the late nineteenth century. According to him, the emerging homosexual and heterosexual roles he discerned in early eighteenth-century London did not differ fundamentally from later nineteenth-century medical psychiatric conceptions of homosexuals or from the way these homosexuals conceived of themselves.[5] In contrast, many other historians have stuck to the late nineteenth century as the era in which both the homosexual and heterosexual identities were born.[6] An exception is Harry Oosterhuis' study of Krafft-Ebing, who carefully created a very useful distinction between the early eighteenth-century sodomite's role and the late nineteenth-century homosexual identity.

Things are even more complicated in the case of the birth of the lesbian identity, since the sources referring to lesbian sex are far scarcer and lesbian subcultures hardly bloomed anywhere. The question of how to prove the historical existence of erotic and sexual relations between women or how to define these precedes the 'identity discussion'. Moreover, the problem of the connection of lesbianism respectively to women who passed as men or female masculinity in general, romantic friendship between women, feminism or the women's movement have turned out to be tricky and difficult.[7] In this historical field there have also been alternative tendencies: to place the emergence of a lesbian identity before the late nineteenth century and out-side a medico-psychiatric context, and to stick to that period and context in search of the modern lesbian identity.[8]

As to early modern lesbian and gay selves, authors such as Trumbach, Van der Meer and Donoghue have demonstrated that the idea of a sodomite or tribade as a specific type of person, with a specific gender role, as a mem-ber of a category that could be named and recognized as such, and finally, as someone who was looking for a justification for his or her sexual acts and inclinations by turning them into an 'inborn' characteristic had already emerged in the eighteenth century. Moreover, for male same-sex-lovers extensive gay subcultures can be discerned in major urban areas. Does this mean that 'the homosexual identity' already existed in gay subcultures and lesbian lives by then, and was only 'reinvented' by medical psychiatry at the end of the nineteenth century? The previous chapter has given strong evidence for the idea that the ways of understanding same-sex desire as something 'inborn' created in early modern, male-to-male urban subcultures must indeed have prompted psychiatrists and physicians to investigate (homo)sexuality as part of someone's genuine personality. After all, in case histories of hermaphrodites – who were generally not part of urban sexual subcultures – physicians hardly initiated ways of investigating the sex of self on their own account. They only acknowledged its importance after the turn of the century, more than three decades after Karl Heinrich Ulrichs's famous phrase 'a female soul trapped in a male body', and the first medico-psychiatric publications on sexual inversion appeared.

Yet, there is a huge difference between the self-understanding developed in relation to persecution and subcultural codes, on the one hand, and the late nineteenth-century homosexual identity, on the other. The major difference does not so much lie in the idea of a separate gay or lesbian type of person. It is evident that such a concept had already started to emerge in the eighteenth century – which by the way certainly does not mean that *all* gender inversion or same-sex sexuality was interpreted as inherent in someone's personal constitution. What differs, however, is the *shape* in which such a 'type of person' or 'personality' was enacted. One and a half centuries of developing ways to express the self through a well-ordered narrative divide the modern homosexual identity from the earlier tribade or sodomite. Casual references to their 'inborn nature' in eighteenth- and early nineteenth-century letters written by sodomites, typical modes of behaviour, dress or speech, words for certain types of sodomites or self-legitimizations during confessions before capital punishment *are not the same* as page-long autobiographical musings on early childhood experiences, lifelong desires and the frustration of desires, dreams, fantasies, experiences and emotions that culminate in an acknowledgement of being 'sexually inverted'. My own work has shown how, towards the end of the nineteenth century, the European tradition of women passing as men transformed from a temporary trespass and deceit into something signifying a person's lifelong pathological identity. The deceit would go with stories plotting the discovery of the masquerade and thus restore order. The identity tales, contrastingly, demand extensive descriptions of a person's lifelong inner drives, desires, emotions, preferences and dreams, as well as a reordering of these elements as symptoms for a certain type of sexual pathological identity.[9] Briefly, I would say that in the case of sodomites and tribades in the eighteenth and early nineteenth centuries, we should talk about a certain type of *person* – with a particular sexual role or script, a certain appearance, who were often labelled as a specific category (molly, tribade) – whereas towards the end of the nineteenth century a lesbian and homosexual *identity* emerged – a dramatic narration with the true, inner sexual self as outcome.

Scripting the (male) homosexual self

Such a scripting of the self, however, was not something people did naturally. Just as the internal physical body was not simply 'there', but had to be entered and 'read' with the help of many routines, practices, techniques, institutions, professional knowledge, etc., so exploring and scripting the inner self required methods of self-reflection, professional psychiatric or psychological skills and knowledge, narrative scripts, and not in the least an 'urge to know'. This section will briefly describe the main characteristics of the development of the complex of practices, routines and techniques involved in narrating one's (homo)sexual self. Klaus Müller and Harry Oosterhuis have with great flair shown how new ways of scripting the self in general influenced the way in which homosexuals scripted their particular selves.

The urge to justify or understand one's own homosexual practices by referring to an unchangeable, lifelong and strong desire, albeit pathological, unnatural or at least deviant, seems to have existed primarily among bourgeois and upper-class men. Women did not show much eagerness to tell their stories, whereas lower-class men seemed to have been relatively less inclined to contact a psychiatrist.[10] Middle-class men probably had a strong motivation to justify and explain sexual behaviour and desires which were so ostensibly at odds with Victorian bourgeois morals, and which seemed to degrade their gender status. For women of all classes, passing and masculinity was always also related to an increase in status, even if it was considered deviant.[11] Working-class men might have been less bothered by Victorian morals, but more likely did not have the time, education and money required for consulting or writing to a psychiatrist.

Klaus Müller has shown how the publication of a huge number of brief male homosexual autobiographies (*Kurzbiographien*) was the result of cooperation between psychiatrists and male same-sex-lovers from 1870 onwards. The autobiographical stories were always published within the framework of psychiatric discourse (otherwise they would not have been published at all). They served as examples in general medico-psychiatric theories, taxonomies or analyses of sexual inversion. Sometimes, such a framework only consisted of just one or two remarks on the part of the psychiatrist, who then left the floor to the homosexual's story. Müller shows how, as a consequence, the narrative was strongly dictated by the codes and form of case histories.[12] For example, the writers demanded precision and strict adherence to the truth from themselves, and built up their story in the sequence of anamnesis, symptoms and therapy.[13] According to Müller, the stories therefore mix confession, aetiology and autobiography, expressing strong feelings of guilt, striving for a sometimes painful 'naked truth', and search for constant characteristics in one's life history, especially with regard to one's sexual desires.[14] Moreover, most autobiographical narrators describe themselves in terms of masculinity and femininity, embracing Ulrich's concept of a feminine soul trapped in a male body while mostly rejecting the idea that their desire for men could be detected from (other/outward) feminine traits.[15]

By publishing these autobiographical short stories in forensic and medico-psychiatric texts, psychiatrists and physicians – notably Krafft-Ebing with his almost annual edition of his famous *Psychopathia Sexualis* – therefore provided a platform for homosexuals to express their own identity and find other people like themselves. Here identity has the double meaning of one's own authentic, idiosyncratic inner self as well as that of belonging to a category of 'identical' people.[16] Such publishing practices, with their standard medical narrative framework and their imitation of other case histories therefore strongly shaped the way homosexuals scripted their identity.

Müller does not clearly explain why, all of a sudden, male same-sex-lovers developed such a desire to speak up, to 'no longer keep secret', to verbalize feelings that hitherto 'didn't have a name'. In his opinion, it was easy to understand, because it was a way for male same-sex-lovers to find words for unknown feelings and identify with others.[17] But was the interest from psychiatrists and other doctors enough to explain their sudden will to tell, to bare their intimate forbidden desires? Had the wish to 'come out' always existed, as something naturally given? I would dare to doubt that. Another explanation Müller has provided for this willingness to tell seems more adequate and interesting to me: the new identity narrative helped to transform the existing guilt and confession discourse into a compulsion to tell the truth about a self which was definitely considered pathological, but was also natural and unchangeable.[18] This, I think, is also of crucial importance in understanding how Barbin's story differed so fundamentally from N. O. Body's.

Harry Oosterhuis has put the emerging autobiographical narration of 'sexual deviants' in the larger framework of the booming interest in autobiographical writing in general. According to him, 'the nineteenth-century fashion for the autobiographical genre' demanded a life history to be a 'voyage of self-discovery', 'interrupted by frequent misdirections and confused by inward struggles'. There was a strong emphasis on the interior, inner truth, which contrasted a 'real self' with the role one played in society.[19] Autobiography was a place where idiosyncratic individual difference could be expressed – even against the rules of Victorian self-control and bourgeois morals – because 'being different and unique was the source and measure of individual worth'.[20] This demanded the awareness of an inner space, of inner motives and desires, and the capacity to reflect on these. Self-discovery entailed processes that were the exact opposite of nineteenth-century middle-class ideals, such as loss of self-control, sexual desire, doubt, etc. One way of getting to know this always deeply hidden self was to revive childhood experiences, to make memory (and forgetting) an object of reflection, and to take dreams seriously. It was in this already existing climate that Freud's theories found such response.[21]

Same-sex-lovers' autobiographical narratives were moulded on this method of self-narration. This can be seen in several characteristics of these narratives, according to Oosterhuis. Childhood experiences were very important, showing sexual desires to be not just temporary impulses but constants in a life history.[22] The stories contained minute observations of people's lives as a means of searching for the hidden truth of their deviant sexual desires. They often claimed that suppression of these desires would be harmful to them, or lamented having to hide their 'real selves'.[23] This is demonstrated by narrating how, after a period of troubles and doubts, the true character of the self appears during a moment of intense crisis. During that crisis, the autobiographical subjects' authentic feelings conflict with the morals of their environment. This often leads to a catharsis, during which negative self-images are transformed into more positive images of one's own authentic truth.[24]

My own analysis of the transformation of a lawsuit against a woman who passed as a man into a psychiatric case history of sexual inversion has furthermore revealed that, within the latter, such a life history was dissected into symptoms which, in turn, constituted the elements of a systematic, psychiatric taxonomy of sexual perversions. A biographical narrative therefore became a fixed identity.[25] Oosterhuis summarized the standardized elements of such a coming-out narrative / sexual identity as follows:

Descent, family background, the retrospective discovery of a peculiar way of
feeling and acting during childhood and puberty, the conviction that one has
always felt the same, the first sexual experiences, the struggle with masturbation
that often raised more anxieties than did sexual contacts with other individuals,
details about sexual fantasies, dreams and behaviour, the exploration of one's
health and gender identity in the past and present, the sense of being overwhelmed by irresistible and 'natural' drives for which one is not responsible,
the (mostly failed) attempts to have 'normal' sexual intercourse (usually with
a prostitute) in order to 'test' the constitutional character of one's sexual preference, the painful knowledge of being different and in conflict with society,
the sense of isolation, the comforting discovery of not being alone, and the
efforts towards moral self-justification.[26]

These new scripts, with their standardized structure and themes, deeply
affected the way N. O. Body told the story of his childhood and adolescence
as a girl and young woman. I believe they also account for the extreme difference in outcome between Barbin's story and his. The transformation these
two hermaphrodites' autobiographical narratives demonstrate reflect Charles
Taylor's hypothesis that, over the last few centuries, the self has become a
'constitutive good' fundamental to the Western moral system.

N. O. BODY

Veracity and true being

'This book is a book of truth'; N. O. Body opens the story of his life with
these words.[27] This truth was initially used in opposition to fantasy or lie, for
the narrator calls the childhood that will be related 'the rarest childhood ever
lived' which despite its strangeness has to be 'believed'.[28] This introduction
contributes to what Philippe Lejeune has called the autobiographical pact –
reassuring the reader that the author, the narrator and the 'I' are identical and
actually exist.[29] The introductory frame of the text has the same effect: Rudolf
Presber reveals the origin of the text and thereby confirms the authenticity
of the story and its author. N. O. Body's text was said to be the exact copy of
the spontaneous and sincere story he had verbally told the author who wrote the
introductory lines. However, to N. O. Body, what was much more important
was that throughout the text truth exists as an essence (or 'inner nature' or
'being'; *Wesen* in German) in opposition to an outward, false appearance:

> I was born a boy, raised as a girl. My life was woven from a twisted muddle
> of threads until, with a powerful blow, the inner essence of my masculinity
> ripped apart the veils, covers and half-truths which upbringing, habit and
> necessity had woven around me. A healthy boy can be raised as feminine as can
> be, a female as manly as can be; this will still never permanently make them
> feel thus inverted.[30]

As Myriam Spörri commented, the theme of truth versus falsehood is reflected by the metaphor of light versus darkness, which is almost omnipresent throughout the book.[31] The struggle between the light of truth and that which covers or conceals it is central to the text.

At this point, N. O. Body's text already diverges markedly from Barbin's as described in chapter 3. Firstly, Barbin's text is about good versus evil, whereas N. O. Body's text centres around the question of truth versus concealment, lies and outward appearance. For Barbin, the category of sex was about *morality*; for N. O. Body, it was a question of *veracity*. Secondly, Barbin talked about his confusion concerning his sex in terms of her right, wrong or impossible *position* within society. N. O. Body referred to this confusion as a contrast between sex as an outward appearance and sex as an inner *being*, an opposition between the sex he was raised as and the sex that had always already defined him from within.[32]

Early youth, school and peers, intimacies

N. O. Body details memories of feeling like a boy from a very early age and recounts memories of exclusion because of his boyish behaviour. In an attempted literary introduction to his early youth, N. O. Body tells the story of a girl excluded from the play of other girls. He sketches a group of children singing and playing in a courtyard:

> All the children are happy and playful except for one, who stands the wrong side of the eaves, letting the falling water drench her boots like a reckless boy. Her eyes wander, half longing, half obstinate over to the little girls, as if she didn't dare join in their games without being asked. And when no-one calls her over, she stamps her little feet obstinately in the puddle to make the water splash up. Now the other children come over, gather round the little girl – this child does at least wear girls' clothes – and shout 'Boy, boy, nasty boy!' This startles the child who runs into the house crying. That child was me.[33]

The standard sexual inversion narrative theme of social isolation, of being 'different' than the others in terms of sex from early childhood on, is apparent here. As the opening scene, it directs N. O. Body's whole life history.

Other tales refer to the boyish games Nora – the name N. O. Body gave the I-protagonist – preferred to play. If there was clay to play with, girls would make bowls and dolls, whereas boys would make animals and bullets, N. O. Body claims; Nora, of course, did the latter.[34] At his fifth birthday there was another clear sign of Nora's boyishness. His favourite aunt was visiting, and brought a large package. In the morning he found out what it was:

> There lay a doll, as big as me. So *that* was the wonderful, fine thing my aunt had promised me? I had been looking forward to *that*? I could have wept, but just in time my gaze fell on a hobby-horse . . . Only then was I really

happy . . . So even back then I had no interest in girls' toys and a very clear
leaning towards the games boys played.[35]

Here, we can clearly discern the 'turn inwards' described in the previous
chapter: what had always been an indication for a person's sexed position in
a sexed moral and social order, was now translated into something defining
a person's fixed inclinations and aversions.

At school, things went relatively well at first, but at a certain point in time
Nora's neighbours Hilde and Lene – who had once played an erotic game
with her during which physical difference had been noticed – plotted against
her with the other schoolgirls. She wanted to join their play, but:

> . . . None of the girls spoke to me, or let me into their circle. Quite nervous, I
> asked, but no-one answered me. Hilde looked away, embarrassed. At last Lene
> blurted out: 'Just go away you horrid boy. We don't want to play with boys!'
> I didn't understand her at all. 'You are a real boy; we know that for sure, and
> Fräulein Stieler says so too, and that's why you can't knit. Just go away and
> play with the boys!'[36]

Shocked by the behaviour of his classmates, Nora started to doubt his sex
seriously for the first time in his life, and drew the conclusion that he indeed
must be a boy.[37] Both the theme of 'being different from the others' and the
fitness for certain occupations from early youth on serve as a proof of one's
'real' self here.

As we have seen in chapter 2, until about the 1860s, the rare examples in
which something was said about the difficulties of changing one's sex, concerned social and moral dislocation, not something psychologically anchored
in the self. This could also be seen in the way in which, in certain cases, a
sudden change of inclinations and aptitude for work, clothing and sexuality
in an adolescent hermaphrodite was narrated. When the rationale of a sex of
self started to become more dominant, such sudden changes were less likely
to be related, as continuity was sought for in the person's inner self. In this
respect, N. O. Body's autobiographical text also clearly differs from that of
Barbin, who never made the most of the characteristics of her childhood to
prove her innate masculine disposition. The same goes for the various ways
in which both authors described their early inclination to girls.

Intimacies

N. O. Body explicitly described his erotic experiences as erotic from very
early on – from a time before he even went to school. Nora and two local
girls, Hilde and Lene, were lying under a big elder on a beautiful spring day.
Sleepy from the heat and the smell of blossom, they started caressing each
other; they couldn't stop feeling under each other's clothes and experienced

a strange sense of well-being. When they also started to explore each other's bodies with their eyes, they discovered the physical differences between them, which would later justify Hilde calling Nora a boy (see above). N. O. Body writes: 'I don't know what led us children to this . . . I [can] remember no incident which would explain these early sexual stirrings in the other, quite normal children.'[38]

Later in life, at the start of puberty, Hilde once again became interested in Nora. All the girls in class were curious about sexual matters, and after Hilde and Nora had got an explanation from the maid, they witnessed a pair of dogs copulating:

> We were possessed by an insane excitement. Hilde threw herself to the ground and laughed hysterically. I was afraid of her laughter, which I could not comprehend; afraid of her eyes and her hands, which sought and clutched me. While I also wanted to feel those hands on my body, the fear of once more revealing my secret to her triumphed over my emotions and drew me away from her loving caresses.[39]

N. O. Body explicitly defined these moments as erotic and sexual; he warned parents and teachers that erotic feelings might arise quite early on in a child's life and that parents should inform their children about sexual matters instead of leaving this to peers and maids.[40] Because of his peculiar build, Nora was of special interest to Hilde and Lene; but N. O. Body does not immediately relate this to his 'true' sex here; he might also be talking about non-gendered infantile eroticism. Further on in the text, however, the connection between the attraction women felt for Nora and his masculine being becomes ever stronger.

A later description of adolescent erotic experiences with a girl accompanied by fantasies and dreams led to desperate doubts about his sex.[41] These doubts gave way again and Nora ascribed her interest in the beauty of female bodies to her artistic inclinations. But N. O. Body – the narrator – names the dreams about one of the girls 'boy's dreams'.[42] These rather vague notices of Nora's erotic feelings as masculine sharpen considerably when N. O. Body describes episodes later in his life. An American student called Harriet, a pretty young woman, was very much attracted to Nora and kissed and hugged him as much as possible. One day, when she was visiting Nora, she threw herself on him and started kissing him frantically while her body 'jolted hysterically'. Nora found this repugnant at first, but then started to answer Harriet's kisses. She left without a word, and Nora – although he dreamt of 'possessing' her – never referred to what had happened again. Nora was afraid of revealing his secret, and thought that Harriet only felt attracted to women; he thought that she would be repelled by him as a man. N. O. Body then comments:

In fact Harriet possessed all the characteristics of a normal girl, had never felt attracted to women and later entered into a normal marriage. It was simply the man in me to which her body had felt instinctively drawn, even though she tried to use all the power of her spirit to combat the hidden drive running deep inside her.[43]

Here N. O. Body acknowledged the existence of the possibility of sexual attraction between women, but used Harriet's future heterosexuality as proof that she had instinctively been attracted to the 'man in him', not to Nora the woman. In other circumstances, he simply presupposed heterosexuality. For example, during the time Nora travelled as a correspondent for a newspaper reporting on the situation of women in Eastern Europe, N. O. Body recalled:

It was often the case that I would share a room with housewives when their husbands were away travelling, and once I had to share a bed with a young girl. At first I found the idea quite frightening. The girl kissed me like mad, but it didn't lead to more intimate relations. She really could feel the man in me. There exists knowledge of the body, stronger than any logic.[44]

Also, the charismatic success of his speeches was attributed to the women's possible subconscious sensual attraction to him.[45]

As for himself, towards the end of the story the impossibility of satisfying his desire for women was increasingly described as unbearable. Nora decided to avoid Harriet in the future, for 'her clutches rendered me weak; I almost passed out. And as I remained insatiate, I was tortured by the wild urges of my whipped-up nerves.'[46]

These interpretations of later erotic and sexual encounters with women were therefore directly linked to Nora's maleness and retrospectively colour the erotic episodes of his youth as heterosexual. The description of unfulfilled erotic desires as increasingly strong and difficult to bear, add to the growing tension of the story. N. O. Body's text therefore carefully builds up the tension by leaving things more confused, misty and unsaid in the beginning, and very slowly working towards a sharper, clearer conflict: his (true) masculine being – sexually and otherwise – contrasting to his (false) appearance as a woman. The story of his intimate relations with women therefore functions completely differently from Barbin's narrative about these relations. Barbin was primarily concerned with the way he might have harmed others by compromising them – desperately and repeatedly directing herself to the reader or to God, asking to put the blame for that on 'fate' or 'the facts of life' more than to her. In contrast, in N. O. Body's text, the first troubled and then increasingly clear feelings for women (and, vice versa, women's feelings for Nora) served as a 'voyage of self-discovery', in which confusion, doubt and misdirection had to be overcome. As we shall see, instead of begging for forgiveness or understanding, others were blamed for their role in concealing the truth.

Finding the true self

N. O. Body's narrative follows the late nineteenth-century coming-out script for sexual inversion to the letter, as it contains almost all the characteristics which Harry Oosterhuis used to describe that narrative.[47] It is marked by a long journey through confusion, doubt and secrecy that finally leads to the truth of self. It is a quest in which finding oneself is the ultimate goal. Doubts about who one truly is thereby structure the story. In N. O. Body's text this question underlies many important and recurring themes of the narrative: the erotic experiences and slowly becoming conscious of these, as we have seen above; moments in which others did not conceive of Nora as a woman, but called her a boy/man, or mannish; the doubts and trouble invoked by the physical characteristics which were unusual for a girl, such as his voice breaking, the absence of menstruation, the appearance of a beard, and his attempts to hide these. These themes centre on a single main question: Who am I – a girl, or not? There are three long passages which describe how Nora was tormented by these doubts. At the age of ten, after having been cruelly rejected by her schoolmates who called her a boy, Nora started wondering whether she really was a girl or not:

> That evening, when I was alone in my little room, I inspected my body. That just wasn't true! I wasn't a boy at all! Mama called me her little girl after all . . . If I was indeed different in nature from the rest of them, why should I not then also be bodily different? I was almost reassured again, then I suddenly had an uncanny awareness: the others down there, they really were quite different from me! And I was gripped by an unnamed panic.[48]

Nora wanted to ask her mother about it the next morning, but then did not dare to. She was frightened to go to school and at home she brooded as to why she had been given a girl's name.[49] On reading the classical story of Achilles, Nora finally found a way out: of course, she was actually a king's son who had been sent to strangers to be raised safely! Nora withdrew from his peers for a while and started living in a fantasy world of classical stories and books. A period of playing wild games with boys followed, a sudden rejection by the boys for being a girl, and a period of renewed friendships with the girls. At the age of fourteen or fifteen, Nora often had erotic fantasies and dreams about women, and started doubting her sex again: 'The old doubts rose once more. What was I exactly? Boy or girl? If I was a girl, why didn't I grow breasts?'[50]

Later on, these explicit doubts about her sex seemed to have disappeared for a while. N. O. Body remarks that at a certain point during adolescence Nora stopped thinking she was a boy. From that moment onwards, most troubles concerning her identity had to do with her relationships with women. They fell in love with her; she was physically attracted and increasingly tortured by unfulfilled sexual desires. She was conscious of her 'uniqueness' (*Eigenart*) and was again troubled by 'the nature of her personality' when she and her friend Lucie started desiring each other.[51] After having fallen madly in love with Hanna Bernhardowna, explicit doubts about his sex re-emerged:

> Worries and doubts continually returned to torment me anew. What was I really then? A man? Oh God, no. That would be an amazing stroke of luck. But miracles do not happen today. I knew nothing any more. My whole life seemed to have worked like a strong suggestion blurring the truth. Everyone saw in me a woman, even my girlfriend called me Nora. How could I have ever thought I was a man? I was an abnormally built girl, that was all! And this feeling? I didn't know, neither of us knew. How could this blissful, compulsive force be a vice? How could the intoxication of pure bliss, the highest beauty in life, be a vice?[52]

At the very end of his narrative he was about to commit suicide together with Hanna. This was a typical, romantic and dramatic act for homosexual couples at the time, also often used as proof of the suffering of homosexuals in campaigns for their emancipation.[53] It was one of the oft narrated cathartic moments in homosexual autobiographies.[54] It is then that Nora was visited by a doctor for having a injured foot. The doctor asked why he was crying so hard, and Nora finally confessed all his misery. After examining her, the doctor affirmed the naturalness of his sexual feelings – for these were heterosexual – and finally the lifelong confusion these feelings was solved:

> My love for my girlfriend was not a vice . . . ; it was a natural feeling. 'If you want to be with your girlfriend and you can offer her a secure future, then go ahead and marry her! You are just as much of a man as I am!'. . . It was as if a dark veil fell from my eyes. The doctor was right. In a bodily sense I was a man. And it had often been said to me that I had a masculine mind . . . Now the dark journey ahead of us was lit by a bright light.[55]

All the prior doubts, troubles, questions and uncertainties suddenly seemed to fall in place. There were still many problems left which were all described by N. O. Body: How to inform his family? How would Hanna react? How to proceed legally? How to find a job without being able to refer to prior education and experiences? How to clothe himself and behave like a man? Even so, the main trouble, the question of who he actually was, had been overcome: the hero had found his goal (his self) and could marry the princess (indeed N. O. Body refers to Hanna as a queen). This closure, of course, stands in marked contrast to the way Barbin's text ended: in total confusion and isolation, fragmented, desperately addressing God and his future readers.

The homosexual story of the 'female soul trapped in a male body' is very similar to N. O. Body's story. Even if N. O. Body also used the physical evidence of his maleness, his inner male *being* was much more important. This is also how Hirschfeld 'read' N. O. Body's story, for he emphatically denied that it was the body that defined N. O. Body's being. The story, Hirschfeld wrote in the epilogue, was a classic example of the struggle between 'inborn disposition' and 'outside influences', and showed how 'certain inner drives' could violently break through the obstacles built up through education and environment. These were the forces of the mind, according to Hirschfeld, for: '*The sex of a human being is located much more in his soul than in his body.*'[56] Therefore, I do not think that N. O. Body's tale simply underwrites the rationale of sex as a proper representation of physical sex. It is more an exemplification of the rationale of sex as an inviolable part of the self. The body – which also in this story has to be dislodged from the person to be diagnosed medically – was a separate object, which here happily corresponds to N. O. Body's being. But the very same stories were told – at least in narratives of sexual inversion – in which such a being 'breaks through' *despite* the characteristics of the body. The medically objectified body then started to play this ambiguous role of either *confirming* the self or being the *counterpoint* against which the self defined itself.[57] The important thing was how the sex of self had become something understood and enacted separately from the sex of the body.

Writing the self: the search for the hidden inside
As we saw in chapter 3, if we turn to the act of writing instead of the plotting of the text, Barbin's text turned out to have changed from primarily being *histoire* to being mostly *discourse*. Instead of leading the reader towards a neat closure which the I-protagonist headed for from the start, control over the story was lost. The text became diary-like, not the plot, but the 'now' of the writing became central, and the reader was addressed directly. Barbin did not use his writing to try and find deeper, unknown layers within himself, I concluded, but kept on trying to restore the disturbed relationship with the outside world by calling a non-existent 'you' into being.

N. O. Body used a quite different strategy to constitute a self and to engage the reader through the act of writing. He extensively explored the inner emotional and erotic life of Nora's childhood and adolescence – detailing certain specific moments, images, dreams and fantasies. Here the self was to be expressed not through communication from subject to subject, but through the scrutiny of one's deepest, most hidden inner space. Typical of N. O. Body's text are the passages in which he *actualizes* the memories and fantasies of his youth – putting himself (and the reader) *in* the situation he described. A clear example thereof is the following:

The first years of my life passed by normally. I have retained a single image from this time, a fleeting, flash-like memory. I must have been very little at the time. *A tall, blonde woman took my nightdress off, making jokes, and put me in a bathtub. I saw, however, that despite her cheery words there were tears in her eyes. Then I was taken to a black cave with a golden star which shed its rays as far as my cot.* Today I can explain this image I held in my memory for so long. It was my mother, who undressed me . . . the woman who had to cry when she saw the body of her child.'[58]

In the first three sentences the first person narrator looks back at his first years of life, at himself at a very young age. Then the text changes (I italicized this): this very young, first-person character looks at a 'tall, blonde woman', etc. The scene is told from little Nora's perspective, including her incomprehension of the situation. The text then returns to the level of reflection of the adult writing, interpreting the image as the mother who bathed her child and took it to bed, and 'had to cry when she saw the body of her child'.[59] Such paragraphs, in which the child's perspective is evoked, are entirely lacking in Barbin's text.

Moreover, in N. O. Body's text it is as if the act of writing spontaneously brought about new memories, more details. It enabled him to put himself in the perspective of the child he once was. The writing works as therapy, or so it seems: more than just writing down an already existing memory, the reader seems to witness this *process* of remembering. For example, 'An evening atmosphere from those years comes to mind', and he subsequently describes how the children cut out figures from magazines.[60] Or he writes: 'That reminds me of a scene . . .'[61] Such phrases suggest that a memory just came to mind while he was writing – which is indeed the way memories are supposed to come: accidentally. Or, he would introduce a story by accentuating the difficulty of remembering it exactly, e.g.:

> I will try to recount how it was back then. It was during a school break. The rain kept us in our classrooms. The girls were playing some kind of singing game; to me at least it is still as if the lost sound of a rhyme is stuck in my ear.[62]

What follows is the painful rejection by the girls in his class because he is a boy – a memory he can apparently only actualize by first going back in his mind to the overall situation in the classroom, by sensing the atmosphere. This style of narration conformed to the convention of authenticity by revealing the sometimes difficult process of remembering.

Above I have already shown that N. O. Body carefully constructed a story in which the significance of Nora's early erotic experiences only very slowly became clear over the course of the story. But he also related things which seemed to escape his own interpretation or which reveal rather nasty fantasies. Some of these are very useful as a piece in the puzzle that is completed at the very end, but some seem rather useless, loose ends that never fit. Consider, for example, his childhood fantasy of taming a tiger:

I had read some story about a boy whose father was a high-ranking Indian . . . [He] tamed a tigress. This made a deep impression on me; I thought the tigress' coat, always depicted next to her master in the book's bright and colourful illustrations, resembled a travelling rug which papa liked to sleep under when he took an afternoon nap. I loved to spread this blanket out in front of me and dream of how I would domesticate the animal.[63]

He only told one girl about these fantasies. Together they made a derelict hen house into the imaginary tiger's cage, and fed it with hay from a nearby stable.

These and other play fantasies abound in N. O. Body's narrative of his childhood. Overall, these stories show how much Nora was already a boy as a child and thus fit neatly into the main plot. But their abundance and detailed description also *escape* this general meaning so that many stories still wait to be deciphered. Why these fantasies about Indian princes (and, elsewhere, wild Negroes)? What made him want to tame the tiger – what did this tiger actually represent? A lot of questions remain unanswered.

Similarly, Nora's adolescent erotic dreams and fantasies were not only mentioned several times, but also described in details that do not *merely* refer to the masculinity of his desires. 'I remember dreams from those days about women, playing in an expanse of water, with soft, white bodies whose undulating lines I saw as a vision appearing from the blue waves. On the seashore stood strange trees.'[64] What were those strange trees doing there on the beach? Why would these women be so white and merge with the blue of the sea so much? There is a depth of self in Nora that we cannot entirely grasp and which also escapes the narrator's final interpretation. N. O. Body surpassed his own carefully constructed narrative with his excessive, detailed writing. Sometimes, this incomprehensible depth is something N. O. Body is ashamed of. For example, when she had nasty, brutal erotic dreams: 'I felt the urge to envelop this girl, to crush and kill her. Then however I was ashamed of these brutal impulses and avoided her on account of them.'[65] The imperative to tell everything in order to find the truth of self, even or especially if it is shameful or disturbing, must have been stronger than the urge to hide such shameful fantasies.

As Harry Oosterhuis has argued, as early as the 1870s and 1880s, psychiatrists and psychologists had considered memory and forgetting a key to the understanding of the self. The inner self was understood to be so vast and well hidden, that special methods were required to reveal its truth. Aspects of the self that were far from valued by bourgeois culture had to be disclosed.

Or rather, the autobiography and other narrations of the self constitute the means *par excellence* by which deviant desires and behaviours could be reconciled with dominant morality. Going back and forth in his mind to trace early memories, dreams and fantasies, it is as if N. O. Body is talking to a psychiatrist, as if there is someone listening out there able to decipher his inner self even better than he is able to himself. This is the way the narrator engages the reader – luring her into trying to find the hidden self in the many stories told. For the most part, this is carefully orchestrated, for the narrator manages to solve most of the riddles in the end: Nora had simply been a boy/man from the very beginning. But the loose ends suggests that there is more to explore, a deeper layer, darker motives, something even better hidden. And that is exactly what defines the modern self: an infinite depth that always escapes complete comprehension.

THE END

N. O. Body's text more or less ends when the decision of sex reassignment is made; only a few pages are used to relate what happened immediately after the decision. Would the story have had quite such a happy ending if N. O. Body had told it ten years later? After all, the true drama of Barbin's narrative only unfolded after the sex reassignment. In other words, is the difference in script of the two autobiographies not merely because of the fact that we do not know how horrible N. O. Body's life was after his sex reassignment?

There is an easy way out of this question: Simon's biographical research has revealed that Karl M. Baer – as he was named after his sex reassignment – led a relatively successful life as a man. Director of one of the Jewish lodges, he had been a prominent member of the Berlin Jewish community, known for his helpfulness and tolerance.[66] There were certainly tragic elements in it: his first wife, Hanna, died three months after their marriage; he remarried later.[67] As a Jew and Zionist he had to flee the Nazi regime in 1938 and went to Palestine.[68] But the sex reassignment had nothing to do with these events.

However, I do not think that the differences between Barbin's and N. O. Body's scripts are simply a question of different realities. Or, to put it even more strongly, I think that the availability of scripts influences the way people make sense of their own lives and inscribe these lives in dominant discourse; indeed, they influence which lives people are actually capable of living. Moreover, the point in time at which the story attains closure is no coincidence; it is related to the story's ultimately moralistic message. What failed Barbin was the coming-out script of sexual inversion, as had just been developed in German-speaking countries between about the 1870s and 1900 – a specific form of *Bildungs*-script in which finding and acknowledging your

true sex *within yourself* (conflicting with the sex of your outward appearance
and upbringing) was the central plot. At the time Barbin was writing her
story, there was as yet no rationale of sex defining it as something ultimately
anchored in the self. Therefore, Barbin's story did not try to discover *who he
truly was* but attempted to justify *his place within society*. The problem connected to this question was not the pain of a damaged and troubled childhood,
but guilt about occupying the wrong place which had compromised the people
he admired and loved. Temporarily, the doctor had taken over the moral
responsibility; his view of the truth about Barbin's sex cut through the knot of
Barbin's moral confusion. In the autopsy report after his suicide, it was held
that this medical decision had returned Barbin 'to his true place in society'.[69]
That should, in the doctor's view, have ended Barbin's trouble. But it did
not solve the disturbance of his social and moral position, and the way this
deeply affected the people he loved. Therefore the story did not end when
his maleness was acknowledged. What was damaged, in Barbin's case, was
never solely and only his own sex of self – for this was inscribed in all sorts
of ways in the social and moral body of which he was part.

In contrast, in N. O Body's text, the fact that the truth of his male self
was concealed for such a long time was attributed to the ignorance, false
shame and hypocrisy of others. When he speaks of his sex assignment at
birth, he hardly conceals his anger towards his father, writing:

> His main concern was to silence the doctor with a handshake and the midwife
> with a large sum of money, so that this 'horribly unpleasant business' would
> not become more widely known. Here his interest ended; may the unfortu-
> nate child figure out how to cope with the world.[70]

Towards the end, N. O. Body follows the humanitarian script which makes
an appeal to the reader to prevent the suffering evoked in the preceding
story:[71]

> All the suffering and all the confusion which have soured my life arises from
> the misguided prudery which veils all things sexual as unclean . . . How much
> suffering and how many struggles I could have been spared if someone at
> home or at school had talked seriously and honestly to me about my sex!
> My youth would not have been so dark and joyless.[72]

In N. O. Body's text *others are blamed* for the fact that he had not been able
to be who he truly was: his parents – especially his father – the midwife,
the family doctor and everybody else who had kept sexual matters secret.
There is no doubt that he himself had been the main victim of their
errors and hypocrisy. So, instead of feeling guilty for having compromised
friends and relatives – whose relationships with Nora all of a sudden appeared
in an entirely different light – instead of pleading innocence in a case of

disruption of the social and moral order, N. O. Body accuses his relatives and friends, and the sanctimoniousness of the culture he lived in about sexuality in general, for having caused him so much suffering and confusion.

There is also a close parallel here to the crucial transformation the homo-sexual autobiography offered: instead of being full of guilt because of one's immoral sexual desires and acts, all of a sudden a 'truth' can be found which has always been wrongfully suppressed or ignored. Just as homosexuals started to do, N. O. Body complained about having had to conceal his 'real self' and started to challenge the dominant sexual ethos and fight the injustice he had had to endure.[73] For Barbin, his inscription in the social and moral body had tormented his conscience, for he felt morally obliged not to disrupt all the existing relations and thereby compromise everybody to whom he felt connected, at the same time as he thought he should tell the (physical) truth. In contrast, in N. O. Body's case, the sex of self triumphantly broke these ties and proved its authenticity and truth exactly by being able to defeat the conventions of upbringing and environment.

This crucial difference between the plot and morality of Barbin and N. O. Body's texts perfectly exemplifies Charles Taylor's assertion that in modern Western culture the self had not only become an inner space which had to be scrutinized and expressed, but had turned into a *constitutive good*. In other words, knowing oneself, expressing oneself and fully becoming oneself has become one of the basic moral values of modern Western culture, which started to replace the religious foundations of morality.[74] It is only against this background that harming someone's true self can be considered more evil than infringing (other) moral rules.

CONCLUSION

How did people come to be classified as a man or woman in cases in which doubt had been raised with regard to their physical sex? This book has shown how in practice different logics were at work to decide on a person's sex (re)assignment: sex as inscription, sex as the body, and sex as the self. These logics often functioned simultaneously, sustaining, contradicting or overlapping each other. The balance between the different logics shifted over time, however. While the logic of sex as body remained the basic logic over the course of time, the logic of sex as self only appeared at the very end of the nineteenth century, while the logic of sex as inscription seemed then no longer to be self-evident. Generally, this can be seen as caused by processes of modernization; in more precise ways, it is related to fundamental changes in medical practice enacting the (sexed) body over the long nineteenth century.

INSCRIPTION

During the first three-quarters of the nineteenth century, and in non-anonymous communities, the dominant rationale of sex turned out to be one of *inscription*. Sex was, in the first place, an inscription of a person's *place in the community*. After the initial categorization according to the appearance and urinary function of their genitals at birth had taken place, in many cases this rationale of inscription prevailed over a rationale demanding sex to be a truthful representation of someone's physical sex. Sex was also inscribed *on the person*, that is, through a name, clothes, public physical appearance and functions, occupations, social relations and space – which were all gendered – a person was known as either male or female.

Fragmentary evidence from medical case histories reveals long periods of silence, secrecy, non-intervention and tolerance before a case of doubtful sex was disclosed to a physician. People with the reputation of being a hermaphrodite, bearded ladies, people publicly switching sex roles, women gossiped about because of their sexual intimacies with other women, people who had raised doubts about their sex as fiancé(e)s or spouses – in many cases they were left alone, for years or even decades. Or, to be a little more precise: no local, legal or medical authorities were called upon to sort out such a person's physical sex by having it medically examined. It is possible that religious authorities – priests or ministers – might have been called upon more easily, but they did not always further disclose the case to authorities or direct it to a physician. Sometimes they only provided moral directions or recommended keeping things secret. The available evidence is necessarily only the tip of the iceberg, as secrecy, non-intervention or talking to a priest do not leave any traces in archives. The extent to which such policies of secrecy and non-intervention were applied, until when and in what sorts of environments, is therefore extremely difficult to estimate.

This does not mean that physical sex was not controlled: only, disclosing a body to a physician and leaving a sex assignment primarily to his judgement was not the logical course to take. People were not used to having their naked bodies examined by a physician, let alone their genitals. There was a lot of shame involved, not only related to an unusual build for one's sex, but also simply in the relation to male doctors and their patients (particularly female ones). Instead, other people such as mothers, midwives, all sorts of healers and same-sex peers had much more easy access to naked bodies. Moreover, a case of publicly noticeable doubtful sex was often watched, ridiculed and gossiped about within a local community. Such surveillance of doubtful sexes did not aim for disclosure, 'truth', and possible (re)assignment of sex, but for *containment*: preventing the doubt from contaminating the moral and social fabric of the entire community. Many hermaphrodites were demonstrably driven to shyness and social isolation by gossip and mockery, and resigned themselves to having lost the prospect of marriage. This protected the community from the possible social and moral disorder relations with hermaphrodites could entail.

A better understanding of these policies of secrecy, non-intervention and containment can, paradoxically, be derived from instances in which they started to come apart, when the legal or medical authorities were finally called in. When did that happen? And what difficulties did such disclosures to physicians cause? Usually, only if hermaphrodites had *already* disrupted the social and moral fabric of relations between the sexes was the option of demanding further disclosure of the physical truth chosen. Or, disclosure to a doctor only happened after containment policies had failed. Mere *individual* doubt never seemed to occasion asking a doctor to decide. Doubting sex, obviously, was more a social or moral problem than something that troubled an individual. When a sex reassignment took place, the medical case histories do not refer in any clear way to the possible damage this might cause to a hermaphrodite's inner sexed self. The way hermaphrodites dealt with such situations clearly shows the problem to be *dislocation*: the loss of place and face. As the memoirs of Barbin make abundantly clear, moreover, everyone related to Barbin was involved in the dishonour caused by her change of civil sex. Therefore, both for the community involved and for the hermaphrodite in question, sex was primarily a *location inscribed* in a social, economic, moral and legal fabric which could only be changed at the very high price of collective disruption and individual uprooting. Such severe consequences of a sex reassignment explain the logic of non-intervention.

I have chosen to distinguish this way of sexing an individual from a modern concept of self by the concept of *person*. Person is defined as having an outward, physical appearance, certain typical characteristics, a specific role and certain rights, but does not refer to an inner self. The concept of person points to precisely the places where an individual and a community meet. Sex, then, was conceived of as something inscribed *on the person* rather than *in the self*, at the same time as it was inscribed as a location within the social and moral fabric of a community.

The dislocation a sex reassignment brought about in every possible respect – loss of status, work, education, honour, biography, social relations, sexual partners or spouses – as well as the awareness of how others were dishonoured retrospectively, could affect a hermaphrodite deeply. Barbin's suicide is easy to understand from these circumstances. However, that does not mean that sex was conceived of as something anchored in an inner self. Nowhere in his memoirs does Barbin refer to a 'true self' – be it male, female or something in between – to legitimize his decisions or to explain his sufferings. What haunted him most was how he had damaged the moral position or honour of others. This did not torment her self, but her conscience. Together with the important role of priests and ministers evident in other case histories, this is a strong reminder of the importance of sex as an inscription in a *moral* fabric.

BODY

However, the rationale of sex as *inscription* as described above, did not rule out the rationale of sex as a due representation of physical sex. After all, each inscription of sex at birth started with that logic, and all the case histories my study is based on came into being because a physician was asked to examine a person's doubtful physical sex. But the way bodily sex *itself* was established in practice underwent major transformations. Even if we assume Thomas Laqueur was right in stating that, conceptually, from the end of the eighteenth century onwards the sexes were considered irreducibly different on the basis of their difference in sexual function, these chapters have shown which fundamental changes took place *within* that framework.

Two developments stand out: firstly, the increasing medical access to bodies; and secondly, the dislodgement of the person from the body in the process. It has become abundantly clear that physicians' access to bodies was far from self-evident. Until around the 1860s, physicians turn out to have hardly used penetrative or extensive palpation techniques during their examinations of hermaphrodites. Instead, they paid a lot of attention to the exact outward appearance of the genitals in order to calculate the possibility for coitus and impregnation. For the actual sexual function, they were mainly dependent on the hermaphrodite's statements. As a consequence, the sexual body enacted under such bedside medicine circumstances was strongly connected to the sex of the *person* of the hermaphrodite (status, appearance, function).

Justine Jumas's case has demonstrated that, even in the context of a legal procedure for the annulment of a marriage, the right to examine a body was highly contested in the 1860s and 1870s in France. While doctors were demanding access to her internal body to disclose its 'truth', in the name of society's protection against moral excesses, legal experts warned against infringing the (newly) protected individual physical integrity. Justine Jumas herself probably fought against the dislocation caused by a possible annulment; but she can possibly also be seen as someone who resisted a medical reading of her body in which she had no say at all. Two opposing strategies of maintaining the sexual order in the case of doubtful sexes could be derived from the Jumas case. One reminds us of the logic of secrecy and non-intervention described in Part I, in which the status quo of the inscribed sex was to be maintained in order not to disturb the social and moral order too much. The other reveals a positivist urge to bring doubtful sexes to light, to disclose their inner gonadal truth and to restore what was considered the natural order of sex.

From about the 1870s onwards, people in general became more willing to visit doctors as well to have their internal bodies examined. Baring the body and permitting penetrative exams became more routine. Apparently, people could temporarily detach their person from their bodies. This must have been even more true for those hermaphrodites who offered doctors proof of their capacity to ejaculate sperm (in or near the consulting room); these often had an apparent interest in proving their masculinity. Many hermaphrodites were still very ashamed of displaying their bodies, however. Anaesthetics turned out to be very helpful in overcoming this shame in order to examine these people. The increase in surgical procedures carried out led to another form of access to the internal bodies of hermaphrodites. In a growing number of cases the hermaphrodite's sex was established through the examination of sections of the gonads under the microscope. These rapidly developing *and* different forms of access to bodies entailed an important shift in the occasion of disclosure of hermaphroditism: in an increasing number of cases, it were not lay people who started to doubt someone's sex but *physicians*.

The extent to which physicians had access to bodies, as well as the way in which they gained it, was in many ways determinative for the manner in which they enacted physical sex. For example, when hardly any internal examination was permitted and any form of 'clinical masturbation' was considered immoral, sexual function was enacted as the verbal declaration of a patient about menstruation, erection, ejaculation and sexual intercourse. In contrast, when evidence of gonadal tissue was acquired through the dissection of histological research, the enactment of sex was devoid of personal experience altogether. Examinations of sex limited to the outside of the body enacted sexual function as a chain of connecting, concrete mechanisms of the genital apparatus, which often included the capacity for sexual excitation. When sexual function was established on the basis of menstruation or ejaculation, many of these mechanisms involved in coitus became irrelevant. In turn, the actual possibility of producing semen or eggs was no longer questioned as soon as scientists started to establish the character of gonadal cells under the microscope. In its many different enactments, therefore, the very same criterion for distinguishing between the sexes (that is, sexual function) could be something entirely different, even contradictory. Parallel to this, hermaphroditism transformed over the nineteenth century from the capacity to have intercourse both as a woman and as a man, to the coexistence of menstruation and ejaculation of sperm, to, as the Germans called it, *Drüsenhermaphroditismus* or hermaphroditism of the sexual glands. Hermaphroditism was not *the same* throughout the nineteenth century; many new forms of hermaphroditism came into being.

The growing medical access to bodies was accompanied by the dislodgement of the person from the body. An increasing number of techniques and routines became available to examine bodies detached from the observations, experience or even the actual body of the person in question. The disciplining of patients had led to more routine examinations of naked and internal bodies, which distanced the hermaphrodite's observations from the physician's. Clinical masturbation transformed the intimate, emotional functions of sex into proof of the presence of functioning male gonads. In particular, the anaesthetics routinely employed from 1900 onwards as well as the extraction of gonadal tissue from living bodies, separated the person from the sex enacted.

Of course, medicine has often been criticized for its removal of the patient's soul, as the German title of Anna Bergman's recent medical history – *Der entseelte Patient* – suggests.[1] Dreger shares this view in her judgement of 'medical men' overlooking the hermaphrodite's own gender identification and sexual inclinations in their assessment of sex. In the medical view only the gonads decided, according to her critique.[2] Apart from the fact that a 'gonad' turns out to have been enacted in multiple ways and is therefore not 'one', I doubt whether contrasting objective criteria with subjective embodiment is a helpful strategy. Contrary to what seems the logical outcome of the history of medicine's increasing capacity to separate the body from the person, this did *not* mean the person of the hermaphrodite disappeared from the clinical encounter altogether. New subjectivities arose and several case histories witnessed the creation of a rationale of sex as a representation of an autonomous, deeply anchored inner sex of self.

SELF

The last part of this book shows the developments in medicine to be one of the major triggers of the emergence of a new rationale of sex, which demanded that the category of sex be a due representation of a person's sense of her or his own sex. With this new rationale of sex, doubting physical sex transformed historically, from something primarily touching the sexed moral, economic and social order in which a person was inscribed, to something troubling an individual person's self in relation to her body. To demonstrate this, three main themes were discussed: the question of sex diagnosis and the shift from legal to clinical procedures, the clinical assessment of a sex of self by means of a 'turn inwards', and the new autobiographical script available for the life history of a person with a so-called 'error of sex'.

The shift from legal to clinical procedures with regard to sex assignment could be seen most clearly in the discussion of the new civil code in Germany and in the international debate on plastic surgery carried out on hermaphrodites. Contrary to what might have been expected, the new diagnostic techniques which provided pathological–anatomical proof of gonadal cells in a living person did not lead to physicians' triumphantly claiming a monopoly on the truth of sex. Unlike earlier assertions from French medical professionals, that only they could establish a person's true sex, many German doctors were not pleased at all with a law that left the decision in cases of doubtful sex entirely up to the medical expert. Not only did they claim that neutral and double sexes existed or complain that finding gonads in a newborn was impossible, some also openly questioned whether the person involved should not (ultimately) define his own sex. As gonadal sex was sometimes so at odds with the person's appearance and self-awareness, leaving the choice to the person would save him from conflicts with his psyche or with morality and the law, these physicians argued. Concepts such as a hermaphrodite's sense of sex, psyche, consciousness, as well as their suffering, happiness or well-being regularly came up in these discussions, and were clearly normative for some of the physicians involved.

In practice, a lot of decisions started to be taken within the clinical encounter and operating theatres, without any interference from the law whatsoever. This was because of a growing capacity for plastic surgery on the genitals and secondary sex characteristics, as well as a corresponding demand from hermaphrodites for the erasure of visible, physical sexual ambiguity. In many a case, there was a discrepancy between what was in all probability the gonadal sex and the hermaphrodite's wishes. In such cases, quite a few surgeons decided to operate in line with the hermaphrodite's wishes, thereby assigning sex in practice. Such decisions were often defended in public, which also evoked a lot of sharp criticism. Within this debate, the sex of self increasingly became something physicians discussed as a separate object concerning which they claimed to have competence. The hermaphrodite's subjective wish thereby transformed into an object physicians discussed and took into account in *their* weighing of physical and psychological factors. From (dis)obeying subjects of civil law, hermaphrodites became implicated in disciplining and normalizing sex. Their demand for surgery as well as some physicians' sincere concern for the well-being of their patients played key roles in this shift.

The growing gap between the everyday appearance of sex and its scientific laboratory enactment evoked a clinical discussion about what to tell the patient. Though full medical disclosure could amount to forcing a patient to take his gonadal sex morally and legally as his actual sex, many physicians had started to think that the question should be considered from the perspective of the hermaphrodite's well-being. They held that in cases in which a person had no doubts about her sex at all, it would dramatically shake her own sense of self and her orientation in the world if a physician would explain that an error in the initial sex assignment had taken place.

This new attention for, and valuing of a hermaphrodite's own sense of sex, did not automatically lead to new routines and techniques to examine such a sex of self. It turns out that the few physicians who tried to make the sex of self into a serious object of a separate clinical examination, primarily used techniques that had been developed in psychiatric case histories of sexual inversion over the previous three decades. Sex thereby turned inwards: what had previously been indicators for a person's sexed position in society, now pointed to lifelong inclinations, preferences and aversions which characterized the sex of a person's inner, genuine being. Existing sexed categorizations of childhood behaviour, interests, capacities, work, clothing, adornment and sexual preferences were projected on to an individual psyche. A model example of such a persistent truth of self can be found in N. O. Body's autobiography *Memoirs of a Man's Maiden Years*. In strong contrast to earlier accounts of errors of sex and subsequent civil sex changes, most notably Barbin's memoirs, N. O. Body 'knew' from his very early youth onwards something was wrong, that he was different from the other girls, loved boys' toys and games and detested girlish pursuits.

With this turn inwards, a new way of guaranteeing the stability and continuity of a sexed social and moral order came into being. The everyday control and regulation of a person's sexed position in the community increasingly relinquished its hold as medicine claimed a monopoly on the interior truth of sex in the name of science and modernity: monitoring sex was thus displaced to the consulting room. But instead of forcing their patients to live according to a strict scientific gonadal criterion of sex ('*true* sex') – which they did not have the authority to do anyway – physicians were often much more pragmatic and strove for a properly functioning *single* sex: a less ambiguous-looking sex. Several aspects of sex, notably the sex of self and the sexual desires of the person in question, were thereby weighed. In the clinic, the first attempts were made to establish a stable relationship between the outward appearance of sex, its functioning in public and private situations, and a stable and genuine sex of self. To that end, both new surgical techniques and methods for determining the sex of self were employed. Diagnostic judgements were thereby replaced by disciplining and normalizing procedures. Medicine also began to make the relationship between pathological–anatomical gonadal sex, on the one hand, and the sex of self, on the other, into a new topic for (statistic) scientific research.

By using the script and standardized themes of autobiographical stories in general and of male homosexuals in particular, N. O. Body managed to make the damage done to his misunderstood masculine self the central theme of his autobiography. Not the disrupted moral and social order in which everyone was involved, as in Barbin's text, but his *individual* suffering was the abuse exposed. The ultimate acknowledgement as a man was not the start of social, economic and moral uprootal, but the final victory of truth over secrecy and sanctimoniousness as well as the happy beginning of a bright future. Within this narrative structure, the self has seemingly become the self-evident basis for moral reasoning: anything damaging to the self or restricting it from being fully acknowledged, developed and expressed is a wrong that has to be fought.

At the turn of the twentieth century, the logic of the category of sex therefore started to be cut off both from outward, physical appearance and from its inscription in a sexed social and moral body: it turned inwards. The sex of self, in these first cases, appears as a phantom limb: the cut-off social and moral body was still felt and projected on to the screen of a genuinely felt stable, inner truth of authentic sexed individuality, while clinicians attempted to create surgically a proper relation of this self to the outer appearance of sex.

NOTES

Quotes from primary sources are translated by Steph Morris (German), Jennifer Gay and Paula Yoni (French) and Wendy Schaffer (Dutch).

INTRODUCTION

1 Mak, Geertje, 1997, *Mannelijke vrouwen. Over grenzen van sekse in de negentiende eeuw* (Meppel and Amsterdam: Boom).

2 I will use the term 'hermaphrodite' throughout the book, as it is the term contemporaries generally used to refer to physical sexes which raised doubts. It should be stressed that modern terms, such as intersex and the more contemporary disorders of sex development (DSDs), are not new terms for the same thing. More particularly, the term hermaphroditism was abandoned during a period (the 1920s) in which it became clear that not all forms of 'doubtful sex' could be recognized from the outside body. I will not adopt the nineteenth century's more precise categorizations of hermaphroditism (such as male pseudo-hermaphroditism, etc.), because the use of 'pseudo-' suggests there to be an essential or true sex which had 'only' not fully developed. This is not to say that such categorization is not interesting in itself (as for example is already shown in Dreger 1998: see below) but that the focus of my study has not been to analyze these concepts.

3 It was Rebecca Jordan Young's excellent – unfortunately not yet published – paper on 'Sexual Rationales – at the 2008 ESSHC conference in Lisbon that helped me to see how different logics were at work within one concept of 'normal' or 'natural' heterosexuality.

4 For reasons that will become clear in this introduction, I have abstained from using the word 'gender' as reference to the 'sex of the self': it is precisely this concept of gender identity which I try to historicize in this study. I will only refer to the term gender in the way Joan Scott introduced it, that is, in an analysis of how structures, ideologies, things, concepts and persons are gendered; Scott, Joan, 1988, *Gender and the Politics of History* (New York, etc.: Columbia University Press).

5 Neugebauer, Franz Ludwig von, 1908, *Hermaphroditismus beim Menschen* (Leipzig: Werner Klinkhardt). Another collection of hermaphrodite case histories, more than a century earlier, can be found in Arnaud, G., 1768. *Mémoires de chirurgie. Sixième mémoire. Dissertation sur les hermaphrodites* (London, Paris: J. Nourse). Just a decade before Neugebauer, Taruffi published a large volume on hermaphrodite

case histories in Italian, which was translated into German: Taruffi, Cesare, 1903. *Hermaphroditismus und Zeugungsfähigkeit. Eine systematische Darstellung der Missbildungen der menschlichen Geschlechtsorgane* (Berlin: R. Teuscher). Neugebauer used both to build up his own collection of cases.

6 See Mak, Geertje, 2011, 'Hermaphrodites on show. The case of Katharina / Karl Hohmann and its use in nineteenth-century medical science', *Social History of Medicine* Advance Access (online 31 March), 10.1093 / shm / hkr050, for a discussion of these cases.

7 See Matta, Christina, 2005, 'Ambiguous bodies and deviant sexualities. Hermaphrodites, homosexuality, and surgery in the United States, 1850–1904', *Perspectives in Biology and Medicine*, 48:1, 74–83, and Reis, Elizabeth, 2009. *Bodies in Doubt. An American History of Intersex* (Baltimore: Johns Hopkins University Press), for many more American case histories; my own research revealed some additional Dutch case histories.

8 Dreger, Alice Domurat, 1998, *Hermaphrodites and the Medical Invention of Sex* (Cambridge, MA, and London: Harvard University Press).

9 See also: for Neugebauer Spörri, Myriam, 2000, 'Die Diagnose des Geschlechts. Hermaphroditismus im sexualwissenschaftlichen Diskurs zwischen 1886 und 1920' (Lizentiatsarbeit, University of Zurich), 48–53.

10 Neugebauer 1908, 705, 698.

11 Next to medical discussions I have used some legal case histories, as well as two hermaphrodite autobiographies.

12 In his study on sexual forensics in Soviet Russia, Dan Healey dedicated chapter 5 to hermaphroditism. He, too, mentioned the remarkable fact that almost one half of the case histories were about the peasantry, a part of the population difficult to reach for modern medicine generally at the time: Healey, Dan, 2009. *Bolshevik Sexual Forensics. Diagnosing Disorder in the Clinic and Courtroom, 1917–1939* (DeKalb, IL: Northern Illinois University Press), chapter 5, esp. 145.

13 Very inspiring and helpful in this respect have been: Duden, Barbara, 1987, *Geschichte unter der Haut. Ein Eisenacher Arzt und seine Patientinnen um 1730* (Stuttgart: Klett-Verlag); Duden, Barbara, 1991. *The Woman Beneath the Skin. A Doctor's Patients in Eighteenth-Century Germany*, trans. Thomas Dunlap (Cambridge, MA, and London: Harvard University Press); Ackerman, Evelyn Bernette, 1990. *Health Care in the Parisian Countryside, 1800–1914* (New Brunswick and London: Rutgers University Press); Lachmund, Jens, 1997. *Der abgehorchte Körper: zur historischen Soziologie der medizinischen Untersuchung* (Opladen: Westdeutscher Verlag).

14 Butler, Judith, 1993, *Bodies that Matter. On the Discursive Limits of 'Sex'* (New York and London: Routledge).

15 Laqueur, Thomas, 1990, *Making Sex. Body and Gender from the Greeks to Freud* (Cambridge, MA and London: Harvard University Press).

16 See for similar arguments: Honegger, Claudia, 1991, *Die Ordnung der Geschlechter. Die Wissenschaften von Menschen und das Weib 1750–1850* (Frankfurt am Main: Campus); Schiebinger, Londa, 1993. *Nature's Body: Gender in the Making of Modern Science* (Boston: Beacon Press).

17 Duden 1987 and 1991; Ackerman 1990. Lachmund 1997; Gowing, Laura, 2003, *Common Bodies. Women, Touch, and Power in Seventeenth-Century England* (New Haven

and London: Yale University Press). Gowing also explicitly criticizes Laqueur for his one-dimensional view on the discourse on sex in the seventeenth century.

18 My tools for the literary analysis of referential historical sources were mainly Mieke Bal's narratology and 'symptomatic reading': Bal, Mieke, 1997. *Narratology, Introduction to the Theory of Narrative* (Toronto: University of Toronto Press). See, for the use of methods of literary analysis in the case of referential texts: Mak 1997, 155–96. See, for English examples of narratological analysis of medical case histories: Mak, Geertje, 2004. 'Sandor/Sarolta Vay: from passing woman to sexual invert', *Journal of Women's History*, 16:1, 54–77; Mak, Geertje, 2005a. ' "So we must go behind even what the microscope can reveal". The hermaphrodite's "self" in medical discourse at the beginning of the twentieth century', *GLQ: A Journal of Lesbian and Gay Studies*, 11:1, 65–94.

19 Hausman, Bernice L., 1995, *Changing Sex. Transsexualism, Technology and the Idea of Gender* (Durham, NC, and London: Duke University Press).

20 This is in line with Joanne Meyerowitz's critique of Hansmann, but I deviate from Meyerowitz in pointing much more to the importance of changing medical technologies for ideas about sex. See part III of this book; and Meyerowitz, Joanne, 2002, *How Sex Changed. A History of Transsexuality in the United States* (Cambridge, MA, and London: Harvard University Press), 14–50.

21 Taylor, Charles, 1989, *Sources of the Self. The Making of the Modern Identity* (Cambridge and New York: Cambridge University Press). See also: Giddens, Anthony, 1991. *Modernity and Self Identity. Self and Society in the Late Modern Age* (Cambridge: Polity Press).

22 Wahrman, Dror, 2004, *The Making of the Modern Self: Identity and Culture in Eighteenth-Century England* (New Haven and London: Yale University Press). See for the shift of masquerades' meaning: 157–65.

23 See Arianne Baggerman's and Rudolf Dekker's contributions to the latter's volume on ego documents in history, Dekker, Rudolf (ed.), 2002a, *Egodocuments and history. Autobiographical Writing in its Social Context since the Middle Ages* (Hilversum: Verloren). For an in-depth study of Dutch autobiographies' marketing 1850–1918, see: Huisman, Marijke, 2008. *Publieke levens: autobiografieën op de Nederlandse boekenmarkt 1850–1918* (Zutphen: Walburg Pers).

24 See e.g. Donoghue, Emma, 1993, *Passions between Women. British Lesbian Culture 1668–1801* (London: Scarlet Press); Trumbach, Randolph, 1998. *Sex and the Gender Revolution. Volume I. Heterosexuality and the Third Gender in Enlightenment London* (London and Chicago: University of Chicago Press); Meer, Theo van der, 2007. 'Sodomy and its discontents. Discourse, desire, and the rise of a same-sex proto-something in the early modern Dutch Republic', *Historical Reflections / Réflections historiques*, 1, 41–67, offers a beautifully nuanced picture of how nineteenth-century identities emerged from earlier notions of male same-sex categories.

25 Halperin, David M., 1990, *One Hundred Years of Homosexuality and Other Essays on Greek Love* (New York and London: Routledge); Müller, Klaus, 1991. 'Aber in meinem Herzen sprach eine Stimme so laut'. *Homosexuelle Autobiographien und medizinische Pathographien im neunzehnten Jahrhundert* (Berlin: Rosa Winkel); Mak, 1997; Oosterhuis, Harry, 2000. *Stepchildren of Nature. Krafft-Ebing, Psychiatry, and the Making of Sexual Identity* (Chicago and London: Chicago University Press).

26 Graille, Patrick, 1987, *Les Hermaphrodites aux XVIIe et XVIIIe siècles* (Paris: Les Belles Lettres); Gilbert, Ruth, 2002. *Early Modern Hermaphrodites. Sex and Other Stories* (Basingstoke and New York: Palgrave); Long, Kathleen, 2006. *Hermaphrodites in Renaissance Europe. Women and Gender in the Early Modern World* (Aldershot and Burlington: Ashgate).

27 See for historical studies: Epstein, Julia, 1995, *Altered Conditions. Disease, Medicine, and Storytelling* (New York and London: Routledge); Hausman 1995; Dreger 1998; Dreger, Alice Domurat, 1999b, 'A history of intersex. From the age of gonad, to the age of consent', in Dreger, Alice Domurat (ed.), 1999a, *Intersex in the Age of Ethics* (Hagerstown, MD: University Publishing Group); Klöppel, Ulrike, 2002a. '"Störfall" Hermaphroditismus und Trans-Formationen der Kategorie "Geschlecht". Überlegungen zur Analyse der medizinischen Diskussionen über Hermaphroditismus um 1900 mit Deleuze, Guattari und Foucault', *Transformationen. Wissen-Mensch-Geschlecht. Potsdamer Studien zur Frauen- und Geschlechterforschung*, 6, 137–50; Klöppel, Ulrike, 2002b. 'XXOXY Ungelöst. Störungsszenarien in der dramaturgie der zweigeschlechtlichen Ordnung', in Jannik Franzen, Ulrike Klöppel, Bettina Schmidt *et al.* (eds), *(K)ein Geschlecht oder viele? Transgender in politischer Perspektive* (Berlin: Querverlag), 153–181; Spörri, Myriam, 2003. 'N. O. Body, Magnus Hirschfeld und die Diagnose des Geschlechts: Hermaphroditismus um 1900', *L'Homme Z.F.G.*, 14:2, 244–61; Alison Redick, 2004. 'American History XY: The Medical Treatment of Intersex, 1916–1955' (PhD thesis New York University); Matta 2005; Herrn, Rainer, 2005. 'Das Geschlecht ruht nicht im Körper, sondern in der Seele. Magnus Hirschfelds Strategien bei Hermaphroditengutachten', in *1-0-1 [one 'o one] Intersex. Das Zwei-Geschlechter-System als Menschenrechtsverletzung* (Berlin: Neue Gesellschaft für Bildende Kunst), 55–71; Klöppel, Ulrike, 2005. '"Strenge Objektivität und extremste Subjektivität konkurrieren" Hermaphroditismusbehandlung in der Nachkriegszeit und die Durchsetzung von "gender by design"', in *1-0-1 [one 'o one] Intersex*, 168–85; Reis 2009; Healey 2009, 134–58. See for studies on current intersex management: Kessler, Susanne J., 1998. *Lessons from the Intersexed* (New Brunswick and London: Rutgers University Press); Dreger 1999b; Fausto-Sterling, Anne, 2000. *Sexing the Body. Gender Politics and the Construction of Sexuality* (New York: Basic Books); Graille 1987; Preves, Sharon E., 2005. *Intersex and Identity. The Contested Self* (New Brunswick, etc.: Rutgers University Press); Karkazis, Katrina, 2008. *Fixing Sex. Intersex, Medical Authority, and Lived Experience* (Durham, NC: Duke); Holmes, Morgan, 2008. *Intersex. A Perilous Difference* (Selinsgrove: Susquehanna University Press); Klöppel 2002a and 2002b focus on scientific theory and not on personal experience. Only Epstein 1995 and Reis 2009 cover more centuries in their studies.

28 Hirschauer, Stefan, 1993, *Die soziale Konstruktion der Transsexualität* (Frankfurt am Main: Suhrkamp); Hirschauer, Stefan, 1998. 'Performing sexes and genders in medical practices', in Annemarie Mol and Marc Berg (eds), *Differences in Medicine. Unraveling Practices, Techniques, and Bodies* (Durham, NC, and London: Duke University Press), 13–27. The English 1998 article is unfortunately only a very brief summary of his detailed 1993 medical ethnography published in German.

29 Hirschauer himself was clearly aware of this historical dimension of that meta-
    morphosis, but confined his chapter on that topic to a profound overview of the
    existing literature at the time. Hirschauer 1993, 66–115.
30 Dreger 1998, 110–38; Dreger 1999b, 6–11.
31 Scott, Joan, 1991, 'The evidence of experience', *Critical Inquiry*, 17:4, 773–97.
    See for a detailed account of the history of the development of the concept of
    'core gender identity': Hausman 1995, 101–5.
32 Rubin, Gayle, 1975, 'The traffic in women. Notes on the "political economy"
    of sex', in Reina R. Reiter (ed.), *Toward an Anthropology of Women* (New York:
    Monthly Review Press), 157–210.
33 See for example: Epstein 1995; Dreger 1999b; Kessler 1998; Fausto-Sterling 2000;
    1-0-1 [one 'o one] Intersex 2005; Reis 2009; *Cardozo Journal of Law & Gender* 2005,
    12:1; Holmes 2008.
34 Butler 1993, 1–16.
35 I think of Hirschauer's ethnographic study of the practice of transsexual trans-
    formations, Hirschauer 1993. See for studies on intersex: Kessler 1998; Fausto-
    Sterling 2000; Karkazis 2008.
36 Though on a very different topic, to me Stoler's argument for reading archives
    'along the grain' in order to understand their implicit logics seemed to represent a
    similar strategic move: Stoler, Ann Laura, 2009. *Along the Archival Grain: Epistemic
    Anxieties and Colonial Common Sense* (Princeton: Princeton University Press).
37 See Dreger 1998; Matta 2005; Reis 2009; Butler, Judith, 2001, 'Doing justice to
    someone: sex reassignment and allegories of transsexuality', *GLQ: A Journal of
    Lesbian and Gay Studies*, 7:4, 621–36.

PART I. INSCRIPTION

1 See e.g. Epstein 1995, 112–13; Dreger 1998, 110–38; Dreger 1999b.
2 Foucault, Michel, 1980, 'Introduction', in *Herculine Barbin. Being the Recently
   Discovered Memoirs of a Nineteenth-Century French Hermaphrodite*, introduced by
   Michel Foucault, trans. Richard McDougall (New York Pantheon Books), vii–x.

CHAPTER 1. SECRECY AND DISCLOSURE.
THE POLITICS OF CONTAINMENT

1 Schweickhard, 1803, 'Geschichte eines lange Zeit für einen Hermaphroditen
   gehaltenen wahren Mannes', *Journal der practischen Heilkunde*, Band XVII:1, 9–52,
   at 11; from the archival sources I have retrieved the full names of the persons
   involved: Generallandesarchiv Karlsruhe, Ehegerichtsprotokoll des Kirchenrates
   1794, Signatur 61/4262.
2 Schweickhard 1803, 13.
3 Schweickhard 1803, 13–14.
4 Ricoux and Aubry, 1899, 'Un prétendu androgyne dans un service de femmes',
   Le Progrès médical, 3rd series, tome X:37, 183–4, at 183.
5 Ricoux and Aubry 1899, 183.

6 Hypospadia is a condition in which the urinary tract does not end at the tip of the penis, but halfway or at the bottom. It often prevents men from urinating in a standing position. Combined with a split scrotum, undescended testicles and/or a small penis, such genitals can look similar to female genitals, especially at birth.

7 Ricoux and Aubry 1899, 184.

8 Virchow, 1856, *Gesammelte Abhandlungen zur wissenschaftlichen Medizin* (Frankfurt Am Main: Meidinger), 770–4, at 770–1.

9 Neugebauer 1908, 624.

10 Weber, Eugen, 1977, *Peasants into Frenchmen: The Modernization of Rural France, 1870–1914* (Stanford: Stanford University Press).

11 Ackerman 1990, 11–59; see chapter 4.

12 Henning, 1819, 'Geschichte eines monströs an den Geschlechtstheilen geborenen Kindes weiblichen Geschlechts, das für einen Knaben bestimmt worden war', *Journal der practischen Heilkunde*, XLII:49, 98–108, at 99, italics added.

13 N. O. Body, 1907, *Aus einem Mannes Mädchenjahren*, foreword by Rudolf Presber, afterward by Magnus Hirschfeld (Berlin: Hesperus Verlag), 20–1.

14 Fronmüller, 1834, 'Beschreibung eines als Mädchen erzogenes männlichen Scheinzwitters', *Zeitschrift für die Staatsarzneikunde*, XIV:27, 205–9, at 206.

15 Parmly, George Dubois, 1886, 'Hermaphrodisme', *American journal of obstetrics and diseases of women and children*, XIX:September, 931–46, at 936.

16 Thompson, R. G. (ed.), 1996, *Freakery: Cultural Spectacles of the Extraordinary Body* (New York and London: New York University Press), 1–19.

17 Wahrman 2004, 202–7.

18 Wahrman 2004, 202.

19 Schweickhard 1803, 17–18.

20 Reverchon, 1870, 'Étude médico-légal sur l'état mental du nommé Ch . . .', *Annales médico-psychologiques*, 5th series, tome IV, XXVIII:November, 377–95, at 380–1. He declared her to be male, and writes about her in the male form. On Marie Chupin, who ended up in an insane asylum after an attempt to kill a three-year-old child, there is a patient dossier available at CESAME – Centre Hospitalier – St Gemmes, Loire, France.

21 Guermonprez, 1892, 'Une erreur de sexe avec ses conséquences', *Annales d'hygiène publique et de médecine légale*, 3rd series, tome XXVIII:September–October, 242–75, 296–306, at 302.

22 See e.g. Eva Elisabeth S., who lived alone as a woman after her marriage was annulled: Schneider and Sommering, 1817, 'Beschreibung einas sehr mekwüdigen Hypospadias', *Jahrbuch der Staatsarzneikunde*, 10, 134–55, at 137; Ursula/Georg Thomasicz, discovered in hospital in Vienna in 1850, led a secluded life, Neugebauer 1908, 256–7; M. C., 'She was very eccentric from girlhood on, and never cared to associate with or enter into play with any children. Since she has been at the asylum she has always scrupulously avoided bathing in the presence of anyone'. Hills, William C., 1873. 'A case of hermaphroditism', *The Lancet*, CI:2578, 129–30; 67-year-old man who had always lived alone in a hovel, Stretton, J. L., 1895. 'So-called hermaphrodite', *The Lancet*, CXLVI:3763, 917.

23 '... Weil die Hebamme angibt, das Kind harne wie ein Mädchen, sei also ein Mädchen': Neugebauer 1908, 624.

24 Traxel, 1856, 'Zeugungsfähigkeit eines Hypospadiacus, dessen Urethra am Perinaeum ausmündet', *Wiener medizinische Wochenschrift*, VI:18, 289–91, at 291.

25 See also another early case which stresses the importance of urination: Larrey, 1859, 'Hermaphrodisme', *Gazette des hôpitaux civils et militaires*, XXXII:115, 459–60. Dan Healey came to similar conclusions for early revolutionary Russia: see Healey 2009, 146, 155.

26 Report from Hoffmann 1877, summarized in Neugebauer 1908, 256–7.

27 '... Mais la conformation anormale de ses organes génitaux externes ... , en l'obligeant à l'attitude de la femme pour uriner, l'aurait gêné beaucoup sous des habits d'homme, et devenait d'ailleurs pour le service militaire un cas prévu de réforme': Larrey 1859, 459.

28 Neugebauer 1908, 442.

29 Schäffler, 1801, 'Beschreibung eines Mannes, dessen fehlerhafte Geschechtstheile sein Geschlecht lange zweifelhaft machten', *Journal der practischen Heilkunde*, Band XIII:1, 114–24, at 123.

30 Schneider and Sommering 1817, 138.

31 Moscucci, Ornella, 1990, *The Science of Woman. Gynaecology and Gender in England, 1800–1929* (Cambridge, New York, Port Chester, etc.: Cambridge University Press), see 112–26; Bynum, W. F., 1994. *Science and the Practice of Medicine in the Nineteenth Century* (Cambridge, New York and Melbourne: Cambridge University Press), see 33–5, 203 and 210 (illustrations of the palpation of women without seeing them); Lachmund 1997, 201: 'Wie problematisch allein schon der Blick des Arztes auf den weiblichen Körper in der Privatpraxis ist, zeigt die Empfelung, den Körper ersatzweise in einem dunklen Zimmer unter dem Rock abzutasten'. See also Lachmund 1997, 79, on the difference between private practice and hospitals; in the latter, even the examination of genitals seemed to have been allowed in the early nineteenth century. For eighteenth-century Germany: Duden 1987, 100–4.

32 *Herculine Barbin. Being the Recently Discovered Memoirs of a Nineteenth-Century French Hermaphrodite*, 1980. introduced by Michel Foucault, trans. Richard McDougall (New York: Pantheon Books), at 68. I am referring here to the page numbers of the English translation of Barbin's memoirs, as I have used the English translation in the rest of this book. The original text can be found in Tardieu, Auguste Ambroise, 1874. *Question médico-légale de l'identité dans ses rapports avec les vices de conformation des organes sexuels* (Paris: J. B. Baillière, 2nd edn).

33 See for the major difference between private practice and hospitals in this respect: Lachmund 1997, 79.

34 Tardieu 1874, 27–8.

35 See e.g. Tourtual, 1856, 'Ein als Weib verheirateter Androgynus vor dem kirchlichen Forum', *Vierteljahrsschrift für gerichtliche und öffentliche Medizin*, 1st series, Band X:1, 18–40, at 25.

36 See further chapter 5.

37 See for the many other practitioners of the body in early eighteenth-century Germany e.g. Duden 1987, 92; for the seventeenth century see Gowing 2003, 3, 17–81. Lachmund 1997, 27–30 and 195–203, has shown that these practices from 'bedside medicine', in which many more people than solely doctors were involved in interpreting a body, continued into the first half of the nineteenth century in Germany and more generally in private practices.

38 Gowing 2003, 17–81.

39 See e.g. Legros, F., 1835, 'Homme hypospade, pris 22 ans pour une femme', *Journal des connaissances médico-chirurgicales*, III:7, 273–6, at 273 ('dont il partageait les jeux et le lit'); Worbe, 1815. 'Sur un individu rendu par jugement á l'état viril, après avoir été vingt-deux ans réputé du sexe féminin; cas médico-légal', *Bulletin de la faculté de médecine de Paris*, XI, 4:10, 479–92, at 488 ('lorsqu'il était couché avec des filles'); Reverchon 1870, 380–1.

40 Loeffler, 1871, 'Zur Kasuistik der Zwitter', *Berliner klininische Wochenschrift*, VIII:26, 309.

41 Neugebauer 1908, 390.

42 From the total of 301 cases analyzed in this book, 223 were registered as female at birth. 47 of these hermaphrodites were reported to have (had) sexual affairs with women during the time they were still assigned the female sex.

43 Schneider and Sommering 1817, 136.

44 Martini, 1861, 'Ein männlicher Scheinzwitter als verpflichtete Hebamme. Amtsmissbrauch und widernatürtliche Unzucht', *Vierteljahrsschrift für gerichtliche Medizin und öffentlichen Sanitätswesen*, XIX, 303–22, at 304.

45 Franz Ludwig von Neugebauer, 1899, 'Cinquante cas de mariages conclus entre des personnes du même sexe, avec plusieurs procès de divorce par suite d'erreur de sexe', *Revue de gynécologie et de chirurgie abdominale*, tome III:2, 195–210, provides an overview of fifty hermaphrodite marriages. The following cases involved long-lasting marriages until 1870, not further discussed in the text: Otto, Adolf Wilhelm, 1824. *Neue seltene Beobachtungen zur Anatomie, Physiologie und Pathologie gehörig* (Berlin: August Rücker), 123–6, 133–5, at 133; Loir, Joseph-Napoléon, 1854. *Des sexes en matière d'état-civil, comment prévenir les erreurs résultant de leurs anomalies, mémoire lu à l'Académie des sciences morale et politiques* (Paris: Cotillon), 19; Neugebauer 1908, 92 (a case from 1860: see also Dreger 1998, 59) and 448, Dailliez, Georges, 1893. *Les sujets de sexe douteux. Leur état psychique. Leur condition relativement au mariage* (Thèse de Paris. Lille: L. Danel), 103–8 (case from 1870); Wallis, Albert W. 1868. 'Sexual malformation', *Medical Times and Gazette. A Journal of Medical Science, Literature, Criticism, and News*, Part II:7, November, 542–3.

46 Neugebauer 1908, 385–6; the 'Jewishness' of the genitals might have referred to a penis that looked circumcised (in cases of hypospadias, the foreskin often did not entirely cover the head of the penis) and/or to its being small, invoking the current prejudice of Jews being effeminate. See Gilman, Sander, 2006. 'Whose body is it, anyway? Hermaphrodites, gays, and Jews in N. O. Body's Germany', in N. O. Body, *Memoirs of a Man's Maiden Years*, trans. Deborah Simon (Philadelphia: University of Pennsylvania Press) vii–xxiv, see xx–xxiv.

47 Neugebauer 1908, 385.

48 See for other examples: Walther, 1902, 'Anomalie génitale', *Bulletins et mémoires de la Société de chirurgie de Paris*, XXVIII, 8 and 15 October, 938–44, 972–5, at 942; Lucas-Championnière, M. J., 1909. 'Présentation des photographies d'un hypospade ayant passé pour une femme, ayant été mariée pendant douze ans, ayant présentée comme femme à barbe et ayant des seins très dévelopés', *Bulletins et mémoires de la Société de chirurgie de Paris*, XXXV:39, 1347–9.

49 '. . . Dass die ihm angetraute Person auch männliche Theile habe, dass sie Mann und Weib zugleich, oder oder besser, nicht vollständig Mann, noch weniger Weib, oder, wie er ein anderes Mal sich ausdrückt, dass sie mehr Mann als Weib sei': Tourtual 1856, 19.

50 Tourtual 1856, 19.

51 Tourtual 1856, 19–20.

52 Tourtual 1856, 20.

53 Tourtual 1856, 20.

54 Schäffler 1801, 114, 118.

55 *Herculine Barbin* 1980, 62.

56 Benoit, Justin, 1840, 'Consultation sur un cas d'hermaphroditisme', *Journal de la Société de médecine pratique de Montpellier*, I: November, 23–37, at 25–6.

57 Worbe 1815, 482.

58 Neugebauer 1908, 135, 527; Stark, Johann Christian, 1799, 'Sonderbare Naturebegebenheit: wirkliche Erscheinung weiblich-männlicher Theile und doch kein Hermaphrodit, wodurch eine andere Weibsperson befruchtet wurde', *Neues Archiv für die Geburtshülfe, Frauenzimmer und Kinderkrankheiten mit Hinsicht auf die Physiologie, Diätik und Chirurgie*, Band I:3, 351–7, at 351; Schneider 1809. 'Der Hermaphroditismus in gerichtlich-medizinischer Hinsicht', *Jahrbuch der Staatsarzneikunde*, 2, 139–68, at 145–6.

59 Fronmüller 1834, 206–7.

60 A very similar example is Marie Raab, described by Marchand, 1883, 'Ein neuer Fall von Hermaphroditismus spurius masculinus', *Archiv für pathologische Anatomie und Physiologie und klinische Medizin*, Band XCII:2, 286–95.

CHAPTER 2. EARLY SEX REASSIGNMENTS AND
THE ABSENCE OF A SEX OF SELF

1 Althusser, Louis, 1977, *Ideologie und ideologische Staatsapparate: Aufsätze zur marxistische Theorie*, trans. Rolf Löper, Klaus Riepe and Peter Schötter (Hamburg and Berlin: VSA); Foucault, Michel, 1972. 'Two lectures', in Colin Gordon (ed.), *Power/Knowledge. Selected Interviews and Other Writings 1972–1977*, trans. Colin Gordon et al., (New York: Pantheon Books), 95–108.

2 Lyons, J. O., 1978, *The Invention of the Self. The Hinge of Consciousness in the Eighteenth Century* (Carbondale, IL: Southern Illinois University Press); Taylor 1989; Porter, Roy (ed.), 1997. *Rewriting the Self* (London and New York: Routledge); Gay, Peter, 1995. *The Naked Heart. The Bourgeois Experience Victoria to Freud* (London and New York: W. W. Norton & Co); Giddens 1991.

3 Dekker, Rudolf, 2002b, 'Introduction', in Rudolf Dekker 2002a, 7–21; Arianne Baggerman, 2002. 'Autobiography and family memory in the nineteenth century', in Dekker 2002a, 161–73.

4 See chapter 9 for an in-depth discussion of developments in the second half of the nineteenth century.

5 Taylor 1989; Giddens 1991.

6 Wahrman 2004, 290.

7 See chapter 4 for an introduction to Laqueur's work.

8 Laqueur 1990, 134–42.

9 Wahrman 2004, 129.

10 Wahrman 2004, 276.

11 Wahrman 2004, 276.

12 Wahrman 2004, 275, 278.

13 Wahrman 2004, 277–8.

14 Mak 1997, 98–163. See also Mak 2004.

15 Schweickhard 1803, 14.

16 Schweickhard 1803, 14.

17 Schallgruber, Joseph, 1825, '[Gerichtliche Medizin]', Zeitschrift für die Staatsarzneikunde, Ergänzungsheft, IV, 309–11, at 310.

18 Virchow 1856, 774.

19 Tourtual 1856, 22.

20 Schäffler 1808, 117–18.

21 Jagemann, 1845, 'Beschreibung einer merkwürdigen Zwitterbildung', Neue Zeitschrift für Geburtskunde, XVII:1, 15–20, at 20.

22 Schneider and Sommering 1817, 156.

23 Worbe 1815, 480. While assigned as a girl at birth and living as such in the period Worbe is narrating, Worbe uses 'he' in the text.

24 Worbe 1815, 481–2.

25 It is a quite familiar nineteenth-century medical opinion that with the descent of the testicles a man erroneously raised a girl would start to experience male sexual desires. See e.g. Debierre, Charles, 1886. 'L'Hermaphrodite devant le code civil. L'hermaphroditisme, sa nature, son origine, ses conséquences sociales', Archives de l'anthropologie criminelle, I, 305–43, at 322; Debierre, Charles, 1891. L'Hermaphroditisme, structure, fonctions, état psychologique et mental, état civil et mariage, dangers et remèdes (Paris: J. B. Baillière), 87–8. Debierres opinion is cited by Guermonprez as an accepted scientific truth: Guermonprez 1892, 272. In 1844, this opinion on the relation between descending testicles and male sexual desires is doubted by Mulder already: Mulder, Jan Andries, [1844]. Aanteekeningen omtrent den hermaphrodiet Maria Rosina, later Gottlieb Göttlich genaamd [n.p.].

26 Worbe 1815, 482–3.

27 Worbe 1815, 488, emphasis in original.

28 Huette, 1856, 'Hermaphrodisme apparent chez le sexe masculin', Gazette médicale de Paris, 3rd series, tome XI, 26:9, 141.

29 Huette 1856.

30 Benoit 1840, 27.

31 Another early example is of the Dutch gynaecologist Mulder [1844]; however, this was a case of a hermaphrodite 'on show', which offered very distinct possibilities for physical and 'psychological' examinations. See Mak 2011, for a discussion of hermaphrodites exhibiting themselves to physicians in exchange for money.

32 Benoit 1840, 24.

33 Benoit 1840, 25.

34 Benoit 1840, 27.

35 Benoit 1840, 27.

36 Benoit 1840, 28.

37 Benoit 1840, 27.

38 Benoit 1840, 35.

39 Worbe 1815, 486–7.

40 Traxel 1856, 289–91.

41 Jones, Joseph, 1871, 'Singular and distressing case of malformation of genital organs', *Medical Record*, IX, 1 July, 198–9.

42 Benoit 1840, 28.

43 Guermonprez 1892, 304.

44 See for discussion among physicians on their relation to the law chapter 5 and Mak, Geertje, 2005b, 'Doubtful sex in civil law: nineteenth and early twentieth century proposals for ruling hermaphroditism', *Cardozo Journal of Law & Gender*, 12:1, 101–15.

45 *Das preußische Landrecht* ('Prussian State Law') section 1, part 1: '§19. If children are born hermaphroditic, the parents decide which sex they shall be raised as; §20. However, at the age of eighteen such a person is free to choose to which sex he wants to belong; §21. This choice determines his future rights; §22. However, if the rights of a third party are dependent on the sex of a putative hermaphrodite, that party may petition to have this person examined by experts; §23. The findings of the experts supersede the choice of the hermaphrodite and his parents. See Wilhelm, Eugen, 1909, *Die rechtliche Stellung der (körperlichen) Zwitter de lege lata und de lege ferenda* (Halle on der Saale: Carl Marhold Verlagsbuchhandlung), 69–70.

46 Schneider 1809, 166; Schneider and Sommering 1817, 137.

47 See e.g. Naegele, D. F. C., 1819, 'Beschreibung eines Falles von Zwitterbildung bei einem Zwillingspaar', *Deutsches Archiv für die Physiologie*, Band V, 136–40, at 137, on the case of the twins Katharina and Maria Manzer; Hoffman 1877, summarized in Neugebauer 1908, 256–7, and the surprisingly late case in *Kölnische Zeitung*, 1903, cited in Neugebauer 1908, 595–6.

48 Worbe 1815, 482.

49 Worbe 1815, 487, emphasis added.

50 Naegele 1819, 136–7.

51 I only collected medical case histories of autopsies in case there was an interesting biography.

52 Schäffler 1801, 118.

53 Follin, 1851, 'D'un cas rémarquable d'hermaphrodisme. Avec quelques considérations sur la détermination du sexe', *Gazette des hôpitaux civils et militaires*, XXIV:140, 561–3, at 561.

54 Report of Hoffmann 1877, summarized in Neugebauer 1908, 256–7.
55 Mayer, 1825, 'Über hermaphroditische Bildungen', *Journal der Chirurgie und Augenheilkunde*, VIII:2, 195–213, at 201.
56 Hufeland, 1801, 'Beschreibung und Abbildung eines zu Berlin beobachteten weiblichen Hermaphroditen', *Journal der practischen Heilkunde*, Band XII:2, 170–2; Stark, Johann Christian, 1801. 'Kurze Beschreibung eines sogenannten Hermaphroditen oder Zwitters, welcher aber mehr zum männlichen, als weiblichen Geschlechte zu rechnen isst, nebst einer Vorerinnerung', *Neues Archiv für die Geburtshülfe, Frauenzimmer und Kinderkrankheiten mit Hinsicht auf die Physiologie, Diätik und Chirurgie*, Band II:3, 538–54; Martens, Franz Heinrich, 1802. *Beschreibung und Abbildung der männlichen Geschlechtsteile von Maria Dorothea Derrier aus Berlin* (Leipzig: Baumgärtnerische Buchhandlung); Schneider 1809; Feiler, Johann, 1820. *Über angeborene menschliche Missbildungen im allgemeinen und Hermaphroditen insbesondere. Ein Beitrag zur Physiologie, pathologischen Anatomie, und gerichtlichen Arzneiwissenschaft* (Landshut: Philipp Krüll), 68–133; Mayer, A. F., 1835. 'Beschreibung des Körperbaus des Hermaphroditen Dürrge (Derrier)', *Wochenschrift für die gesammte Heilkunde*, Band III:50, 801–13; Neugebauer 1908, 154–6, 181.
57 Schmidt, C. H., 1821, 'Beschreibung eines weiblichen Hermaphroditen, nach seinen äussern und innern Geschlechtstheilen', *Journal der practischen Heilkunde*, Band XLVI:6, 101–7; Loir 1854, 12–3; DaCorogna, 1864. 'Hermaphroditisme apparent chez une personne du sexe féminin', *Bulletins de la Société anatomique de Paris*, 2nd series, tome IX, 39: November, 481–8, esp. 481; Leblond, 1885. 'Du pseudohermaphrodisme comme impédiment médico-légal de la déclaration du sexe dans l'acte de naissance', *Annales d'hygiène publique et de médecine légale*, 3rd series, tome XIV:3, 293–302, esp. 293 and 299; Debierre 1891, 69–83; Neugebauer 1908, 101–3, 151; Dreger 1998, 54–7.
58 Froriep, Robert, 1833a, 'Beschreibung eines Zwitters nebst Abbildung der Geschlechtstheile desselben', *Wochenschrift für die gesammte Heilkunde*, Band I:3, 61–70; Froriep, Robert, 1833b. 'Miscellaneous', *Frorieps Notizen*, Band XXXVI:9, 137–8; Mulder [1844]; Neugebauer 1908, 196, 458–60; Dreger 1998, 52–4.
59 See Mak 2011 for hermaphrodites exhibiting themselves, in particular Hohmann.
60 Virchow, 1872, 'Vorstellung eines Hermaphroditen', *Berliner klininische Wochenschrift*, IX:49, 585–8, at 588.
61 Legros 1835, 273.
62 Wahrman 2004, 168. Wahrman uses both the indications 'socially' and 'outwardly'.
63 *Shorter Oxford English Dictionary* (5th ed., 2002).

CHAPTER 3. HERCULINE BARBIN

1 In this chapter, the page numbers in the notes refer to the text re-edited by Foucault and translated by Richard McDougall; I will refer to this text as *Herculine Barbin* 1874 (1980). The original is to be found in Tardieu 1874.
2 Foucault 1980, xi.
3 Foucault 1980, vii–x.
4 Foucault 1980, x.

5 Goujon, 1869, 'Étude d'un cas d'hermaphrodisme bisexuel imparfait chez l'homme', *Journal de l'anatomie et de la physiologie normales et pathologiques de l'homme et des animaux*, VI, 599–615, at 599, 'L'autopsie . . . a permis . . . de confirmer l'exactitude du diagnostic qui l'avait en dernier lieu remis à sa véritable place dans la société'; translation in *Herculine Barbin* 1874 (1980), 131.

6 See e.g. Foucault, Michel, 1976, *La Volonté de savoir. Histoire de la sexualité*, 1 (Paris: Gallimard).

7 *Herculine Barbin* 1874 (1980), 62.

8 *Herculine Barbin* 1874 (1980), 78.

9 Goujon 1869; Tardieu 1874.

10 Wahrman 2004, 42–4, quotation 42–3.

11 *Herculine Barbin* 1874 (1980), 3.

12 *Herculine Barbin* 1874 (1980), 3.

13 *Herculine Barbin* 1874 (1980), 98, emphasis in original.

14 *Herculine Barbin* 1874 (1980), 98.

15 Taylor 1989, 368–92.

16 The references to himself with the pseudonym Camille at certain points in the text, as well her regular reference to future readers, indicate this.

17 See e.g. Butler, Judith, 1990, *Gender Trouble. Feminism and the Subversion of Identity* (New York and London: Routledge), 93–106; Weeks, Jeffrey, 1991. *Against Nature: Essays on History, Sexuality and Identity* (London: Rivers Oram), 164; Epstein 1995, 111–14; Dreger 1998, 16–19, 28–9, 51–2;

18 Only Hausman 1995, 76, very briefly questions the correctness of talking in terms of gender disorder in the case of Barbin, as the term 'gender disorder' has only come up in a late twentieth-century context of medical treatments of transsexuals.

19 See for the history of autobiography: Lyons 1978; Nussbaum, Felicity A., 1989, *The Autobiographical Subject. Gender and Ideology in Eighteenth-Century England* (Baltimore and London: Johns Hopkins University Press); Taylor 1989; Gay 1995; Oosterhuis 2000, 215–30; Dekker 2002b; Porter, Roy, 2003. *Flesh in the Age of Enlightenment* (London: Allen Lane).

20 Pascal, Roy, 1960, *Design and Truth in Autobiography* (Cambridge, MA, and London: Harvard University Press), 5, 9, 39, quoted in Nussbaum 1989, 7.

21 Buckley, Jerome, 1984, *The Turning Key. Autobiography and the Subjective Impulse since 1800*, (Cambridge, MA, and London: Harvard University Press), 52, 39–40, quoted in Nussbaum 1989, 6 and 227, n. 11.

22 Nussbaum 1989, see also Porter 1997, 12; Flint, Kate, 1997. ' ". . . As a rule, I does not mean I" ', in Porter 1997, 156–66; Stanton, Domna C., 1987, 'Autogynography: is the subject different?', in Domna C. Stanton (ed.), *The Female Autograph: Theory and Practice of Autobiography from the Tenth to the Twentieth Century* (Chicago: Chicago University Press), 3–20; Steedman, C., 2000, 'Enforced narratives. Stories of another self', in T. Cosslett, C. Lury and P. Summerfield (eds), *Feminism and Autobiography: Text Theories Methods* (London and New York: Routledge), 24–39.

23 Blau DuPlessis, Rachel, 1985, *Writing beyond the Ending: Narrative Strategies of Twentieth-Century Women Writers* (Bloomington: Indiana University Press), chapter 1.

24 See Dekker 2002b, 13–15; Baggerman 2002, 163–6.
25 See Lyons 1978, Nussbaum 1989; Taylor 1989; Gay 1995; Oosterhuis 2000, 215–30; Dekker 2002a; Porter 2003.
26 Oosterhuis 2000, 218–20.
27 *Herculine Barbin* 1874 (1980), 8; see also 30, where Barbin, notes Camille's increasing aversion and inaptness to handicrafts and preference for reading; these inclinations are not gendered explicitly.
28 See for other examples: Mak 1997, 72.
29 *Herculine Barbin* 1874 (1980), 10.
30 *Herculine Barbin* 1874 (1980), 12.
31 *Herculine Barbin* 1874 (1980), 27.
32 *Herculine Barbin* 1874 (1980), 28.
33 *Herculine Barbin* 1874 (1980), 33.
34 *Herculine Barbin* 1874 (1980), 34.
35 *Herculine Barbin* 1874 (1980), 35.
36 Compare also *Herculine Barbin* 1874 (1980), 36.
37 *Herculine Barbin* 1874 (1980), 35.
38 *Herculine Barbin* 1874 (1980), 44.
39 *Herculine Barbin* 1874 (1980), 51.
40 *Herculine Barbin* 1874 (1980), 52.
41 *Herculine Barbin* 1874 (1980), 57.
42 *Herculine Barbin* 1874 (1980), 57–8, italics original.
43 *Herculine Barbin* 1874 (1980), 54.
44 *Herculine Barbin* 1874 (1980), 61.
45 *Herculine Barbin* 1874 (1980), 63.
46 *Herculine Barbin* 1874 (1980), 75.
47 *Herculine Barbin* 1874 (1980), 79.
48 *Herculine Barbin* 1874 (1980), 91–2.
49 *Herculine Barbin* 1874 (1980), 95–6.
50 *Herculine Barbin* 1874 (1980), 96.
51 *Herculine Barbin* 1874 (1980), 94–5.
52 *Herculine Barbin* 1874 (1980), 95.
53 Foucault 1980; Butler 1990, 93–106; Weeks 1991, 164.
54 This cannot be traced in the English translation as only the French language marks certain adverbs linked to a person as female or male.
55 This would be consistent with Valerie Traub's findings for early modern England: Traub, Valerie, 2002, *The Renaissance of Lesbianism in Early Modern England* (Cambridge: Cambridge University Press), 158–87.
56 Goujon in *Herculine Herculine Barbin* 1874 (1980), 130.
57 *Indépendant de la Charente-Inférieure*, 21 July 1860, cited in *Herculine Barbin* 1874 (1980), 145.
58 *Herculine Barbin* 1874 (1980), 91.
59 *Herculine Barbin* 1874 (1980), 93.
60 *Herculine Barbin* 1874 (1980), 94.
61 *Herculine Barbin* 1874 (1980), 78.

62 *Herculine Barbin* 1874 (1980), 80–1.
63 *Herculine Barbin* 1874 (1980), 101.
64 *Herculine Barbin* 1874 (1980), 110.
65 *Herculine Barbin* 1874 (1980), 110–11.
66 See among many others: Connell, R. W., 1995, *Masculinities* (Cambridge: Polity Press); Tosh, John, 2005. *Manliness and Masculinities in Nineteenth-Century Britain: Essays on Gender, Family and Empire* (Harlow, etc.: Pearson).
67 *Herculine Barbin* 1874 (1980), 90.
68 *Herculine Barbin* 1874 (1980), 95–6, 101.
69 *Herculine Barbin* 1874 (1980), 99.
70 *Herculine Barbin* 1874 (1980), 99.
71 *Herculine Barbin* 1874 (1980), 100.
72 See also *Herculine Barbin* 1874 (1980), 101 and 105–6 for his desire of partaking of the erotic life of the city, and his immediate repudiation.
73 *Herculine Barbin* 1874 (1980), 106.
74 *Herculine Barbin* 1874 (1980), 106–7.
75 *Herculine Barbin* 1874 (1980), 103.
76 *Herculine Barbin* 1874 (1980), 99.
77 Foucault 1980, xxi: 'elegant, affected and allusive style, that is somewhat turgid and outdated'; Butler 1990, 98: 'sentimental and melodramatic tone'; Epstein 1995, 112: 'highly rhetorical sentiment'; Dreger 1998, 17: 'thick dramatic prose'.
78 *Herculine Barbin* 1874 (1980), 59.
79 Culler, Jonathan, 1981, *The Pursuit of Signs* (Ithaca: Cornell University Press), 141.
80 *Herculine Barbin* 1874 (1980), 102–3.
81 *Herculine Barbin* 1874 (1980), 100.
82 *Herculine Barbin* 1874 (1980), 100.
83 Culler 1981, 141.
84 Culler 1981, 157.
85 Laqueur, Thomas, 1989, 'Bodies, details, and the humanitarian narrative', in Lynn Hunt (ed.), *The New Cultural History* (Berkeley, Los Angeles and London: University of California Press), 176–206.

PART II. BODY

1 Laqueur 1990, 1–148. Laqueur has been severely criticized for only paying attention to Galenic views, leaving Aristotelian opinions aside for convenience's sake. This includes his all too positive view on the position of hermaphrodites, which he incidentally shared with Foucault. See e.g. Park, Katharine, and Nye, Robert, 1991, 'Destiny is anatomy.' (Essay review of *Making Sex: Body and Gender from the Greeks to Freud*, by Thomas Laqueur), *The New Republic*, 204, 18 February, 53–7; Daston, Lorraine, and Park, Katharine, 1996, 'The hermaphrodite and the orders of nature: sexual ambiguity in early modern France', in Louise Fradenbury and Corla Freccero (eds), *Prenodern Sexualities* (London and New York: Routledge), 117–36; Park, Katharine, 1997, 'The rediscovery of the clitoris. French medicine and the tribade, 1570–1620', in David Hilman and Corla Mazzio (eds), *The Body*

in Parts: Fontasies of Corporeality on Early Modern Europe (London and New York: Routledge), 170–93; Stolberg 2003; Gowing 2003.

2 Laqueur 1990, 149–93.

3 Dreger 1998, 139–66.

4 Mol, Annemarie, 2002, *The Body Multiple. Ontology in Medical Practice* (Durham, NC, and London: Duke University Press), 1–51.

5 Please also refer to Mak, Geertje, 2006, 'Doubting sex from within. A praxiographic approach to a late nineteenth-century case of hermaphroditism', *Gender & History* 18:2, 360–88, for this argument.

CHAPTER 4. HOW TO GET THE SEMEN TO THE NECK OF THE WOMB

1 Schweickhard 1803, 14.

2 Schweickhard 1803, 14–15.

3 Schweickhard 1803, 15–16.

4 Schweickhard 1803, 16.

5 Schweickhard 1803, 18.

6 Schweickhard 1803, 21.

7 Schweickhard 1803, 22–3.

8 Gowing 2003, 17–51; Duden 1987, 26–30, and, see for the difficulties of establishing pregnancy, 181–94.

9 Duden 1987, 20–4, 140–71; Gowing 2003, 29, 52–81.

10 Gowing 2003, 48–51.

11 Duden 1987, 94, 100–4.

12 Duden 1987 (English translation 1991) consists of a thorough analysis of the language of the body in the interaction between an early eighteenth-century German doctor and his female patients; see also Lachmund 1997, 27–51; Foucault, Michel, 2003 (orig. French 1963). *The Birth of the Clinic. An Archaeology of Medical Perception* (London and New York: Routledge), xi; Jewson, N. D., 1976. 'The disappearance of the sick-man from medical cosmology, 1770–1870', *Sociology*, 10:2, 232–4; Bynum 1994, 33–4.

13 Originally, these terms stem from N. D. Jewson's ground-breaking article of 1976, which triggered a great deal of discussion about the historically changing relationship between doctors, patients and medical science (Bynum 1994, 232).

14 Lachmund 1997, 52–100.

15 Lachmund 1997, 194–203.

16 Ackerman 1990, 11–59.

17 Lachmund 1997, 37–41.

18 Poovey, Mary, 1987, ' "Scenes of an indelicate character". The medical "teatment" of Victorian women', in Catharine Gallagher and Thomas Laqueur (eds), *The Making of the Modern Body* (Berkeley and Los Angeles: University of California Press), 137–68; Moscucci, 112–27; Schoon, Lidy, 1995. *De gynaecologie als belichaming van vrouwen. Verloskunde en gynaecologie 1840–1920* (Zutphen: Walburg Pers), 32–63.

19 Moscucci 1990, 75–81; Schoon 1995, 37–41.

20 Kapsalis, Terri, 1997, *Public Privates. Performing Gynecology from Both Ends of the Speculum* (Durham, NC, and London: Duke University Press), 31–57.

21 Moscucci 1990, 112–27; Bynum 1994, 33–5, 203 and 210 (illustrations of how to palpate women without seeing their bodies); Lachmund 1997, 201: 'Wie problematisch allein schon der Blick des Arztes auf den weiblichen Körper in der Privatpraxis ist, zeigt die Empfehlung, den Körper ersatzweise in einem dunklen Zimmer unter dem Rock abzutasten'; see also 79 on the difference between private practice and hospitals, at which even the examination of the genitals seems to have been allowed in the early nineteenth century.

22 Benoit 1840, 33.

23 Stark was one of the first physicians to dismiss theoretically the ability of all other genital parts to be decisive for the determination of someone's sex, except for the testicles and ovaries; in his own research he did not practise what he preached, as he only very superficially palpated Durrgé's alleged testicle (Stark 1801). The well-known anatomist Johann Müller stated in 1830 that only the presence of 'Saamenkanälchen' in testicular tissue or 'Graafschen Follikeln' in ovarian tissue could establish someone's sex. Müller, Johannes, 1830. *Bildungsgeschichte der Genitalien aus anatomischen Untersuchungen an Embryonen des Menschen und der Thiere, nebst einem Anhang über die chirurgische Behandlung der Hypospadia* (Düsseldorf: Arnz); Neugebauer 1908, 343.

24 Schweickhard 1803, 16–17.

25 Schweickhard 1803, 17–18.

26 Schweickhard 1803, 25: '. . . mag er sich vario situ et applicatione zu helfen wissen)'.

27 Schweickhard 1803, 34–5.

28 Schweickhard 1803, 36–7.

29 Schweickhard 1803, 37.

30 Schweickhard 1803, 37–8.

31 Schweickhard 1803, 44–5.

32 Schweickhard 1803, 46.

33 This conclusion of the case is to be found in the archival sources: Generallandesarchiv Karlsruhe, Ehegerichtsprotokoll des Kirchenrates 1794, Signatur 61/4262, Resolution Markgrafen Karl Friedrich, 17 December 1794.

34 Schweickhard 1803, 52.

35 Schweickhard 1803, 9–10.

36 Schweickhard 1803, 34.

37 Other first-hand case-histories in which the characteristics of early nineteenth-century examinations of the sexual functioning of hermaphrodites described can be found include: Desgenettes 1791, 'Testicules passés de l'abdomen dans le scrotum, à l'âge de seize à dix-sept ans; et verge mal conformée: observation présentée, et lue à la Société royale des sciences de Montpellier, le 4 août 1790', *Journal de médecine, chirurgie et pharmacie*, tome XXXVIII: July, 81–4; Schäffler 1801; Worbe 1815, 491–2; Schneider and Sommering 1817, 136–7, 141–2; Joseph Schallgruber, 1823. *Abhandlungen im Fache der Gerichtsarzneikunde* (Grätz: Miller), 131; Mayer 1825; Froriep 1833a, 68–70; Fronmüller 1834, 206–9;

Coste, 1835. 'Conformation vicieuse des organes génitaux chez une femme. Operation', *Journal des connaissances médico-chirurgicales*, 3:7, 276–7; Naegele 1819; Jagemann 1845, 19–21; S. H. Harris, 1847. 'Case of Doubtful Sex', *American Journal of the Medical Sciences*, XXI: July, 121–4; Traxel 1856, 290; Tourtual 1856, 33–7; Huette 1856, 141; Virchow 1856, 774; Martini 1861. Some case histories refer to these characteristics, but differ in interesting ways: Mulder [1844], Benoit 1840. Benoit will be discussed below in more detail, Mulder is a case of a hermaphrodite exhibiting himself, a topic I discuss elsewhere (Mak 2011). Some French case-histories treat sexual attraction more as a social aspect of sex, which will also be discussed below.

38 Fronmüller 1834, 206–7.
39 Fronmüller 1834, 208–9.
40 Worbe 1815, 491–2, 489–90.
41 Schneider 1809, 164–5.
42 Schäffler 1801, 120.
43 Huette 1856, 141.
44 Traxel 1856, 290.
45 Healey 2009, 148, noted that Soviet physicians, who usually abstained from talking about sexual pleasure, in cases of hermaphroditism suddenly had to discuss these aspects of physical sex. Partly, they could do so because they considered hermaphroditism a physical, not a psychological phenomenon (Healey 2009, 140). But maybe this way of discussing sexual dysfunction also followed from the fact that many of the cases concerned peasants who had hardly been in contact with modern medicine.
46 In some cases, such information was (also) obtained through the other people involved. See e.g. Schneider and Sommering 1817, 136–7, 141–2; Martini 1861, 303–4, 308–10.
47 See e.g. 'Es liess sich durch Friktion leicht in Erektion bringen': Stark 1801, 548; '. . . die Neigung und Kraft zur Erection muss aber in jedem Fall sehr schwach seyn, da sie nach vorhergegangenem Reiben sehr wenig zu bemerken war': Schäffler 1801, 117; 'Es richtete sich bey Berührung, auch beym blossen Anblick eines Mannes auf': Schallgruber 1823; 'Bei diesem Experiment, das einen sichtlichten Reiz auf die Geschlechtsorgane ausübt, erhebt sich das bis dahin nach unten schlaff herabhängend Glied, schwillt an, nimmt an Länge und Dicke zu, und behält, wenn es vollständig rigid geworden ist, nur noch eine kaum merkliche Krümmung nach unten': Jagemann 1845, 19.
48 Benoit 1840, 34.
49 Tourtual 1856, 34–5.
50 Tourtual 1856, 35.
51 Martini 1861, 318–19, emphasis added.
52 Martini 1861, 321.
53 Martini 1861, 322.
54 Laqueur 1990, 177.
55 Laqueur 1990, 49–52.
56 Dreger 1998, 139–66.

57 Reis 2009, 53–4.
58 Reis 2009, 54.
59 This is, by the way, just one possible example to show that Reis's suggestion that this was not the case in Europe ('In this country [the USA] the tendency to proclaim hermaphroditism "impossible" began long before the age of gonads': Reis 2009, 54) is completely mistaken.
60 Schweickhard 1803, 19.
61 This interest in the ovaries is an exception to the rule that physicians were generally not all that interested in establishing their presence or absence; he made no attempt to palpate them, however: Jagemann 1845, 19–20.
62 Jagemann 1845, 20.
63 Schallgruber, 131.
64 Froriep, 1833a, 70.
65 Coste 1835, 276–7.
66 Tourtual 1856, 36.
67 Schneider and Sömmering 1817, 137.

CHAPTER 5. JUSTINE JUMAS: CONFLICTING BODY POLITICS

1 Laurent, François, 1870, *Principes du droit civil français*, vol. 2 (Paris and Brussels: A. Durand and Pedone, Lauriel / Bruyland-Christophe), 397, quoted in Jalabert 1872, 135–6.
2 Hunt, Lynn, 2007, *Inventing Human Rights. A History* (New York and London: Norton & Company), 15–34.
3 Hunt 2007, 113–45.
4 See, for the impotency trials in France in the early modern period, Darmon, Pierre, 1986, *Le Tribunal de l'impuissance: virilité et défaillances conjugales dans l'ancienne France* (Paris: Seuil); McLaren, Angus, 2007. *Impotence: A Cultural History* (Chicago: Chicago University Press); McClive, Cathy, 2009, 'Masculinity on trial: penises, hermaphrodites and the uncertain male body in early modern France', *History Workshop Journal*, 68, 45–68.
5 Tardieu 1874, 18.
6 Foucault 1980, viii–ix.
7 The original sentences can be found in Archives Départementales du Gard, jugements du tribunal d'Alès 29 avril 1869 (7 U 1/91) and 28 janvier 1873 (7 U 1/90), l'arrêt de la cour impériale de Nîmes du 29 novembre 1869 (4 U 3/212), and in Archives Départementales de l'Hérault, l'arrêt de la cour d'appél du 8 mai 1872 (2 U 139). The sentences are extensively quoted in Tardieu 1874. For convenience's sake I here refer to the pages in Tardieu's text instead of the archival original; I have however taken the liberty of changing the initials used in Tardieu's text to the full name for the sake of intelligibility.
8 Darmon 1986, see for 'trial by congress' and its final abolition during the French Revolution: 186–209; see also McLaren 2007 for a cultural approach to the history of impotency.
9 Tardieu 1874, 7.

10 Tardieu 1874, 7.

11 Tardieu 1874, 8.

12 Tardieu 1874, 8–9.

13 Courty, Amédée, 1872, 'Consultation médico-légale à l'appui d'une demande en nullité de mariage', *Montpellier médical*, tome XXVIII:6, 473–88, at 474.

14 Italics in original. Tardieu 1874, 14 and in Courty 1872, 474.

15 Tardieu 1874, 10.

16 The sources are not clear about who exactly appealed.

17 Tardieu 1874, 11.

18 Tardieu 1874, 12.

19 Tardieu probably referred to: Briand, J., and Chaudé, Ernest (ed.) *Manuel complet de médecine légale, contenant un traité élémentaire de chimie légale par J. Bouis* (Paris: J.-B. Baillière et fils, 1869); Tardieu 1874, 18.

20 Tardieu 1874, 21.

21 Courty 1872, 487.

22 Jalabert, Philippe, 1872, 'Examen doctrinal de jurisprudence civile', *Revue critique de législation et de jurisprudence*, new series, tome II:22, 129–49, at 148.

23 Jalabert 1872, 148.

24 According to Tardieu, the annulment was made on the grounds that did not touch the fundamental questions of the case. Unfortunately, I do not have the text of the annulment at my disposal.

25 Cited in Tardieu 1874, 23.

26 Jalabert 1872, 137–8.

27 Courty 1872, 484.

28 Jalabert 1872, 148–9.

29 Cited in Tardieu 1874, 27.

30 Cited in Tardieu 1874, 27–8 (in Tardieu's text it is wrongly 'octobre', but in the original archival sentence it reads rightly 'novembre').

31 See Tardieu 1874, 27–8.

32 Tardieu 1874, 28–9, emphasis added.

33 Courty 1872, 473.

34 Courty 1872, 473–4.

35 Courty 1872, 480–1.

36 Tardieu 1874, 12.

37 Tardieu 1874, 13.

38 Tardieu 1874, 14.

39 Tardieu 1874, 15.

40 Jules de Laugardière, 1866, *Guide de l'officier de l'état civil*, (Colmar: C. M. Hoffmann, 2nd edn), 161, quoted in Jalabert 1872, 133.

41 Laurent 1870, 397.

42 Jalabert 1872, 129.

43 Jalabert 1872, 135.

44 Jalabert 1872, 149.

45 Jalabert 1872, 134.

46 Jalabert 1872, 134–5.

47 In a footnote, Jalabert refers to Bannier, *Des preuves*, 3ème éd., t. I., no. 110, 327, note, Jalabert 1872, 135.
48 Jalabert 1872, 136.
49 Jalabert 1872, 148.
50 Loir 1854, 1.
51 Loir 1854, 1, 28.
52 Loir 1854, 16.
53 Loir 1854, 28.
54 Garnier, P. 1885, 'Du pseudo-hermaphrodisme comme impédiment médico-légal à la déclaration du sexe dans l'acte de naissance', *Annales d'hygiène publique et de médecine légale*, 3rd series, tome XIV:3, 285–93, at 287–8.
55 Garnier 1885, 289.
56 Garnier 1885, 292.
57 Garnier 1885, 292.
58 Garnier 1885, 293.
59 Debierre 1886, 335–6.
60 Debierre 1886, 337–8.
61 Tardieu 1874, 28.
62 Dalloz, D. (ed.), 1882, *Jurisprudence Générale* (Paris: Bureau de la Jurisprudence Générale), vol. 2, 155–6.
63 Dalloz 1882, 156.
64 Dalloz 1882, 156.
65 Dalloz 1882, 156.
66 Debierre 1886, 341.
67 Debierre 1886, 340.
68 A very interesting critical discussion of this standpoint, showing the difficulty of claiming that 'nature' should decide, can be found in Brouardel, Paul, 1904. 'Malformation des organes génitaux de la femme. Y a-t-il lieu de reconnaître l'existence d'un troisième sexe?', *Annales d'hygiène publique et de médecine légale*, 4th series, tome I:3, 193–204.
69 De María Arana, Marcus, 2005, http://www.sf-hrc.org/ftp/uploadedfiles/sfhumanrights/Committee_Meetings/Lesbian_Gay_Bisexual_Transgender/SFHRC%20Intersex%20Report%281%29.pdf

CHAPTER 6. THE DISLODGEMENT OF THE PERSON

1 See Mak 2011.
2 These findings of an increasing willingness of patients to visit a doctor correspond with Edward Shorter's rather rough impression: Shorter, Edward, 1985. *Bedside Manners. The Troubled History of Doctors and Patients* (New York: Simon & Schuster), 57–62, 118–21. For a much more precise appreciation of a rural French population's willingness to visit a doctor during the nineteenth century, see Ackerman 1990, 11–59.
3 McGrath, Roberta, 2002, *Seeing Her Sex. Medical Archives and the Female Body* (Manchester: Manchester University Press), 100–44.

4   See Dreger 1998, 110–14; Mak 2006.

5   Guermonprez 1893, 252–3.

6   See Mak 2011.

7   References to the examination of ejaculated sperm were found nineteen times in my database; only two of these cases date back to before 1883. Two cases refer to the impossibility of obtaining sperm, one because of the hermaphrodite's refusal, the other because of the young age of the hermaphrodite.

8   Marchand 1883, 291.

9   Marchand 1883, 291.

10 Citation: Descoust, 1886, 'Sur un cas d'hermaphrodisme', *Annales d'hygiène publique et de médecine légale*, tome XVI, 87–90, at 89; the other case histories: Reverdin, Auguste, 1905. 'Note sur un cas d'hypospadie', *Annales des maladies des organes génito-urinaires*, XXIII: 15 January, 138–45, at 140; Walther 1902, 941; Pozzi, Samuel, 1884. 'Homme hypospade considéré depuis 28 ans comme femme', *Annales de gynécologie*, tome XI: April, 257–68, at 263–4.

11 Blondel, M. R., 1899, 'Observation de pseudohermaphroditisme', *Bulletins et mémoires de la Société obstétricale et gynécologique de Paris*, XV:January, 3–12, at 8.

12 Kösters, Johannes, 1898, *Ein neuer Fall von Hermaphroditismus spurius masculinus* (Berlin: Gustav Schade), at 22.

13 Messner, 1892, 'Ein neuer Fall von Hermaphroditismus verus (Hermaphrodismus verus unilateralis?) am Lebenden untersucht und beschrieben', *Archiv für pathologische Anatomie und Physiologie und klinische Medizin*, Band CXXIX:2, 203–13, at 209–10. In this case, there is no wish to reassign sex. I am not sure whether this is not actually a case of display in exchange for money. Although the man in question suffered from heavy pains during menstruation, there is no sign of a demand for treatment. Moreover, he had been seen by several other physicians at several other hospitals.

14 Weissbart, 1902, 'Ein männlicher Scheinzwitter', *Monatsschrift für Geburtshülfe und Gynäkologie*, March, 266–72, at 269; Hirschfeld, Magnus, 1906. 'Drei Fälle von irrtümlicher Geschlechtsbestimmung', *Medizinische Reform, Wochenschrift für soziale Medizin*, XIV:51, 614–17, at 615.

15 Neugebauer, Franz Ludwig von, 1896, 'Ein junges Mädchen von männliches Geschlecht. Verhängnisvolle Folgen einer irrtümlichen Geschlechtsbestimmung. Verhandlung vor dem Strafrichter', *Internationale photographische Monatsschrift für Medizin und Naturwissenschaften*, III: August–September, 259–67, at 262, italics added.

16 Neugebauer, Franz Ludwig von, 1904a, 'Mann oder Weib? Sechs eigene Beobachtungen von Scheinzwittertum und "Erreur de sexe"', *Zentralblatt für Gynäkologie*, XXVIII:2, 33–51, at 49.

17 Although a case beyond the time span I have chosen, I decided not to leave it out for it is the only one which describes in detail how sperm was obtained during a consultation.

18 Hirschfeld, Magnus, 1912, *Geschlechts-Umwandlungen. Irrtümer in der Geschlechtsbestimmung. Sechs Fälle aus der forensischen Praxis* (Berlin: Adler Verlag), 30.

19 Hirschfeld 1912, 30.

20 Hirschfeld 1912, 24.

21 Laqueur, Thomas, 2003, *Solitary Sex. A Cultural History of Masturbation* (New York: Zone Books), 276–302.

22 Kapsalis 1997, 11–30; see Henslin, James M., and Biggs, Mae E., 1971, 'Dramaturgical desexualisation: the sociology of the vaginal examination', in James M. Henslin (ed.), *Studies in the Sociology of Sex* (New York: Appleton-Century-Crafts), 243–72.

23 Pernick, Martin S., 1985, *A Calculus of Suffering. Pain, Professionalism, and Anesthesia in Nineteenth-Century America* (New York: Columbia University Press), 35–76; Pernick shows that although the technique of anaesthesia was quickly adopted by all hospitals in the USA and Europe, its use remained selective until 1880, that is, under different circumstances and for various groups anaesthesia was applied differently (237–8).

24 Pernick 1985, 59.

25 Pernick 1985, 58–62.

26 Pernick 1985, 84–5, 228–34.

27 Hirschauer, Stefan, 1991, 'The manufacture of bodies in surgery', *Social Studies of Science*, 21:2, 279–319, see 305, 286–9 and 305–14 for a description of how patient bodies turn into objects, and how the two different meanings of that body are dealt with (its meaning in everyday life and its meaning as an anatomical object) by certain routines or rituals.

28 Kirsten Rehwinkel presented a paper in Berlin at the ESSH Conference in 2004 in which she described the introduction of anaesthesia as an artificial follow-up to cases of 'apparent death', pointing to the fundamental change this brought about with regard to the relation of the doctor to a body from which the individuality had temporarily disappeared.

29 Dreger 1998, 91–2.

30 Marchand 1883, 289.

31 Fancourt Barnes, 1888, '[Meeting of the British Gynaecological Society, April 25, 1888]', *British Gynaecological Journal*, IV:April, 205–12, 231, see 206 n., 210; see for other examples Siebourg-Barmen, 1898. 'Ueber einen Fall von Pseudohermaphroditismus masculinus completus', *Monatsschrift für Geburtshülfe und Gynäkologie*, July, 73–5, and Geijl, A. 1902. 'Over operatief ingrijpen bij pseudohermaphroditismus masculinus of femininus externus', *Medisch weekblad van noord- en zuid-Nederland*, IX:22–38, 281–4, 326–30, 381–8, 397–404, 413–20, 433–5, 464–71, 494–501, 512–19, 555–8, 567–70, 586–91, 632–9, see 282.

32 Only one of these cases happened to be French (Descoust 1886, 88), so possibly the development of using narcosis for the purpose of diagnosis (or the use of narcosis in general) was more rapid in Germany and the Netherlands than in France.

33 Pernick 1985, 228–30.

34 Neugebauer 1904a, 45.

35 Schneller, 1894, 'Ein Fall von Pseudohermaphroditismus', *Münchener medizinische Wochenschrift: Organ für amtliche und praktische Ärzte*, LXI:33, 655–6, at 655.

36 Alberti, 1905, 'Kasuïstiek zu Hypertrichosis universa acquisita und Veränderungen der Sexualorgane', *Beiträge zur Geburtshilfe und Gynäkolologie*, IX:3, 339–44, at 340.

37 Alberti 1905, 340.

38 Alberti 1905, 340.

39 See e.g. Neugebauer 1908, 422; see for use of narcosis in order to be able to take pictures also: Henrotay, J. 1901. 'Hypospade pénoscrotal élevé en femme jusqu'à 24 ans', *Bulletin de la Société royale belge de gynécologie et d'obstrétrique*, XI:4, 103–5, at 104.

40 Alberti 1905, 341.

41 Neugebauer, Franz Ludwig von, 1902, 'Ein interessanter Fall von zweifelhaftem Geschlecht eines als Frau verheirateten Scheinzwitters', *Zentralblatt für Gynäkologie*, XXVI:7, 171–5, see 173.

42 See e.g. Neugebauer 1908, 426.

43 In Anglo-Saxon case-histories I have found two cases of the removal of gonadal tissue at the hermaphrodite's request, two to lessen the pain in the groin, and only one in which it was stated that 'it would be a singularly unfortunate thing for a person with all the outward appearance of a female to develop into a man as to internal organs and feelings': Buchanan, George, 1885. 'Hermaphrodite, aged 9, in whom two testicles were excised from the labia majora [meeting Medical-Chirurgical Society 9 January 1885]', *Glasgow Medical Journal*, XXIII: March, 213–17, at 214.

44 I cannot explain why the number of laparotomies in Neugebauer's overviews did not change between 1903 and 1908. I have tried to work out whether he had possibly changed his categories of counting (there are some difficulties there) but I still cannot find the reason why there is no increase at all.

45 See, for the emergence of medical photography and its impact on the medical enactment of the female body, McGrath 2002, 100–44.

46 Differences between my figures and Neugebauer's derive from the fact that my figures are a selection from his cases, restricting myself to cases written in French, German, English or Dutch and to hermaphrodites who were alive while their sex was doubted (except for a few examples). The twenty-seven hermaphrodites mentioned here therefore survived surgery.

47 See Part III for an extensive discussion of this issue.

48 See also Spörri 2000 (57–64) on this matter of techniques of looking.

49 Dreger 1998, 150, has also pointed this out, showing that pictures of true hermaphrodites had become pictures of gonadal tissue under a microscope.

50 See Spörri 2000, 57–64; Dreger 1998, 146–50.

51 See Spörri 2000, 57–64; Dreger 1998, 146–50.

52 Pick, L., 1905, 'Über Adenome der männliche und weibliche Keimdrüse bei Hermaphroditismus verus und spurius nebst Bemerkungen über das endometriumähnliche Adenom am inneren weiblichen Genitale', *Berliner klininische Wochenschrift*, XLII:17, 502–9.

53 Pick 1905, 50.

54 Pick, 1905, 508.

55 See Mol 2002 for the specificity of the technique with which – in her case arthero-sclerosis, in my case hermaphroditism – was enacted, Mol 2002, 29–33.

PART III. SELF

1 Hirschauer 1993, 21–65, 321–51; see, for a brief English article on the topic, Hirschauer 1998, 14, 23–4.
2 Hirschauer 1993, 66–115.
3 See Kessler 1998, Fausto-Sterling 2000, 45–77, Hirschauer 1998, 23–4. Hirschauer regards the medical practices as a 'displacement of contradiction' which trans-form social conflicts into theoretical controversies.
4 Hausman 1995, 14.
5 Dreger 1998, 110–66; see, for a summary, Dreger 1999b, 6–11. Both Foucault and Laqueur suggested the coming into being of a strictly medically defined 'true sex', but they did not trace the narrowing down of that definition as precisely as Dreger.
6 Dreger 1998, 113.
7 Dreger 1998, 157–8.
8 Scott 1991.
9 See Foucault 1972, 78–109, for a criticism of 'suppression', in particular 108.
10 Dreger 1998, 79–109; Reis confusingly switches constantly from referring to the physician's difficulties in defining sex to pointing to their heteronormative standard. If sex cannot be defined, what is the heteronomative standard? Reis 2009, 55–114.
11 Dreger 1998, 110–38; Reis 2009, 55–81.
12 See Jewson 1976.
13 Geijl 1902, 328–9, emphasis added.
14 See, e.g., Kessler 1998, 21–24; Alexander, Tamara, 1999. 'Silence = death', in Dreger, 1999a, 103–10; Fausto-Sterling 2000, 63–6, Preves 2003, 60–86; Karkazis 2008, 58–60, 89–92, 186–91.
15 Meyerowitz 2002, 21–2; see also Doyle, J., 2007, 'Historicising surgery: gender, sex and the surgical imaginary', *Social Semiotics*, 17:3 (special issue: 'Body Modifications'), 341–59.

CHAPTER 7. SEX ASSIGNMENT AROUND 1900.
FROM A LEGAL TO A CLINICAL ISSUE

1 See for an extensive discussion of laws with regard to hermaphrodites and physician's discussions thereof in Germany and France, Mak 2005b.
2 Kösters 1898, 26.
3 Landau, Theodor, 1903, 'Ueber Hermaphroditen. Nebst einigen Bemerkungen über die Erkenntnis und die rechtliche Stellung dieser Individuen', *Berliner klininische Wochenschrift*, XL:15, 339–43, at 342–3.
4 See, for a full quotation and discussion of the entire proposal, Mak 2005b, 201–9.
5 Wilhelm 1909, 59.

 6 Wilhelm 1909, 6–8.
 7 Wilhelm 1909, 59.
 8 See for this case also the previous chapter and Mak 2006.
 9 Guermonprez 1892, 302.
10 Guermonprez 1892, 304, capitals in original. Cf. chapter 2 p. xxx (n. 43) above.
11 Neugebauer 1908, 401.
12 Zangger, H., 1905, 'Über einen Fall von Pseudohermaphroditismus masculinus externus in pathologischanatomischer, psychologischer und forensischer Hinsicht', *Schweizerische Zeitschrift für Strafrecht*, XVIII, 303–14, at 312.
13 Zangger 1905, 311–14.
14 Wilhelm 1909, 62; the quoted phrase is from Zangger.
15 Neugebauer, Franz Ludwig von, 1916, *Hermaphroditismus und Pseudohermaphroditismus* (Wien: Braumüller), 292.
16 See chapter 6, table 2.
17 These discussions on surgery for hermaphrodites would continue in the first half of the twentieth century; see, for the USA, Redick 2004; for Soviet physicians, Healey 2009, 148–54. Healey suggests more of an opposition between the West and the Soviet Union than I can see; in both contexts, a gonadal diagnostic criterion (sometimes including diagnostic surgery) was often in conflict with plastic surgery meant to help the patient create a less ambiguous sex. Exceptional, though, is the way the Soviet physician Andreeva takes sexual pleasure into account: Healey 2009, 152–4.
18 Epstein 1995, 122.
19 Lynds, J. G., 1905, 'Clinical Cases', *Journal of the Michigan State Medical Society*, IV: March, 122–6, at 123.
20 Lynds 1905, 124.
21 Lynds 1905, 124.
22 Blondel 1899, 11.
23 Blondel 1899, 11.
24 Delore, Xavier, 'Des étapes de l'hermaphrodisme,' in *L'Écho médicale de Lyon*, 4 (1899), 193–205, 225–32, 229, described in Dreger 1998, 125–6.
25 Geijl 1902, 282.
26 Geijl 1902, 284.
27 Geijl 1902, 326; elsewhere in the same article he wrote: 'To determine the sex of an hermaphrodite and our practical treatment of its bearer, the constitution of the gonads is of lesser value than the condition of the organs of copulation and the nature of the inner life and soul of the person concerned.' (590)
28 Neugebauer, Franz Ludwig von, 1904b, '[Letter to the editor]', *Interstate Medical Journal St Louis*, XI: May, 317–18, at 318; see also Neugebauer 1908, 62.
29 Landau 1903, 340.
30 Neugebauer 1904a, 43.
31 See on diagnostic laparotomy Dreger 1998, 86, 92–3, 149–50; see for the issue of diagnostic laparotomy also: Myriam Spörri 2002, 249–50.
32 In Neugebauer's register 1908, I can find four laparotomies that were carried out for diagnostic reasons, but three of them do not mention biopsies and two were

carried out alongside a herniotomy; only one (carried out by Neugebauer himself)
was exclusively intended as a biopsy. However, six times a herniotomy had been
performed in order to do a biopsy. In the literature, the *possibility* of performing
a biopsy is mentioned regularly. See for example: Taussig, 1904c. 'Rejoinder to
Dr Goffe's letter', *Interstate Medical Journal St Louis*, XI: May, 316–17, esp.
316, where he counters Goffe's argument that diagnostic surgery would automatically entail castration, referring to five diagnostic laparotomies, mentioned by
Neugebauer, Franz Ludwig von, 1904c. 'What value has the knowledge of
pseudo-hermaphroditism for the practitioner?', *Interstate Medical Journal St Louis*,
XI:February, 103–24, see 118–19. Dreger already mentioned that Guermonprez
was attacked by a colleague in 1892 for not having performed diagnostic surgery,
and that Xavier Delore in 1899 advised performing a laparotomy in cases of a
doubtful sex (Dreger 1998, 92–3; Guermonprez 1892, 343). See also Landau, who
agreed to diagnostic operations by means of an incision in the groin (herniotomy),
but not to laparotomy (because of the life-threatening danger involved): Landau
1903, 341; Westerman, C. W. J., 1903. 'Over miskend pseudohermafroditisme',
Nederlandsch tijdschrift voor Geneeskunde, XXXIX:18, 1009–12, at 1011, also speaks
about removing 'a little piece' from the gonads to perform microscopic examination as a regular practice. Also see for descriptions of diagnostic operations:
Neugebauer, 1908, 429–30 (herniotomy with biopsy) and 431–3 (laparotomy with
biopsy); Péan, 1895. 'Faux hermaphrodite', *Gazette des hôpitaux civils et militaires*,
LXVIII:41, 404–5 (diagnostic laparotomy without biopsy).

33 See for a French discussion: Guermonprez 1893, 255.
34 Landau, Theodor, 1904, 'Mann oder Weib', *Zentralblatt für Gynäkologie*, XVIII:7,
203–4, at 204. This brief reaction to Neugebauer's diagnostic laparotomy is
extraordinary sharp in distinguishing between the clinical and the scientific aims
of an operation.
35 Landau 1903, 343.
36 What follows is a rewritten part of Mak 2005a.
37 Goffe, J. Riddle, 1903, 'A pseudohermaphrodite, in which the female characteristics predominated. Operation for removal of the penis and the utilization of
the skin covering it for formation of a vaginal canal', *American Journal of Obstetrics
and Diseases of Women and Children*, 48:6, 755–63, at 757.
38 See Mak 2005a for more details of the surgery. Lynds (mentioned above) copied
this technique.
39 Goffe 1903, 762–3, italics added.
40 Goffe 1903, 755–7.
41 Goffe 1903, 757.
42 Goffe 1903, 757, italics added.
43 For further details also see Mak 2005a.
44 Goffe 1903, 759.
45 See above for Geijl 1902 and Lynds 1905; Green 1898 (quoted in Neugebauer
1908, 214) removed the functioning testicles of a young woman who wished
to remain female: 'The question now arose, as to what should be done, as the
patient in mind and habit is more a woman that [*sic*] a man, and is illegal for him

to remain as he is in female attire, he expressed a desire to have the testicles removed and continue a woman and it seems to me, that is the best solution of the difficulty.'

46 See, for a thorough analysis of this 'age of idiosyncracy', Redick 2004.

47 Goffe 1903, 762–3, italics added.

48 See, for another critical remark, James M. West from New York, who wrote: 'I consider it unwise and unfair to tamper with these ill-developed organs, endeavouring, for instance, to convert the uncertain sex into a female by amputating the rudimentary penis and establishing an artificial vagina. Grant that the operation has been so far successful as to make a somewhat close approach to the female organs, is it not bitterly unfair to the other party to be joined by holy wedlock to such a being?' (West, James N., 1904. 'Sterility from vaginal causes', Medical News, LXXXV, 58–61, at 59).

49 Taussig, Fred J., 1904a, 'Shall a pseudo-hermaphrodite be allowed to decide to which sex he or she shall belong?', American Journal of Obstetrics and Diseases of Women and Children, 49:2, 162–5.

50 Taussig 1904a, 162, italics added.

51 Taussig 1904a, 163, italics added.

52 Taussig, Fred J., 1904b, 'Editorial comment', Interstate Medical Journal St Louis, XI:Feb, 134.

53 Kösters 1898.

54 Taussig 1904c, 316.

55 Neugebauer 1904b, 318.

56 Taussig 1904a, 162–3.

57 The terms used in the English sources, 'psycho-sexual feelings', 'psychological sex' or 'psychological sexuality' do not always make it clear whether they refer to the category of sex or sexual preferences or both. This confusion is another indication that those concepts were hardly distinguished at the time.

58 Taussig 1904a, 163.

59 Howard, William Lee, 1904, 'Sex perversion in America', American Journal of Dermatology and Genito-Urinary Diseases, January, cited in Goffe 1904, 314–15.

60 Taussig, 1904c, 316.

61 Taussig, 1904c, 317.

62 See for these developments, Hausman 1995, 72–109; and for a more extensive description of the first half of the century as the 'age of idiosyncracy' with regard to intersex, Redick 2004 and also Reis 2009, 82–114.

CHAPTER 8. THE TURN INWARDS

1 See also on this subject Epstein 1995, where she discusses modern epistemological questions with regard to the difference between the 'outside' and the 'inside' of the body: Epstein 1995, 117–18.

2 See e.g. Kessler 1998, 21–4; Alexander 1999; Fausto-Sterling 2000, 63–6; Preves 2003, 60–86; Karkazis 2008, 58–60, 89–92, 186–91.

3 Clark, Andrew, 1898, 'A case of spurious hermaphroditism (hypospadias and undescended testes in a subject who had been brought up as a female and been married for sixteen years)', *The Lancet*, CLI:3889, 718–19, at 719.

4 Clark 1899, 719.

5 Westerman 1903, 1009.

6 Westerman 1903, 1011.

7 Westerman 1903, 1011.

8 Westerman 1903, 1011.

9 Westerman 1903, 1011.

10 Guermonprez 1893, 275.

11 Guermonprez 1893, 297.

12 Guermonprez 1893, 298.

13 Guermonprez 1893, 300, italics added.

14 Zangger 1905, 303–14.

15 See also Mak 2005b.

16 Zangger 1905, 312; see also chapter 7.

17 West 1904, 59.

18 König's letter, cited in Neugebauer 1908, 604–5.

19 König's letter, cited in Neugebauer 1908, 606–7.

20 König cited in Neugebauer 1908, 606.

21 König cited in Neugebauer 1908, 607.

22 Neugebauer, 1908, 607.

23 It also deviates remarkably from Healey's description of Neugebauer; the discussion among physicians on disclosure as a whole is more similar to the way Soviet physicians dealt with it than Healey suggests: Healey 2009, 148–51.

24 Geijl 1902, 330.

25 Geijl 1902, 330–1.

26 Geijl 1902, 633.

27 Hirschauer 1993, 189–203; Hirschauer 1998, 15–17.

28 Hirschfeld, Magnus, 1899, 'Die objective Diagnose der Homosexualität', *Jahrbuch für sexuelle Zwischenstufen unter besonderer Berücksichtigung der Homosexualität*, I, 4–35. After this first publication, the questionnaire was re-edited as a separate publication under the title *Psychobiologischer Fragebogen* in 1903 which was reprinted at least five times. See also Müller 1990, 303–6.

29 See for these new techniques for diagnosing 'identity' in case histories of sexual inversion: Müller 1990, 155–268, 292–325; Hacker 1987, 33–69; Oosterhuis 2000, 43–72, 139–151; Mak 1997, 197–243; Mak 2004a.

30 Kösters 1898, 15.

31 See also for this interrogation Mak 2006.

32 Kösters 1898, 17.

33 Hirschfeld, Magnus, 1905, 'Ein Fall von irrtümlicher Geschlechtsbestimmung (Erreur de sexe)', *Monatsschrift für Harnkrankheiten und sexuelle Hygiene*, II:1, 53–9, at 54.

34 Wahrman 2004, 207 and 318.

35 'Alle Handarbeiten' in German at the time refers for women, to needlework and sewing, and for men, to masculine manual labour, such as carpentry and construction. Because he was brought up as a girl, and because of the 'but' in the text which supposes a contradiction, I have chosen to translate it as 'needlework and sewing'.
36 Hirschfeld 1905, 53.
37 Hirschfeld 1905, 54.
38 Hirschfeld 1906, 614–15.
39 See for example the case histories of Benoit 1840 and Mulder [1844] and the many descriptions of Katharina/Karl Hohmann in Mak 2011.
40 See Oosterhuis 2000 and Müller 1991 for these developments from Krafft-Ebing, and for the analysis of this very change in one case of 'female sexual inversion', Mak 1997, 197–243 and Mak 2004.
41 Hirschfeld 1906, 615.
42 Hirschfeld 1906, 615.
43 Hirschfeld 1905, 55.
44 Hirschfeld 1905, 55.
45 Mak 1997, 223; see also Oosterhuis for 'testing' the constitutional character of one's homosexuality by attempts to have 'normal' sexual intercourse: Oosterhuis 2000, 229.
46 Proof for this statement can be found in Hirschfeld 1912, in which he described six cases of both hermaphroditism and transvestism. In one case he supposed a female lesbian cross-dresser to be a hermaphrodite on the basis of an as yet undiscovered internal hermaphroditic build, possibly ovotestis (see 9–14, esp. 12). See: Mak 1997, 316–51 and Mak, Geertje, 1998. ' "Passing women" im Sprechzimmer von Magnus Hirschfeld. Warum der Begriff "Transvestit" nicht für Frauen in Männerkleidern eingeführt wurde', Österreichische Zeitschrift für Geschichtswissenschaften. Homosexualitäten, 9:2, 384–99, esp. 396.
47 Zangger 1905, 307.
48 Zangger 1905, 307–8, footnotes removed from text.
49 Zangger 1905, 310.
50 Fausto-Sterling 2000; Jordan-Young, Rebecca M., 2010, Brain Storm. The Flaws in the Science of Sex Differences (Cambridge, MA and London: Harvard University Press).
51 Mulder [1844] 16–17, contesting this general opinion; Debierre 1886, 322; Debierre 1891, 87–8; Guermonprez 1892, 272.
52 Klebs, Edwin, 1876, Handbuch der pathologischen Anatomie. I.2. Pancreas, Nebenniere, Harn- und Geschlechtsapparat (Berlin: Hirschwald), 718–48.
53 Klöppel 2002, 142–9.
54 Neugebauer 1908, 673.
55 Neugebauer 1908, 674, 698–702.
56 Neugebauer 1908, 358.
57 Hausman 1995; Redick 2004.
58 Hausman 1995; Kessler 1998.
59 Notably Trumbach, Randolph, 1994, 'London's sapphists: from three sexes to four genders in the making of modern culture', in Gilbert Herdt (ed.), Third Sex,

NOTES   263

Third Gender. Beyond Sexual Bimorphism in Culture and History (New York: Zone
Books), 111–37; Trumbach 1998, 18–19; Donoghue 1993, 1–8; and Van der Meer
2007.

CHAPTER 9. SCRIPTING THE SELF. N. O. BODY'S AUTOBIOGRAPHY

1 I have used the original German text, translated by Steph Morris, because when
   I started this project no English translation was available. The English edition
   appeared in 2005, with an introduction by Sander L. Gilman. I will not discuss
   this introduction here, as it is too fuzzy in its use of core concepts to be helpful
   or clarifying. In particular, the use of the concept of 'third sex' as a metaphor
   for any transgression of gender identity, sexual identity or physical sex is only
   confusing.
2 Gilman 2006, xx–xxiv; Simon, Hermann, 1993, 'Wer war N. O. Body?', in Hermann
   Simon (ed.), *N. O. Body, Aus einem Mannes Mädchenjahren* (Berlin: Edition Hentrich),
   167–246, see 179–80; Simon, Hermann, 2006, 'Afterword. In search of Karl
   Baer', in N. O. Body, *Memoirs of a Man's Maiden Years*, trans. Deborah Simon
   (Philadelphia: University of Pennsylvania Press), 113–36; Gilman, Sander, 1999.
   Making the Body Beautiful: A Cultural History of Aesthetic Surgery (Princeton: Princeton University Press), 281–2.
3 Foucault 1976.
4 Meer, Theo van der, 1995, *Sodoms zaad in Nederland: het ontstaan van homoseksualiteit in de vroegmoderne tijd* (Nijmegen: Sun); for English publications based on
   this extended study of the sodomite trials in the Dutch Republic see Meer, Theo
   van der, 1994. 'Sodomy and the pursuit of a third sex in the early modern period',
   in Gilbert H. Herdt (ed.), *Third Sex, Third Gender: Beyond Sexual Dimorphism in
   Culture and History* (New York: Zone Books), 137–212, and Van der Meer 2007.
5 Trumbach 1998, 18–19.
6 Müller 1991; Mak 1997 and 2004, Halperin 1990; Halperin 1995.
7 To name but a few of these studies: Smith-Rosenberg, Carroll, 1985, *Disorderly
   Conduct. Visions of Gender in Victorian America* (New York: Oxford University Press);
   Hacker, Hanna, 1987. *Frauen und Freundinnen. Studien zur 'weiblichen Homosexualität' am Beispiel Österreich 1870–1938* (Weinheim and Basel: Beltz Verlag);
   Vicinus, Martha, 1989. ' "They wonder to which sex I belong." The historical
   roots of the modern lesbian identity', in Dennis Altman *et al.* (eds), *Homosexuality,
   Which Homosexuality?* (Amsterdam and London: Schorer / An Dekker / GMP
   Publishers), 215–38; Donoghue 1993; Everard, Myriam, 1994. *Ziel en zinnen. Over
   liefde en lust tussen vrouwen in de tweede helft van de achttiende eeuw* (Groningen:
   Historische Uitgeverij); Trumbach 1994; Bonnet, Marie-Jo, 1995. *Les relations
   amoureuses entre les femmes du XVIe au XXe siècle: essai historique* (Paris: Jacob);
   Mak 1997; Mak, Geertje, 1999. 'Wo das Sprechen zum Schweigen wird. Zur
   historischen Beziehung zwischen "Frauen" und "Lesben" ', in Kati Röttger and
   Heike Paul (eds), *Differenzen in der Geschlechterdifferenz / Differences within Gender
   Studies. Aktuelle Perspektiven der Geschlechterforschung* (Berlin: Erich Schmidt
   Verlag), 316–99; Traub 2002.

8 See for early modern studies Donoghue 1993; see for nineteenth-century studies Hacker 1987, Vicinus 1989, Mak 1997.

9 Mak 1997 and Mak 2004.

10 Oosterhuis 2000, 150–1, 204–8; see for an explanation in the case of women: Mak 1997, 197–243, 316–51; Mak 1998.

11 Mak 1997, 316–51; Mak 1998.

12 Müller 1991, 229–30.

13 Müller 1991, 211.

14 Müller 1991, 254–6.

15 Müller 1991, 223–4.

16 See for a beautiful description of these two meanings of identity: Wahrman 2004, xii.

17 Müller 1991, 230.

18 Müller 1991, 254–6.

19 Oosterhuis 2000, 216–17.

20 Oosterhuis 2000, 217.

21 Oosterhuis 2000, 216–20.

22 Oosterhuis 2000, 223.

23 Oosterhuis 2000, 225.

24 Oosterhuis 2000, 226.

25 Mak 2004.

26 Oosterhuis 2000, 229. Oosterhuis also based this list on Müller 1991, 208–30.

27 N. O. Body 1907, 8. The page numbers refer to the reissue published in 1993, edited by Hermann Simon.

28 N. O. Body 1907, 8.

29 Lejeune 1975.

30 N. O. Body 1907, 8.

31 Spörri, 122–3.

32 I have chosen to refer to N. O. Body with he and him, because he so emphatically claimed this to be the truth from early childhood on. As Nora is the protagonist of his story, I will also refer to that name to indicate the fact that he was raised a girl. Barbin is an entirely different case, referring to herself in both ways (f/m), with a clear shift from more female to more male over the course of the text.

33 N. O. Body 1907, 9–10.

34 N. O. Body 1907, 38.

35 N. O. Body 1907, 27.

36 N. O. Body 1907, 42.

37 N. O. Body 1907, 43.

38 N. O. Body 1907, 24–5.

39 N. O. Body 1907, 69–70.

40 N. O. Body 1907, 25, 156–7; it is clearly a theme important to him.

41 N. O. Body 1907, 79.

42 N. O. Body 1907, 94.

43 N. O. Body 1907, 113.

44 N. O. Body 1907, 130.

45 N. O. Body 1907, 126.

46 N. O. Body 1907, 113; see also 123: 'Immer mehr litt ich unter dem wilden Begehren meiner jungen, aufgeregten Sinne'.

47 See Oosterhuis quoted above: Oosterhuis 2000, 229.

48 N. O. Body 1907, 42–3.

49 N. O. Body 1907, 44.

50 N. O. Body 1907, 79.

51 N. O. Body 1907, 123.

52 N. O. Body 1907, 136.

53 Hirschfeld refers to the many suicides of adolescents in his appraisal of N. O. Body's text: N. O. Body 1907, 163; his *Jahrbuch für sexuelle Zwischenstufen* contains many newspaper articles recording homosexual suicides (often as a couple).

54 Oosterhuis 2000, 226–7.

55 N. O. Body 1907, 146–7.

56 Hirschfeld 1907, 163, emphasis in original.

57 I would like to thank Annemarie Mol for her explanation of this double role the objectified body often plays in modern medicine.

58 N. O. Body 1907, 12, italics added.

59 N. O. Body 1907, 12.

60 N. O. Body 1907, 36.

61 N. O. Body 1907, 36, 77.

62 N. O. Body 1907, 42.

63 N. O. Body 1907, 55.

64 N. O. Body 1907, 81–2.

65 N. O. Body 1907, 113; see for another passage 94.

66 Simon 1993, 219–20.

67 Simon 1993, 214–15.

68 Simon 1993, 221–2.

69 Goujon 1869, 601.

70 N. O. Body 1907, 11. See for other reproaches towards his parents who did not discuss the subject at all, 79–80.

71 See for the script of a humanitarian narrative: Laqueur 1989.

72 N. O. Body 1907, 157–8.

73 Oosterhuis 2000, 225–8.

74 Taylor 1989, 305–20.

CONCLUSION

1 Bergmann, Anna, 2004, *Der entseelte Patient* (Berlin: Aufbau-Verlag).

2 Dreger 1998, 110–38; Dreger 1999b.

BIBLIOGRAPHY

ARCHIVAL SOURCES

Archives Départmentales de l'Hérault
2 U 139, l'arrèt de la our d'appel du 8 mai 1872.
Archives Départmentales du Gard
7 U 1/90, 7 U 1/91, jugements du tribunal d'Alès des 29 avril 1869 et 28 janvier 1873;
4 U 3/212, l'ârret de la cour impériale de Nîmes du 29 novembre 1869.
CESAME – Centre Hospitalier – St Gemmes, Loire, France
Dossier du patient Marie Chupin.
Generallandesarchiv Karlsruhe
Ehegerichtsprotokoll des Kirchenrates 1794, Signatur 61/4262.

PRINTED PRIMARY SOURCES

Alberti, 1905. 'Kasuïstiek zu Hypertrichosis universa acquisita und Veränderungen der Sexualorgane', *Beiträge zur Geburtshilfe und Gynäkologie*, 9:3, 339–44.

Arnaud, G., 1768. *Mémoires de chirurgie. Sixième mémoire. Dissertation sur les hermaphrodites* (London and Paris: J. Nourse).

Benoit, Justin, 1840. 'Consultation sur un cas d'hermaphroditisme', *Journal de la Société de médecine pratique de Montpellier*, I: November, 23–37.

Blondel, M. R., 1899. 'Observation de pseudohermaphroditisme', *Bulletins et mémoires de la Société obstétricale et gynécologique de Paris*, XV: January, 3–12.

Brouardel, Paul, 1904. 'Malformation des organes génitaux de la femme. Y a-t-il lieu de reconnaître l'existence d'un troisième sexe?', *Annales d'hygiène publique et de médecine légale*, 4th series, tome I:3, 193–204.

Buchanan, George, 1885. 'Hermaphrodite, aged 9, in whom two testicles were excised from the labia majora [meeting Medical-Chirurgical Society 9 January 1885]', *Glasgow Medical Journal*, XXIII: March, 213–17.

Clark, Andrew, 1898. 'A case of spurious hermaphroditism (hypospadias and undescended testes in a subject who had been brought up as a female and been married for sixteen years)', *The Lancet*, CLI:3889, 718–9.

Coste, 1835. 'Conformation vicieuse des organes génitaux chez une femme. Operation', *Journal des connaissances médico-chirurgicales*, 3:7, 276–7.

Courty, Amédée, 1872. 'Consultation médico-légale à l'appui d'une demande en nullité de mariage', *Montpellier médical*, tome XXVIII:6, 473–88.

DaCorogna, 1864. 'Hermaphroditisme apparent chez une personne du sexe féminin', *Bulletins de la Société anatomique de Paris*, 2nd series, tome IX, 39: November, 481–8.

Dailliez, Georges, 1893. *Les sujets de sexe douteux. Leur état psychique. Leur condition relativement au mariage* (Thèse de Paris. Lille: L. Danel).

Dalloz, D. (ed.), 1882. *Jurisprudence générale* (Paris: Bureau de la Jurisprudence Générale), vol. 2.

Debierre, Charles, 1886. 'L'Hermaphrodite devant le code civil. L'hermaphroditisme, sa nature, son origine, ses conséquences sociales', *Archives de l'anthropologie criminelle*, I, 305–43.

Debierre, Charles, 1891. *L'Hermaphroditisme, structure, fonctions, état psychologique et mental, état civil et mariage, dangers et remèdes* (Paris: J. B. Baillière).

Descoust, 1886. 'Sur un cas d'hermaphrodisme', *Annales d'hygiène publique et de médecine légale*, tome XVI, 87–90.

Desgenettes, 1791. *Journal de médecine, chirurgie et pharmacie*, tome XXXVIII: July, 81–4.

Fancourt Barnes, 1888. '[Meeting of the British Gynaecological Society, April 25, 1888]', *British Gynaecological Journal*, IV: April, 205–12, 231.

Feiler, Johann, 1820. *Über angeborene menschliche Missbildungen im allgemeinen und Hermaphroditen insbesondere. Ein Beitrag zur Physiologie, pathologischen Anatomie, und gerichtlichen Arzneiwissenschaft* (Landshut: Philipp Krüll), 68–133.

Follin, 1851. 'D'un cas rémarquable d'hermaphrodisme. Avec quelques considérations sur la détermination du sexe', *Gazette des hôpitaux civils et militaires*, XXIV:140, 561–3.

Fronmüller, 1834. 'Beschreibung eines als Mädchen erzogenes männlichen Scheinzwitters', *Zeitschrift für die Staatsarzneikunde*, XIV:27, 205–9.

Froriep, Robert, 1833a. 'Beschreibung eines Zwitters nebst Abbildung der Geschlechtstheile desselben', *Wochenschrift für die gesammte Heilkunde*, Band I:3, 61–70.

Froriep, Robert, 1833b. 'Miscellaneous', *Frorieps Notizen*, Band XXXVI:9, 137–8.

Garnier, P. 1885. 'Du pseudo-hermaphrodisme comme impédiment médico-légal à la déclaration du sexe dans l'acte de naissance', *Annales d'hygiène publique et de médecine légale*, 3rd series, tome XIV:3, 285–93.

Geijl, A. 1902. 'Over operatief ingrijpen bij pseudohermaphroditismus masculinus of femininus externus', *Medisch weekblad van noord- en zuid-Nederland*, IX:22–38, 281–4, 326–30, 381–8, 397–404, 413–20, 433–5, 464–71, 494–501, 512–19, 555–8, 567–70, 586–91, 632–9.

Goffe, J. Riddle, 1903. 'A pseudohermaphrodite, in which the female characteristics predominated. Operation for removal of the penis and the utilization of the skin covering it for formation of a vaginal canal', *American Journal of Obstetrics and Diseases of Women and Children*, 48:6, 755–63.

Goffe, J. Riddle, 1904. 'Hermaphroditism and the true determination of sex', *Interstate Medical Journal St Louis*, XI: May, 314–15.

Goujon, 1869. 'Étude d'un cas d'hermaphrodisme bisexuel imparfait chez l'homme', *Journal de l'anatomie et de la physiologie normales et pathologiques de l'homme et des animaux*, VI, 599–615.

Guermonprez, 1892. 'Une erreur de sexe avec ses conséquences', *Annales d'hygiène publique et de médecine légale*, 3rd series, tome XXVIII: September–October, 242–75, 296–306.

Harris, S. H., 1847. 'Case of doubtful sex', *American Journal of the Medical Sciences*, XXI: July, 121–24.

Henning, 1819. 'Geschichte eines monströs an den Geschlechtstheilen geborenen Kindes weiblichen Geschlechts, das für einen Knaben bestimmt worden war', *Journal der practischen Heilkunde*, Band XLII:49, 98–108.

Henrotay, J. 1901. 'Hypospade pénoscrotal élevé en femme jusqu'à 24 ans', *Bulletin de la Société royale belge de gynécologie et d'obstrétrique*, 11:4, 103–5.

Herculine Barbin. Being the Recently Discovered Memoirs of a Nineteenth-Century French Hermaphrodite, 1980. introduced by Michel Foucault, trans. Richard McDougall (New York: Pantheon Books).

Hills, William C., 1873. 'A case of hermaphroditism', *The Lancet*, CI:2578, 129–30.

Hirschfeld, Magnus, 1899. 'Die objective Diagnose der Homosexualität', *Jahrbuch für sexuelle Zwischenstufen unter besonderer Berücksichtigung der Homosexualität*, I, 4–35.

Hirschfeld, Magnus, 1905. 'Ein Fall von irrtümlicher Geschlechtsbestimmung (Erreur de sexe)', *Monatsschrift für Harnkrankheiten und sexuelle Hygiene*, II:1, 53–9.

Hirschfeld, Magnus, 1906. 'Drei Fälle von irrtümlicher Geschlechtsbestimmung', *Medizinische Reform, Wochenschrift für soziale Medizin*, XIV:51, 614–17.

Hirschfeld, Magnus, 1912. *Geschlechts-Umwandlungen. Irrtümer in der Geschlechtsbestimmung. Sechs Fälle aus der forensischen Praxis* (Berlin: Adler Verlag).

Huette, 1856. 'Hermaphrodisme apparent chez le sexe masculin', *Gazette médicale de Paris*, 3rd series, tome XI, 26:9, 141.

Hufeland, 1801. 'Beschreibung und Abbildung eines zu Berlin beobachteten weiblichen Hermaphroditen', *Journal der practischen Heilkunde*, Band XII:2, 170–2.

Jagemann, 1845. 'Beschreibung einer merkwürdigen Zwitterbildung', *Neue Zeitschrift für Geburtskunde*, XVII:1, 15–20.

Jalabert, Philippe, 1872. 'Examen doctrinal de jurisprudence civile', *Revue critique de législation et de jurisprudence*, new series, tome II:22, 129–49.

Jones, Joseph 1871. 'Singular and distressing case of malformation of genital organs', *Medical Record*, IX, 1 July, 198–9.

Klebs, Edwin, 1876. *Handbuch der pathologischen Anatomie. I.2. Pancreas, Nebenniere, Harn- und Geschlechtsapparat* (Berlin: Hirschwald), 718–48.

Kösters, Johannes, 1898. *Ein neuer Fall von Hermaphroditismus spurius masculinus* (Berlin: Gustav Schade).

Landau, Theodor, 1903. 'Ueber Hermaphroditen. Nebst einigen Bemerkungen über die Erkenntnis und die rechtliche Stellung dieser Individuen', *Berliner klininische Wochenschrift*, XL:15, 339–43.

Landau, Theodor, 1904. 'Mann oder Weib', *Zentralblatt für Gynäkologie*, XVIII:7, 203–4.

Larrey, 1859. 'Hermaphrodisme', *Gazette des hôpitaux civils et militaires*, XXXII:115, 459–60.

Laugardière, Jules de, 1866. *Guide de l'officier de l'état civil* (Colmar: C. M. Hoffmann, 2nd edn).

Laurent, François, 1870. *Principes du droit civil français*, vol. 2 (Paris and Brussels: A. Durand and Pedone Lauriel / Bruyland-Christophe).

Leblond, 1885. 'Du pseudohermaphrodisme comme impédiment médico-légal de la déclaration du sexe dans l'acte de naissance', *Annales d'hygiène publique et de médecine légale*, 3rd series, tome XIV:3, 293–302.

Legros, F., 1835. 'Homme hypospade, pris 22 ans pour une femme', *Journal des connaissances médico-chirurgicales*, III:7, 273–6.

Loeffler, 1871. 'Zur Kasuistik der Zwitter', *Berliner klininische Wochenschrift*, VIII:26, 309.

Loir, Joseph-Napoléon, 1854. *Des sexes en matière d'état-civil, comment prévenir les erreurs résultant de leurs anomalies, mémoire lu à l'Académie des sciences morales et politiques* (Paris: Cotillon).

Lucas-Championnière, M. J., 1909. 'Présentation des photographies d'un hypospade ayant passé pour une femme, ayant été mariée pendant douze ans, ayant présentée comme femme à barbe et ayant des seins très dévelopés', *Bulletins et mémoires de la Société de chirurgie de Paris*, XXXV:39, 1347–9.

Lynds, J. G., 1905. 'Clinical Cases', *Journal of the Michigan State Medical Society*, IV: March, 122–6.

Marchand, 1883. 'Ein neuer Fall von Hermaphroditismus spurius masculinus', *Archiv für pathologische Anatomie und Physiologie und klinische Medizin*, Band XCII:2, 286–95.

Martens, Franz Heinrich, 1802. *Beschreibung und Abbildung der männlichen Geschlechtsteile von Maria Dorothea Derrier aus Berlin* (Leipzig: Baumgärtnerische Buchhandlung).

Martini, J., 1861. 'Ein männlicher Scheinzwitter als verpflichtete Hebamme. Amtsmissbrauch und widernatürtliche Unzucht', *Vierteljahrsschrift für gerichtliche Medizin und öffentlichen Sanitätswesen*, XIX, 303–22.

Mayer, 1825. 'Über hermaphroditische Bildungen', *Journal der Chirurgie und Augenheilkunde*, VIII:2, 195–213.

Mayer, A. F., 1835. 'Beschreibung des Körperbaus des Hermaphroditen Dürrge (Derrier)', *Wochenschrift für die gesammte Heilkunde*, Band III:50, 801–13.

Messner, 1892. 'Ein neuer Fall von Hermaphroditismus verus (Hermaphrodismus verus unilateralis?) am Lebenden untersucht und beschrieben', *Archiv für pathologische Anatomie und Physiologie und klinische Medizin*, Band CXXIX:2, 203–13.

Mulder, Jan Andries, 1844. *Aanteekeningen omtrent den hermaphrodiet Maria Rosina, later Gottlieb Göttlich genaamd* [n.p.].

Müller, Johannes, 1830. *Bildungsgeschichte der Genitalien aus anatomischen Untersuchungen an Embryonen des Menschen und der Thiere, nebst einem Anhang über die chirurgische Behandlung der Hypospadia* (Düsseldorf: Arnz).

Naegele, D. F. C., 1819. 'Beschreibung eines Falles von Zwitterbildung bei einem Zwillingspaar', *Deutsches Archiv für die Physiologie*, Band V, 136–40.

Neugebauer, Franz Ludwig von, 1896. 'Ein junges Mädchen von männliches Geschlecht. Verhängnisvolle Folgen einer irrtümlichen Geschlechtsbestimmung. Verhandlung vor dem Strafrichter', *Internationale photographische Monatsschrift für Medizin und Naturwissenschaften*, III: August–September, 259–67.

Neugebauer, Franz Ludwig von, 1899. 'Cinquante cas de mariages conclus entre des personnes du même sexe, avec plusieurs procès de divorce par suite d'erreur de sexe', *Revue de gynécologie et de chirurgie abdominale*, 3:2, 195–210.

Neugebauer, Franz Ludwig von, 1900a. 'Une nouvelle série de 29 observations d'erreur de sexe', *Revue de gynécologie et de chirurgie abdominale*, 4:2, 133–74.

Neugebauer, Franz Ludwig von, 1900b. 'Quarante-quatre erreurs de sexe révélées par l'opération. Soixante-douze opérations chirurgicales d'urgence, de complaisance ou de complicité pratiquées chez des pseudo-hermaphrodites et personnes . . .', *Revue de gynécologie et de chirurgie abdominale*, 4:4, 457–518.

Neugebauer, Franz Ludwig von, 1902. 'Ein interessanter Fall von zweifelhaftem Geschlecht eines als Frau verheirateten Scheinzwitters', *Zentralblatt für Gynäkologie*, XXVI:7, 171–5.

Neugebauer, Franz-Ludwig von, 1903. 'Chirurgische Überraschungen auf dem Gebiete des Scheinzwittertums', *Jahrbuch für sexuelle Zwischenstufen*, V:1, 205–424.

Neugebauer, Franz Ludwig von, 1904a. 'Mann oder Weib? Sechs eigene Beobachtungen von Scheinzwittertum und "Erreur de sexe"', *Zentralblatt für Gynäkologie*, XXVIII:2, 33–51.

Neugebauer, Franz Ludwig von, 1904b. '[Letter to the editor]', *Interstate Medical Journal St Louis*, XI: May, 317–18.

Neugebauer, Franz Ludwig von, 1904c. 'What value has the knowledge of pseudohermaphroditism for the practitioner?', *Interstate Medical Journal St Louis*, XI: February, 103–24.

Neugebauer, Franz Ludwig von, 1908. *Hermaphroditismus beim Menschen* (Leipzig: Werner Klinkhardt).

Neugebauer, Franz Ludwig von, 1916. *Hermaphroditismus und Pseudohermaphroditismus* (Wien: Braumüller).

N. O. Body, 1907. *Aus einem Mannes Mädchenjahren*, foreword by Rudolf Presber, afterward by Magnus Hirschfeld (Berlin: Hesperus Verlag).

Otto, Adolf Wilhelm, 1824. *Neue seltene Beobachtungen zur Anatomie, Physiologie und Pathologie gehörig* (Berlin: August Rücker), 123–6, 133–5.

Parmly, George Dubois, 1886. 'Hermaphrodisme', *American Journal of Obstetrics and Diseases of Women and Children*, XIX: September, 931–46.

Péan, 1895. 'Faux hermaphrodite', *Gazette des hôpitaux civils et militaires*, LXVIII:41, 404–5.

Pick, L., 1905. 'Über Adenome der männliche und weibliche Keimdrüse bei Hermaphroditismus verus und spurius nebst Bemerkungen über das endometriumähnliche Adenom am inneren weiblichen Genitale', *Berliner klininische Wochenschrift*, XLII:17, 502–9.

Pozzi, Samuel, 1884. 'Homme hypospade considéré depuis 28 ans comme femme', *Annales de gynécologie*, tome XXI: April, 257–68.

Reverchon, 1870. 'Étude médico-légal sur l'état mental du nommé Ch . . .', *Annales médico-psychologiques*, 5th series, tome IV, XXVIII: November, 377–95.

Reverdin, Auguste, 1905. 'Note sur un cas d'hypospadie', *Annales des maladies des organes génito-urinaires*, XXIII:15 January, 138–45.

Ricoux and Aubry, 1899. 'Un prétendu androgyne dans un service de femmes', *Le Progrès médical*, 3rd series, tome X:37, 183–4.

Schäffler, 1801. 'Beschreibung eines Mannes, dessen fehlerhafte Geschechtstheile sein Geschlecht lange zweifelhaft machten', *Journal der practischen Heilkunde*, Band XIII:1, 114–24.

Schallgruber, Joseph, 1823. *Abhandlungen im Fache der Gerichtsarzneikunde* (Grätz: Miller), 131.

Schallgruber, Joseph, 1825. '[Gerichtliche Medizin]', *Zeitschrift für die Staatsarzneikunde*, Ergänzungsheft, IV, 309–11.

Schmidt, C. H., 1821. 'Beschreibung eines weiblichen Hermaphroditen, nach seinen äussern und innern Geschlechtstheilen', *Journal der practischen Heilkunde*, Band XLVI:6, 101–7.

Schneider, 1809. 'Der Hermaphroditismus in gerichtlich-medizinischer Hinsicht', *Jahrbuch der Staatsarzneikunde*, 2, 139–68.

Schneider and Sömmering, 1817. 'Beschreibung eines sehr merkwürdigen Hypospadias', *Jahrbuch der Staatsarzneikunde*, 10, 134–55.

Schneller, 1894. 'Ein Fall von Pseudohermaphroditismus', *Münchener medizinische Wochenschrift: Organ für amtliche und praktische Ärzte*, LXI:33, 655–6.

Schweickhard, 1803. 'Geschichte eines lange Zeit für einen Hermaphroditen gehaltenen wahren Mannes', *Journal der practischen Heilkunde*, Band XVII:1, 9–52.

Siebourg-Barmen, 1898. 'Ueber einen Fall von Pseudohermaphroditismus masculinus completus', *Monatsschrift für Geburtshülfe und Gynäkologie*, July, 73–5.

Solowij, A., 1899, 'Ein Beitrag zum Hermaphroditismus', *Monatsschrift für Geburtshülfe und Gynäkologie*, Band IX, 210–1.

Stark, Johann Christian, 1799. 'Sonderbare Naturbegebenheit: wirkliche Erscheinung weiblich-männlicher Theile und doch kein Hermaphrodit, wodurch eine andere Weibsperson befruchtet wurde', *Neues Archiv für die Geburtshülfe, Frauenzimmer und Kinderkrankheiten mit Hinsicht auf die Physiologie, Diätik und Chirurgie*, Band I:3, 351–7.

Stark, Johann Christian, 1801. 'Kurze Beschreibung eines sogenannten Hermaphroditen oder Zwitters, welcher aber mehr zum männlichen, als weiblichen Geschlechte zu rechnen isst, nebst einer Vorerinnerung', *Neues Archiv für die Geburtshülfe, Frauenzimmer und Kinderkrankheiten mit Hinsicht auf die Physiologie, Diätik und Chirurgie*, Band II:3, 538–54.

Stretton, J. L., 1895. 'So-called hermaphrodite', *The Lancet*, CXLVI:3763, 917.

Tardieu, Auguste Ambroise, 1874. *Question médico-légale de l'identité dans ses rapports avec les vices de conformation des organes sexuels* (Paris: J. B. Baillière, 2nd edn).

Taruffi, Cesare, 1903. *Hermaphroditismus und Zeugungsfähigkeit. Eine systematische Darstellung der Missbildungen der menschlichen Geschlechtsorgane* (Berlin: R. Teuscher).

Taussig, Fred J., 1904a. 'Shall a pseudo-hermaphrodite be allowed to decide to which sex he or she shall belong?', *American Journal of Obstetrics and Diseases of Women and Children*, 49:2, 162–5.

Taussig, Fred J., 1904b. 'Editorial comment', *Interstate Medical Journal St Louis*, XI: Feb, 134.

Taussig, 1904c. 'Rejoinder to Dr Goffe's letter', *Interstate Medical Journal St Louis*, XI: May, 316–17.

Tourtual, 1856. 'Ein als Weib verheirateter Androgynus vor dem kirchlichen Forum', *Vierteljahrsschrift für gerichtliche und öffentliche Medizin*, 1st series, Band X:1, 18–40.

Traxel, 1856. 'Zeugungsfähigkeit eines Hypospadiacus, dessen Urethra am Perinaeum ausmündet', *Wiener medizinische Wochenschrift*, VI:18, 289–91.

Virchow, 1856. *Gesammelte Abhandlungen zur wissenschaftlichen Medizin* (Frankfurt an Main: Meidinger), 770–4.

Virchow, 1872. 'Vorstellung eines Hermaphroditen', *Berliner klininische Wochenschrift*, IX:49, 585–8.

Wallis, Albert W., 1868. 'Sexual malformation', *Medical Times and Gazette. A Journal of Medical Science, Literature, Criticism, and News*, Part II:7, November, 542–3.

Walther, 1902. 'Anomalie génitale', *Bulletins et mémoires de la Société de chirurgie de Paris*, XXVIII, 8 and 15 October, 938–44, 972–5.

Weissbart, 1902. 'Ein männlicher Scheinzwitter', *Monatsschrift für Geburtshülfe und Gynäkologie*, March, 266–72.

Westerman, C. W. J., 1903. 'Over miskend pseudohermaphroditisme', *Nederlandsch tijdschrift voor Geneeskunde*, XXXIX:18, 1009–12.

West, James N., 1904. 'Sterility from vaginal causes', *Medical News*, LXXXV, 58–61.

Wilhelm, Eugen, 1909. *Die rechtliche Stellung der (körperlichen) Zwitter de lege lata und de lege ferenda* (Halle an der Saale: Carl Marhold Verlagsbuchhandlung).

Worbe, 1815. 'Sur un individu rendu par jugement á l'état viril, après avoir été vingt-deux ans réputé du sexe féminin; cas médico-légal', *Bulletin de la faculté de médecine de Paris*, XI, 4:10, 479–92.

Zangger, H., 1905. 'Uber einen Fall von Pseudohermaphroditismus masculinus externus in pathologischanatomischer, psychologischer und forensischer Hinsicht', *Schweizerische Zeitschrift für Strafrecht*, XVIII, 303–14.

SECONDARY SOURCES

Ackerman, Evelyn Bernette, 1990. *Health Care in the Parisian Countryside, 1800–1914* (New Brunswick and London: Rutgers University Press).

Alexander, Tamara, 1999. 'Silence = death', in Alice Domurat Dreger (ed.), *Intersex in the Age of Ethics* (Hagerstown, MD: University Publishing Group), 103–10.

Althusser, Louis, 1977. *Ideologie und ideologische Staatsapparate: Aufsätze zur marxistische Theorie*, trans. Rolf Löper, Klaus Riepe and Peter Schötter (Hamburg and Berlin: VSA).

Baggerman, Arianne, 2002. 'Autobiography and family memory in the nineteenth century', in Rudolf Dekker (ed.), *Egodocuments and History. Autobiographical Writing in its Social Context since the Middle Ages* (Hilversum: Verloren).

Bal, Mieke, 1997. *Narratology, Introduction to the Theory of Narrative* (Toronto: University of Toronto Press).

Bergmann, Anna, 2004. *Der entseelte Patient* (Berlin: Aufbau-Verlag).

Blau DuPlessis, Rachel, 1985. *Writing beyond the Ending: Narrative Strategies of Twentieth-Century Women Writers* (Bloomington: Indiana University Press).

Bonnet, Marie-Jo, 1995. *Les relations amoureuses entre les femmes du XVIe au XXe siècle: essai historique* (Paris: Jacob).

Butler, Judith, 1990. *Gender Trouble. Feminism and the Subversion of Identity* (New York and London: Routledge).

Butler, Judith, 1993. *Bodies that Matter. On the Discursive Limits of Sex* (New York and London: Routledge).

Butler, Judith, 2001. 'Doing justice to someone: sex reassignment and allegories of transsexuality', *GLQ: A Journal of Lesbian and Gay Studies*, 7:4, 621–36.

Bynum, W. F., 1994. *Science and the Practice of Medicine in the Nineteenth Century* (Cambridge, New York and Melbourne: Cambridge University Press).

Cardozo Journal of Law & Gender, 2005. 12:1.

Connell, R. W., 1995. *Masculinities* (Cambridge: Polity Press).

Culler, Jonathan, 1981. *The Pursuit of Signs* (Ithaca: Cornell University Press).

Darmon, Pierre, 1986. *Le Tribunal de l'impuissance: virilité et défaillances conjugales dans l'ancienne France* (Paris: Seuil).

Daston, Lorraine, and Park, Katharine, 1996. 'The hermaphrodite and the orders of nature: sexual ambiguity in early modern France', in Louise Fradenburg and Corla Freccero (eds), *Prenodern Sexualities* (London and New York: Routledge), 117–36.

Dekker, Rudolf (ed.), 2002a. *Egodocuments and History. Autobiographical Writing in its Social Context since the Middle Ages* (Hilversum: Verloren).

Dekker, Rudolf, 2002b. 'Introduction', in Rudolf Dekker (ed.), 2002a, *Egodocuments and History. Autobiographical Writing in its Social Context since the Middle Ages* (Hilversum: Verloren), 7–21.

De María Arana, Marcus, 2005. http://www.sf-hrc.org/ftp/uploadedfiles/sfhumanrights/Committee_Meetings/Lesbian_Gay_Bisexual_Transgender/SFHRC%20Intersex%20Report%281%29.pdf

Donoghue, Emma, 1993. *Passions between Women. British Lesbian Culture 1668–1801* (London: Scarlet Press).

Doyle, J., 2007. 'Historicising surgery: gender sex and the surgical imaginary', *Social Semistics*, 17:3 (special issue: 'Body Modifications'), 341–59.

Dreger, Alice Domurat, 1998. *Hermaphrodites and the Medical Invention of Sex* (Cambridge, MA, and London: Harvard University Press).

Dreger, Alice Domurat (ed.), 1999a. *Intersex in the Age of Ethics* (Hagerstown, MD: University Publishing Group).

Dreger, Alice Domurat, 1999b. 'A history of intersex. From the age of gonads to the age of consent', in Dreger, Alice Domurat (ed.), *Intersex in the Age of Ethics* (Hagerstown, MD: University Publishing Group), 5–22.

Duden, Barbara, 1987. *Geschichte unter der Haut. Ein Eisenacher Arzt und seine Patientinnen um 1730* (Stuttgart: Klett-Verlag).

Duden, Barbara, 1991. *The Woman Beneath the Skin. A Doctor's Patients in Eighteenth-Century Germany*, trans. Thomas Dunlap (Cambridge, MA, and London: Harvard University Press).

Epstein, Julia, 1995. *Altered Conditions. Disease, Medicine, and Storytelling* (New York and London: Routledge).

Everard, Myriam, 1994. *Ziel en zinnen. Over liefde en lust tussen vrouwen in de tweede helft van de achttiende eeuw* (Groningen: Historische Uitgeverij).

Fausto-Sterling, Anne, 2000. *Sexing the Body. Gender Politics and the Construction of Sexuality* (New York: Basic Books).

Flint, Kate, 1997. ' ". . . As a rule, I does not mean I" ', in Roy Porter (ed.), *Rewriting the Self* (London and New York: Routledge), 156–66.

Foucault, Michel, 1972. 'Two lectures', in Colin Gordon (ed.), *Power/Knowledge. Selected Interviews and Other Writings 1972–1977*, trans. Colin Gordon *et al.*, (New York: Pantheon Books), 78–109.

Foucault, Michel, 1976. *La Volonté de savoir. Histoire de la sexualité*, 1 (Paris: Gallimard).

Foucault, Michel, 1978. *The Will to Knowledge. The History of Sexuality*, vol. 1, trans. Robert Hurley (New York: Pantheon Books).

Foucault, Michel, 1980. 'Introduction', in *Herculine Barbin. Being the Recently Discovered Memoirs of a Nineteenth-Century French Hermaphrodite*, introduced by Michel Foucault, trans. Richard McDougall (New York: Pantheon Books).

Foucault, Michel, 2003 (orig. French 1963). *The Birth of the Clinic. An Archaeology of Medical Perception* (London and New York: Routledge).

Gay, Peter, 1995. *The Naked Heart. The Bourgeois Experience Victoria to Freud* (London and New York: W. W. Norton & Co).

Giddens, Anthony, 1991. *Modernity and Self Identity. Self and Society in the Late Modern Age* (Cambridge: Polity Press).

Gilbert, Ruth, 2002. *Early Modern Hermaphrodites. Sex and Other Stories* (Basingstoke and New York: Palgrave).

Gilman, Sander, 1999. *Making the Body Beautiful: A Cultural History of Aesthetic Surgery* (Princeton: Princeton University Press).

Gilman, Sander, 2006. 'Whose body is it, anyway? Hermaphrodites, gays, and Jews in N. O. Body's Germany', in N. O. Body, *Memoirs of a Man's Maiden Years*, trans. Deborah Simon (Philadelphia: University of Pennsylvania Press), vii–xxiv.

Gowing, Laura, 2003. *Common Bodies. Women, Touch, and Power in Seventeenth-Century England* (New Haven and London: Yale University Press).

Graille, Patrick, 1987. *Les Hermaphrodites aux XVIIe et XVIIIe siècles* (Paris: Les Belles Lettres).

Hacker, Hanna, 1987. *Frauen und Freundinnen. Studien zur 'weiblichen Homosexualität' am Beispiel Österreich 1870–1938* (Weinheim and Basel: Beltz Verlag).

Halperin, David M., 1990. *One Hundred Years of Homosexuality and Other Essays on Greek Love* (New York and London: Routledge).

Halperin, David M., 1995. *Saint Foucault: Towards a Gay Hagiography* (New York, etc.: Oxford University Press).

Hausman, Bernice L., 1995. *Changing Sex. Transsexualism, Technology and the Idea of Gender* (Durham, NC, and London: Duke University Press).

Healey, Dan, 2009. *Bolshevik Sexual Forensics. Diagnosing Disorder in the Clinic and Courtroom, 1917–1939.* (DeKalb, IL: Northern Illinois University Press).

Henslin, James M., and Biggs, Mae E., 1971. 'Dramaturgical desexualisation: the sociology of the vaginal examination', in James M. Henslin (ed.), *Studies in the Sociology of Sex* (New York: Appleton-Century-Crafts), 243–72.

Herrn, Rainer, 2005. 'Das Geschlecht ruht nicht im Körper, sondern in der Seele. Magnus Hirschfelds Strategien bei Hermaphroditengutachten', in *1-0-1 [one 'o one] Intersex. Das Zwei-Geschlechter-System als Menschenrechtsverletzung* (Berlin: Neue Gesellschaft für Bildende Kunst), 55–71.

Hirschauer, Stefan, 1991. 'The manufacture of bodies in surgery', *Social Studies of Science*, 21:2, 279–319.

Hirschauer, Stefan, 1993. *Die soziale Konstruktion der Transsexualität* (Frankfurt am Main: Suhrkamp).

Hirschauer, Stefan, 1998. 'Performing sexes and genders in medical practices', in Annemarie Mol and Marc Berg (eds), *Differences in Medicine. Unraveling Practices, Techniques, and Bodies* (Durham, NC, and London: Duke University Press), 13–27.

Holmes, Morgan, 2008. *Intersex. A Perilous Difference* (Selinsgrove: Susquehanna University Press).

Honegger, Claudia, 1991. *Die Ordnung der Geschlechter. Die Wissenschaften von Menschen und das Weib 1750–1850* (Frankfurt an Main: Campus).

Huisman, Marijke, 2008. *Publieke levens: autobiografieën op de Nederlandse boekenmarkt 1850–1918* (Zutphen: Walburg Pers).

Hunt, Lynn, 2007. *Inventing Human Rights. A History* (New York and London: Norton & Company).

Jewson, N. D., 1976. 'The disappearance of the sick-man from medical cosmology, 1770–1870', *Sociology*, 10:2, 225–44.

Jordan-Young, Rebecca M., 2010. *Brain Storm. The Flaws in the Science of Sex Differences* (Cambridge, MA, and London: Harvard University Press).

Kapsalis, Terri, 1997. *Public Privates. Performing Gynecology from Both Ends of the Speculum* (Durham, NC, and London: Duke University Press).

Karkazis, Katrina, 2008. *Fixing Sex. Intersex, Medical Authority, and Lived Experience* (Durham, NC, and London: Duke University Press).

Kessler, Suzanne J., 1998. *Lessons from the Intersexed* (New Brunswick and London: Rutgers University Press).

Klöppel, Ulrike, 2002a. ' "Störfall" Hermaphroditismus und Trans-Formationen der Kategorie "Geschlecht". Überlegungen zur Analyse der medizinischen Diskussionen über Hermaphroditismus um 1900 mit Deleuze, Guattari und Foucault', *Transformationen. Wissen-Mensch-Geschlecht. Potsdamer Studien zur Frauen- und Geschlechterforschung*, 6, 137–50.

Klöppel, Ulrike, 2002b. 'XXOXY Ungelöst. Störungsszenarien in der Dramaturgie der zweigeschlechtlichen Ordnung', in Jannik Franzen, Ulrike Klöppel, Bettina Schmidt *et al.* (eds), *(K)ein Geschlecht oder viele? Transgender in politischer Perspektive* (Berlin: Querverlag), 153–81.

Klöppel, Ulrike, 2005. ' "Strenge Objektivität und extremste Subjektivität konkurrieren" Hermaphroditismusbehandlung in der Nachkriegszeit und die Durchsetzung von "gender by design" ', in *1-0-1 [one 'o one] intersex. Das Zwei-Geschlechter-System als Menschenrechtsverletzung* (Berlin: Neue Gesellschaft für Bildende Kunst), 168–85.

Lachmund, Jens, 1997. *Der abgehorchte Körper: zur historischen Soziologie der medizinischen Untersuchung* (Opladen: Westdeutscher Verlag).

Laqueur, Thomas, 1989. 'Bodies, details, and the humanitarian narrative', in Lynn Hunt (ed.), *The New Cultural History* (Berkeley, Los Angeles and London: University of California Press), 176–206.

Laqueur, Thomas, 1990. *Making Sex. Body and Gender from the Greeks to Freud* (Cambridge, MA, and London: Harvard University Press).

Laqueur, Thomas, 2003. *Solitary Sex. A Cultural History of Masturbation* (New York: Zone Books).

Long, Kathleen, 2006. *Hermaphrodites in Renaissance Europe. Women and Gender in the Early Modern World* (Aldershot and Burlington: Ashgate).

Lyons, J. O., 1978. *The Invention of the Self. The Hinge of Consciousness in the Eighteenth Century* (Carbondale, IL: Southern Illinois University Press).

Mak, Geertje, 1997. *Mannelijke vrouwen. Over grenzen van sekse in de negentiende eeuw* (Meppel and Amsterdam: Boom).

Mak, Geertje, 1998. ' "Passing women" im Sprechzimmer von Magnus Hirschfeld. Warum der Begriff "Transvestit" nicht für Frauen in Männerkleidern eingeführt wurde', *Österreichische Zeitschrift für Geschichtswissenschaften. Homosexualitäten*, 9:2, 384–99.

Mak, Geertje, 1999. 'Wo das Sprechen zum Schweigen wird. Zur historischen Beziehung zwischen "Frauen" und "Lesben" ', in Kati Röttger and Heike Paul (eds), *Differenzen in der Geschlechterdifferenz / Differences within Gender Studies. Aktuelle Perspektiven der Geschlechterforschung* (Berlin: Erich Schmidt Verlag), 316–99.

Mak, Geertje, 2004. 'Sandor/Sarolta Vay: from passing woman to sexual invert', *Journal of Women's History*, 16:1, 54–77.

Mak, Geertje, 2005a. ' "So we must go behind even what the microscope can reveal". The hermaphrodite's 'self' in medical discourse at the beginning of the twentieth century', *GLQ: A Journal of Lesbian and Gay Studies*, 11:1, 65–94.

Mak, Geertje, 2005b. 'Doubtful sex in civil law: nineteenth and early twentieth century proposals for ruling hermaphroditism', *Cardozo Journal of Law & Gender*, 12:1, 101–15.

Mak, Geertje, 2006. 'Doubting sex from within. A praxiographic approach to a late nineteenth-century case of hermaphroditism', *Gender & History*, 18:2, 360–88.

Mak, Geertje, 2011. 'Hermaphrodites on show. The case of Katharina/Karl Hohmann and its use in nineteenth-century medical science', *Social History of Medicine Advance Access* (online 31 March) 10.1093/shm/hkr050.

Matta, Christina, 2005. 'Ambiguous bodies and deviant sexualities. Hermaphrodites, homosexuality, and surgery in the United States, 1850–1904', *Perspectives in Biology and Medicine*, 48:1, 74–83.

McClive, Cathy, 2009. 'Masculinity on trial: penises, hermaphrodites and the uncertain male body in early modern France', *History Workshop Journal*, 68, 45–68.

McGrath, Roberta, 2002. *Seeing Her Sex. Medical Archives and the Female Body* (Manchester: Manchester University Press).

McLaren, Angus, 2007. *Impotence: A Cultural History* (Chicago: Chicago University Press).

Meer, Theo van der, 1994. 'Sodomy and the pursuit of a third sex in the early modern period', in Gilbert H. Herdt (ed.), *Third Sex, Third Gender: Beyond Sexual Dimorphism in Culture and History* (New York: Zone Books), 137–212.

Meer, Theo van der, 1995. *Sodoms zaad in Nederland: het ontstaan van homoseksualiteit in de vroegmoderne tijd* (Nijmegen: Sun).

Meer, Theo van der, 2007. 'Sodomy and its discontents. Discourse, desire, and the rise of a same-sex proto-something in the early modern Dutch Republic', *Historical Reflections / Réflections historiques*, 1, 41–67.

Meyerowitz, Joanne, 2002. *How Sex Changed. A History of Transsexuality in the United States* (Cambridge, MA, and London: Harvard University Press).

Mol, Annemarie, 2002. *The Body Multiple. Ontology in Medical Practice* (Durham, NC, and London: Duke University Press).

Moscucci, Ornella, 1990. *The Science of Woman. Gynaecology and Gender in England, 1800–1929* (Cambridge, New York, Port Chester, etc.: Cambridge University Press).

Müller, Klaus, 1991. '*Aber in meinem Herzen sprach eine Stimme so laut'. Homosexuelle Autobiographien und medizinische Pathographien im neunzehnten Jahrhundert* (Berlin: Rosa Winkel).

Nussbaum, Felicity A., 1989. *The Autobiographical Subject. Gender and Ideology in Eighteenth-Century England* (Baltimore and London: Johns Hopkins University Press).

Oosterhuis, Harry, 2000. *Stepchildren of Nature. Krafft-Ebing, Psychiatry, and the Making of Sexual Identity* (Chicago and London: Chicago University Press).

1-0-1 [one 'o one] Intersex. Das Zwei-Geschlechter-System als Menschenrechtsverletzung, 2005. (Berlin: Neue Gesellschaft für Bildende Kunst).

Park, Katharine, and Nye, Robert, 1991. ' "Destiny is anatomy" '. (Essay review of *Making Sex. Body and Gender from the Greeks to Freud*, by Thomas Laqueur), *The New Republic*, 204, 18 February, 53–7.

Park, Katharine, 1997. 'The rediscovery of the clitoris. French medicine and the tribade, 1570–1620', in David Hilman and Corla Mazzio (eds), *The Body in Parts: Fantasies of Corporeality in Early Modern Europe* (London and New York: Routledge), 170–93.

Pernick, Martin S., 1985. *A Calculus of Suffering. Pain, Professionalism, and Anesthesia in Nineteenth-Century America* (New York: Columbia University Press).

Poovey, Mary, 1987. ' "Scenes of an indelicate character". The medical "treatment" of Victorian women', in Catharine Gallagher and Thomas Laqueur (eds), *The Making of the Modern Body* (Berkeley and Los Angeles: University of California Press), 137–68.

Porter, Roy (ed.), 1997. *Rewriting the Self* (London and New York: Routledge).

Porter, Roy, 2003. *Flesh in the Age of Enlightenment* (London: Allen Lane).

Porter, Roy, and Lesley Hall, 1995. *The Facts of Life. The Creation of Sexual Knowledge in Britain, 1650–1950* (New Haven and London: Yale University Press).

Preves, Sharon E., 2005. *Intersex and Identity. The Contested Self* (New Brunswick, etc.: Rutgers University Press).

Redick, Alison, 2004. 'American History XY: The Medical Treatment of Intersex, 1916–1955' (PhD thesis, New York University).

Reis, Elizabeth, 2009. *Bodies in Doubt. An American History of Intersex* (Baltimore: Johns Hopkins University Press).

Rubin, Gayle, 1975. 'The traffic in women. Notes on the "political economy" of sex', in Reina R. Reiter (ed.), *Toward an Anthropology of Women* (New York: Monthly Review Press), 157–210.

Schiebinger, Londa, 1993. *Nature's Body: Gender in the Making of Modern Science* (Boston: Beacon Press).

Schoon, Lidy, 1995. *De gynaecologie als belichaming van vrouwen. Verloskunde en gynaecologie 1840–1920* (Zutphen: Walburg Pers).

Scott, Joan, 1988. *Gender and the Politics of History* (New York, etc.: Columbia University Press).

Scott, Joan, 1991. 'The Evidence of Experience', *Critical Inquiry*, 17:4, 773–97.

Shorter, Edward, 1985. *Bedside Manners. The Troubled History of Doctors and Patients* (New York: Simon & Schuster).

Simon, Hermann, 1993. 'Wer war N. O. Body?', in Hermann Simon (ed.), *N. O. Body. Aus einem Mannes Mädchenjahren* (Berlin: Edition Hentrich), 167–246.

Simon, Hermann, 2006. 'Afterword. In search of Karl Baer', in N. O. Body, *Memoirs of a Man's Maiden Years*, trans. Deborah Simon (Philadelphia: University of Pennsylvania Press), 113–36.

Smith-Rosenberg, Carroll, 1985. *Disorderly Conduct. Visions of Gender in Victorian America* (New York: Oxford University Press).

Spörri, Myriam, 2000. 'Die Diagnose des Geschlechts. Hermaphroditismus im sexualwissenschaftlichen Diskurs zwischen 1886 und 1920' (Lizentiatsarbeit, University of Zurich).

Spörri, Myriam, 2003. 'N. O. Body, Magnus Hirschfeld und die Diagnose des Geschlechts: Hermaphroditismus um 1900', *L'Homme Z. F. G.*, 14:2, 244–61.

Stanton, Domna C., 1987. 'Autogynography: is the subject different?', in Domna C. Stanton (ed.), *The Female Autograph: Theory and Practice of Autobiography from the Tenth to the Twentieth Century* (Chicago: Chicago University Press), 3–20

Steedman, C., 2000. 'Enforced narratives. Stories of another self', in T. Cosslett, C. Lury and P. Summerfield (eds), *Feminism and Autobiography: Texts Theories Methods* (London and New York: Routledge), 24–39.

Stolberg, Michael, 2003. *Homo patiens. Krankheits- und Körpererfahrung in der Frühen Neuzeit* (Köln: Böhlau).

Stoler, Ann Laura, 2009. *Along the Archival Grain: Epistemic Anxieties and Colonial Common Sense* (Princeton: Princeton University Press).

Taylor, Charles, 1989. *Sources of the Self. The Making of the Modern Identity* (Cambridge and New York: Cambridge University Press).

Thompson, R. G. (ed.), 1996. *Freakery: Cultural Spectacles of the Extraordinary Body* (New York and London: New York University Press).

Tosh, John, 2005. *Manliness and Masculinities in Nineteenth-Century Britain: Essays on Gender, Family and Empire* (Harlow, etc.: Pearson).

Traub, Valerie, 2002. *The Renaissance of Lesbianism in Early Modern England* (Cambridge: Cambridge University Press).

Trumbach, Randolph, 1994. 'London's sapphists: from three sexes to four genders in the making of modern culture', in Gilbert Herdt (ed.), *Third Sex, Third Gender. Beyond Sexual Bimorphism in Culture and History* (New York: Zone Books), 111–37.

Trumbach, Randolph, 1998. *Sex and the Gender Revolution. Volume I. Heterosexuality and the Third Gender in Enlightenment London* (London and Chicago: University of Chicago Press).

Vicinus, Martha, 1989. ' "They wonder to which sex I belong." The historical roots of the modern lesbian identity', in Dennis Altman et al. (eds), *Homosexuality, Which Homosexuality?* (Amsterdam and London: Schorer / An Dekker / GMP Publishers), 215–38.

Wahrman, Dror, 2004. *The Making of the Modern Self: Identity and Culture in Eighteenth-Century England* (New Haven and London: Yale University Press).

Weber, Eugen, 1977. *Peasants into Frenchmen: The Modernization of Rural France, 1870–1914* (Stanford: Stanford University Press).

Weeks, Jeffrey, 1991. *Against Nature: Essays on History, Sexuality and Identity* (London: Rivers Oram).

INDEX

Ackerman, Evelyn 9, 24, 99
Alexina B. *see* Barbin, Herculine
Alexina X. 53, 78
ambiguity, labels for 19–20, 27–8
  see also reputation
amputation of clitoris/penis 112–13,
  152, 166, 171–80, 183, 194, 256n44,
  260n48
anaesthesia 148–51
Anna Barbara Meier (A.B.M.) 19–20,
  25–7, 29, 31, 36, 38–9, 50–1, 95–7,
  100–5, 107, 111
Anna Laabs 197–9, 205
  see also N.O. Body
Anna Regina Märker 33, 109
autobiographical writing 12–13, 66–73,
  206–12, 219–22, 230
autobiography 66–89, 205–24

Barbin, Herculine 66–70, 73–89, 117,
  164, 194, 205–7, 211–13, 216,
  218–24, 231–2
bearded women 6, 11, 19–21, 25–8,
  40, 67, 95–6, 150, 194, 217, 225
  see also outer appearance
bedside medicine 94, 97–102, 109, 113,
  119, 136–7, 162, 181, 228, 240n37
biopsy 175, 203, 258–9n32
  see also diagnostic surgery
body
  access to 93–100, 116–18, 123–7, 132–3
  enactment of 6–10, 46, 92–4, 115,
  138, 143, 147

history of 97–100
integrity of 116–18, 123–7
multiple 6–7, 92–4
person and 3, 55, 93–4, 115, 134,
  136–156, 161, 163, 187, 200, 219,
  228–9
self and 1, 48, 52, 54, 57–8, 64, 93,
  114–15, 136–8, 157–64
social fabric and 115, 161
surveillance of 29–32, 127–131
  see also physical examination
Body, N.O. *see* N.O. Body
Butler, Judith 8, 14, 91, 247n77

category of sex 1–5, 14–16, 19, 40,
  43, 57, 65, 70, 92, 131, 185,
  189, 192, 202, 213, 230–2,
  260n57
clitoris (enlarged) 4, 15, 34, 129, 142,
  144, 146, 198, 247n1
  see also amputation of clitoris/penis
clothing *see* outer appearance
coitus (capacity for) 20, 27, 34–5, 93,
  105, 108–14, 119, 136, 160, 162,
  172, 178, 190, 197–8, 228–9
containment policies 32, 41–3, 226
core gender identity 10, 13, 46, 158,
  237n31
  see also gender identity
court, hermaphrodite cases before 21,
  30, 36, 59, 67, 95–8, 101, 104,
  109–10, 116–35, 144
Courty, Amédée 120–5

Darbousse-Jumas, Justine *see* Jumas,
    Justine
Debierre, Charles 128–30, 163, 166,
    201, 242n25
Dekker, Rudolf 49
diagnostic surgery 150–2, 155, 175, 190,
    203, 256n44, 258n31, 258–9n32
disclosure 21–3, 29–34, 37–40, 138–41,
    155–6, 186–93
dishonour *see* reputation, loss of
dislocation 61, 81–4, 133–4, 206
doubtful sex, legal category of 116,
    127–31, 166–71
Dreger, Alice Domurat 5, 13, 92–3,
    111–12, 141, 149, 151, 154, 159–60,
    175, 229, 233n2, 256n49, 257n5
Duden, Barbara 9, 97

E.C. 176–82
Emma R. 189–90
enactment *see* body; physical
    examination; sex of self; sexual
    function
Epstein, Julia 164
exhibition of hermaphrodites 62–3, 136,
    143, 152, 234n6

Finon 20–3, 26–8
Foucault, Michel 11–12, 18, 44, 66–70,
    80, 98, 100, 117, 159, 160, 166,
    204–9
Friederike S. 195

Garnier, Paul 128–32, 166
Geijl, A. 162, 173–80, 191–2, 255
gender ambiguity 2, 14, 70
gender identity 1, 10, 13, 15, 18, 46–8,
    57, 63–72, 77, 80, 157–8, 182, 184,
    195, 205–6, 209, 211, 233n4, 237n31
    see also identity; person; sex of self;
    subjectivity
gender scripts 84–7, 89, 205–24
gender, sex and 7–9
    see also sex of self; body and, person;
    subjectivity; sex-gender system

genitals *see* physical examination
Goffe, J. Riddle 176–82, 258–9n32
gonadal standard 68, 92, 111, 136, 141,
    151–3, 160, 164, 168–9, 176–84,
    201, 228
    discussion of 168–71, 174–9, 182–4,
    191–3
    see also Dreger, Alice Domurat
gonads, examination of *see* physical
    examination
gossip and mockery 19–21, 26, 28, 32–3,
    39, 49, 61–3, 82–4, 114, 133, 144,
    225–6
    see also reputation
Guermonprez 141–3, 168–9, 188–9,
    194, 201

Hanna O. 24, 31–2, 39, 51, 105
Hausman, Bernice 10, 158–9, 245n18,
    260n62
Healey, Dan 234n12, 239n35, 250n45,
    258n17, 261n23
hernia 52, 112, 142, 190
herniotomy 112, 141–2, 151–2, 175,
    190, 258–9n32
heterosexual order 14–15, 40, 76, 93,
    111, 160, 186, 193, 216, 233n3
    see also same-sex marriage, fear for
Hirschauer, Stefan 13, 137, 148–9, 158,
    193, 237n29, 237n35, 257n3
Hirschfeld, Magnus 5, 145–6, 193–200,
    104–5, 219
Holmes, Morgan 236n23, 237n33
Holzheid, Elizabetha 21–2, 26–7, 34
homosexual/lesbian identity 11–12, 15,
    164, 201, 204, 206–12, 261n29
    see also lesbianism; marriage;
    same-sex intimacies; sexual drives
homosexuality 160, 164, 189–90, 193,
    197, 204, 207–9
hospital medicine 98–101, 117
humanitarian (narrative) 89, 162, 166,
    175, 223, 247n85, 265n71
human rights 117–18, 133
Hunt, Lynn 117–18

hypospadia 21, 28–9, 106–7, 152, 171, 188, 238n6

identity 43–9, 264n16
    see also gender identity; homosexual/ lesbian identity
impotency trials 117–120, 124, 130, 251n4, 251n8
inscription, sex as 3, 17–19, 25, 41, 43, 65–9, 73, 78, 81, 115, 131, 135, 157–9, 185, 192–4, 224–7

Jalabert, Philippe 120–7
Johanna K. 28–9, 38, 51, 107
Jordan-Young, Rebecca 200, 233n3
Justine Jumas 30, 115–36, 165–6, 205, 228

Karkazis, Katrina 236n23, 237n33, 257n14, 260n2
Kessler, Suzanne J. 236n23, 237n33, 237n35, 257n3, 257n14, 260n2, 262n58
Klöppel, Ulrike 201, 236n27, 262n53
König 189–90, 196

laboratory medicine 141, 156, 162, 203, 231
Lachmund, Jens 9, 98–100, 239n31, 249n21, 249n37
Landau, Theodor 166–8, 175–6, 179–80, 191
laparotomy 150–2, 155, 175, 256n44, 258n31, 258–9n32
Laqueur, Thomas 8–9, 48, 68, 89, 91–3, 110–11, 154, 227, 234n17, 247n1, 257n5
Law 60–1, 118–23, 166–171, 175, 188–9, 230–1
    France 118–23, 168
    Germany 166–71
    physician's discussion of 123–31, 166–71, 230
    physician's power and 60–1, 168
    sex (re)assignment and 60–1

see also court, hermaphrodite cases before; impotency trials; marriage, annulment of
legal category of 'doubtful sex' 116, 127–31, 166–71
legal definition of marriage 116, 118–21, 126, 128–31, 169–71
legal definition of sex 120–3, 166–71
    see also court, hermaphrodite cases before
lesbianism 80–1, 207–9
    see also homosexual/lesbian identity; same sex intimacies
location, sex as see position, sex as
logics of sex see rationales of sex
Loir, Joseph-Napoléon 127–8, 132, 166
Louise-Julia-Anna 141–3, 168, 188–9, 194

Maria Katharina Ulmerin 36, 51, 62
Maria Raab 144, 241n60
Marie B. 37–8, 55–7, 60, 108
Marie Chupin 28, 238n20, 266
Marie (-Marguerite) 51–3, 59, 61, 106
Marriage
    annulment of 34–6, 61, 63, 101, 114, 116–35, 228
    clinical discussion of 160–1, 163, 168–9, 171–4, 187–92
    see also same sex marriage, fear for
Matta, Christina 234n7, 326n27, 237n37
medical case histories as historical source 4–5, 9–10, 17–18, 22–4, 58–63, 136–7, 143, 153, 171, 210, 225, 230
medicine, history of 91–4, 97–102, 136–8, 148–9, 161–4
    see also bedside medicine; hospital medicine; laboratory medicine
Meer, Theo van der 207–8, 235n24, 263n4
menstruation 25, 229
    absence of 67, 112, 118, 123, 217
    see also physical examination
Meyerowitz, Joanne 163, 235n18, 235n20, 257n15

midwives 6, 19, 23–5, 28, 30–3, 37, 40,
    96–100, 109, 116, 118–19, 121–4,
    128, 132–4, 223, 226
Mol, Annemarie 6, 92–3, 138, 257n55,
    265n57
monstrosity 24–5, 32, 93, 124, 129, 164
moral order/fabric 11, 13, 41, 43,
    64–6, 69, 86, 114–15, 118,
    127–31, 161, 165, 168, 183,
    185–8, 192–3, 202–3, 224,
    226–8, 231
Müller, Klaus 209–10, 264n26

nature 8, 11, 14, 48–50, 54, 57, 68, 114,
    131, 208
Neugebauer, Franz Ludwig von 3–6,
    22, 28, 32, 145, 149–152, 167–81,
    186, 189–91, 201–2
N.O. Body 24, 197–9, 205–7, 212–24
non-anonymous social environments
    27, 41–2, 64–5, 157, 161
non-intervention 19–25, 29–37, 40–3,
    63–5, 225–8

one sex system 8, 48, 91–3
    see also Laqueur, Thomas; two sex
    system
Oosterhuis, Harry 73, 207, 209, 211,
    217, 221, 262n45
outer appearance 40, 52, 96, 100–2,
    115, 232
    ambiguous 25–9, 32, 40–1, 62, 70,
    114, 163, 171–2, 177, 182–3,
    231–2
    see also bearded women; urinating
ovaries see gonadal standard; ovotestis;
    physical examination
ovotestis 154–6, 262n46

penis see amputation of clitoris/penis;
    hypospadia; physical examination
person (as concept) 45, 63–5, 115
    body and 3, 55, 93–4, 115, 134,
    136–56, 161, 163, 187, 200, 219,
    228–9

photography 136–7, 149–50, 152–3,
    178, 241n48, 256n49
physical examination
    anaesthesia
    diagnostic surgery and see diagnostic
    surgery
    ejaculation and 104–10, 113, 136,
    143–7, 229
    gonads and 6, 136–8, 151–5, 160,
    166–7, 171, 174, 176–7, 180,
    184–8, 200–3, 228–30
    menstruation and 100, 107, 118,
    122–3, 134, 136, 229
    microscope and 92–3, 137–8, 144–7,
    152–8, 160, 169, 175, 181–2, 188,
    201, 226, 229
    outer genitals and 100–10
    see also physical examination,
    penis/clitoris; physical
    examination, vagina
    ovaries and 6, 102–3, 105, 108, 112,
    117–18, 122, 125, 130, 137, 140,
    149, 151–5, 175, 177, 249n23,
    251n61
    palpation and 7–8, 97, 100–3, 110,
    134, 136–7, 141–3
    patients' statements and 95–8, 102–5
    penetration and 7–8, 97, 100–3,
    141–3
    penis/clitoris and 8–9, 34, 96, 102–9,
    112–13, 188, 190, 238n6, 240n46,
    251n4
    photography and 136–7, 149–50,
    152–3, 178, 241n48, 256n49
    shame and 30, 93–101, 134, 137–8,
    143–52, 156, 226, 228
    techniques and routines and 5–8, 12,
    92–4, 97–102, 136–7, 141–3, 147,
    155, 161, 163–4, 184, 186, 228–9
    testicles and 6, 101, 106, 112, 139,
    144, 154–5, 162, 173, 175, 177,
    179, 188, 191, 249n23
    vagina and 96, 101–10, 113, 119, 125,
    130, 142, 147, 153, 172, 255n22
place, sex as see position, sex as

plastic surgery 15, 151–2, 159, 163, 166, 171–84, 230, 258n17
see also amputation of clitoris/penis; surgery
position, sex as 57–63, 66–9, 81–7, 133, 193, 202–3, 225–7
practices see enactment; physical examination; praxeographic approach
praxeographic approach 6–10, 71–3, 87–9, 92–4
pregnancy after intercourse with hermaphrodite 19–20, 28–9
procreation 34–5, 93, 103, 105–11, 114, 192
as norm for marriage 123, 130
psychic trauma 1, 57, 65, 67, 170–1, 185, 189
see also dislocation
psychological sex 5, 13, 18, 46, 50, 157–8, 161–4, 167–8, 170–1, 175–6, 179–204, 230–1
see also sex of self

rationales of sex 2–3, 15, 17–18, 40–3, 65, 68, 91–4, 115, 157–8, 192, 225
reassignment of sex see sex reassignment
Reiss, Elizabeth 111, 160, 251n59, 257n10
reputation, of being hermaphrodite 19–20, 27–8, 33, 40, 60, 63, 226
loss of 24–5, 32–4, 61, 67, 76–81, 86, 134
see also ambiguity, labels for; Zwitter
routines see physical examination; sex of self
rural communities 5, 23–4, 27–8, 41–2, 84–5, 99

same-sex intimacies 30–2, 40–1, 73–6, 214–17
same-sex marriage, fear for 120, 126–31, 168–9, 188–9,
see also heterosexual order; marriage
Schneider 106, 114

Schweickhard 96, 104–6
Scott, Joan 13, 159, 233n4
secondary sex characteristics see bearded women; outer appearance
secrecy 19–42, 133–5, 165, 168, 172, 210, 215, 217, 223, 225–8, 232
see also social isolation
self 43–5, 157–164
ancien regime of 46
autobiographic writing and 12–13, 66–73, 206–12, 219–22, 230
body and 1, 48, 52, 54, 57–8, 64, 93, 114–15, 136–8, 157–64
history of 11, 45–9, 57–8
modern 45–9, 54, 70–3, 87
socially turned 46–7, 51, 63
see also gender identity; person (concept of); sex of self; subjectivity
sex dichotomy 2, 14–15, 91
see also two sex system
sex, enactment of 117, 92–4, 134, 136–8, 143, 147, 151, 155–6, 162–3, 183, 185, 201–2, 225, 228–31
sex-gender system 14, 48, 186
sex of self 3, 30, 13–14, 43–65, 86, 157–166, 181, 184, 185–6, 188, 193–5, 200–4, 206, 208, 214, 219, 223–4, 230–2, 241
absence of 1, 12, 18, 43–65
body and 64–8, 133–5, 157–66, 179–88, 200–2
enactment of 12–13, 46, 71, 164, 185, 193, 200, 203–8, 219
routines and techniques of 58, 209, 231
sexual desires and 51, 54, 56, 73–81, 107–15
see also gender identity; person (concept of); self; subjectivity
sex reassignment 36, 43, 45, 49–65, 67, 78–84, 101, 114, 134, 169, 194, 196, 204–6, 222, 226
forced 59–61
see also dislocation; psychic trauma
sexual abuse 33

sexual drives (direction of) 53–6, 73–6,
107–14, 179–182
sexual function 51, 56, 93, 102–115
enactment of 93–4, 110, 115, 137–8,
229
see also coitus; procreation; sexual
drives; sexual relations
sexual glands *see* gonads
sexual inversion 46, 158, 161, 164, 181,
193, 197–9, 204, 206–13, 217, 219,
222, 231, 261n29
see also homosexual / lesbian identity;
sexual drives (direction of)
sexual relations 32–40, 38–9, 41, 65,
73–81, 114, 185, 207
shame 7, 17, 19–25, 31, 40, 50–1, 63,
75, 77, 79, 83–5, 200, 221, 223
see also physical examination;
social isolation
single sex 165, 177–8, 182, 232
social isolation 41, 63, 81–9, 114, 172,
206, 212–13, 216, 226
see also secrecy; shame
social order / fabric 13, 41, 43, 64–5, 69,
114–15, 127–31, 165, 168, 183,
185–8, 194, 224, 226–7, 292
subject(ivity) and 44–5, 59, 63, 87–9,
135, 157, 163, 165, 172
surgery 29, 136–8, 140, 148–52, 155,
158–63, 165–6, 169–84, 187, 189,
191, 201, 203, 230–1, 234n7,
255n27, 257n15, 258n17,
258–9n32, 259n38
see also diagnostic surgery

Tardieu, Ambroise 67–8, 89, 116–17,
120–1, 124–5, 163, 205, 239n32
Taussig, Fred J. 178–82
Taylor, Charles 11, 46, 48, 69, 193,
212, 224
techniques *see* physical examination;
sex of self

testicles
amputation of 151, 153–4, 190,
256n43, 258n32, 259–60n42
late / undescended 21, 51, 140, 151,
189, 201, 238n61, 242n25
see also ovotestis; physical
examination
third sex *see* ambiguity, labels for;
legal category of doubtful sex
Tourtual 35, 50, 108–9, 113
transsexual(ity) 13–14, 16, 157–8, 193,
235n19n20, 236n18, 237n35n37,
245n18
trauma *see* psychic trauma
Traxel 28–9, 107
true sex 18, 32, 66–70, 92, 111, 117, 123,
128–9, 157–65, 174–82, 199, 215,
230, 232–3
Foucault and 18, 70
see also Dreger, Alice; gonadal
standard; single sex
Trumbach, Randolph 207–8
two sex system 9, 48, 54, 91–4, 110–11,
138
see also Laqueur, Thomas; one sex
system

urinating 20–1, 28–9, 40–1, 51, 65, 103,
105, 107, 152, 176, 179, 185, 225,
238n6, 239n23, 239n25

Wahrman, Dror 11, 26, 45–55, 63, 68,
70–1, 196, 264n16
Westerman, C. W. J. 187–8, 196
Wilhelm, Eugen 167–8, 170
Wilhelmina K. 166, 168, 194–5

Zangger, Heinrich 169, 189–91, 196,
199–200
Zwitter 19–20, 27, 40, 109
see also ambiguity, labels for;
reputation of being hermaphrodite